THE
UNITED STATES
IN
WORLD AFFAIRS
1950

SOME PUBLICATIONS OF THE

COUNCIL ON FOREIGN RELATIONS

THE
UNITED STATES
IN
WORLD AFFAIRS
1950

By Richard P. Stebbins
and the Research Staff of the
Council on Foreign Relations
with an introduction by
Lewis W. Douglas

Published for the
COUNCIL ON FOREIGN RELATIONS
by
HARPER & BROTHERS
NEW YORK
1951

The Council on Foreign Relations is a non-profit institution devoted to study of the international aspects of American political, economic and strategic problems. It takes no stand, expressed or implied, on American policy.

The authors of books published under the auspices of the Council are responsible for their statements of fact and expressions of opinion. The Council is responsible only for determining that they should be presented to the public.

THE UNITED STATES IN WORLD AFFAIRS, 1950

Copyright, 1951, by Council on Foreign Relations, Inc.
Printed in the United States of America

All rights reserved, including right to reproduce
this book or any portion thereof in any form.

For information address Council on Foreign Relations,
58 East 68th Street, New York 21

FIRST EDITION

American Book–Knickerbocker Press, Inc., New York

COUNCIL ON FOREIGN RELATIONS

OFFICERS AND DIRECTORS

R. C. LEFFINGWELL
Chairman of the Board

ALLEN W. DULLES
President (on leave)

HENRY M. WRISTON
Acting President

FRANK ALTSCHUL
Secretary

CLARENCE E. HUNTER
Treasurer

WALTER H. MALLORY
Executive Director

GEORGE S. FRANKLIN, JR.
Assistant Executive Director

FRANK D. CARUTHERS, JR.
Assistant Treasurer

COMMITTEE ON STUDIES

HENRY M. WRISTON
Chairman

ACKNOWLEDGMENTS

THE cooperative effort which produced this volume has laid its author under heavier obligations than can be fully acknowledged in a one-page note. Among those on whose encouragement and advice I have depended most are Percy W. Bidwell, Director of Studies, and Walter H. Mallory, Executive Director of the Council on Foreign Relations; Hamilton Fish Armstrong, the Editor of *Foreign Affairs;* and Dr. Henry M. Wriston and the members of the Council's Committee on Studies.

The burdens of authorship have been materially lightened by the sympathetic and intelligent collaboration of my secretary, Inez Viterbo. Particular thanks are due also to Carl Rodman for his work on the chronology and the index, to Gustav Schweizer of the American Geographical Society for the maps, and to Rudolph de Harak for the organizational charts. Richard K. Carlton, Mary MacPherson, Mr. Rodman, Isador Schlachter, Marilyn Talman, and Thetis Touliatou lent valuable aid in the gathering and organization of material, a process in which the expert assistance of Ruth Savord and the Council's library staff was, as always, both indispensable and freely given. My colleagues of the research staff and various other authorities, both official and unofficial, have been more than generous with help and criticism. The business office headed by Frank D. Caruthers, Jr. has maintained its record of unobtrusive efficiency.

Amid such varied obligations it seems almost presumptuous to claim sole responsibility for the finished volume. Its shortcomings, at any rate, must be laid to my charge and not to that of the Council on Foreign Relations or any of my counselors or collaborators.

R. P. S.

INTRODUCTION

BY LEWIS W. DOUGLAS

THIS book is an opportune reminder of the way our country's vital interests have become entangled in events in the farthermost parts of the world—whether in the Far East where a flood of violent nationalism, joined with the lurid and empty promises of Communism, has already carried China into an alliance with the Soviet and threatens like developments in other areas of the Far East; whether in Southeast Asia and Indonesia where the reaction against Western influence has already swept away many of the old relationships; whether in the subcontinent of Asia where the creation of new nation states has given rise to a host of new problems; whether in the Middle East where a succession of disturbances has disclosed the vulnerability of that region; whether in North Africa, South America, the South Pacific, or Europe.

The 1950 story describes the disorder in Southeast Asia, in the Middle East and the conflict within Europe. It covers the wars in the Orient. It sharply silhouettes the extent to which the old focal points of power have moved from their prewar orbits. It discloses an unbalance of power which the last war created on a worldwide scale unprecedented in modern history. It shows how this unbalance of power, combined with Soviet military strength and the ideological paraphernalia of Communism, is producing a situation which threatens the entire structure of the civilized community. The meaning of this shift in the world balance of power may perhaps be suggested by the question: "Would there now be a war in Korea, would the French now be engaged in open hostilities with Communist forces in Indochina, would the satellite states within the sphere of Soviet influence in Europe be pressing against the boundaries, and would indigenous subversive orders operating under Kremlin control be attempting to upset the internal regimes of the Western World, if a French army comparable in strength to the army of the 30's were now in existence, if the Japanese Army of the 30's were under arms, and if German military strength were as it was in '36?" The absence of any one of these elements of power compounded by the division of Germany into its East and West spheres has created an international environment within which the ideas and dogma of Communism, reinforced by skillful Communist devices of deception and by the power of Soviet arms, have been able to subjugate a large part of Asia and to expose Europe, the Middle East and other areas to constant threat.

The United States during 1950 continued in the role of principal defender of the faith. We emerged from the war as the repository of an amount of industrial authority which made us the envy of the Western World and the source from which Europe derived an infusion of hope for her recovery.

The vigor of the intricate and complicated economic and industrial system peculiar to America; the resourcefulness of its managerial and proprietary personnel in overcoming obstacles; the vitality which characterized the incessant drive for technological improvements in production; and the ingenuity with which problems—some self-imposed—were resolved, all together made it possible for the United States to play the important role which she played in international affairs. They make us one of the few nations which can inspire others to join in the task of redressing the unbalance of power which the war caused and thereby of restoring some sort of order in the world. They make us as respected by the Soviet as they make us feared by them. Taken together with other factors they have so far deterred the Soviet from directly committing itself to the final test of arms.

The influence of the United States in world affairs is, therefore, intimately and irrevocably related to the vitality of our peculiar American scheme. If we would continue to derive benefits from the former, we must vigilantly nurture the vigor of the latter.

PREFACE

THE year 1950 marked a decisive turning point in the history of the United States as a world power and opened a climactic phase in the resistance of free nations to the aggressive tendencies of Stalinist Communism. With the entrance of Communist China upon the international stage, the "cold war" between East and West broadened rapidly into a global conflict involving large-scale military collisions in the Far East and a serious threat of atomic world war. The Communist regimes in Moscow and Peking held the initiative throughout the year, maintaining the appearance of unbroken solidarity while maneuvering the free nations into a situation of disunity and acute peril. Concurrently, the gradual strengthening of the North Atlantic alliance system was offset by an increasing strain in United States relations with friendly governments. The close of the year found this country growing in material power but internally divided and, in the Far East at any rate, more nearly isolated from other nations than at any time since World War II.

The present volume essays to recount these developments in a manner appropriate to a series whose aim is dispassionate analysis of American world policy as it develops from year to year. Like its predecessor volumes, it makes no pretense at definitive history nor at exhaustive treatement of any particular segment of United States foreign relations. What it does attempt is to aid in the understanding of contemporary affairs through a balanced, impartial interpretation in which recent happenings are brought into intelligible focus and related to the broad, underlying tendencies that are shaping the modern world. By subordinating particular events to the over-all picture, it aspires to supplement—though hardly to substitute for —the more detailed information which is readily available from other sources.

The attempt to discern a coherent pattern in the welter of daily events is not an easy one, and not everyone will be equally satisfied with the results achieved in any one year. The growing interrelation of developments in all parts of the world poses extraordinarily difficult problems of interpretation, organization, and space allotment. The need of keeping the treatment within manageable bounds entails rigorous condensation everywhere and leaves only a sentence or two for the discussion of such episodes as the retirement of the King of the Belgians and the revolution in Nepal, in which no obvious United States interest was involved. The compensating advantage of the method, if any, lies in the fact that the really decisive forces in the world situation are enabled to stand out more prominently in the absence of encumbering detail.

At a time when foreign policy has become the most bitterly controversial public issue of the day, it is appropriate to remind the reader that this series is concerned neither with defending nor attacking particular individuals, organizations, or policies. Its only purpose is to present the record, fully and fairly, in its relation to American interests and objectives throughout the world. This does not mean, of course, that the author has attempted the impossible task of excluding the element of personal judgment from his narrative. It is impracticable to devote one's time to the study of international affairs without forming certain opinions about them, and the reader is entitled to know in a general way what those opinions are. Most readers of this volume will probably agree that the test of an opinion is not who holds it or how vigorously it is expressed, but how well it will stand up under the scrutiny of history.

R. P. S.

New York, April 1951.

CONTENTS

MAPS AND CHARTS

CHAPTER ONE

TWO WORLDS IN CONFLICT

FOR GENERATIONS we Americans have been conditioned to think of our country not only as the perfect realization of man's dream of freedom but also as the foremost champion of liberty and progress throughout the world. It is certainly a fact that American influence and power have often been exerted in support of other peoples struggling against tyranny and oppression. American missionaries, doctors, educators, and engineers have tirelessly carried the benefits of Western thought and science to the inhabitants of remote parts of the earth. This record of humanitarian action, largely disinterested and often contrasting with the more egoistic policies of older nations, has given the United States an enviable reputation which still lingers in many countries, but has sharply declined within the last few years.

In recent decades the stock picture of the United States as a practically unique embodiment of progressive and humanitarian values has seemed increasingly questionable. The American people, perhaps, have lost none of their innate faith in human nature, but have quite naturally acquired a certain interest in the avoidance of radical change. Meanwhile the demands of the rest of the world have grown. Political democracy, once considered a virtual American monopoly, has become the acknowledged standard of political organization throughout much of the world and no longer fully satisfies man's restless striving to improve his condition. New peoples have become aware of their national identity, and imperiously claim the right to manage their affairs without foreign interference. New theories of economic and social democracy have come into vogue, to which Americans, with their extraordinary standards of popular welfare achieved under free enterprise, have remained indifferent and in some cases even hostile. Secure in the enjoyment of its own system, the United States, by imperceptible degrees and almost without knowing it, has been transformed from one of the more radical to one of the most conservative among the world's major nations.

Analysis of the causes, variations, and possible justifications of this national outlook would transcend the limits of the present discussion, which is concerned only with examining its effects upon our foreign relations. Its fundamental significance in this connection results from the culmination of two major historical trends which reached their climax in the period of the Second World War and the ensuing years of world confusion. One was the increasing responsibility for leadership in the world community which devolved upon the United States as the result of its vast material power, its relative inaccessibility to hostile military action, and its forthright detestation of totalitarianism and aggression, whether Hitlerite or Stalinist. The other was a profound radicalization in the thinking of great masses of the world's people, particularly in the colonial and "underdeveloped" countries of Asia and the Far East.

In the spring of 1945, while the accredited representatives of 50 legal governments were setting up the United Nations organization at San Francisco, millions of human beings who had survived the hazards and privations of World War II awaited the overthrow of Axis tyranny in a distinctly revolutionary mood. The greater part of humankind had always lived in conditions of barely tolerable hardship, oppression, hunger, and disease. Conventional restraints, their own weakness, and the police power of their rulers, whether indigenous or foreign, had made them tractable instruments of the existing order. The difference in 1945 was that many of them had ceased to accept this state of affairs as inevitable. The war had disclosed the feebleness of constituted authority and diffused

the idea that old grievances could be remedied by direct action
—all the more readily if disinterested outside help was available.

Neither the United States nor its allies in Western Europe
were in a position to grasp the full significance of this revolutionary ferment, still less to view it with enthusiasm. Stabilization and recuperation from the ordeal of war were obviously
the world's immediate needs. An upsurge of revolutionary
passions, unaccompanied by any sense of realism or discipline,
could only complicate the task of restoring peace to a sorely
tried humanity. Undoubtedly significant concessions to the
popular temper would be necessary, and the United States, in
particular, was by no means backward in advocating the adoption of liberal policies by the European colonial nations. Its
contributions to UNRRA and other economic relief programs,
meanwhile, helped greatly to alleviate the most acute physical
distress among some of the affected peoples.

None of the Western democracies, however, seemed disposed to take measures of a scope commensurate with that of
the revolutionary movement as it has since revealed itself. In
Europe, there remained a considerable body of disaffection,
much of which tended to gravitate into the orbit of national
Communist parties which claimed to represent the interests
of the broad masses of the people. In Asia, the unrest born
of social tensions combined with anti-imperialist feeling failed
to abate, despite the emancipation of the Philippines by the
United States, the British grant of independence to India,
Pakistan, Ceylon, and Burma, the Dutch offer of independence to the East Indies under the Netherlands crown, the
French proposals of limited autonomy in Indochina, and American efforts to promote an accommodation between China's
Nationalist government and the powerful Communist movement which for two decades had been fighting it as an instrument of domestic reaction and foreign imperialism.

Only one government unaffectedly welcomed the new conditions. This was the government of the Union of Soviet Socialist Republics, which based its policy on the revolutionary doctrines of Marx and Lenin and operated simultaneously as a state administration and as the general staff of the Communist revolutionary movement throughout the world. To the men in Moscow's Kremlin, discontent with existing conditions and authorities provided the ideal climate for furthering the uncompromisingly revolutionary cause in which they had been nurtured, and which they had not renounced even when tactical necessities obliged them to deemphasize it in the interest of cooperation with the governments of "capitalist" nations. The world's political and social ferment gave them an unrivaled opportunity to fortify and extend their own totalitarian system while endeavoring to supplant the United States as the main hope of those in every country who looked forward to better days.

1. Stalinism and the West

That the postwar aims of Premier Joseph V. Stalin and his associates would diverge radically from those of the other United Nations governments was assured by the ironclad view of history and society to which they had been committed since their entry into the revolutionary movement against Tsarist Russia more than a generation earlier. That view was built on the notion of a fundamental, unalterable opposition between rival social classes and the national governments they supposedly controlled—between the world proletariat and the world bourgeoisie, and between the Soviet Union and the "imperialist" governments which were considered to serve as the instruments of "predatory" capitalism. The ultimate, preordained outcome of this antagonism, in the Soviet view, was to be the institution of proletarian dictatorships, the destruction of the bourgeoisie, and the establishment of a classless, communistic society in all countries of the world.[1]

This millennial goal, however, would not be attained without struggle. The most bitter and irreconcilable hostility on the part of the capitalist world was taken for granted by the

[1] The affectation of placing quotation marks around such familiar Marxist terms as "capitalist," "bourgeois," "imperialist," etc. has generally been avoided in the confidence that the reader will recognize when they are being employed in their specialized ideological sense.

founders of the Soviet Union and their disciples. "We are living not merely in a state but in a system of states," V. I. Lenin had pointed out in 1919, "and the existence of the Soviet Republic side by side with imperialist states for a long time is unthinkable. One or the other must triumph in the end. And before that end supervenes, a series of frightful collisions between the Soviet Republic and the bourgeois states will be inevitable." [2]

Furthermore, Lenin and his followers had no intention of passively awaiting the outcome of historical necessity. To them the world revolution was a living, dynamic thing which demanded their fullest active support. In another famous passage written as far back as 1915 Lenin had sketched the way in which a revolutionary victory in one country—Russia, as it turned out—would be utilized to promote the revolutionary cause in all countries. "The victorious proletariat of that country, having expropriated the capitalists and organised its own socialist production, would *confront* the rest of the capitalist world, attract to itself the oppressed classes of other countries, raise revolts among them against the capitalists, and, in the event of necessity, come out even with armed force against the exploiting classes and their states." [3]

The continuous republication of these and similar statements in the Soviet Union, and Stalin's approving citations and elaborations of them in his own writings, constitute but one among many indications that Lenin's revolutionary conception remained central to the Soviet world outlook. In retrospect it seems sufficiently obvious that the ultimate world-revolutionary goal was never lost to sight, even through the years of Stalin's consolidation of power in Russia, the concentration on "socialism in one country," the "popular front" era of the 1930's, the Stalin-Hitler pact of 1939, and the wartime alliance with the imperialist nations of the West. The limited wartime collabora-

---

[2] V. I. Lenin, "Report of Central Committee at 8th Party Congress," *Selected Works* (New York, International Publishers, 1943), VIII, 33; quoted by J. Stalin in *Problems of Leninism* (Moscow, Foreign Languages Publishing House, 1940), 156.
[3] Lenin, "United States of Europe Slogan," *Selected Works*, V, 141; quoted by Stalin in *Problems of Leninism*, 158.

tion—or "cobelligerency"—of the U.S.S.R. with Great Britain and the United States in 1941–1945 was not the prelude to a reconciliation of interests which the Soviets felt in their hearts to be irreconcilable, but a temporary expedient dictated by a mortal threat to the survival of the Soviet Union. The termination of hostilities brought the period of collaboration to an almost immediate end and revealed once more the persistent ideological chasm which the smoke of conflict had temporarily obscured.

As seen through Soviet eyes, the victorious conclusion of World War II opened a new and highly promising epoch of world history. It was true that the crushing of Germany and Japan, while reducing the number of the U.S.S.R.'s imperialist enemies, also diminished the opportunities for playing off one group of capitalist states against another. The supposedly ineradicable hostility of the remaining capitalist powers might still necessitate a policy directed in the first instance at preventing any possibility of "capitalist encirclement." The power of the United States, which Soviet theorists long had viewed as the predestined leader of an anti-Soviet crusade, had increased both relatively and absolutely; and its unfriendly disposition toward the U.S.S.R. had been confirmed, to the satisfaction of the Soviet leaders, by its unwillingness to subordinate the military and political conduct of the war to Soviet desires. After Hitler's overthrow the Politburo undoubtedly felt that it had to be on its guard against hostile moves by the United States and its associates. The whole postwar policy of the Soviet Union was sometimes explained—not altogether implausibly— as an essentially defensive reaction to the presumed hostility of the capitalist world.

In reality, however, it is very doubtful that Soviet motivations can be adequately interpreted in terms of the conventional distinction between "defensive" and "aggressive" aims. From the point of view of the Soviet leaders there is no essential difference between working to protect the Soviet system at home and working to extend it to new areas of the earth's surface. Both are integral parts of the long-term, life-and-death struggle with world capitalism. And after 1945 the over-all balance of forces in the world, the "correlation between the socialist and capitalist systems," as Soviet theoreticians called it, had changed in such a way that the Soviet Government no longer needed to confine itself to a strictly "defensive" policy such as it had followed in the 1930's. Capitalism itself had now been thrown on the defensive, the Soviet leaders reasoned. The imperialist countries faced economic chaos and a strong possibility of collapse. Bourgeois domination over the oppressed proletariats had weakened. Even more important, the war had undermined imperialist control of hundreds of millions of colonial peoples. These weaknesses gave the Kremlin an unparalleled opportunity to strengthen the security of the U.S.S.R., advance the frontiers of socialism, and bring closer the day of final victory for the world revolution.[4]

Covered with the world-wide prestige earned for it by the Red Army, the Soviet Union possessed very considerable assets for such an enterprise despite the wartime impairment of its never very strong industrial and technological base. Its revolutionary apparatus united the explosive force of an idea, the dynamic qualities of a powerful nation, and the devotion of an international army. The idea, which found the root of poverty, exploitation, war, and all other evils in the capitalist system of production, had demonstrated its persuasiveness and vitality through practically a century. The Russian nation, expansionist in its traditions and unremittingly inoculated with a messianic doctrine for a generation, was the world's largest in area, stood next to China and India in population, and was second only to the United States in developed resources and productive power. At its leaders' command was a disciplined, international body of agitators and organizers, trained in conspiratorial methods, fanatically and unquestioningly devoted to the Soviet cause, and subject to no ethical restraints in promoting its interests.

These advantages would have counted for less if the Soviet

[4] An illuminating reflection of this outlook is the article of B. L. Leontyev, "The Struggle for Peace—Mighty Movement of Modern Times," *Voprosy filosofii*, No. 1, 1950, 21-34 (abstracted in *Current Digest of the Soviet Press*, II, No. 38, November 4, 1950, 3-8).

Union and Communism had everywhere been viewed with the suspicion and repugnance they have traditionally aroused in the United States. In reality Communism, even in its Stalinist dress, possessed a measure of genuine appeal which it would be unrealistic to overlook. A minority of individuals in every country were captivated by its doctrinal boldness, its fanaticism, and its atmosphere of perpetual struggle. A larger number were swayed by its promise to correct real abuses and its vision of a future of universal peace and abundance. Finally, it held a strong potential appeal for the socially disinherited of this world—for countless thousands in every climate who had received no great share of capitalist abundance, had grown weary of privation and indignity, and had become ripe victims of any movement that promised a better future, however visionary. The overcrowded hovels of Asia and the Far East, in particular, teemed with people whose condition recalled Karl Marx's century-old summons to those who had "nothing to lose but their chains."

A further advantage to the Kremlin flowed from uncertainty and divided counsels among its presumed adversaries. Outside the Soviet Union, many people of undoubted intelligence and integrity hesitated to believe that Soviet activities seriously threatened the civilization they knew. It seemed next to incredible that reasonable men could dedicate themselves to a revolutionary program which was based on the conscious rejection of ordinary morality and whose realization required the most systematic and ruthless terrorism. It was painful to imagine that the Soviet Union's magnificent resistance to German Nazism foreshadowed a determined attempt to spread another form of totalitarianism, more highly systematized and certainly not less destructive of all that Western civilization considered most valuable in the human personality. A well-meant disposition to rationalize and find excuses for Soviet conduct served to weaken and delay world reaction to the long series of aggressive acts by which, from 1944 onward, the Soviet leaders disclosed their bad faith and their expansionist ambitions.

At the other extreme were those whose detestation of Communism led them to misapprehend its real nature and the real dangers it concealed. Fear and hatred sometimes obscured the fact that advancing Communism, for all its ruthlessness, relied only partly on physical force and could not conceivably be stemmed solely by forcible measures. Frontal attack on an enemy position was exceptional in Soviet-Communist tactics. To its intended victims Communism presented itself not as an enslaving but as a liberating movement, and as one dedicated to the liquidation of real, familiar grievances. The pupils of the dissolved Comintern were past masters in the subtle techniques of infiltration, subversion, and erosion by propaganda and deception, cunningly attuned to the realities of each particular situation. Against such methods the soldier and the policeman were at an equal disadvantage. Communism, in the last analysis, was a state of mind, and attempts to fight it with conventional weapons served only to encourage Moscow's thundering denunciations of capitalistic "reaction," "barbarity," and "militarism." Only a strategy of great versatility and flexibility, based on an appreciation of the full range of Soviet methods and of the popular emotions on which they played, would have much chance of countering Soviet tactics and exploiting any weaknesses that might appear in the Soviet position.

The most striking feature of these tactics, as they revealed themselves through the later 1940's, was their diversity and, at the same time, their complete subordination to the aim of protecting and extending the area controlled by the U.S.S.R. in Europe and Asia. One of the axiomatic features of Communism, deeply ingrained in Leninist revolutionary ideology, is the utilization of any means whatever for the furtherance of the Communist cause. In its struggle against "imperialism" the Soviet Union thus felt free to resort to a far greater variety of weapons than the repertoire of any non-Communist country could conceivably include. Diplomatic pressure and deception, propaganda, legalistic quibbles, economic bargaining, political obstruction, labor agitation, civil disorder, guerrilla warfare, and even direct military intervention were utilized according to circumstances by the Soviet Government and its foreign supporters, whose efforts, despite their alleged independence of control from Moscow, all too clearly dovetailed into a universal plan.

Certain underlying features of this activity emphasized its common inspiration and also suggested some of the mental characteristics, at once cautious and bold, imaginative and limited, and above all opportunistic, of the man who directed it. Its basic preoccupation appeared to be the strengthening of the Soviet Union itself, which Stalin had once described as "a mighty base" for the further development of the world revolution.[5] In the pursuit of this aim it recklessly sacrificed both the international good will which had been one of the Soviet Union's major assets at the war's end, and the short-range interests of the foreign revolutionary groups which served as the advance guard of international Communism. It treated loyal servants of the revolution with almost the same measure of distrust as it did the "ruling circles" of the capitalist world. It regularly availed itself of the "big lie" technique which imputed its own motives to its adversaries, and beclouded each new act of aggression and repression with talk of the "peace" and "democracy" which the Soviet Union claimed to be defending against the nefarious designs of Wall Street. Sensing the latent distrust of the United States which existed among foreign peoples, it spared no effort to build up the fiction of a bloodthirsty and profit-hungry American capitalism bent on world enslavement through the Marshall Plan and the atomic bomb.

The internal policies of the U.S.S.R. itself formed an integral part of this global design, the root purpose of which was not so much the welfare of the world proletariat as the strengthening of the Soviet Union for a showdown which Communists frankly believed to be inevitable. Whether or not the search for military preparedness that dominated the postwar life of the Soviet Union was spurred by delusive expectations of a

5 "The October Revolution and the Tactics of the Russian Communists" (1924), in *Problems of Leninism*, 116-117.

capitalist attack, there was no mistaking the warlike posture of the Soviet armed forces after 1945 or the concern for military potential which inspired the Fourth Five-Year Plan for the reconstruction and expansion of the Soviet economy. Not only the labor of the Soviet peoples, "voluntary" or forced, but also the capacities of hundreds of thousands of war prisoners and the industrial loot of occupied areas in Europe and the Far East were mobilized for the task of overcoming the deficiencies of Soviet transportation, power, and heavy industry. While millions of young men continued to fill the swollen cadres of the Soviet army, Soviet and "captive" foreign scientists pressed their experiments with atomic energy, guided missiles, submarines, and other phases of modern warfare.

Meanwhile the Soviet people, still restricted to a minimum of personal comforts, renewed acquaintance with the peacetime rigors of the fully developed police and propaganda state. Increasingly cut off from every source of independent knowledge of the outside world, their only possible course was rigid social and mental conformity. Those who failed to respond to the incitements of the official propaganda responded to the terror wielded, in their name, by the agents of the Ministry of Internal Affairs.

To dispassionate observers a movement governed by such methods seemed unlikely to add much to the sum total of human happiness, either now or at some future date when the world proletariat might come into its own. These, however, were the characteristic features of the system which was already being introduced in rudimentary fashion in those foreign areas in Europe which the advancing Red Army had brought under Soviet control. *Mutatis mutandis,* the same system would shortly make its appearance in China, as that country's old-established Communist party prepared to reap the fruit of its military victories. The same militancy, the same rigid subordination, the same carelessness of individual rights, the same uncompromising dedication to a visionary goal could be discerned in the actions of the Communist parties that were still operating in the outer darkness of the capitalist world. Such characteristics went deeper than mere tactics, which might be altered from month to month. They were rooted in the mentality of the men and women who had turned to Communism and stayed with it. Often combined with keen intelligence and resourcefulness, they formed the durable strength of the movement and its danger for the majority who could not share its apocalyptic vision.

Continuous pressure against all of the enemy's weak points was the rationale of Soviet-Communist expansionism; but its strategic directives were a profound secret, and it was sometimes easier to describe the effects of a given move than to elucidate the line of thought which prompted it. No outsider could say with assurance, in 1950, how far the results of five years' effort in Europe and elsewhere corresponded to the expectations and intentions of the Soviet leaders. In fact, the revolution had been carried forward to the limits of the Red Army's westward advance, and there stopped. The "Iron Curtain" had been established along a line which split Germany in two and which excluded Western influence from the broad band of European territory stretching from the Elbe to the Soviet frontier. The countries to the east, with the single exception of Finland, were methodically remolded in the Soviet image; those to the west, some of which had seemed ripe for revolution in the years after 1945, were left to rehabilitate themselves with the aid of the United States or to succumb to the internal "contradictions" of capitalist society, stimulated by the destructive zeal of the local Communist parties.

Whether the Soviet Union viewed the temporary subsidence of the revolutionary movement in Western Europe with equanimity must remain a matter of conjecture. There is on record a published Soviet statement which praises the revolutionary services of the French and Italian Communist parties and attributes their failure to the fact that "unfortunately the Soviet army did not and could not render . . . assistance," as it allegedly had done in the case of Yugoslavia, by creating the conditions necessary for them to take power.[6] The implication that the French and Italian Communists could not have come to power without Soviet armed assistance may correspond to the facts, but fails to explain why the U.S.S.R. gave them no greater encouragement to exploit their initial revolutionary successes in 1945–1947. The question remains unanswered whether the Soviet Union, always wary of independent foci of power within the Communist camp, really wanted them to come to power without the restraining presence of Soviet armed forces.

No such misgivings appear to have attended Soviet policy toward Germany, which lay directly on the borders of the Soviet area of control and had been recognized since before 1917 as a decisive center of the world proletarian struggle. Though forced to accept a complicated division of the conquered country into allied occupation zones and sectors, the Russians undoubtedly hoped for a restoration of German unity (minus extensive territorial amputations in the east) and a quick withdrawal of occupation forces under conditions which would favor continued prosecution of the revolutionary struggle throughout the country. Once Germany was brought under Soviet control, extension of the revolution to the rest of Western Europe would follow almost as a matter of course. Soviet moves in Eastern Germany, which paralleled the revolutionary process that was going forward in Eastern Europe, clearly had the additional motive of establishing a base for the revolutionizing of Germany as a whole. This broad conception explained the violent Soviet resistance to the establishment of a separate German government in the American, British, and French zones of occupation, a step necessitated by Soviet noncooperation with the three Western occupying powers. It also accounted for the persistence of Soviet and German Communist spokesmen in sounding the theme of German "unity" even after separate governments had been set up in both Western and Eastern Germany in 1949.

[6] Letter from the Central Committee of the Soviet Communist party to the Central Committee of the Yugoslav Communist party, May 4, 1948, in *The Soviet-Yugoslav Dispute: Text of the Published Correspondence* (London and New York, Royal Institute of International Affairs, 1948), 51.

With the stalling of the revolutionary offensive in Europe, Soviet-Communist attention appeared to shift increasingly to the unexploited potentialities afforded by the anti-Western, anticolonial struggle of indigenous peoples in the Far East. To some extent this appearance of a shift may have been illusory. Kremlin strategy had always been based on what Stalin once called the "alliance of the proletarian revolution [in industrialized countries] with the liberation movement in the colonies and the dependent countries," [7] and the revolutionary forces in Burma, Malaya, Indochina, Indonesia, and above all China had certainly not lacked Soviet encouragement in their postwar battles against the reimposition of the old order. By 1949, however, the imminence of a Communist victory in China made it urgently necessary to regulate the status of the Chinese Communist party and at the same time offered the possibility of quick additional conquests and a consolidation of Communist power over large parts of the Asiatic continent. While Soviet-sponsored activities in Europe dwindled to a virtual holding operation, the entire Asiatic front entered upon a period of feverish activity which was to persist throughout the ensuing year.

The extension of Soviet influence far beyond the Russian frontiers, and the means and methods by which it had been accomplished, raised a question whether the Kremlin was actually engaged in prosecuting a world revolution or was simply pursuing a modernized form of the old-fashioned Russian imperialism. A false distinction was sometimes made between Communism, which was held to be an internal affair of the Russians, and imperialist expansionism, which threatened other nations and was therefore a matter of legitimate international concern. In reality the two concepts appeared hardly separable. Marxist-Leninist Communism, as the rationalization of a specific mental attitude, was expansionist by its very nature, and seemed incapable of accepting for any length of time the conventional restraints to which the old-fashioned imperialism had been subject. So long as Stalin preferred a method of expan-

[7] "The Foundation of Leninism" (1924), in *Problems of Leninism,* 60.

sion into contiguous areas, using the Soviet army and Soviet diplomacy as his main instruments, the outward aspects of the Soviet drive to world power were bound to duplicate the classical imperialist pattern. The content of the imperialist undertaking, however, was revolutionary. The fate of each successive victim showed that the aim was not merely the extension of influence and power, but the complete transformation of society in the Soviet image.

Not the least important battleground of this undeclared war against the "imperialist" world order, which governed every phase of Soviet foreign policy, was the United Nations organization. The Soviet Government had entered the United Nations in 1945 with few illusions about its professed aims of international peace, harmony, and progress. Lasting peace and harmony between imperialist and socialist states, according to the Soviet gospel, was impossible. Despite its success in bargaining for an advantageous voting position, the U.S.S.R. was bound to regard the United Nations, like the League of Nations before it, as an organization dominated by the imperialist powers and their client states. Participation in such an organization had definite advantages from the Soviet point of view, if only to prevent its being transformed into an anti-Soviet coalition. But the Soviets were doomed from the outset to an opposition role, and their behavior in the "town meeting of the world" recalled the tactics prescribed by Lenin for the "revolutionary utilization of reactionary parliaments."

Though Stalin occasionally referred to the United Nations as a "serious instrument" for the preservation of international peace and security, his practice indicated that he regarded it primarily as a means of blocking any "capitalist crusade" against the U.S.S.R.—and, incidentally, as an incomparable device for the world-wide dissemination of Soviet propaganda. Far from helping to make it an effective instrument of peace and security, the U.S.S.R. habitually used it as a means of disrupting, confusing, and delaying concerted international action and constructive efforts for peace. Its chief interest in collective security seemed to lie in preventing any effective collective action against itself or one of its satellites. These tactics served to alienate a growing number of nations whose original inclination toward the Soviet Union had been cautiously friendly. They thus accentuated the diplomatic isolation of the Soviet bloc and, in a practical sense, rendered Soviet participation increasingly ineffective. Nevertheless the Soviet Union chose to remain a member of the United Nations for the sake of its propagandistic potentialities and the Charter provisions which gave the Soviet delegate a veto power over the most crucial area of the organization's work.

Though the protagonists of this effort to destroy the bourgeois world recognized no subjective or ethical limitations, their success inevitably was conditioned by the limitations of the human material with which they worked. "A war for the overthrow of the international bourgeoisie," Lenin had warned, was "a hundred times more difficult, prolonged and complicated than the most stubborn of ordinary wars between states." [8] For those who rejected Lenin's and Stalin's interpretation of historical necessity, there would always remain a question whether the goal they had set was not actually beyond the reach of mere human beings. The most casual observation of conditions within the "camp of democracy and peace" disclosed innumerable points at which human nature and capacity were falling short of requirements. The central role of repression and terror in the entire Soviet system showed that the masses had not responded to the revolutionary gospel as positively as the revolutionaries of 1917 had expected. Overt opposition was virtually impossible; but two thin streams of migration, one toward the "corrective labor" camps of the Soviet Union and the other toward the displaced persons centers of Western Germany and Austria, revealed a persistent undercurrent of rebelliousness against the conditions of Soviet life.

Signs of disaffection could also be perceived in the revolutionary vanguard outside the Soviet frontiers. Many who had flocked to the Communist standard in the years around 1945

[8] "'Left-Wing' Communism, an Infantile Disorder," *Selected Works*, X, 111.

were frightened off again as the ruthlessness, deadly determination, and cynical opportunism of Soviet methods disclosed themselves. Even some veteran Communists who had rounded every bend of the party line in the 1920's and 1930's were antagonized by Stalin's invariable practice of sacrificing the foreign Communist parties to the immediate interests of the Soviet Union. The latent tension between the Russian and international aspects of the movement came to a head in 1948 with the dramatic revolt of Marshal J. B. Tito and the Yugoslav Communist party, which was essentially a gesture of protest against the Kremlin's claim to infallibility in regulating local Communist affairs down to the last detail. The dangerous potentialities of Tito's contumacy, which struck at the root principle of centralized revolutionary direction and had profound repercussions throughout the Bolshevik family, could be gauged by the violence of the Kremlin's reaction and the diligence with which it endeavored to hunt down anyone who could be suspected of similar leanings.

The unmeasured fury of this purgative process in Soviet-controlled areas after 1948 drew attention to a still greater danger which dogged the footsteps of those who presumed to regard themselves as the chosen instruments of historical destiny. This was the danger of one of those arrogant miscalculations which had eventually sealed the doom of Hitler, Mussolini, and many another would-be world conqueror. Stalin, as he entered his seventy-first year, was still known for his level head and cool nerves, but it had yet to be shown that he and his henchmen could conduct an action on the world stage with the same judgment and finesse they had brought to the conquest of power in Russia. Their ideological weapons were sufficiently potent to redeem any number of minor tactical blunders, but a false move on the grand scale could have consequences infinitely dangerous for the "socialist fatherland" as well as for humanity at large.

Finally, the Kremlin had to reckon with the latent powers of resistance of the civilization it was bent on destroying. The Soviet Government's initial postwar advances had caught the "free world" off guard, at a time when long-term cooperation with the Soviet Union had still seemed a serious possibility. Its own policies, however, soon dissipated official and popular good will in the United States and other democracies, and began a process of slow rapprochement among those nations which rejected the Soviet view of life and politics. Potentially the U.S.S.R. and its satellites were faced with a coalition of free nations vastly superior in material resources, and linked by a belief in individual freedom and dignity which might yet prove its superiority to the shallow deceptions of the Stalinist creed.

2. The Free World Discovers Itself

In prosecuting their life-and-death struggle with world capitalism, the Soviet leaders placed heavy reliance on the effects of internal conflicts and "contradictions" within the enemy camp. These internal cleavages, according to Soviet theory, were ineluctably preparing the way for the downfall of the whole capitalist system; it was the task of the revolutionary movement to exploit and aggravate them, thus hastening the process decreed by history and ensuring that it reached its appointed end. Communist propaganda and agitation were therefore directed unremittingly to playing upon and intensifying the latent conflicts which abounded in the non-Soviet world —class conflict between exploiters and exploited, political and racial conflict between imperialist and colonial nations, and, not least, conflicting interests among the imperialist nations themselves. Many of these antagonisms were really severe and could be made to look even more so. Since the war Communism had worked upon them with considerable effect, predisposing large masses of humanity to believe that the Soviet Union was their friend and that their real enemies were nearer home.

But, if Soviet tactics enjoyed some success in the effort to split up and dissolve the outer world into its mutually antagonistic elements, they also produced another tendency quite opposite to what the Soviet leaders aimed at. The expansionist policies of the Soviet Government, by making the free nations aware of their common interests in face of a common peril, went far toward counterbalancing the disintegrating effects of Communist tactics on the level of propaganda and mass action. What the Soviet Union might have gained by posing as the friend of the downtrodden and oppressed it largely threw away by revealing itself as the enemy of legality and free government everywhere. The key to postwar world history lay in the interaction of these two trends: a movement toward disintegration of the established order, continuously stimulated by Communist agitation, but continuously checked and counterbalanced by revelations of the imperialistic tendencies of the Soviet Union itself.

The "free world'" which gradually became cognizant of itself during the postwar years reflected a growing awareness that the Soviet Government was intent on destroying the international order built up through centuries of modern history. "Free world" was a term of courtesy and convenience rather than an accurate description of the congeries of nations which acknowledged the threat of Soviet imperialism. These nations, from Britain, and the United States to Nicaragua, Japan, Afghanistan, and Yemen, represented more varied traditions and a greater diversity of political and social forms than did even the nations of the postwar Soviet bloc. Not all of them regarded each other as friends, nor did they uniformly acknowledge the sanctity of the individual and the other tenets that made up the liberal-democratic creed. On many international issues they bitterly opposed each other. What they had in common was the fact that none of them repudiated the principles of individual liberty as did the followers of Lenin and Stalin, and that their governments, often reluctantly but nevertheless explicitly, condemned the aggressive actions directed from Moscow in the name of "peace" and "democracy."

The "free world" as it existed in 1949 and 1950 had been evoked by Soviet imperialism and formed by American encouragement. The United States, which as early as March 1947 had acknowledged a vital interest in supporting "free peoples who are resisting attempted subjugation by armed minorities or by outside pressures," [9] was predestined by all the facts of international life to take the lead in organizing whatever resistance was to be offered to Soviet efforts. Because of its favorable geographic position and latent economic and military strength—vastly increased by the very war which had largely shattered the economies of its European friends—this country alone possessed unutilized resources which could be applied to stiffening the tottering foundations of the Old World. The same considerations marked it out for the special enmity of the Soviet Union, whose dogmatists had long foreseen the emergence of the United States as the supreme embodiment of capitalism.

Although the advance of the Stalinist tide was recognizably incompatible with America's larger interests in the world, this country was by no means eager to take up the responsibility of arresting it. Our postwar foreign policies as elaborated in the closing years of the great conflict had been geared to a world at peace, not to a life-and-death ideological and power struggle with one of our most valiant allies. World pacification, chastisement of the former aggressor nations, and promotion of expanding democracy and welfare through the United Nations and its ancillary agencies such as the proposed International Trade Organization—these had been the aims, which were not entirely surrendered even when the demands of the new power conflict became inescapable. Such objectives were attuned to the conception of an international order that would represent "one world," politically as well as geographically. Such a conception was far more congenial to most Americans than the alternative, "two-world" doctrine of irreconcilable antagonism, which was accepted slowly, skeptically, and, for the most part, reluctantly.

To an increasing degree, nevertheless, resistance to Soviet and Communist encroachments became the primary object of American policy, based on the conviction that, as President Truman said in his message to Congress of March 12, 1947,

[9] Message of President Truman to Congress, March 12, 1947.

"If we falter in our leadership, we may endanger the peace of the world—and we shall surely endanger the welfare of our own Nation." That this conviction was well founded seems, in the light of subsequent developments, as little open to doubt as the fact that American action in the ensuing years actually did stave off an imminent peril to Europe and indirectly to the entire free world. From the Truman Doctrine and the Marshall Plan in 1947 to the North Atlantic Treaty and the Mutual Defense Assistance Program in 1949, American policy was directed explicitly and, on the whole, successfully, to re-establishing the foundations of a world threatened by imminent collapse.

History, which may be counted upon to assess this record in its full significance, will undoubtedly record a number of shortcomings which robbed American action in these years of its full potential effectiveness. Many of the failures and half-successes of American postwar policy were accounted for by the novelty and extraordinary difficulty of a world situation governed by the operation of tremendous forces which were largely beyond control of ordinary statesmanship. Others could be attributed to deficiencies in the preparation of the American people and their government for an enterprise of such un-exampled complexity. Among the assumptions on which American action seemed to be based were some which suggested an inadequate grasp of the issues at stake and which could be corrected only in the light of bitter and costly experience. Although such partial miscalculations were in no way peculiar to the United States, this country's leading position made them even more conspicuous than similar manifestations elsewhere in the free world.

Probably the most fundamental limitation on American action in the years 1947–1950 was a widespread tendency to underestimate the magnitude of the effort—mental as well as material—which would be required if the free world was to survive. If the majority of Americans were in little doubt about the reality of the Stalinist threat, they sometimes displayed a lack of perceptiveness concerning its nature, methods, and scope. It took time for them to realize that resistance to Soviet expansionism was an undertaking of global dimensions, in which the abandonment of any one position would only provide a springboard for further Communist advance, at the same time encouraging the Kremlin's partisans throughout the world and diminishing the will of other threatened peoples to resist.

It was even more difficult to realize what heavy demands this global resistance would make on our resources, our military power, and, not least, our political understanding. Throughout American statements and actions from 1947 to 1950 there seemed to run a feeling that the problem could somehow be dealt with by a limited effort, without sacrifice of a rising standard of living at home and without radical political or social changes in the free world. In the light of all existing precedents, American action in these years was certainly not lacking in foresight, generosity, and courage. But the events of 1950 were to show how inadequate these actions had been in terms of the actual world conditions which international Communism was feverishly exploiting for its own ends.

Two reflections of this tendency to underrate and oversimplify the problem deserved special attention because of their profound influence on American relations with the other members of the free world. One was a widespread disposition to rely on mechanical expedients of one kind or another to defeat a movement which was essentially not mechanical but psychological in character. This propensity was most conspicuous in the realm of military affairs. Sections of the government, of Congress, and of public opinion, equating Soviet expansionism with the expansionism of earlier imperialist states, tended to think of it as a movement that relied primarily on force and could be checked by the application of superior force. People of this turn of mind, though far from agreed on the specific measures required, correctly pointed out that the Soviet Union's tremendous postwar military establishment demanded a comparable effort on the part of this country. The vital point that was often overlooked was that military force was only one of the weapons in the Soviet arsenal, and not necessarily the principal one. Except in China, the main Communist onslaughts between 1945 and 1950 were delivered not on the military but on the political and social level, and directed less against the armies of the free world than against its social, economic, and psychological weak points. Even in China, the collapse of the Nationalist armies—despite the possession of considerable American equipment—showed how inadequate military force could be if the moral and spiritual foundations were open to attack.

The same indifference to psychological factors was evident in American attitudes toward friendly nations. Since the United States in resisting Soviet encroachments was acting not only in its own interest but in that of the free world as a whole, it was generally taken for granted that other free nations must subordinate their particular interests and policies to this overriding identity of aim. The reasoning no doubt was logical, but action based upon it always ran the danger of antagonizing friendly countries which felt that their legitimate interests were being unnecessarily disregarded. Other nations, conscious though they might be of the Soviet menace, were not prepared to follow American policy in all its details. Not a few foreign observers still regarded American action in world affairs as so erratic, so impetuous, and so self-aggrandizing in tendency as to be almost as great a danger to world tranquility as the policies of the U.S.S.R. itself. Readiness to neglect the susceptibilities of our friends and to take their solidarity as a matter of course assisted the unremitting efforts of Soviet propaganda to ascribe postwar world tensions to an alleged American desire for world domination.

The possibility of misunderstandings between the United States and its friends was accentuated by the prevalence of certain unfavorable opinions and half-truths about American policy which were as widespread as they were inexact. An example was the traditional European view concerning the capriciousness and instability of American foreign policy. This impression lingered despite the evidence of the 1948 presidential campaign that neither major party had then favored a retreat to isolationism. Still more prevalent, and infinitely more damaging in the postwar atmosphere, were two dogmas which presupposed that the United States had turned its back on isolationism and was capable of pursuing a consistent, purposeful foreign policy. One of these held that American policy was basically "militaristic" and directed toward war with the Soviet Union; the other, which did not exclude the first, that American policy was essentially "reactionary" and "imperialistic" in its inspiration and objectives.

Americans might reject these assertions as preposterous, but could not escape the fact that they were widely accepted abroad, with consequences highly detrimental to this country and the free world as a whole. No beliefs could possibly be more noxious in a period whose chief emotional preoccupations were fear of a new war and revulsion against colonialism and exploitation. In Europe particularly, this country's outspoken antipathy to the U.S.S.R., its obvious tendency to think of the Soviet menace in military terms, and its known reliance on a single and terrible weapon, the atomic bomb, bred a feeling of profound mistrust which went far to offset the positive effects of American material assistance. The prospect of becoming an East-West battleground and a target for atomic bombardment predisposed Europeans against American "atomic diplomacy," as Communists called it, and guaranteed an audience for Communist propaganda representing the United States as the chief danger to the peace.

The allegedly reactionary and imperialist nature of American policy was also highly suspect to those Europeans—perhaps a majority in Western Europe—who had lost faith in free enterprise as a solution of their own problems and sometimes tended to make the mistake of identifying American capitalism with support of out-and-out fascist regimes like that of Generalissimo Francisco Franco in Spain. An even greater dubiety about the real aims of the United States reigned in large parts of Asia and the Far East, where many millions of men had recently forced their way to independent nationhood and other millions were eager to throw off what remained of

European colonial rule. The leaders of opinion in these countries, dissatisfied with the limited extent of American assistance in their emancipation efforts, suspected the United States of secretly siding with the European colonial powers and opposing their aspirations. Meanwhile Latin Americans evinced no small resentment over the existing influence of the United States in their affairs and the preference accorded to other areas in the allocation of United States resources.

Such attitudes, however lacking in discrimination, were standing obstacles to that mobilization of spiritual forces in the free world which was essential if the Stalinist offensive was to be effectively combated. In a polarized world, those who were not solidly in one camp became involuntary allies of the other side. The situation was one that American policies and actions in the postwar years had unintentionally helped to create, but one which, in turn, seriously impeded the realization of American policy objectives.

Two phases of postwar United States policy, both of which seemed to foreign critics to combine a militaristic with an imperialist-reactionary trend, exemplified this vicious circle in a special degree. One concerned the treatment of the former enemy states, Germany and Japan; the other was the American attitude in China's civil war.

The postwar evolution of American policy toward Germany and Japan reflected with the utmost clarity the transition from a "one-world" to a "two-world" concept of international affairs. Early allied actions toward the vanquished aggressor states were based on the apparent expectation of a long period of peace, and certainly did not contemplate their participation in any new power alignment. Yet within five years or less the United States, spurred by Soviet aggressiveness and followed somewhat haltingly by its democratic allies, had swung around to a point at which it seemed to regard the regeneration of both Western Germany and Japan as far enough advanced to warrant their inclusion—conceivably even their rearmament— within a coalition of defensive forces directed at curbing the expansionism of the U.S.S.R. A concomitant of this reversal was a relaxation of the pressure against those entrenched economic and social groups in the former enemy states which, though perhaps not directly implicated in the Nazi and Japanese aggressions, had merited the epithets "reactionary," "nationalistic," and "imperialistic" and now seemed to be regaining some of their former influence.

Although a good argument could be made for the necessity of these concessions in the light of the over-all East-West power balance, their effect on foreign opinion was not reassuring. The peoples and governments of those countries which had directly experienced Axis aggression displayed grave misgivings over a trend that threatened, in effect, to cancel out the victory achieved in World War II. In this attitude they found themselves at one with the loudly professed though somewhat hypocritical stand of the U.S.S.R. and the governments of the Soviet bloc. Led by France in Europe and by the Philippines and Australia in the Pacific, this country's non-Communist allies of the Second World War endeavored to apply the brakes and to limit the effect of American policies which they did not approve but at the same time could not wholly repudiate.

Responsibility for the government of the conquered countries was so distributed that this country's allies had little choice except to follow, however protestingly, the lead of the United States. In China, a country 13 times as large and three times as populous as Germany and Japan together, they were bound by no such considerations. The American policy of aid to Chiang Kai-shek's Nationalist government, and of refusal to deal with the victorious Chinese Communists, was one which other free nations had no power to oppose but recognized no obligation to support. Thus by late 1949, when the Communists had gained control of virtually the entire China mainland and established a "People's Republic" claiming sovereignty over the whole of China, the United States found itself in some danger of being left practically alone in continuing to recognize the fugitive Nationalist regime on the island of Formosa—which had begun as the ally of all the Western powers and technically still represented China as one of the five great powers in the United Nations.

The causes of this anomaly were to be sought as much in the domestic politics of the United States as in any special peculiarities of the Far Eastern situation. To many foreign observers, however, American policy toward China seemed to betray not only a lack of realism but also an unwarranted preoccupation with military factors and a regrettable attachment to the political-social status quo. In Asia particularly, support of Chiang Kai-shek's dictatorship was equated with opposition to the whole reformist trend which had reached revolutionary dimensions in so many sections of that continent. American postwar policy in Southeast Asia, India, and the Middle East, though by no means oblivious to local aspirations, had not espoused them vigorously enough to dispel this impression. Thus the Chinese civil war, which annexed the world's most populous country to the camp of international Communism, had the further effect of driving a wedge between the United States and its allies and alienating in some degree the sympathies of other Asiatic countries.

This brief enumeration naturally does not exhaust the list of larger and smaller tensions that existed between the United States and its friends in the free world. In focusing on the United States, moreover, it conveys a one-sided impression of American wrong-headedness and ignores both the political eccentricities of other nations and the more general social and political "contradictions" which Soviet policy was striving to accentuate. These contradictions, extending throughout the length and breadth of the free world, were of many kinds. Each national state had its internal struggle of competing parties, classes, and ideologies. In what remained of the colonial world, pressure for the overthrow of foreign rule continued to build up, while new internal tensions germinated in the newly liberated countries. Individual nations continued to pursue their special interests, subordinating them with difficulty if at all to the need for common action. Clashes of national interest had more than once led to sharp military conflict, and there were smoldering quarrels—between the Arab states and Israel, for example, and between Pakistan and India—which held a constant threat of new, uncontrollable conflagrations.

And yet, amid all these tensions and open and latent quarrels, there were occasions when the free world seemed to become conscious of itself and to function as a true community united by a common interest. In 1948–1949 the principal nations of Western Europe and North America had determined to unite their efforts in establishing an effective, integrated defense against the eventuality of aggression from any quarter. The free nations outside the North Atlantic nucleus, however they might bicker among themselves and curse the very existence of an East-West conflict, were also united on the key issue of opposition to Soviet-Communist aggression. When that issue was posed without possibility of evasion, not only the North Atlantic allies but all the nations of the non-Communist world showed a clear understanding of where their interest lay. The General Assembly of the United Nations, the most comprehensive forum of the postwar world, was the customary scene of these demonstrations. They reached a climax on December 1, 1949 when 53 nations—including every non-Communist member of the world body—voted to adopt an Anglo-American resolution calling on all nations to return to the peaceful principles of the United Nations Charter.

The regularity with which a majority of the United Nations followed the American lead on issues connected with direct Soviet aggression was not the result of coercion or even, primarily, of the expectation of American favors. On other issues —including China—the non-Communist delegations were not too hesitant about voting against the United States. Their stand on the specific issue of Soviet policy came from a reluctant realization that Soviet tactics were in fact a threat to every free nation, and that the problem of the United States was also their own problem.

The Kremlin, in its preparations to destroy the free world, had thus in reality driven the free world into a reluctant act of self-recognition. Yet the solidarity that found expression at certain critical moments was provisional and highly precarious. The free world lived from crisis to crisis. Between crises, the old doubts, distrusts, and antagonisms, always stimulated by Communist propaganda, continued to eat away at its foundations. It would need a still graver crisis to disclose whether the free world believed in itself sufficiently to defend its freedom by methods which the adversary would respect.

3. Fronts in a Global Struggle

Opinions differed about the imminence of a crisis which would put the free world's solidarity to the test, but it was plain that the possibility of an armed clash was recognized on both sides and that the Soviet leaders were in a position to throw down the gauntlet at any time. As though fascinated by the expectation of catastrophe, the Soviet bloc and the North Atlantic Treaty powers worked feverishly to marshal their strength while the global "cold war" between them raged with undiminished violence. "If history is any guide," wrote John Foster Dulles in a book published early in 1950, "war will come out of this situation. . . . Future generations will look back with amazement if war is averted. It will be an achievement without precedent. Yet that is our task. It is a task that requires an effort like the one required to win a great war." [10]

The winter of 1949–1950 was not too bad a moment for taking stock of the situation which promised to make such heavy demands in the time ahead. No distracting crisis of the first magnitude was at hand. Relations between the two camps, though chronically tense, seemed well below the boiling point despite the recent revelation that the Soviet Union was in a position to explode atomic bombs. At the moment the U.S.S.R. seemed mainly preoccupied with celebrating Stalin's seventieth birthday and pressing forward the work of national industrialization and militarization. Emulating these endeavors, the Com-

[10] John Foster Dulles, *War or Peace* (New York, The Macmillan Company, 1950), 3.

munist governments of Eastern Europe were conducting new purges and intensifying the long-standing pressure against Western interests within their territories; in China the new Communist government of Mao Tse-tung had entered a similar path, closely guided by Soviet advisers and technicians.

In the West, the nations of the five-nation Brussels treaty and the Atlantic pact were accelerating their planning for "collective defense" of the North Atlantic area, and for utilization of the American equipment that was tardily entering the transatlantic pipelines under the Mutual Defense Assistance Program enacted in October 1949. Authorities responsible for the Marshall Plan were proclaiming the virtues of "economic integration" as a means of setting Western Europe on a firm economic basis which would seal the gates against Communist disruption. Each month found the new Federal Republic in Western Germany a little stronger, and the opposition to its association in these collective efforts a little weaker. Outside of Europe, American and allied officials touched and retouched their plans for economic and military reinforcement of threatened areas of the free world.

While the two camps continued to prepare themselves against an eventuality whose outlines could be but dimly perceived, the battle lines between them continued fluid. As yet neither side could claim possession of the decisive areas. Between the Soviet and non-Soviet zones in Europe stretched a band of countries—Germany, Austria, and Yugoslavia—whose permanent allegiance was still in dispute and which embraced the heart of the Continent. To the southeastward, Turkey, Iran, and the Middle East were provisionally beyond Soviet reach, but by no means beyond the scope of Soviet ambitions. In the Far East, while Japan recuperated under the benevolent administration of General Douglas MacArthur, the revolutionary impetus which had carried Mao Tse-tung's armies across China had not yet spent itself. Burma, Thailand, Malaya, Indochina, Tibet, and the Republic of Korea all lay on the fringes of the newly enlarged Sino-Soviet realm and could be subjected to intolerable pressure at a moment's notice. These were the areas in which the East-West competition was to be keenest in the coming months, while the struggle in the European and Middle Eastern theaters proceeded along lines which had already become familiar.

The prominence of the Far Eastern theater of conflict in late 1949 and 1950 certainly betokened no loss of interest in Europe on the part of either the Kremlin or the United States and its allies. Europe, with its highly developed economy and its cultural preeminence, probably continued to outweigh the Far East not only in the minds of Europeans but in the opinions of Moscow and Washington. But, whereas in the Far East the conquest of China had laid open tempting avenues for Communist exploitation, in Europe the Communist advance had been at least temporarily checked. There all that remained for the Kremlin, short of actual aggression or quasi-aggression, was to maintain its forces in being, coordinate their activities with the requirements of its global strategy, and await a more propitious opportunity for resuming the struggle on a large scale. This situation implied nothing like inactivity for Western European Communists, who continued to maintain an unremitting, "legal" pressure of demonstrations and propaganda against their governments, while their ardent and effective espousal of the Soviet "peace" crusade grew more noticeable as their power to create major disturbances waned.

In Germany, routine Communist activities of this order were coordinated with the campaign for German "unity" through which the Kremlin hoped, eventually, to capture control of those parts of Hitler's former Reich which it had not already annexed, occupied, or bestowed on its Polish satellite. Possession of Germany, now precariously divided between the Western-supported Federal Republic and a Soviet-controlled "Democratic Republic" in the East, might very well tip the balance in Europe as between East and West. Thus, while the U.S.S.R. and the Western occupying powers worked to incorporate their parts of Germany into their respective politico-economic systems, each side made efforts to mobilize German sentiment as a whole against the other party. In this paradoxical competition for the German mind, the representatives of both Western democracy and Stalinist Marxism found themselves appealing to sentiments not wholly unrelated to those that had sustained Adolf Hitler's march toward world conquest.

Similar but perhaps less crucial tugs of war went on in Austria and in Yugoslavia, which together held the keys to the Danube and southeastern Europe. In Austria the Soviet Union, insensitive to the desire of the Austrians to resume their historic place in the Western family of nations, prolonged the four-power military occupation from year to year by refusing, on one tenuous pretext after another, to conclude a treaty restoring the country to normal conditions. Here it confined itself to the essentially passive role of dog in the manger; but toward Communist Yugoslavia, whose crime had been defiance of Kremlin authority and ultimate secession from the Soviet bloc, it omitted no form of menace short of armed invasion. The Western powers, which elsewhere in Eastern Europe had been virtually reduced to a strategy of unheeded protests, also viewed Yugoslavia as an area of primary strategic and ideological significance. As a sequel to the rout of the Communist guerrillas in Greece in mid-1949, the United States, with some British support, had embarked on a policy of limited but open encouragement to Marshal Tito in his lone fight against the international Bolshevik machine.

Yugoslavia's experience, by disclosing the psychological Achilles' heel of the Stalinist system, was generally considered to have an important bearing on the destiny of China, another country with potentialities for independent existence and the only "great power" to succumb to Communism since 1917. Despite the unequivocal professions of loyalty to the Soviet Union with which China's new masters capped their military victory, neither tradition nor local circumstances had seemed to fit China for easy absorption into the Soviet bloc. Communism in its Stalinist format had seemed inconsistent with the strongly marked individualism of the Chinese people; even their Communist leaders looked back on some three decades of autonomous action with a minimum of supervision from Moscow. Some able observers of the Far Eastern scene had even regarded the Chinese Communist movement as one that would be as ready to work with the United States as with the Soviet Union.

Whatever merit such views might have possessed, their submission to the test of experience had been made impossible by the weight of contrary opinion that was brought to bear on the government of the United States. Any idea of cultivating the friendship of a Communist China had been buried under an avalanche of protest from those Americans whose antipathy to Far Eastern Communism was so great that they continued to agitate for large-scale assistance to Chiang Kai-shek long after the responsible officials had concluded that the Generalissimo's cause was a hopeless one. Largely as a result of this pressure, American policy toward China took an opposite course from American policy toward Yugoslavia. Instead of trying to encourage autonomist and "deviationist" tendencies among the Chinese Communists, the United States chose to take President Mao Tse-tung's statements at face value, insisted that Chinese Communism was cut directly from Moscow's cloth, and made it clear that the Peking regime could expect no advantages, diplomatic or economic, from this country. Not unexpectedly, the results produced were also diametrically opposed. While the gulf between Tito and the Soviet bloc continued to widen, relations between Peking and Moscow seemed to become more intimate every day.

Although their deliberately highhanded treatment of American interests contributed greatly to this outcome, the disadvantages for China of an exclusively Soviet orientation must have been perfectly evident to the Chinese Communist leaders themselves. China's immense backwardness and devastated condition placed it in the front rank of countries that required large-scale foreign assistance for reconstruction and development. Such aid in adequate amounts the Soviet Union would be unable to supply for many years; the long-term credit of $300 million extended in connection with the Sino-Soviet treaty which Mao Tse-tung signed in Moscow on February 14, 1950 would be barely visible against the backdrop of China's requirements. Soviet aid, moreover, was a two-edged implement, invariably extended in such a way as to strengthen Soviet control of the beneficiary's affairs. The published agreements of February 14, temporarily extending Soviet rights in the Chinese Changchun Railway, Port Arthur, and Dairen, would tend to perpetuate the direct influence the U.S.S.R. was already exercising in Manchuria and North China. Subsequent agreements establishing joint Sino-Soviet companies for Chinese civil aviation, mineral exploitation in Sinkiang, and operation of the Changchun Railway revealed the application to China of the notorious "50–50 companies" device which had been used so successfully in the exploitation of Soviet Eastern Europe.[11]

A logical consequence of China's inclusion in the Soviet bloc was a growing harassment of Western individuals and interests within Chinese territory. This phenomenon could be viewed either as a Chinese counterpart of the similar persecutions taking place in Eastern Europe or, because of its special emphasis on Americans, as a Soviet-inspired campaign to eliminate American prestige in China and complete the alienation of the two countries. Whatever its motives, there could be no doubt that incidents like the year-long detention of Consul Angus Ward and his staff in Mukden in 1948–1949 served to harden American antipathy to the Chinese Communists and make any kind of accommodation between the two governments that much the more difficult. When the Communists climaxed these provocations in January 1950 by requisitioning certain American and other foreign consular properties in Peking, in defiance of both treaty rights and official protests, the United States retaliated by ordering the recall of all official

---

[11] The texts of the Sino-Soviet treaty of friendship, alliance and mutual assistance and the accompanying agreements on Manchuria and Soviet credits are printed in *USSR Information Bulletin*, X, February 24, 1950, 108-110; the official summary of the March 27 agreements establishing joint companies appears *ibid.*, April 14, 1950, 202-203. For a digest of State Department information on the "strategic detachment" of northern areas of China by the U.S.S.R. see *Department of State Bulletin*, XXII, February 6, 1950, 218-219, and April 10, 1950, 568.

American personnel in Communist China.[12] This move, comparable to a break in diplomatic relations, severed the last official American link with a regime which clearly expected to function in China for the indefinite future.

American withdrawal from continental China highlighted the contrast between this country's attitude and that of most other governments interested in Chinese affairs. The American stand evoked little sympathy among our European allies and still less among the peoples of Asia, all of whom were directly affected by the Chinese overturn. While American-Chinese relations had been moving toward a formal rupture, other governments had been preparing to come to terms with China's new rulers and salvage what they could of their former interests from the wreck of the old regime. The standard American arguments against diplomatic recognition of the Chinese Communists [13] carried little weight outside the United States. Great Britain offered on January 6, 1950 to establish relations with Peking; Norway, Denmark, Sweden, Switzerland, and the Netherlands were among the friendly European governments that followed the British example. Leading non-Communist governments in Asia, headed by Burma, India, Pakistan, and Israel, had taken the initiative even earlier. These latter governments were representative of a prevalent trend of thought which deplored the "ideological" struggle of the great powers and tended to think of China's new regime as at least somewhat preferable to the one that had preceded it.

---

[12] *Department of State Bulletin,* XXII, January 23, 1950, 119-123; the difficult story of the evacuation is recounted in later issues of the same publication.

[13] These arguments were succinctly stated in a letter from Herbert Hoover to Senator William F. Knowland of California, made public on January 2, 1950, in which the former President advocated continued recognition and support of the Chinese Nationalists on the following grounds: "(1) a wall against communism in the Pacific; (2) the defense of Japan and the Philippines; (3) the prevention of Chinese legations and consulates in the United States (and such other countries as agree with us) becoming nests of Communist conspiracies; (4) the prevention of another Communist permanent member of the United Nations Security Council with its dangerous implications to that body; (5) the dangers of Chinese Communist participation in formulating peace with Japan; (6) by maintaining at least a symbol of resistance we would have a better basis for salvation of southeastern Asia; (7) there would be at least a continued hope of sometime turning China in the path of freedom again."

The immediate practical effects of this cleavage within the free world were not particularly spectacular; in fact, the Chinese Communists affected such an aloofness in the matter that it was months before any Western government could even consummate an exchange of diplomatic representatives. The chief significance of the issue lay in its revelation of divergent attitudes on the whole Far Eastern situation—divergences which, if permitted to continue, might take on real importance in the event of a crisis. More was at issue than a question of diplomatic technique, more, even, than the momentous question of China's future place in the international community. For the United States, where voices could still be heard advocating military intervention against the Chinese Communists, it raised the question how far we could afford to separate ourselves from other friendly nations on whose cooperation our own security presumably depended. For all of the Atlantic powers it raised the problem of finding a mutually acceptable basis for cooperation with each other and with Asia in the effort to turn back the Stalinist tide.

Because of their proximity to a new Communist power center, the problem of Asian attitudes loomed especially large in all the countries that ringed China on the east, south, and west. Chiang Kai-shek still held the formerly Japanese-ruled island of Formosa, together with Hainan—until the latter position gave way before Communist amphibious attacks in April and May 1950. The Communists proclaimed their principal remaining objectives to be the "liberation" of Formosa and Tibet, to both of which China had considerable legal claims; but this definition of aims did not lessen the possible menace to other, wholly non-Chinese areas which presumably also had their places on the Stalinist timetable. The Republic of Korea, for example, bordered directly on Communist-held territory, and the hostile Korean Communist regime north of the 38th parallel was always open to reinforcement from Manchuria or the Soviet maritime province. The conquest of South China in the fall of 1949 had brought the Communists to the borders of Burma and Indochina and given them the possibility of intervening directly in an area where local Communist-led groups had already precipitated conditions of virtually full-scale civil war.

In no area was an understanding of Communist methods more essential than in these and the other countries of Southeast Asia, where Communist agents were merely the catalysts in an already revolutionary situation. Here, if anywhere, success for either side depended on ability to ride the wave of popular feeling and satisfy popular aspirations for independence and a better life. Military force was worth comparatively little in Southeast Asia if it was exerted in opposition to, rather than in furtherance of, these wishes—as the French in Indochina, and the Dutch in Indonesia, had already discovered. Varying local situations in Burma, Malaya, Thailand, Indochina, and Indonesia failed to obscure the underlying, common realities. The people of these countries had little love for the West, which had blocked the realization of their aspirations in the past; they had no particular antipathy toward the Soviet Union and Communism, which promised them liberation from a multitude of present evils; they would not resist Communist infiltration effectively unless convinced that in so doing they were defending their own interests, not those of foreign imperialists or a parvenu native ruling class.

It was largely with situations like this in mind that the United States had developed the Point Four program for promoting the economic growth of underdeveloped areas. The encouragement of technological assistance and capital investment in underdeveloped countries, one of the foremost economic preoccupations of the postwar world, had been described in President Truman's inaugural address of January 20, 1949 as a major phase of the American program for safeguarding peace and freedom against the challenge of Communism. Greatly expanded activity along these lines, both nationally and through the United Nations, was contemplated as soon as Congress had enacted the necessary legislation. Meanwhile, in Southeast Asia, the United States and other friendly nations

were already entering a race to alleviate the most critical manifestations of poverty and want before that area was completely
submerged by Communist-supported violence. Ministers of the
British Commonwealth countries met at Colombo, Ceylon, in
January 1950 and laid the foundations for a comprehensive
economic development program in Southern and Southeast
Asia, based on the tacit assumption that American assistance
would be available in its execution. In February, American
diplomats in the Far East gathered at Bangkok, Thailand, to
consider "the affirmative steps which could be taken by the
United States to carry out its announced policies of extending
friendly support to the states in Asia which may desire such
assistance." [14]

Participants in both the Colombo and Bangkok conferences
were obsessed with the realization that Communist gains in
Southeast Asia had reached a point where economic assistance
no longer could be considered a remedy sufficient in itself. The
political and military aspects of the problem were especially
prominent in French Indochina, where Communist-led resistance to the French had entered a more dangerous phase with
the Communist conquest of South China and the recognition
of the Vietminh insurgents by Peking and Moscow in January
1950.

Indochina, especially the eastern territories which formed the
state of Vietnam, reproduced in a small way the dilemma
which had split the free nations over China. Here again they
were forced to choose between a Communist movement with
real popular appeal and a "legitimate" but scarcely popular
government associated with the old regime, in this case French
imperialism. Here, as in China, the United States opted for the
"legal," anti-Communist contender; on February 7 it recognized the French-supported Vietnam government of Emperor
Bao Dai, accompanying the announcement with an intimation
that Vietnam could expect economic and military as well as
diplomatic support in its effort to cope with "internal dissen-

[14] *Department of State Bulletin*, XXII, March 27, 1950, 502.

sion fostered from abroad." [15] Britain and various Western European states which were impressed with the military threat of Vietminh likewise recognized Bao Dai; but professedly anti-imperalist nations like India and Pakistan, which regarded the French policy in Indochina with the utmost skepticism, remained aloof and mistrustful.

These differences on Far Eastern policy represented a growing threat to the unity of free Europe and free Asia, and an opportunity which the Kremlin was not slow to recognize. Though each particular segment of the Far Eastern problem tended to produce a slightly different alignment among the free nations, the dilemma of the West was really identical throughout the area. How was the necessity for stemming the Communist tide in Asia to be reconciled with the need of recapturing the allegiance of Asia's peoples? The Communist movements in Asia had identified themselves with real popular needs to such a point that it was difficult for the West to oppose Communism without seeming to oppose popular interests as well. Opposition to Mao Tse-tung in China and Ho Chi Minh in Indochina, partiality to their rivals Chiang Kai-shek and Bao Dai, were not easy to explain in Asia. Instead of freedom versus totalitarianism, Asians tended to think in terms of imperialism versus national liberation. There were times when Western—especially United States—policies in Asia struck them as being not merely anti-Communist but perilously close to anti-Asiatic.

In exploiting this basic cleavage the Kremlin made full use of all the varied means at its disposal: diplomacy, propaganda, even military action by its puppets and supporters. Nowhere did it publicize the issue more dramatically than in the United Nations organization, conventionally utilized by Moscow as a gigantic sounding board for the slogans of its political warfare. The China problem, which embodied the conflicting tendencies on the largest scale, was ideally suited for a psycholog-

[15] Ibid., February 20, 1950, 291-292. Technically, U.S. recognition was extended simultaneously to Vietnam, Laos, and Cambodia (the Associated States of Indochina), whose status as independent states within the French Union had received official French approval on February 2.

ical trial of strength between Stalinism and the West, with the Asian peoples and the masses throughout the world as umpire. Throughout the meetings of the General Assembly in the fall of 1949, this tendency to play to the Asian gallery had been evident in the contumely which Soviet representatives heaped on China's "reactionary Kuomintang clique" and its American supporters. It became even more prominent with the opening of the new year and the commencement of a determined Soviet campaign to oust the "Kuomintang representative" and seat a Communist delegate in the United Nations Security Council as the "legitimate" representative of the Chinese people.

This campaign, which was to become a major element in the U.S.S.R.'s political warfare and which seemed during the first half of 1950 to be digging a sorry grave for the world organization established with such high hopes a scant five years earlier, was open to conflicting interpretations. Pressure for Peking's admission to the United Nations could be viewed as a natural sequel to the action of the Soviet and other governments in recognizing the Communist "People's Republic" as the government of all China. China, as a "great" power, was a permanent member of the Security Council; a Communist delegate at Lake Success would presumably vote with the Soviet Union and attenuate the effects of the latter's isolation in that key body. On the other hand, it was theoretically possible that a Chinese Communist delegation, once installed, would display undesired tendencies toward independence. Some well-qualified observers, impressed by the excessive violence of the Soviet campaign, held that its true object was the contrary of its professed one—i.e., to make the seating of a Communist delegate impossible and thus preserve Moscow's complete control of Chinese Communist foreign policy.

Whatever the inner motivations of the Soviet Union in boycotting the United Nations over this issue for a period of almost seven months, from January 13 until August 1, 1950, the primary historical significance of the incident would seem to lie in its relation to the continuing East-West struggle for the mind of Asia. When Soviet delegate Yakov A. Malik stalked out of the Security Council chamber on January 13, declaring that the Soviet Union would neither participate in the Security Council nor recognize the legality of its decisions until "the representative of the Kuomintang group" had been removed, he was not only blackmailing the world organization but also renewing the Soviet Union's bid for the support of "progressive," anti-Kuomintang Asian opinion. The same underlying purpose could be discerned in all subsequent Soviet maneuvers, before and after Mr. Malik's return to the Security Council in August.

Trygve Lie, the Secretary-General of the world organization, uttered a memorable understatement when he declared on January 20 that the situation signalized by Malik's withdrawal was "not a happy one for the United Nations." In the preceding week the Soviet boycott had spread to half a dozen other United Nations bodies, including the Atomic Energy Commission, the Military Staff Committee, and various committees of the Economic and Social Council. In each case the Soviet delegate, accompanied by any other delegates from the Soviet bloc who were present, had withdrawn in protest when their attempts to unseat the Chinese Nationalist delegate were overruled. No Soviet delegation was present when the Trusteeship Council convened in Geneva on January 19.

Since the Russians and their supporters were normally in a minority at all United Nations gatherings, their absence did not necessarily prevent the transaction of business. Actions that required their cooperation were impossible anyway; for those that did not, ways could be found of surmounting the legal difficulties created by their absence. The real significance of the boycott was at once vaguer and more important. It showed, more dramatically than any previous incident, the contemptuous indifference of the Kremlin to the accepted international ideals of the time. And it offered a disquieting suggestion of the lengths to which Moscow might go in trying to impose its will on nations that disagreed with it.

The wisdom of the Soviet move from Moscow's own point of view was another matter. Like other manifestations of Soviet truculence, it produced secondary effects which tended to get in the way of the original objective. Governments which had been reconciled to accepting Communist China into the United Nations conceived fresh doubts, which might or might not have been anticipated by the Politburo strategists. More broadly, this new proof of contempt for the world organization helped to rally wavering minds and redirect attention to the basic issues of legality and orderly process in world affairs. This was one of the occasions when the free world, which the Kremlin aimed to divide and conquer, became dimly aware of its underlying community of interest. Which were stronger, the bonds that united the free world or the forces that divided it? This was a fundamental question of our era, to which time alone held the answer.

CHAPTER TWO

CONFUSION ON THE HOME FRONT

BY THE middle of the twentieth century it was sufficiently obvious that the future of Western civilization would be largely governed by the manner in which the United States would henceforth exercise its unique power and influence. At least one observer had pointed out that there was a direct correlation between the national behavior of the United States and the prospects of the revolutionary movement which threatened that civilization most immediately. Stalinist aims, this observer held, would be frustrated to the extent that the United States could "create among the peoples of the world . . . the impression of a country which knows what it wants, which is coping successfully with the problems of its internal life and with the responsibilities of a World Power, and which has a spiritual vitality capable of holding its own among the major ideological currents of the time." Conversely, however, "exhibitions of indecision, disunity and internal disintegration within this country have an exhilarating effect on the whole Communist movement. At each evidence of these tendencies, a thrill of hope and excitement goes through the Communist world; a new jauntiness can be noted in the Moscow tread; new groups of supporters climb on to what they can only view as the band wagon of international politics; and Russian pressure increases all along the line in international affairs." [1]

This analysis, made public at a time when the Marshall Plan was the novelty of the hour and the fate of Western Europe

[1] X, "The Sources of Soviet Conduct," *Foreign Affairs*, XXV, July 1947, 581-582.

hung precariously in the balance, was abundantly substantiated in the years that followed. The vision and determination which produced the European Recovery Program, the Vandenberg Resolution of 1948, the Atlantic Pact, and the military assistance program inestimably strengthened the collapsing structure of international relations and administered a severe setback to Communist aims. Yet, despite the large measure of congressional and public support which facilitated the inauguration of these key measures, the friends and enemies of the United States were justified in asking how far they were really to be taken as the expression of a unified national will. The voices of dissent which accompanied their enactment betrayed the existence within the national body politic of disagreements which extended not merely to the execution of foreign policy but to the first principles of American participation in world affairs.

While the American Government was laboring year in and year out to reestablish the free world on secure foundations, at home these voices of dissent had swelled to a loud and angry chorus. By 1950 they had reached a crescendo which literally threatened to drown out the words of the President and the Secretary of State. Ordinary language is scarcely adequate to characterize the indiscriminate nature of some of the attacks that were made during this tumultuous period on the foundations as well as the constitutional executants of American foreign policy. A kind of frenzy seemed to take possession of sections of the Congress, and caused such echoes throughout the country as to raise questions about the national capacity for discriminating judgment on foreign policy matters.

Manifestations of discontent with the trend of our foreign relations came from no single source and were not confined to any single aspect of foreign policy. Indeed, the various objections raised had little in common except their almost uniformly emotional tone and their suggestion of deep-rooted uncertainty and confusion in the national mind. They reached a pitch of violence in relation to certain allegations of Communist influence in the State Department, put forward in connection with the dispute over Far Eastern policy which had racked the United States ever since it became clear that Chiang Kai-shek's armies were incapable by themselves of preventing a Communist victory in the Chinese civil war. In reality, however, they reflected differences of temperament and principle which might, under other circumstances, have asserted themselves just as vigorously in relation to Europe, South America, or the Arctic.

It would be misleading to link these dissensions to any single organized antagonism between political parties, occupational or social groups, or sectional interests. Subordinate loyalties of this kind contributed something to the heat of conflict, and the political plight of a party which had been out of office for nearly 18 years was responsible for some of the most virulent attacks on the national foreign policy as it had evolved under the Truman administration. But popular response to the tactics sanctioned by the Republican high command indicated that important segments of the American people were actually out of sympathy with the actions that had been taken in their name, and ready to impute the worst intentions to the men who had taken them. Nor was the agitation by any means confined to Republican quarters. Nonpartisan and Democratic spokesmen found fault with the administration in a manner that flatly challenged its claim to represent the national will in matters of foreign policy.

The administration itself was by no means free of internal differences having to do with some of the same issues. Each of the several departments and agencies concerned with foreign affairs—the State and Defense departments, the Economic Cooperation Administration, the Treasury, the Department of Commerce—had its specialized approach to foreign policy questions, and their disagreements were sometimes aggravated by personal rivalries and competition for the ears of influential congressmen. A lack of coordination and teamwork was apparent throughout the foreign affairs area of the government, and would be only partially remedied by such measures as the appointment of W. Averell Harriman to serve as a special

FOREIGN AFFAIRS ORGANIZATION OF THE EXECUTIVE BRANCH, 1950

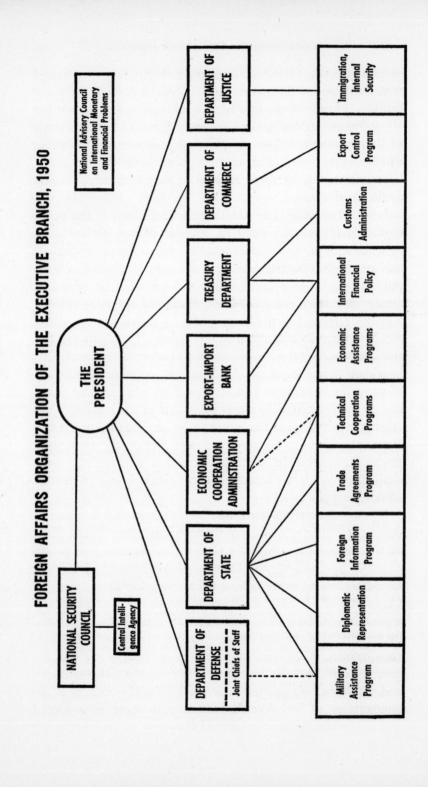

assistant to the President on foreign policy matters and the naming of a commission under Gordon Gray to develop the outlines of an integrated foreign economic policy. Doubts about the quality and integrity of the officials in some branches of the administration, moreover, made it easier to question the validity of administration objectives in other fields.

Secretary of State Dean Acheson tried to assure a London audience on May 10, 1950 that the "strange and confusing dissonance" crowding the transatlantic frequencies from the United States was a part of the normal process by which the American people were accustomed to reach their more difficult national decisions. The disconcerting feature of such an analysis, however—apart from its disregard of the serious personal attacks that were being made on Acheson and his advisers— was the fact that so much of the controversy related to decisions which were supposedly already made and nationally accepted. The issues in question extended far beyond the details of American policy toward China and the integrity of the State Department. Implicitly they involved irreconcilable assumptions concerning the nature of the contemporary world crisis and, indeed, the whole basis of American participation in organized international life. On various fronts the responsible authorities found themselves defending clear-cut positions

NOTE ON CHART OPPOSITE: This simplified diagram shows the principal departments and agencies concerned with foreign policy and indicates the nature of their responsibility, under the President, for the administration of specific foreign policy programs. Of the numerous interdepartmental committees designed to ensure coordination on both policy and working levels, only the two most important are shown. The *National Security Council,* which is resposible for advising the President on the integration of domestic, foreign, and military policies relating to the national security, comprises the President, the Vice President, the Secretaries of State and Defense, and the Chairman of the National Security Resources Board. The *National Advisory Council* has the task of coordinating the policies and operations of U.S. representatives on the International Bank and Fund, the Export-Import Bank, and all other agencies to the extent that they engage in foreign loan operations or foreign financial, exchange, or monetary transactions; its members are the Secretary of the Treasury (Chairman), the Secretaries of State and Commerce, the Chairman of the Board of Governors of the Federal Reserve System, the Chairman of the Board of Directors of the Export-Import Bank, and the Economic Cooperation Administrator.

which had been taken up on the assumption that they answered to the national interest and would be supported by public opinion. Whether the administration was right or wrong in specific instances was less significant than the fact that its over-all appraisal of the world situation, built on the experience of five postwar years, was so far short of having gained general acceptance.

Viewed in the broadest historical perspective, the confusion of 1950 might be understandable as a phase in America's slow and painful adaptation to new responsibilities and a new world position. It was, after all, only recently that the United States had turned its back on isolation and accepted the United Nations; the clarification of postwar power relationships, and of the leading role which would devolve on this country, were even more recent. The process of readjustment had been rendered incomparably more difficult by the concurrent emergence of the Soviet menace, a completely novel phenomenon which further refracted the already divergent American attitudes on world affairs in general and forced the United States to embark on actions of fateful magnitude while still a novice in the arts of world leadership. The events to be described in this chapter bore witness to the perilous difficulties of this evolution. They did not necessarily preclude the return of a more responsible frame of mind in which administration, Congress, and the people could resume in some measure of harmony their collective search for genuine solutions of real problems.

1. Bipartisanship in the Balance

The legislative program which President Truman outlined to Congress in his State of the Union Message on January 4 made no direct allusion to the political tempests already gathering on Capitol Hill. Both of our great political parties, said the President, were "committed to working together"—and, he added, he was "sure they will continue to work together"—to achieve the national objective of "peace." The major business of the session, he implied, would lie in "carrying out the

specific programs for peace which we have already begun"—
wholehearted support of the United Nations; maintenance of
"a strong and well-balanced defense organization"; continued
participation "in the common defense of free nations against
aggression"; and continued efforts for world economic recovery and expanded world trade, with emphasis on the renewal
of the European Recovery Program, prompt accession to the
International Trade Organization, and adoption of the Point
Four legislation to increase the flow of technical assistance and
capital investment to underdeveloped areas.

The program had a familiar ring. Each of the items mentioned had engaged congressional attention in the 1949 session; some of them had been the subject of intermittent debate over a period of years. Important details might be open to
question, but the underlying principles seemed clear, and the
specific legislation requested would be a logical implementation of purposes which had animated all American foreign
policy since 1945 or earlier.

The moment, however, was singularly unpropitious for the
enactment of even a routine foreign policy program. Although
the administration could theoretically count on Democratic majorities in both houses, the mood of Congress was such that no
recommendation from the executive branch was likely to be
received with sympathy or deference. Factors which had impelled Congress to support the administration in the past
seemed to have lost much of their force, while the administration's more outspoken critics were gaining daily in strength
and confidence. Especially in the Senate, action on legislative
issues was relegated to the background while the senior legislators indulged in a prolonged free fight extending to virtually
every phase of foreign policy, past, present, and future.

A major influence in the sequence of events in Congress was
the difficult situation of the Republican party after nearly two
decades in opposition. For that party's most influential representatives, foreign policy loomed as a matter of life-and-death
significance. The organized future of the party seemed to depend on discovering a formula to rekindle public enthusiasm

and outbid the entrenched Democrats for the support of the electorate. The presidential campaign of 1948, fought primarily on domestic issues, had failed to loosen the Democratic hold. With the congressional election of 1950 in the offing, most Republican leaders drew the conclusion that an equally vigorous assault in regard to foreign policy was both necessary and justified.

The divergent response of individual Republicans to this situation illustrated the dilemma which any opposition party must face in times which demand a maximum of national unity in face of an external danger. Sharply as they might differ on domestic matters, the two major American parties were in reality not deeply divided in their conception of the national interest in foreign affairs. Both had recognized the inherent threat to the security of the United States in the policies of Nazi Germany and the postwar policies of Soviet Russia, and both had been virtually at one in the determination to resist them. Concerning the main trend of American foreign policy through the 1940's, therefore, there had been little room for disagreement. Through the procedural devices which came to be identified with the "bipartisan foreign policy," such leading Republicans as Senator Arthur S. Vandenberg and John Foster Dulles played a constructive role in the preparation of several crucial acts of American policy, notably in relation to the United Nations, the Inter-American Treaty of Reciprocal Assistance, the European peace settlements, the Marshall Plan, and the North Atlantic Treaty.

Inestimable as was the value of bipartisanship to the country at large, there can be little doubt that such a narrowing of the area open to opposition criticism was a political handicap to the minority party, and one which the administration did not fail to exploit. Recriminations over the administration's frequent failures to take the minority party into its confidence, and sharp criticism of the administration policy in areas like China where the bipartisan principle had never been applied, were a poor substitute for the right of unlimited opposition which the Republicans had tacitly surrendered by subscribing to those major national policies which had been formalized by legislative action. Republican discomfort was accentuated by recurrent signs that the administration placed a lower value on Republican participation than did Republicans themselves.

By late 1949, therefore, the focus of intraparty discussion among Republicans was shifting away from the proper application of the bipartisan principle to the merits of the principle itself. More and more frequently it was asserted that bipartisanship had been tried and failed. The ailing Senator Vandenberg had urged the maintenance of what he preferred to call an "unpartisan" foreign policy; but such leaders as Senator Kenneth S. Wherry of Nebraska, a frequent spokesman for the more restive elements in the party, manifested their disagreement in terms that suggested a determination to have done with artificial restraints and regain complete freedom of action.

While the official status of bipartisanship hung in the balance, its underlying spirit was rapidly disintegrating under a barrage of Republican attacks directed against the administration's policy in China. As an area on which Republican views had never been sought, China was a "legitimate" field for criticism and had been so utilized since before the 1948 election. The magnitude of the subsequent Communist victory, and its still unforeseeable implications for the entire Far East, seemed to many Republicans to substantiate their assertions that Washington was heavily to blame for the disasters that had overtaken the Chinese Nationalists. Each fresh refusal to intervene in what the administration considered a hopeless cause could be interpreted as new evidence of that "softness" toward Communism with which opposition spokesmen had long taxed the administration and particularly the State Department. The prevailing temper of American opinion in 1950 made it possible to imply, and later to assert openly, that United States policy in the Far East *was actually made by Communist agents.*

The specific grounds of the domestic dispute over China had shifted with each deterioration of Nationalist fortunes. By the beginning of 1950, when the Nationalist foothold had shrunk to a few islands off the Chinese coast, the administration was being attacked primarily on two counts: (1) its supposed readiness to extend diplomatic recognition to the Chinese Communist regime and support its admission to represent China in the United Nations; and (2) its refusal to provide assistance to Chiang Kai-shek in order to repel a threatened Communist attack on Formosa, supposedly as a preliminary to an eventual Nationalist reconquest of the mainland. Whereas the administration had long since announced its decision not to extend further military assistance to the Nationalist government, Republican spokesmen vociferously demanded that this policy be reversed and that Formosa be protected by American naval units or other suitable means.

On the specific issue of Formosa the administration itself was by no means of one mind. Prominent military authorities like Secretary of Defense Louis Johnson and General of the Army Douglas MacArthur, Commander in Chief of United States Forces in the Far East, were known to share the Republican view that so important a strategic position, midway between the American bases on Okinawa and in the Philippines, ought at all costs to be kept out of Communist hands. The State Department, on the contrary, feared the effect on Chinese and world opinion of any American intervention on an island which had belonged to China until its conquest by Japan in 1895, had been promised to China at Cairo in 1943 and at Potsdam in 1945, and was considered an integral part of China by Communists and Nationalists alike.

This latter view, combined with a lack of readily available means to ensure the protection of the island, had prevailed in discussions in the National Security Council. On January 5 the President positively announced that the United States had no intention of interfering in the present situation, or of seeking to acquire special rights or privileges or to establish military bases on Formosa "at this time." "At this time," Secretary Acheson explained, meant that "in the unlikely and unhappy event that our forces might be attacked in the Far East, the

United States must be completely free to take whatever action in whatever area is necessary for its own security." [2]

Close on the heels of this decision, Acheson began the work of elucidating the positive side of the policies which had been developed to meet the new situation in the Far East. These were policies in which military force would play an important but not necessarily a preponderant part, and which would be governed by objective possibilities and subordinated to an underlying identity of interest between the people of the United States and the peoples of Asia. In a series of public pronouncements Acheson spoke of an American "defensive perimeter" extending from the Aleutians via Japan and the Ryukus to the Philippines, which would be protected by the United States under all circumstances; of our determination to persevere in the work of democratic reconstruction we had so promisingly begun in Korea (which, however, was offered no guarantee against military attack); of our readiness to help the newly independent nations of Southeast Asia to realize their aspirations for a better life; and of the conviction that American interference in China would only incur the hostility of the Chinese and divert their attention from the imperialistic depredations being carried out by the U.S.S.R. and its Chinese servants. [3]

This policy resembled the program of the administration's critics in so far as it aimed at promoting the interests of the United States through actions taken in distant countries to stem the advance of Communism in the Far East. It differed from them in its choice of locale, in its greater concern for choosing actions that would be palatable to the peoples affected, and in its view of military force as one possible element in an integrated program rather than as a primary weapon. But such ideas, whatever their intrinsic value, had little chance of acceptance by the now thoroughly aroused pro-Nationalist congressmen. Once their demands for action in Formosa had been de-

[2] *Department of State Bulletin*, XXII, January 16, 1950, 81.
[3] See especially Acheson's speech at the National Press Club, Washington, January 12 (summarized in *The United States in World Affairs, 1949*, 462-464), and the more finished presentation of the same line of thought in his address to the Commonwealth Club, San Francisco, March 15, 1950.

nied, the critics of the administration's Far Eastern policy
embarked on a wholesale campaign to discredit it finally and
completely in the eyes of the nation. For the first time it was
seriously asserted not only that this policy had failed to serve
the national interest, not only that it had promoted the successes of world Communism, but that it was actually inspired
by Communists for Communist ends.

In taking this tack, anti-administration forces sought to
utilize a current of public mistrust which had been gathering
force for several years, not without the encouragement of certain congressmen. Allegations of Communist activity in the
State Department and other branches of the federal government were an old issue in Washington, and one in which Congress and the public habitually took a more poignant interest
than they did in providing the encouragement and facilities
the government needed to do an effective job. Loose talk about
the "Communists and fellow travelers" who were supposed to
enjoy a free run of the Department of State had helped to give
that institution an unholy glamor that contrasted strangely with
the sober reality. Lack of understanding and confidence between
the public and the hard-worked, frequently maligned personnel
of the State Department was an incidental symptom of this
country's incomplete adjustment to its new world position.

Despite sustained, energetic efforts to eliminate disloyal elements from the federal service, there occurred in 1949 and early
1950 a number of sensational developments which offered a
measure of vindication to those who had insisted that the Truman administration was a paradise for Communists and spies.
In October 1949 virtually the entire leadership of the American Communist party had been found guilty of criminally conspiring to advocate the forcible overthrow of the United States
Government. In January 1950 the second trial of Alger Hiss
concluded with a jury finding that the former State Department official had committed perjury in denying that he had
passed confidential government documents to the representative of a Communist spy ring a dozen years earlier. Secretary
Acheson, who like many other public men had been a personal

friend of the defendant, enraged congressional critics and heightened the clamor for his own resignation by quoting the founder of Christianity and announcing that, whatever the outcome of any appeal procedure, "I do not intend to turn my back on Alger Hiss."

A few weeks later another jury found a Department of Justice analyst and a Soviet employee of the United Nations guilty of conspiring to commit espionage and remove classified documents for the benefit of the U.S.S.R., this time as recently as 1949. Again the State Department, which had infuriated the U.S.S.R. by refusing to recognize the Soviet defendant's claim to diplomatic immunity, incurred equally vehement criticism at home by moving to have him deported rather than imprisoned.[4] Capping the excitement, a British scientist, German-born Dr. Klaus Fuchs, who had worked on American atomic projects for prolonged periods between 1943 and 1947, was arrested in England in February and readily admitted having passed numerous atomic secrets to the U.S.S.R.

These incidents went far to refute the administration dismissals of past espionage investigations as political "red herrings." The Americans involved had been convicted on evidence which, though it left serious questions unanswered, could leave no doubt as to the seriousness of the problem. Their convictions were an invitation to sober thought about one of the most perplexing questions of the age—how a free society can protect itself against modern, highly sophisticated forms of disloyalty without extinguishing the essential freedom which nourishes its own life.

Such rarefied speculations, however, were far from the minds of most members of Congress. While the proponents of strong anti-Communist policies worked to tighten the espionage laws and devise new Communist-control measures, an-

[4] The recommendation had the stated objective of avoiding any "misunderstanding" on the part of the U.S.S.R. which could result in "prejudicing the situation of American citizens now in Eastern Europe, including diplomatic officers and other government officials" (*Department of State Bulletin*, XXII, March 20, 1950, 445). On the serious plight of U.S. representatives in Communist countries at this period cf. *The United States in World Affairs, 1949*, 273, 430-431.

other group set out to discredit as thoroughly as might be the Secretary of State, the State Department, the national administration, and the established foreign policy of the United States. As the personification of everything they were fighting they selected Dean Acheson, a man who did in a sense embody the main trend of postwar American policy, and one whose personal and intellectual qualities had never evoked great appreciation on Capitol Hill.

Amid mounting demands for the resignation of Acheson as the man who allegedly tolerated Communists in his Department, Senator Joseph R. McCarthy, a Wisconsin Republican, made a series of speeches during February in which he implied that the State Department was "thoroughly infested" with Communists and that he could name 205, 57, or 81 individuals —the number varied constantly—"who were known to the Secretary of State as being members of the Communist party and who nevertheless are still working and shaping the policy of the State Department." [5] The State Department immediately challenged McCarthy to present his evidence, something the Senator was never persuaded to do with reference to this or any of the other astounding allegations he was to make in the coming weeks. Persons familiar with Washington loyalty investigations were reasonably certain that any "list" the Senator might possess was neither new nor up-to-date. Proof, however, seemed to be the least of McCarthy's worries. His customary tactic when pressed was to assert that substantiation of all his charges would be found in the Federal Bureau of Investigation loyalty files, which the President refused to surrender on constitutional and security grounds.

Repeated with bewildering variations, the McCarthy charges immediately became a first-rate political issue. Had Americans forgotten how to laugh? A special subcommittee of the Senate Foreign Relations Committee was promptly set up to reinvestigate the loyalty of State Department employees. To this

[5] For an analysis of these and subsequent charges cf. Alfred Friendly, "The Noble Crusade of Senator McCarthy," *Harper's Magazine*, CCI, August 1950, 34-42.

body Senator McCarthy elaborately doled out the names of various departmental employees, former employees, occasional consultants, and special representatives at international conferences. Most prominent among them were Ambassador-at-Large Philip C. Jessup, whom McCarthy—always speaking under conditions that would ensure his immunity against libel action—branded with an "unusual affinity for Communist causes," and Owen Lattimore, a well-known authority on the Far East whom the Senator identified by implication as "the architect of our Far Eastern policy" and the "top Russian espionage agent in the United States."

Both Jessup and Lattimore were abroad when these allegations were made. Jessup was just completing an official tour in the Far East, and Lattimore was heading a United Nations technical assistance mission in Afghanistan. Both hastened to return to Washington for personal appearances before the subcommittee, where they demolished the McCarthy charges as convincingly as could be expected in a not very orderly proceeding which put the entire burden of proof on the accused persons. In Lattimore's case it was also made clear that, far from having been an "architect" of United States Far Eastern policy, he had had no regular connection with the Department of State and his direct influence on policy had been less than negligible. McCarthy's other charges stood up no better in face of the refutations offered by the persons accused.

But the naming of Jessup and Lattimore had carried the McCarthy crusade into the main stream of the Republican agitation on Far Eastern policy and assured it the explicit support of such leading Republicans as Senators Wherry, Robert A. Taft of Ohio, and Styles Bridges of New Hampshire. Through March and April the turmoil grew and grew. Wherry declared that the Secretary of State "must go" because he was "a bad security risk." Taft lashed out against "the pro-Communist group in the State Department who surrendered to every demand of Russia at Yalta and Potsdam, and promoted at every opportunity the Communist cause in China. . . ." The President, in turn, castigated McCarthy, Bridges, and Wherry as saboteurs of American foreign policy, announced an extension of Jessup's governmental assignment, and said he did not think Lattimore was a spy.

Amid signs of growing distaste in Democratic and some Republican quarters, but to the loud acclaim of various sections of the American public, McCarthy continued through the spring to tantalize the Senate subcommittee with hints of further sensational disclosures. Not until July did the subcommittee complete its work, which had been equally hampered by the tactics of the accuser, the unavailability of governmental loyalty files, and the hysterical atmosphere in which the inquiry took place. In a formal report signed only by the subcommittee's Democratic majority, all persons who had been publicly accused were exonerated and McCarthy's charges and methods were denounced as "a fraud and a hoax . . . perhaps the most nefarious campaign of half-truths and untruth in the history of this republic." The subcommittee's two Republican members refused to sign on the ground that the investigation had been "superficial and inconclusive." The Senate accepted the report on July 20 in a strict party-line vote.

There is no way to determine how far the more uncritical supporters of this campaign were actuated by individual credulity, by party zeal, or by less reputable influences such as the mysterious "China lobby," which was said to shrink from no means of punishing those who had opposed all-out aid to Chiang Kai-shek. It is equally futile to speculate about how far the Kremlin, plotting its own course in the Far East, was encouraged by this exhibition of disunity at the heart of the free world. But the careful student is bound to conclude that the effects of the episode, though largely intangible, were seriously detrimental to American prestige and to the attainment of national aims to which even the administration's extreme critics professed to subscribe.

Although the campaign did not overtly change administration policy toward China or dislodge the Secretary of State, it certainly weakened the general conduct of the nation's foreign affairs as well as precluding any positive readjustment of our

Far Eastern policy which would bring it into closer alignment with the policies of allied and friendly nations. By creating fresh obstacles to the diplomatic recognition of Communist China, it helped set the stage for the grave crisis in Chinese-American relations that was to occur later in the year. In the meantime it aggravated public confusion at home, undermined the reputation of honest and able officials, aggravated the sense of personal insecurity that pervaded the government service, and contributed to a wave of anti-Communist hysteria which already threatened to engulf the country. By its methods it offered confirmatory evidence to those abroad who professed to see in the United States a land of thinly veiled reaction. It probably accentuated a real tendency in American world policy to develop along lines that took little account of foreign public opinion and thus ran the risk of alienating foreign support which might be needed some day.

The White House and the State Department were not unconscious of the dangers of the situation, both for the Democratic administration and for the nation at large. While refusing to compromise on matters which they deemed essential, they recognized the necessity of taking the congressional temper into account where no vital principle was involved. Foreign policy in a democracy had, after all, to be responsive to the national mood, and there was no mistaking the general trend of articulate American opinion in the first half of 1950. The prevailing tendency was to see the world situation in terms of sharply contrasted forces, pro-Communist and anti-Communist; to execrate the former and indiscriminately embrace the latter, whether or not they answered to any rigid "democratic" standard or were favorably regarded by the peoples of other friendly nations. Thus the furor over China helped to confirm various trends in American policy which have already been identified as a source of tension between the United States and the rest of the free world.

It would be too much to describe this tendency as a conscious attempt at congressional appeasement, or a capitulation to the views of such conservative Democrats as Senator Tom Connally, the Texan chairman of the Foreign Relations Committee. World conditions were such that the United States, irrespective of domestic considerations, could not afford to subordinate its foreign policy entirely to any doctrinaire criterion. As Acheson remarked, "We are not dealing here with the kind of situation where we can go from one country to another with a piece of litmus paper and see whether everything is true blue, whether the political, economic, and social climate is exactly, in all its details, the kind that we would like to have either for them or for us." [6]

But as issues continued to arise in which the administration was forced to choose between possible anti-Communist support and straightforward democratic principle, familiarity with the situation in Washington inevitably strengthened the tendency to resolve each such dilemma in the same way. From Vietnam to Yugoslavia, opposition to Stalin had come to outweigh every other consideration. An identical trend could be discerned in the State Department's gradual thawing toward Franco Spain and its rapproachement with the Argentine dictatorship of General Juan D. Perón. The same attitude was ever more strikingly manifest in American policy toward Germany and Japan, whose potential contribution to the free world's material strength obviously prompted more official concern than did their still incomplete regeneration as peace-loving democratic states.

These were matters with which the nations of the free world would have to wrestle in the months ahead. A more immediate necessity was to try to rescue at least something of the bipartisan spirit from the wreckage of the congressional free-for-all. The President, in his public statements, distinguished sharply between the McCarthy faction and other Republican Senators in whose leadership he continued to express confidence. In addition, he appealed to the patriotism of qualified individuals in the Republican party who possessed experience of postwar diplomacy and were capable of viewing the international situa-

[6] Remarks made at a meeting of the Advertising Council at the White House, February 16, released to the press March 9, 1950.

tion with balance and detachment. John Sherman Cooper, a former Republican Senator from Kentucky and a delegate to the United Nations General Assembly in 1949, agreed early in the spring to serve as a consultant to Secretary Acheson in forthcoming meetings of the North Atlantic Treaty powers. At the suggestion of Senator Vandenberg, John Foster Dulles was approached and in April accepted appointment as a special consultant to advise the Secretary both on "broad problems" and on "specific lines of action" in relation to "Europe, the Far East, and other areas of the world." [7]

From both ends of Pennsylvania Avenue, meanwhile, tentative efforts were made to improve liaison arrangements and create a better mutual understanding on foreign policy matters.[8] Foundations were being laid which might support a new structure of cooperative relationships once the fury of the tempest had abated. But it would be many months before the storm had blown itself out.

2. The H-Bomb and "Total Diplomacy"

Those who had joined the anti-administration chorus seemed to be prompted by various motives but to share certain basic attitudes regarding contemporary international affairs. In some ways the fervor of their anti-Communist declamations recalled the outlook of an earlier and simpler time, before America had experienced the awakenings and the disillusionments that go with direct involvement in the world's troubles. Their outlook, in fact, bore definite resemblances to the isolationism of previous decades, now transformed into a kind of supernationalism which demanded a "forceful" world policy and attached minimum importance to the cooperation of other nations. They differed from the official administration view not so much in their identification of the perils that faced this country as in their estimate of the nature of those perils and in their choice

[7] *Department of State Bulletin*, XXII, April 10, 1950, 572; April 24, 1950, 661-662; May 8, 1950, 720-721.
[8] *Ibid.*, June 19, 1950, 1003.

of methods to combat them. In administration eyes they were guilty of overestimating the efficacy of pure force, and of grossly disregarding the "human factors" that were ultimately decisive in every political situation. And, of course, they sometimes made the further mistake of classifying among the primary enemies of the United States all those who failed to share their particular views.

There was another current in American thinking, not quite so articulate during these turbulent months but perhaps equally tenacious and even more lasting in its effects on American world policy. This was the attitude which distrusted the effects of physical force; which placed its primary faith not in power and compulsion, but in man's unquenchable thirst for freedom and human dignity; and which hesitated to attribute total depravity even to the sworn enemies of the United States. People of this more "idealistic" turn of mind, many of whom had placed great hope in the United Nations, had been uncomfortable in the "two-world" atmosphere of the later 1940's. Realizing the disastrous course which any new world war would be sure to take, they reacted with distress to any move by either side that seemed to bring war closer. They preferred the Marshall Plan to the Atlantic Pact, and the Point Four program to military assistance. They did not exclude the possibility of a change of heart in Moscow which would permit genuine negotiation and a solution of East-West differences.

Among the aspects of United States postwar policy which most disturbed Americans of this "idealistic" disposition, none had been productive of greater dismay than the official attitude regarding that most fateful product of modern technology, the atomic bomb. While some observers (and officials) had taken undisguised satisfaction in this country's monopoly of the atomic weapon and professed to consider it a sufficient means of crushing any potential enemy, others suffered persistent misgivings over its original use against Japan and experienced fresh pangs at every indication that the United States was persevering in atomic development and counted heavily on the devastating effects of the bomb in the strategy of any future conflict. The vast destructive powers of the A-bomb took it out of the category of ordinary weapons of war and seemed to raise an independent moral issue, all the more pressing since it was assumed from the first that the Soviet Union, too, would be able to begin producing atomic bombs within a few years.

The national administration, though seemingly untroubled by scruples of this order and determined to exploit whatever political advantages might flow from this country's lead in the atomic arms race, had itself been without any clear-cut notion concerning the implications of the new weapon and its relation to the larger strategic picture. There was a widespread feeling in the years after 1945 that the blast over Hiroshima had rendered all previous military thinking and experience obsolete; that atomic bombardment was capable almost by itself of producing speedy and total military victory, even against so vast and geographically decentralized a power as Russia; and that this country's industrial preeminence actually made atomic bombardment an economical as well as an effective way of waging war. Comparatively little attention was given either to the world-wide psychological implications of atomic warfare or to the fact that this country was far more vulnerable to atomic attack than was its principal potential enemy. Despite growing murmurs of dissent—which naval spokesmen brought to a climax in sensational House hearings on military policy in the fall of 1949—these assumptions profoundly influenced the development of strategic planning both on the national level and in the North Atlantic Treaty organization. "We have repeatedly recognized in this country," as General Omar N. Bradley explained to a congressional committee in July 1949, "that the first priority of the joint defense is our ability to deliver the atomic bomb." [9]

The Russians, who entered the postwar era with neither an atomic bomb nor a strategic air force to deliver it, were well equipped to exploit the inherent weaknesses of the American

[9] *Mutual Defense Assistance Act of 1949: Hearings* on H.R. 5748 and H.R. 5895 before the House Foreign Affairs Committee, 81st Congress, 1st Session (Washington, 1949), 71.

position. They themselves had never been in the habit of staking everything on a single weapon. Their strategy, in war and in peace, relied on the intimate cooperation of *all* weapons, military, political, and psychological. When and if they managed to develop an atomic bomb, they were unlikely to make it the centerpiece of their strategy, still less to announce the fact to a shuddering world. For the time being their military policy would rely primarily on the maintenance of ground forces large enough to give them an assured preponderance of military power on the European Continent. Thus they had everything to gain by playing upon the apprehensions which the American attitude had aroused in Western Europe and elsewhere. Year in, year out, their lurid denunciations of American "atomic diplomacy" kept these fears alive and, incidentally, helped to distract world attention from the 175-odd divisions of their own mobilized ground forces.

Soviet tactics in the United Nations extracted every possible advantage from the fact that the United States, largely disarmed in other respects, was literally forced to cling to the atomic bomb as the principal guarantor of its security and that of Western Europe in the years immediately ahead. While rejecting any workable plan for international inspection and control of atomic facilities, Soviet spokesmen called at every opportunity for the unconditional prohibition of atomic weapons and the destruction of existing bomb stocks. Acceptance of this demand by the United States was impossible, because it would have wiped out the American lead in the atomic field and eliminated what many believed was the chief deterrent to an advance of the Soviet army across Europe. But its rejection, even though supported by a large majority of the United Nations, enabled the U.S.S.R. to pose with some effectiveness as the champion of threatened humanity against the bloodthirsty designs of United States "ruling circles."

Two developments in the second half of 1949 brought the simmering disquietude over this situation to boiling point. President Truman revealed on September 23 that the Soviet Union, anticipating official American calculations by three to

five years, had produced an "atomic explosion." A few weeks
later it became known that the United States itself now had
an atomic bomb of vastly increased effectiveness and was
working on a "super-bomb"—presently to be known as the
hydrogen bomb, H-bomb, or tritium bomb—which might have
as much as 1,000 times the power of the 1945 weapon. The war
of universal extermination which had hitherto been a vague
theoretical possibility was suddenly brought frighteningly
close. The desire to exorcise this horrible prospect dominated
the fall session of the General Assembly, which, however,
was no more successful than its predecessors in persuading
the great powers to agree on any workable plan for the
international control of atomic energy. The obstinate refusal of
the Soviet Union to permit international inspection of atomic
activities within its territory was generally recognized at Lake
Success as the chief barrier to an effective international agreement; but the position of the United States, which continued
to insist on the rigid control plan already endorsed by the
Assembly, aroused considerable dissatisfaction both at home
and abroad.[10]

The adjournment of the Assembly left the United States
facing the problem of whether or not to proceed with the development of the hydrogen bomb, the practicability of which
still remained to be determined. Scientific, military, political,
and moral factors all entered into the decision, and the novelty
of the project left the men responsible for it with no assured
basis of judgment on any of these grounds. Unlike the atomic
bomb, the hydrogen bomb depended not on the fission but on
the fusion of atoms, and its potential destructiveness was believed to be limited only by the carrying capacity of the aircraft
or submarine which would presumably deliver it. Some spoke
of flash burns which would kill every living being within a
radius of 20 miles of an explosion, coupled with destruction
from radioactivity over a much wider area. A few imaginative
scientists speculated on the possibility of igniting the atmosphere and literally setting the world on fire. Such sensational

[10] For fuller discussion see *The United States in World Affairs, 1949,* 292-301.

pronouncements, in a field completely beyond the understanding of all but a few specialists, contributed greatly to public agitation but did little to clarify the issues on which any rational decision would have to be based.

Whether the advent of hydrogen bombs would work out to the national advantage of the United States—assuming that such old-fashioned concepts as "national advantage" still had relevance to the situation that would then exist—depended on a host of unforeseeable factors, among them the costs of production and delivery, the ability of the U.S.S.R. to produce an equivalent weapon, the relative vulnerability of the two powers and their allies to H-bomb attack, and their relative adeptness in using the bomb as an instrument of political persuasion or blackmail. The psychological impact, at home and abroad, could not be disregarded, and the United States would have to reckon with the demonstrated skill of the Kremlin in distorting this country's most innocent moves into monstrous acts of warmongering. The possible influence on the Kremlin would have to be balanced against the restiveness which had been growing in Western Europe ever since Russia's possession of an A-bomb became known.

But painstaking analysis of these and other factors was excluded by what seemed the political necessities of the moment. Russia had breached the American atomic monopoly, belying the assurances of American leaders. American defenses against atomic attack were virtually nil. Previous efforts at atomic agreement with the U.S.S.R. had only thickened the wall of distrust that separated the two governments, and the Soviet walk-out from the United Nations in January had interrupted all contact between them on atomic matters. The American people were deemed to need some psychological reassurance against the destruction of their cities, and the masters of the Kremlin a warning against untimely adventures. In the midst of rumors that disagreement was rife within the Atomic Energy Commission and that a new attempt would be made to reach an atomic control agreement with the Soviet Union, President Truman served notice on January 31 that he had directed the commission "to continue its work on all forms of atomic weapons, including the so-called hydrogen or super-bomb." Like all other work in the atomic field, added the President, "it is being and will be carried forward on a basis consistent with the over-all objectives of our program for peace and security."

For a good many Americans this decision confirmed the moral liability the United States had already incurred in inaugurating the age of atomic warfare. To innumerable others it brought home the terrifying prospect of a world cataclysm that staggered the imagination. Inevitably it reinvigorated the clamor for a new approach which would somehow spare mankind this fate. Demands for an international agreement to outlaw atomic weapons were put forward with redoubled energy. This spontaneous movement was not confined to religious, pacifistic, leftist, or any other specific groups. It penetrated the walls of the Capitol and took possession of unsentimental members of Congress. This was one of the occasions when habitual behavior patterns are obliterated by a tide of powerful emotion.

Unlike the concurrent objection on Far Eastern policy, manifestations of discontent with the administration stand on atomic energy proceeded largely from Democratic quarters which apparently did not share the official skepticism regarding the chances of fruitful negotiation with the Soviet Union. Senator Connally, one of those who had urged the development of the hydrogen bomb, announced that he also favored another attempt to negotiate an atomic control agreement. Senator Brien McMahon of Connecticut, chairman of the Joint Congressional Committee on Atomic Energy, told the Senate in a dramatic speech on February 2 that the "severe realities" of the present-day world had left us no alternative to proceeding with the H-bomb; but, he said, it was now necessary to move heaven and earth to end the atomic armaments race, establish "worldwide atomic peace," and make possible "atomic-created abundance for all men." A "moral crusade for peace" was his recommendation—a vast campaign to gain the ears of people on both sides of the Iron Curtain, plus a $50 billion "global Marshall

Plan" under which all nations, including the U.S.S.R., would accept effective international control of atomic energy and devote two-thirds of their present armaments expenditures to constructive tasks of economic development.

Four days later Senator Tydings, chairman of the Armed Services Committee, offered a different plan—convocation by the President of a world disarmament conference to deal with both atomic and conventional weapons, from H-bombs down to rifles. There was "more than a faint hope" of a positive response to such an appeal, the Senator suggested; if the Russians were to turn down "a fair proposition," we should at least know where we stood. While Senators McMahon and Tydings continued to urge their respective solutions, two other important proposals were thrown into the mill. Harold Stassen, President of the University of Pennsylvania and a former Republican presidential aspirant who had interviewed Stalin in 1947, publicly called on President Truman to request "a major mid-century conference with the leaders of the Soviet Union"; Senator Connally talked of a possible atomic peace conference among the American, British, and Soviet Foreign Ministers.

Such proposals, which the Soviet press gleefully summed up as a "growing mass movement" for a new departure in American-Soviet relations, were by no means confined to the United States. Suggestions of a break in the great-power deadlock always aroused the keenest interest in Europe, where memories of the destruction caused by conventional bombs lent peculiar terrors to the new weapons that were discussed so freely across the Atlantic. Tenuous indications that the Soviet Government might be receptive to new American proposals served to heighten the tension. The idea that atomic warfare—perhaps all warfare—could be exorcised by a dramatic move from Washington was bound to be a popular one. The absence of such a move would lend support to the Soviet contention that official intransigence in the United States was the root of the world's ills. Even for those most familiar with Soviet methods, moreover, it was difficult to take the responsibility of assuming in advance that a new approach would be fruitless. No less an

authority than Winston Churchill, certainly no optimist where
the intentions of the Kremlin were concerned, suggested in a
political speech on February 14 that it was difficult "to see how
things could be worsened" by "another talk with Soviet Russia
on the highest level."

To policy-making officials in Washington, already under
such strong attack in other fields, this pressure was a further
source of embarrassment. They had not forgotten the sorry
results of the proposal to send Chief Justice Fred M. Vinson to
Moscow at the height of the 1948 election campaign,[11] nor the
President's occasional assertions that he would be glad to meet
Stalin at the White House, but nowhere else. A more fundamental obstacle, however, was the conviction that no fresh
approach to the U.S.S.R. could alter the permanent realities of
the situation. Unless the United States was prepared to make
far-reaching unilateral concessions for the sake of registering
a delusive "agreement," the only result of soliciting contact
with the Kremlin would be false hopes followed by disappointment.

While the President reiterated his belief in the United Nations plan of atomic energy control and in the adequacy of the
United Nations as a negotiating forum, Secretary Acheson
outlined the views which had induced the administration to
hold tight to its established positions. The philosophy he presented was of exceptional significance because it was to govern
the administration attitude toward other proposals for East-
West negotiations which would be put forward under even
graver circumstances.

Speeches like those of Senators McMahon and Tydings,
Acheson told the press on February 8, reflected a basic American urge for peace but did not necessarily represent the best
means of achieving it. "If we could reach our goal by agreement," he said, "that would be highly desirable and the simplest and easiest way to do it. But I think four years of experience have brought us the realization that that is not possible.
. . . Agreements reached with the Soviet Government are useful

[11] *The United States in World Affairs, 1948–1949,* 502-503.

when those agreements register facts or a situation which exists, and . . . they are not useful when they are merely agreements which do not register the existing facts."

In dealing with the Soviet Union, Acheson emphasized, it was essential to realize both its purposefulness and its capacity for adjusting itself to realities. The only road to agreement with the Soviet Government was the long and infinitely difficult one the United States had already chosen—that of converting "situations of weakness" into "situations so strong that they can be recognized and out of them can grow agreement." The creation of strength instead of weakness, he intimated, had been the basis of American policy in Germany, in Japan, in Western Europe, and indeed throughout the world. This method, the only one that was workable in the long run, demanded "purpose, continuity of purpose, perseverance, sacrifice, and . . . more than almost anything else, very steady nerves."

The advent of the H-bomb, Acheson warned, altered none of these facts; but it did mean that "we must be even more calm and even more steady than we have been in the past, because the responsibilities and the consequences of not being calm and not being steady are more terrible than they were before." Nor must we carry the process of self-examination and self-criticism to the point where it became mere self-reproach, "because that attitude of mind is apt to bring paralysis in the field of action," and "action is essential along the lines I have been discussing."

It was in a further discussion of this same problem that Acheson coined the phrase "total diplomacy" to characterize the demands of a struggle which, he insisted, was "just as crucial from the point of view of the continued existence of our way of life" as the total war of a few years earlier. This second talk, originally delivered off the record to a small private group,[12] was a plea to his hearers not to underestimate the enemy and not to yield to the temptation to look for short cuts and easy answers. "We are struggling against an adversary that

[12] Remarks at a meeting of the Advertising Council at the White House, February 16, released to the press March 9, 1950.

is deadly serious. We are in a situation where we are playing for keeps. Moreover, we are in a situation where we could lose without firing a shot." The methods of the old-fashioned imperialism were "kid stuff compared to the methods we are up against." But the only answer to these methods was the one that had been outlined so many times before: We "must be prepared to meet wherever possible all thrusts of the Soviet Union," even though "it will not always be possible to anticipate where those thrusts will take place, and we will not always be able to deal with them with equal effectiveness"; and we must work "to create those economic, political, social, and psychological conditions that strengthen and create confidence in the democratic way of life."

"No good would come from our taking the initiative in calling for conversations at this point," Acheson averred. "Such an effort on our part would raise false hopes among some people and fears among others. The Russians would know that there was a public expectancy of results of some kind, and those results could only be achieved by dangerous concessions on our part. Only the Russians would benefit from such a step. The Russians know that we are ready, always have been ready, to discuss with them any outstanding issue. We have discussed with them all important outstanding issues, not once, but many times. It is clear that the Russians do not want to settle those issues as long as they feel there is any possibility they can exploit them for their own objectives of world domination. It is only when they come to the conclusion that they cannot so exploit them that they will make agreements, and they will let it be known when they have reached that decision."

In a formal address at the University of California on March 16 the Secretary presented these views once again. The statement was more finished, and he outlined in some detail the fields—Germany, Austria, Japan, Korea, Eastern Europe, the United Nations, international Communist activities, diplomatic practices, hostile propaganda—in which the Soviet leaders had a continuing opportunity to demonstrate their desire for friendly relations. The underlying idea, however, was unchanged. Though always ready to discuss, to negotiate, to agree, we were "understandably loath to play the role of international sucker." "We must not, in our yearning for peace, allow ourselves to be betrayed by vague generalities or beguiling proffers of peace which are unsubstantiated by good faith solidly demonstrated in daily behavior." "I see no evidence that the Soviet leaders will change their conduct until the progress of the free world convinces them that they cannot profit from a continuation of these tensions."

By the time this address was delivered, the initial sensation of the hydrogen bomb had yielded to the earthy theatricality of the McCarthy campaign. American agitation for a direct approach subsided, but there persisted a strong undercurrent of discontent with a policy which had frankly lost faith in negotiation and seemed content to leave the psychological initiative to the Russians. Many Americans and even more foreigners obviously failed to share the administration's invincible pessimism regarding the outlook of the Politburo. Their misgivings provided fertile soil for the intensified "peace" campaign with which Moscow was to greet the advent of spring. But meanwhile Americans had to grapple with still other aspects of their new relationship to a perplexing world.

3. What Kind of Internationalism?

The foreign policy debates of early 1950 disclosed a widespread uncertainty concerning both the outstanding diplomatic problems of the day and the underlying principles from which any attempt to solve specific problems would have to proceed. Certain formulas like peace, anti-Communism, "a strong and well-balanced defense organization," resistance to Soviet encroachments, and support of the United Nations were generally acceptable as emotional symbols. But as soon as a problem arose which involved translating one of these generalities into definite action, it became apparent that different people attached radically different meanings to the same words.

This situation was peculiarly noticeable in reference to those foreign policy questions which concerned the relationship of the United States to the United Nations, the principal embodiment of the twentieth-century urge toward world organization. Because of the importance and scope of its functions the United Nations exerted an influence on every phase of American foreign policy and frequently acted as a kind of catalyst of American feeling. All the supposedly stock attitudes of the American public—nationalist and internationalist, isolationist and participationist, practical and idealistic, one-world and two-world, realistic and sentimental—had a way of crystallizing on any issue that concerned the adaptation of the United States to organized life in this multinational body. On its most elementary level the process could be witnessed in the quarrels that convulsed several American communities during 1950 over the display of the United Nations flag in proximity to the Stars and Stripes. More complex in their origins and implications were the proposals for a drastic remodeling of the United Nations which were considered by the Senate Foreign Relations Committee in the course of the same year.[13]

Dissatisfaction with the existing status of the United Nations was to be expected in view of its conspicuous position at the center of a generally unsatisfactory world situation. For many Americans to whom the United Nations was a symbol of their conversion to an international outlook, the failure of the world organization to produce international peace and harmony was as disappointing as the original hopes placed in it had been exaggerated. Yet, although the shortcomings of the United Nations were impossible to ignore, it was not so easy to determine precisely what was wrong. Some felt that the United States itself had done much to weaken the world body by taking important foreign policy actions outside its purview, and/or by saddling it with problems it could not solve; others

[13] *Revision of the United Nations Charter: Hearings* before a subcommittee of the Senate Foreign Relations Committee, 81st Congress, 2nd Session (Washington, 1950); see also *To Seek Development of the United Nations into a World Federation: Hearings* on H. Con. Res. 64 before the House Foreign Affairs Committee, 81st Congress, 1st Session (Washington, 1950).

pointed to the Russians and their use of the veto in the Security
Council as the source of every difficulty. This latter view became increasingly prevalent as evidence accumulated that the
United Nations could not function to the satisfaction of the majority until some means was found of getting around the
habitual sabotage of the Soviet delegation. Its validity seemed
sufficiently demonstrated when Mr. Malik abandoned the
Security Council in January 1950, a move that marvelously
cleared the atmosphere in that body but at the same time
reduced its area of theoretical effectiveness and raised some
question about the validity of actions taken by the Council in
the absence of a permanent member.

Preoccupation with the problem of Soviet tactics provided
such common denominator as existed among the various ingenious proposals that had been offered for perfecting the
United Nations structure and making its operations as nearly
foolproof as possible. That they reflected widespread and
genuine perturbation over the existing state of affairs was apparent from the fact that one or another of them was supported
by nearly half the members of the Senate and over 100 members of the lower house. Just as striking, however, was the lack
of anything approaching a consensus with regard to methods
by which the situation might be corrected. The nature of the
recommendations pointed to a widespread faith in mechanical
expedients but a great diversity of opinions concerning the
nature of the problem and the realistic possibilities of improvement.

Two of the plans, reflecting the ideas respectively of the
United World Federalists and the Committee to Frame a
World Constitution, proposed to grasp the nettle firmly and go
forward from the present feeble United Nations to a "world
federation" or a "true world government" endowed, as a
minimum, with adequate powers to preserve peace and prevent
aggression. How the U.S.S.R. and its satellites were to be induced to enter such an association was not elaborated upon by
the resolutions' sponsors. Other proposals were addressed to
the more immediate problem of finding ways to realize United

Nations objectives without radically altering the existing Charter. Though varying widely among themselves, they showed a definite trend toward the idea of supplementary agreements among like-minded member states *outside* the United Nations, an expedient sanctioned by the Charter and already adopted in the Inter-American Treaty of Reciprocal Assistance, the Brussels Treaty of 1948, and the North Atlantic Pact.

Two such proposals merited special attention because of their distinguished sponsorship and their attempt to build realistically on foundations already established—in one case on the North Atlantic Treaty, in the other on the United Nations organization itself. The first of these was the so-called Atlantic Union resolution (S. Con. Res. 57) introduced by Senator Estes Kefauver, Democrat, of Tennessee and backed by such figures as former Supreme Court Justice Owen J. Roberts, Harold C. Urey, William L. Clayton, and Clarence K. Streit. Its aim was to convert the existing North Atlantic alliance into a political federation. It called on the President to invite the "democracies which sponsored the North Atlantic Treaty [14] to name delegates . . . to meet this year with delegates of the United States in a federal convention to explore how far their peoples and the peoples of such other democracies as the convention may invite . . . can apply among them, within the framework of the United Nations, the principles of free federal union."

Strengthening of the United Nations on a universal rather than a regional basis was the aim of the Thomas-Douglas Resolution (S. Con. Res. 52), also known as "The Article 51 Pact" because it called for a supplementary agreement for collective self-defense under Article 51 of the United Nations Charter.[15] The object of this resolution, whose supporters in-

[14] Belgium, Canada, France, Luxembourg, Netherlands, U.K., and U.S.
[15] Article 51, which provided the legal basis of the Brussels Treaty and the North Atlantic Pact, reads in part: "Nothing in the present Charter shall impair the inherent right of individual or collective self-defense if an armed attack occurs against a Member of the United Nations, until the Security Council has taken the measures necessary to maintain international peace and security."

cluded Democratic Senator Paul H. Douglas of Illinois, Quincy Wright, Hamilton Fish Armstrong, Arthur N. Holcombe, Stephen M. Schwebel, and Clark M. Eichelberger, was to provide the United Nations with machinery and armed forces that could be used to repel an attack even if a Soviet veto prevented the Security Council from "fulfilling its duties." Signatories to the proposed agreement, which would be open to all members of the United Nations, would undertake both to maintain specified armed forces for the immediate use of the United Nations and to come to the aid of a victim of attack if so requested by a two-thirds vote of the General Assembly (including three of the five great powers).

Finally, Senator Homer Ferguson, Republican, of Michigan had introduced a more conservative resolution (S. Con. Res. 72) listing various means by which the United Nations might be strengthened in cooperation with other governments: "by interpretation of the Charter, by action taken or usages developed under the Charter, by supplementary agreements among nations who desire thus to further the purposes of the Charter, or, ultimately, by amendment of the Charter." Among particular fields for action, mention was made of voluntary agreement to limit the use of the veto; admission to the United Nations of all states qualified for membership; elimination of reservations, by the United States and other countries, on the compulsory jurisdiction of the International Court of Justice; development of the United Nations Field Service; renewed efforts to provide the United Nations with armed forces; and "utilization by all members . . . of suitable measures for collective self-defense under article 51 . . . as necessary to maintain peace and security." The resolution was supported, among others, by Mr. Eichelberger and by Professor Clyde Eagleton of New York University.

The method of development and growth within the existing Charter, as suggested by Senator Ferguson, was one that had already proved its value on many occasions. This was decidedly the method preferred by the State Department, which, painfully aware though it was of the shortcomings of the present

United Nations mechanism, was not prepared to face the domestic and international complications involved in a major revision of the Charter or negotiation of a major supplementary agreement among United Nations members.

When Deputy Under-Secretary of State Dean Rusk appeared to testify before the Senate subcommittee, he laid great emphasis on these potentialities of organic growth and the dangers of "turning in any irresponsible or whimsical fashion to new forms of organization or formulae for perfection." "We have by no means exhausted the possibilities of the existing Charter," he insisted. "There are large and comparatively unexplored regions of the Charter which are available to its members for further cooperation and joint action. The United Nations has demonstrated a flexibility, a response to practical situations by the development of custom and practice, and the power to adjust its procedures. . . . There is no question but that the Charter can carry much more traffic if its members desire to have it do so." [16]

Of the seven specific proposals before the Foreign Relations subcommittee,[17] the State Department expressed itself as generally favorable to the Ferguson resolution but found more or less serious objections to all the others. Assistant Secretary John D. Hickerson politely characterized the various plans for world federation, world government, and fundamental remodeling of the United Nations as being probably impracticable in themselves, unlikely to solve the outstanding problems of the day, and dangerous to the gains already made under existing instrumentalities. While paying particular tribute to the interest of those who sponsored the "Article 51 pact," he argued that a special agreement to exercise the right of collective self-defense was unnecessary because the General Assembly already possessed ample power to deal with cases of

[16] *Revision of the United Nations Charter: Hearings,* 380, 385.
[17] In addition to the proposals already described, the subcommittee was considering a resolution on the political federation of Europe sponsored by Senators J. William Fulbright and Elbert D. Thomas (S. Con. Res. 12), and a resolution from Senator John Sparkman calling for modification of the veto and establishment of an international police force (S. Res. 133).

aggression in which the Security Council failed to function.[18] In addition to freezing the exercise of the right of self-defense into a rigid pattern and perhaps arousing delusive expectations of military assistance throughout the world, he feared that such a pact would have unfavorable repercussions on the developing structure of the North Atlantic Treaty organization.

One method of reforming the United Nations was conspicuously absent from the proposals considered by the Foreign Relations subcommittee, but was bound to have a certain appeal because it avoided the subtleties of Charter interpretation and struck directly at the most conspicuous source of the world organization's difficulty. This was the method of expelling the Soviet Union and its satellites and reorganizing the United Nations without them. Hitherto this course had had few open advocates. The Charter of the United Nations was, as Mr. Rusk had pointed out, "our basic over-all agreement with the Soviet Union." It contained "provisions which, if loyally carried out, would assure the peace." [19] So long as it remained in effect, a basis existed for the improvement of relations if ever the Soviet Government should wish them to improve. Its abrogation would signify the final break with the one-world concept of San Francisco, and would tend to convert whatever might remain of the world body into an anti-Soviet alliance. Before the Malik walk-out in January, such a program would not have found many overt supporters in the United States. Its enunciation in the spring of 1950 was one more evidence of the increasingly anti-Soviet trend of American opinion.

Not surprisingly, the most notable proposal on these lines came from the same source as had some of the strongest demands for a more energetic policy in the Far East. Former President Herbert Hoover, speaking in New York on April 27, made the blunt "suggestion . . . that the United Nations should be reorganized without the Communist nations in it. If that is

[18] Machinery for the exercise of these powers was created, largely on the initiative of the United States, at the autumn session of the General Assembly. Cf. below, pp. 369-371.
[19] *Revision of the United Nations Charter: Hearings*, 385.

impractical" the senior Republican statesman continued, "then a definite New United Front should be organized of those peoples who disavow communism, who stand for morals and religion, and who love freedom." The world, Mr. Hoover affirmed, "needs mobilization" against the tide of Red agnosticism, slavery, and imperialism. "The United States needs to know who are with us in the cold war against these practices, and whom we can depend on."

This speech caused consternation in United Nations quarters, indignation among American advocates of a stronger United Nations, and perceptible embarrassment in Washington. President Truman congratulated Mr. Hoover on his speech but omitted any reference to its crucial sentence. Mr. Hickerson assured the press once again that the United Nations was "the cornerstone of our foreign policy." Congressional quarters appeared somewhat at a loss for comment, but the State Department's new Republican advisers sharply dissociated themselves from the Hoover proposal. Mr. Dulles saw "no occasion to destroy the universality of the United Nations"; Mr. Cooper felt that it "would take away all hope of peace and lead to a freezing of the present situation [and] a hopeless view of the future," as well as signifying a failure by the United States to live up to its international commitments.[20]

Although the Hoover proposal was made several weeks after the Senate hearings had closed, something of the state of mind which inspired it was also discernible among various private witnesses who had appeared before the subcommittee. Several of these had opposed all resolutions tending toward world government or even substantial strengthening of the United Nations. Spokesmen for various patriotic societies showed a lively apprehension of any "superstate" or "international bureaucratic dictatorship." Their arguments were adequately summarized in the report of the Foreign Relations Committee: [21]

[20] *New York Times*, April 29, 1950.
[21] *Revision of the United Nations Charter:* Senate Report 2501, 81st Congress, 2nd Session, September 1, 1950 (Washington, 1950), 49-50.

1. The United Nations is an organization of sovereign states. Therefore we can support the United Nations as now constituted. The United States must not, however, support any amendments of the Charter or any new organization which would abridge United States sovereignty.

2. The United States has always depended upon itself. It should do so now. We must not squander our economic and military strength abroad on untrustworthy partners—some of whom are socialistic. In fact, our military and economic aid to foreign governments weakens us at home and we may thereby become victims of enemies from within the United States.

3. Attempts to create a world federation are part of an international conspiracy designed eventually to turn the United States over to the Communists.

4. It is fallacious to believe that we can have just a little world government. If we create any supergovernment with limited powers it will be only a matter of time until it takes over all of our freedoms. Thus a world government with "power to take jurisdiction over all matters that bear on war and peace would be capable of taking jurisdiction over everything." . . .

5. Practically any of the proposals under consideration would "supersede and extinguish the Constitution of the United States."

6. If the United States were in a world government, the American people could expect "to support all other members of our world family." . . .

Such views were to become more prevalent before the year was out. As of mid-1950, however, the committee was more impressed on the whole by the apparent strength of the positive movement for active United States participation in international collaboration. There was some evidence, it felt, that the State Department might have "underestimated the willingness of the American people to accept the burdens that go with the position of leadership in the free world." But it was equally struck by the great diversity of opinions as to the course the United States should follow. "The principal consensus of opinion was that the world is in trouble and something needs to be done. There was no agreement as to what to do, who should do it, what the results of specific proposals would be; nor was there evidence that the American people are aware of the full implications of the various proposals." [22]

[22] *Ibid.,* 4, 51.

Under the circumstances, the committee did not give its endorsement to any of the specific resolutions before it, nor did it attempt to evolve a composite resolution of its own. Most of the proposals involved serious constitutional questions on which the committee thought it improper to take a position "until the issues have been debated, discussed, and understood the length and breadth of this land." The abnormal situation created by the East-West struggle, and the unexpected effectiveness of the United Nations in dealing with the Communist aggression in Korea, were additional factors deterring the committee from attempting a final judgment. In its interim report it expressed the hope that "democratic consideration and debate of the ideas and issues developed during the hearings will temper some visionaries with practicality and some realists with idealism." Thus there might develop "a consensus of opinion that will make it possible for the Executive or the Congress to propose a course of action that will be generally acceptable to the American people as the one most likely to lead to peace and freedom." [23]

While the inconclusive debate on possible major reorganization of the United Nations went forward, Congress was also considering a number of important matters affecting the nature of American participation in the world body as it existed in 1950. Some of these involved extension of United Nations authority and responsibility, others the support of activities already under way. The specific issues and interests involved were highly diverse, and do not readily lend themselves to unified treatment. One identical question, however, stood at or near the heart of each discussion: How far was the United States prepared to go in adjusting its national policies to the present requirements of the international community? To what extent was it prepared to seek the fulfillment of American aims within a wider international framework, and to what extent did it insist on retaining full freedom to pursue them in its own way?

Action on concrete United Nations problems offered a con-

[23] *Ibid.*, 5, 53-54.

tinuing test of how far the American nation had really modified
its former isolationist attitude. The matter was of more than
academic importance, because every indication of the American
outlook was watched with the keenest interest by foreign
nations whose whole future depended in one way or another
on the course the United States might take. It was vital for
them to know whether the United States, which never tired of
calling for union among the other free nations, was itself
willing to accept any real limitations on its freedom of action
within the international community. It was equally vital to
know whether the American initiative to which they were accustomed at international conferences represented a genuine
national conviction or merely the ideas of a few officials who
would later be repudiated by Congress and the public.

A case in point was the Convention on the Prevention and
Punishment of the Crime of Genocide, which had been unanimously adopted by the United Nations General Assembly on
December 9, 1948 and awaited ratification by the world's
governments. Drawn up largely on American initiative, this
convention declared genocide (attempted destruction of a
national, ethnical, racial, or religious group) to be a crime
under international law, justiciable either by national courts or
by an international tribunal which might be established by
subsequent agreement; and it obligated the states which accepted it to enact legislation providing effective penalties for
persons found guilty. The convention would come into force
90 days after 20 nations had ratified it; by mid-September 1950
it had been signed by 43 and ratified by 24 governments.

President Truman sent the convention to the Senate in June
1949, and a subcommittee of the Foreign Relations Committee
held hearings on it in January and February 1950. An overwhelming majority of witnesses expressed themselves in favor
of ratification; organizations supporting the convention included the American Federation of Labor, the American
Legion, the Congress of Industrial Organizations, the New
York City Bar Association, and numerous social, religious,
and cultural groups. The principal objection came from a group

within the American Bar Association (its nine-man Committee on Peace and Law through the United Nations) which disagreed with the assurances of government officials, and of other groups within the association, that the convention was fully compatible with the American Constitution and would not supersede domestic law. On April 12, the Senate subcommittee recommended that the convention be ratified, subject to four "understandings" or clarifying interpretations designed to obviate constitutional difficulties; but no action was taken by the full Foreign Relations Committee, despite an appeal from the President for ratification before the next session of the General Assembly.[24]

Comparable problems were involved in the Charter for an International Trade Organization, on which Congress also took no definite action during its 1950 session. This international code of fair trade practices, largely inspired by the United States but unacceptable to important interests in this country, is more suitable for discussion in the section on foreign economic policy which concludes the present chapter. The same is true of Congress' halting and incomplete action on the Point Four program of aid to economically underdeveloped areas, and of its appropriations or non-appropriations in support of various United Nations relief and welfare programs. On the positive side, mention must be made here of the Senate's ratification of the convention establishing the Intergovernmental Maritime Consultative Organization, a specialized agency of the United Nations, and of the action of both houses in passing an amended Displaced Persons bill which would ease the task of the International Refugee Organization in winding up its work of resettlement of European refugees.[25]

[24] *The Genocide Convention: Hearings* before a subcommittee of the Senate Foreign Relations Committee, 81st Congress, 2nd Session, on Executive O (Washington, 1950); report of subcommittee action in *New York Times,* April 13, 1950; letter from the President to Senator Connally, August 26, in *Department of State Bulletin,* XXIII, September 4, 1950, 379.

[25] Public Law 555, 81st Congress, eliminated the discriminatory features in the 1948 Displaced Persons Act, increased to 341,000 the number of displaced persons eligible to enter the United States outside the immigration quota, and extended the time limit for the operation to June 30, 1951. For background cf. *The United States in World Affairs, 1949,* 102-103.

Most of these actions involved highly technical problems as well as issues of principle, and a judgment on their merits would carry us beyond the limits of the present discussion. The significant point to be noted here is that the over-all performance was an exceedingly checkered one, shot through with reversals, inconsistencies, and half measures. Its net effect was to confirm the impression that Congress, and presumably the public, possessed a general belief in the United Nations idea but no settled convictions about what this implied in the way of positive cooperation within the international community. It left open the larger question whether the United States yet recognized a firm commitment to common action among nations that wanted to remain free.

4. What Kind of Economic Policy?

The underlying uncertainty of the American people concerning the requirements of their world position was peculiarly marked in the domain of economic policy. The crucial role of economic factors in world affairs had been demonstrated a hundred times over, in depression, in war, and in postwar readjustment. The vital relationship of the American economy to any hope of establishing a more stable international order was scarcely debatable. American economic policy was consciously directed toward reorienting the world economy along lines which would serve the interests both of the United States and of the larger world with which its fate was indissolubly linked. Yet the detailed policies developed to this end were by no means universally accepted. Each of them was subject to heavy and recurrent pressure for abandonment, curtailment, or substantial modification. Not infrequently this pressure became so heavy as to constitute a substantial repudiation of the basic policy.

In its simplest terms the problem of American economic policy was to find an adjustment between the interests of particular groups of Americans—businessmen, manufacturers, farmers, wage-earners, taxpayers—and the larger, world-wide interests that affected the security and prosperity of the nation as a whole. For many years the national administration had seen the key to this adjustment in the expansion of trade and general economic activity throughout the world. Unable to live comfortably on its own resources, the United States would always require a considerable exchange of commodities and services with other countries. Expansion of these exchanges on a multilateral basis, it was reasoned, would make for high levels of prosperity both at home and abroad and lessen the economic tensions which might otherwise seek relief in war. "Peace through trade," combined with opportunities for American enterprise, was the underlying objective of the Reciprocal Trade Agreements program initiated in the 1930's and of the various international economic organizations and agreements—the International Bank and Fund, the International Trade Organization, and the General Agreement on Tariffs and Trade—promoted by the United States during and after World War II.

Pursuit of this objective in the postwar years was complicated by three types of conditions, each of which necessitated modifications, compromises, and temporary postponements. First and possibly most fundamental was the marked indifference of large sections of the American public, which tended to shy away from economic abstractions, gave the official policy little affirmative support, and offered no effective counterpoise to those who had special reasons for backing or resisting it. As a result, economic policy was more affected by special group interests than any other phase of foreign policy. Since this was a field in which Congress exercised decisive influence, advocates and opponents of each program habitually mobilized all the familiar means of pressure on Capitol Hill. Legislation on economic policy, when it emerged from the congressional mill, tended to reflect the relative persuasiveness of those who stood to gain or lose directly rather than any settled conclusions as to its relation to the national interest and the over-all requirements of American foreign policy.

Further complications arose from the extraordinarily disturbing effects of the world war and the ensuing turmoil on every continent. Wartime destruction and dislocation of the world economy compelled the United States to set aside its long-run objectives and undertake a monumental relief and reconstruction effort, carried out partly through national and partly through international channels, in order to ward off sheer collapse in many areas of the world. Until the world economy had been securely reestablished, it was impossible to progress far toward the ultimate goal of a nondiscriminatory, multilateral system of expanding world trade. Meanwhile other nations found innumerable cogent reasons to maintain exchange controls, import quotas, and other restrictive devices which ran directly counter to this objective and involved frequent discrimination against American goods and services. Almost from the beginning of the recovery process American officials were preoccupied by a latent conflict between two major aims of American economic policy: (1) the rebuilding of the economies of friendly nations, which at least temporarily involved their retention of trade barriers under a loose interpretation of the most-favored-nation principle; and (2) the rebuilding of world trade on a basis of free competition with no discrimination against American or any other products. Hopes that general economic recovery would lead to a rapid abandonment of restrictive practices were only very partially realized.

The emergence of the East-West political struggle introduced new factors into the situation and made a solution more difficult because it necessitated the weighing of every move in terms of its political and military as well as its economic implication. From the standpoint of the United States, the dangers of Communist infiltration supplied a new motive for assisting economic recovery and promoting economic cooperation, particularly in Europe. On the other hand, distrust of the Soviet Union resulted in a demand for actions which in some instances ran counter to the over-all recovery objective. Military requirements were a standing threat to the satisfaction of economic requirements. There was also a growing tendency to discourage our European partners from carrying on large-scale trade with the U.S.S.R. and the various countries which had fallen under its domination. The technical aspects of this policy, which originated in a natural reluctance to add to the military potential of the Soviet bloc, were vigorously debated in Europe and to a minor extent in this country. Less debatable was the fact that partial closure of the Eastern market increased Western Europe's dependence on the United States, thus interfering with the economic aim which Paul G. Hoffman, head of the Economic Cooperation Administration, had picturesquely described as "getting Europe on its feet and off our back."

All of these factors had a bearing on the fundamental problem of the so-called "dollar gap," which was another way of describing the chronic disparity between exports and imports in American exchanges with the rest of the world. In the four years 1946–1949, this country's export surplus of goods and services had amounted to $29 billion, or nearly half the total value of American exports during the period. Meanwhile the necessary imports of Western Europe, Japan, and certain other areas from the United States continued to be financed largely by governmental grants and loans, which totaled approximately $22 billion during the same period.[26] This, however, was a method that no responsible American statesman was willing to continue indefinitely. The European Recovery Program, the largest of the foreign aid programs, had been designed to bring Europe's payments into balance by 1952; and administration and congressional leaders, even if they conceded that some selective foreign aid might be required after that date, were unanimous in declaring that the program must end on schedule.

Yet there might be weighty objections to any abrupt modification of policies which, whatever their burden on the United States, had unquestionably served to keep the European and world economy from foundering in its most difficult period. If economic aid were simply cut off, European and other countries would have to limit their future imports from the

[26] *Report to the President on Foreign Economic Policies* (Washington, November 10, 1950), 25.

dollar area to whatever they could pay for with their own exports—a course which might be disastrous to the American as well as foreign economies. Among other undesired effects it might well result in lowered living standards around the world, accentuate distress and social tension, and reopen the floodgates of Communist agitation. Thus the logical corollary of ending American aid would be the development of alternative policies, adequate to maintain the gains already made and promote further progress in the same direction.

The problem was not necessarily insoluble, provided all parties understood what was at stake and were willing to make the necessary adjustments. Action would be required on several fronts. The non-dollar countries, especially in Europe, would have to sell more to the dollar area, at the same time pursuing policies that would bring lowered costs, greater productivity, and a stronger competitive position. The dollar countries would have to maintain a high level of private foreign investment and—as was explicitly recognized by the United States and Canada at the Washington financial conference in September 1949 [27]—would have to modify some of their own protective commercial policies in the interests of buying more from the non-dollar world. Both groups would have to redouble their efforts to promote economic development and build up purchasing power in the underdeveloped countries, not only to alleviate popular unrest and bar the door to Communist expansion but also to promote the growth of world trade on a multilateral basis.

The nature of these problems was to be substantially modified in the course of 1950 by the commencement of a large-scale rearmament effort in response to the Soviet-sponsored aggression in Korea. Some familiar phenomena like the over-all dollar gap were virtually to disappear; others, like the conflict between military and civilian requirements in the allocation of resources, were to assume greater importance. These developments, however, could not be foreseen during the months when Congress was working over the economic policy legislation pro-

[27] *The United States in World Affairs, 1949,* 127-128.

posed for enactment at the 1950 session. An examination of its record is still pertinent because not only the actual legislation but also the attitudes and opinions that left their mark upon it continued to influence the course of developments during the second half of the year.

That the administration program encountered exceedingly rough sledding was no surprise in view of the rising demand for economy and the election-year political climate already described. What struck the observer most forcibly was not the violence of partisan conflict but the extraordinary confusion and uncertainty of purpose which seemed to extend equally to both sides of the legislative chambers. Nothing in the nature of a struggle between two rival economic philosophies was discernible. Opponents of the administration program, whether Republican or Democratic, seldom had any clear-cut alternatives to suggest. Rejecting some administration ideas out of hand, they ostensibly accepted others while in reality doing their best to nullify them by amendments and limiting conditions. Individual issues were decided—or left undecided— neither on their merits nor on their relation to any underlying principle, but solely by the play of contradictory pressures and waves of feeling. The legislation that emerged, whatever might be thought of its adequacy, could by no stretch of imagination be termed the reflection of a consistent national policy.

As between economic assistance programs and general measures to promote world trade, the latter fared worse. Having narrowly passed the basic measure to extend the Reciprocal Trade Agreements Act in the fall of 1949, Congress sat back and did substantially nothing to implement the administration's plans for reducing trade barriers and reviving multilateralism. A number of congressmen continued to display keen interest in the reduction of trade barriers within Western Europe, but their enthusiasm failed to carry over into the larger field where the commercial policies of the United States itself were involved. A part of the responsibility for this negative record undoubtedly lay with the administration, whose bill to streamline and modernize United States customs procedure—

the so-called "Customs Simplification Act of 1950" (H.R. 8304) —did not reach the House Ways and Means Committee until May 1, too late to escape sidetracking by urgent tax legislation. On the other hand, Congress showed its usual reserve toward the Charter for an International Trade Organization, which had been submitted to both houses in April 1949—a year after signature—with a request for its urgent approval by joint resoluction. The House Foreign Affairs Committee held exhaustive hearings in May and June,[28] but submitted no recommendation, and no action was taken in the Senate. Since other governments were unwilling to bind themselves to the liberal provisions of this largely American-inspired document until the United States itself led the way, congressional inaction effectually halted progress toward international outlawry of discriminatory trade practices. In December the administration was to shelve the Charter for the indefinite future as a casualty of the Korean crisis.

The temper in which Congress approached its annual task of legislating for economic assistance to other countries was strongly influenced by the magnitude and unbalanced nature of the budget submitted to it early in January. In his budget message for the fiscal year 1950–1951 the President asked Congress to approve a total outlay of $42.4 billion, as contrasted with estimated budgetary receipts of only $37.3 billion. A part of the $5.1 billion deficit, he said, would be made up by projected adjustments in the tax laws. As usual, the largest items in the budget were national defense ($13.5 billion), veterans' services and benefits ($6.1 billion), and international affairs and finance ($4.7 billion); together these three classifications accounted for 71 percent of the total. The request for international affairs and finance included new appropriations of $3.1 billion for the third year of the European Recovery Program, $115 million for economic aid to Korea, $35 million for technical assistance to underdeveloped areas, and $648 million

[28] Membership and Participation of the United States in the International Trade Organization: Hearings on H. J. Res. 236 before the House Foreign Affairs Committee (Washington, 1950).

(plus $500 million in new contract authority) for the Mutual Defense Assistance program. This last item, the President commented, would "remain substantial" for several years, and expenditure for stimulating foreign economic development would "increase somewhat" as conditions grew more favorable. The huge expenditures for foreign recovery and relief, on the other hand, were due to "diminish rapidly as recovery programs near completion, although new measures may become necessary to attain specific objectives in particular areas." [29]

This qualified reassurance was much too vague to enlist congressional enthusiasm. Only the military assistance program, which will be considered in the next chapter, swept through comparatively undamaged on the wave of militancy that followed the aggression in Korea. Foreign economic assistance, on the contrary, sustained an intense battering as it ran the usual gantlet of committee and floor debate in both houses. The eventual results were embodied in three distinct legislative enactments: (1) the Far Eastern Economic Assistance Act of 1950 (Public Law 447, approved February 14), authorizing economic assistance to Korea and Nationalist China in the fiscal year 1950; (2) the Foreign Economic Assistance Act of 1950 (Public Law 535, approved June 5), providing legislative authorization for aid to Europe, Korea, China, Palestine refugees, underdeveloped areas, and United Nations children's programs in the fiscal year 1951; and (3) the General Appropriation Act, 1951 (Public Law 759, approved September 6), which provided funds for all but one of those programs in the new fiscal year. The consolidated nature of the legislation, especially the inclusion of all regular appropriations for 1950–1951 in one omnibus appropriation bill, was a new departure. The processes by which Congress arrived at the substance of each measure, however, varied little from the practice of earlier years.

The Far Eastern Economic Assistance Act originated as an attempt to remedy Congress's failure to pass legislation at its

[29] The full text of the President's budget message for 1951 appeared in *New York Times*, January 10, 1950.

previous session in implementation of the responsibility the United States had assumed for economic support of the Republic of Korea.[30] Almost without warning the needs of this small outpost of the "free world," inconsequential in economic terms but important in relation to United States world policy, became dangerously involved in the larger controversies over governmental economy and especially Far Eastern policy. On January 19 the administration's request for $60 million of new economic aid to Korea up to June 30, 1950 was flatly rejected by a House vote of 193–191, reflecting an alignment of Southern Democrats with Republicans who were smarting over the administration's negative position on the Formosa issue. A querulous statement by Korean President Syngman Rhee evidenced the distress of a government whose whole future rested on steady American support. Secretary Acheson, voicing the "concern and dismay" of the State Department, drew attention to probable adverse effects not only in Korea but also "in other parts of the world where our encouragement is a major element in the struggle for freedom." [31]

The solution, worked out in the House Foreign Affairs Committee, was frankly described by one Democratic Congressman [32] as "a sop to people who are more interested in our China policy than in what we are trying to do in Korea." The bill was rewritten to include Nationalist China, where authority to expend some $104 million in economic aid funds left over from the China Aid Act of 1948 was about to expire. These funds were now made usable up to June 30, 1950, and under its new title the bill passed both houses comfortably early in February.

All of this was in the nature of unfinished business relating to the fiscal year 1950. For fiscal year 1951 Korea eventually was allotted an additional $100 million in economic aid funds, and the residue still remaining from the China aid program was assigned to various uses in non-Communist China and its

[30] The United States in World Affairs, 1949, 87-88, 434, 436.
[31] Department of State Bulletin, XXII, February 6, 1950, 212.
[32] Representative Mike Mansfield of Montana, February 7, 1950.

"general area." [33] In sanctioning the new allocation for Korea, Congress was encouraged by various administration statements reflecting confidence in the Republic's ability to survive despite the threat to its existence from the Soviet-supported regime north of the 38th parallel. The Korean fighting which began in June showed the inadequacy of these estimates, and also made it probable that if the Republic survived at all its economic assistance needs in the next year would be far in excess of $100 million.

In the legislation extending the European Recovery Program for the third year of its four-year span, Congress faced few basic problems which had not been minutely thrashed out in the debates of 1948 and 1949. The program, as Mr. Hoffman and other administration spokesmen made clear, had been spectacularly successful in two of its primary aims, the halting of Communism and the revival of production in Western Europe. What remained was to push forward with the elimination of trade barriers within Europe and facilitate readjustments which would make the Marshall Plan countries as nearly as possible independent of extraordinary outside assistance by mid-1952. Steps toward European economic integration, Mr. Hoffman reported, had so far been "disappointing" but not "discouraging"; the chief innovation planned for 1950–1951 was the use of $600 million in E.C.A. funds to promote a European Payments Union and other devices to liberalize European trade.[34]

Twenty-seven weeks, from February 21 to August 28, were consumed in congressional consideration of the program. Few congressmen questioned its general merits; Hoffman's administration, it appeared, had gained widespread approval. On the other hand, many hesitated to go along with his detailed recommendations. Some felt that the job of the United States was substantially completed, or could be wound up on a much

[33] Estimated to total $94 million, these funds were allocated to non-Communist China including Formosa (at least $40 million); non-Communist areas in the "general area" of China (not over $40 million); famine relief in China ($8 million); and education of Chinese students in the U.S. ($6 million).

[34] *Extension of European Recovery—1950: Hearings* on S. 3101 before the Senate Foreign Relations Committee, 81st Congress, 2nd Session (Washington, 1950), 3-13.

smaller scale. Senator Taft, who led Republican efforts to reduce the administration's "tighter than tight" request for $2.95
billion in new funds,[35] told the Senate on April 27 that E.C.A.
had done a good job, but that its figures for the new year were
taken "out of the air" with no "justification." "It is difficult to
say how much it should be cut," he said, "but I have finally
come to the conclusion that a 20 percent cut of $600 million
. . . would be reasonable, and would not hamper seriously the
operation of the program." Other Republican Senators—Kem
of Missouri, Hickenlooper of Iowa, Ives of New York, and
Bridges of New Hampshire—proposed cuts ranging from $1
billion down to $250 million, the figure finally accepted in May
by both Senate and House. The appropriations committees then
sharpened their weapons and for the next several weeks the
program underwent a further course of lacerations, emerging
late in August for the President's signature at the level of
$2.25 billion (plus $277 million remaining from the previous
year's appropriation).

During its passage through Congress the E.C.A. legislation
became the object of the usual number of amendments, some of
constructive intent and others frankly designed to make the
Marshall Plan serve other purposes than those for which it
was originally conceived. Conspicuous in the latter class were
various proposals to subordinate European recovery to the direct interests of sections of the American economy—notably a
strong but unsuccessful attempt in the House to require E.C.A.
to spend $1 billion of its limited funds in procuring surplus
agricultural products in this country. Senator Connally, who
shared the widespread irritation over discrimination against
American petroleum products by the United Kingdom, introduced an amendment (later shifted to the policy declaration of
the act) directed generally against undue restrictions on American imports by Marshall Plan countries. Also included in the
final text of the law was an amendment by Senator Lodge of
Massachusetts which took the opposite tack by urging E.C.A. to
reduce the amount of dollar purchases by Marshall Plan coun-

[35] Plus $150 million left over from the previous appropriation.

tries in order to lessen the dollar costs of the program and minimize the burden on the American taxpayer.

Another class of amendments and threatened amendments was notable as revealing a real tendency to dictate to the Marshall Plan countries and ride roughshod over their political sensitivities. In one extreme instance the House, sitting as a Committee of the Whole, adopted by 99-66 an amendment which would have withheld aid from the United Kingdom as long as the "partition" of Ireland continued. (Later the amendment was repudiated, 226-60.) Senator Kem and Senator Malone of Nevada made the usual attempts to deny aid to countries which strayed from the path of free enterprise. Kem and Wherry proposed unsuccessfully to stiffen further the requirement against exportation of goods with any possible military potential from Western Europe to the U.S.S.R. and its satellites.

Finally, and with results that reflected the increasingly conservative trend of American thinking, Senator McCarran of Nevada renewed his campaign to include Franco Spain among the beneficiaries of the Marshall Plan. Despite strong and repeated discouragement by the administration and a first rejection by the Senate in April, a mandatory loan to Spain in the amount of $62.5 million was included in the omnibus appropriation bill that reached the White House late in August. Rather than veto the entire measure at that stage, the President announced that he would treat the McCarran rider as an "authorization"—not a "directive"—and would lend money to Spain only if satisfactory terms were available and the foreign policy of the United States would be promoted thereby.[36]

The Point Four legislation for underdeveloped countries encountered roughly similar treatment on its second submission to Congress, except that its greater novelty entailed even greater legislative difficulties and the outcome was even more in doubt until the appropriation bill had passed its last hurdle. The philosophy of the "bold new program," which sought by

[36] *Department of State Bulletin*, XXIII, September 25, 1950, 517. As approved by the Senate on August 1 by 65-15, the McCarran rider called for a loan of $100 million; the amount was reduced to $62.5 million in the Senate-House conference on the appropriation bill.

inexpensive methods to raise economic levels and thus counter the appeal of Communism in economically underdeveloped areas, had been voluminously expounded to Congress the year before, though too late for action. Congressional skepticism toward the concept announced with so much fanfare in the President's inaugural address had caused the administration some embarrassment in its relations with the United Nations during 1949, and had forced a postponement of the United Nations Technical Assistance Conference which was to ascertain the means available for carrying out what American officials had steadly maintained was a joint United States-United Nations enterprise.[37] This omission was repaired in 1950, but not before a series of legislative mishaps had deepened the skepticism in United Nations and other quarters about the reality of American interest in purposeful action to raise world living standards.

Nevertheless the "Act for International Development," which eventually became Title IV of the Foreign Economic Assistance Act, was a significant milestone in the evolution of American world policy. For the first time it was declared to be the policy of the United States "to aid the efforts of the peoples of economically underdeveloped areas to develop their resources and improve their working and living conditions by encouraging the exchange of technical knowledge and skills and the flow of investment capital to countries which provide conditions under which such technical assistance and capital can effectively and constructively contribute to raising standards of living, creating new sources of wealth, increasing productivity and expanding purchasing power." To this end Congress authorized United States participation in both multilateral and bilateral "technical cooperation" programs, including those operated under the United Nations, the Organization of American States, and other international organizations; directed the President to appoint an officer responsible for planning, implementing, and managing the programs, together with a policy advisory board representing interested private groups; and authorized the appropriation of $35 million (including $10

[37] *The United States in World Affairs, 1949, 91-102, 332-347.*

million already appropriated under existing technical cooperation programs) to support these activities up to June 30,
1951. In the later appropriation act this amount was reduced
to $34.5 million—$26.9 million of new money plus $7.6 mil-
lion already appropriated.

The most striking feature of this act was its almost exclusive
concentration on the element of technical assistance and its
omission of anything more than a passing reference to the
need for increased capital investment in the underdeveloped
countries. This omission reflected an important divergence between articulate opinion in the underdeveloped countries and
prevailing sentiment in the United States. Spokesmen for the
underdeveloped countries showed comparatively little interest
in technical assistance but laid great stress on their requirements for investment capital, which, they held, must come
mainly from public, preferably United Nations, sources. American business interests, on the contrary, strenuously opposed
public loans and grants of all kinds, professed a general willingness to invest in underdeveloped countries, but insisted that
the latter must first create a favorable "climate" by promising
equitable treatment to the foreign private investors. The inability of the State Department to bridge this gulf was responsible for a somewhat arbitrary emphasis on technical assistance
as the one phase of the program which had some chance of
general American support.[38]

Much of the heat generated by the Point Four bill in its
passage through Congress could be traced to this unresolved
conflict. Critics of the measure seemed convinced that it committed the United States to a policy of large-scale beneficence
without obligating the underdeveloped countries to improve
their treatment of foreign business. Perhaps sensing the relevance of the program to the whole problem of reconstructing
the world economy, various congressmen voiced the suspicion
that Point Four was intended to take the place of E.C.A. when
the latter went out of business. Senator Taft, who professed to

[38] A bill designed to encourage private investment in underdeveloped countries
by authorizing the Export-Import Bank to offer limited guarantees of such investments against certain nonbusiness risks (H.R. 8083) passed the House on
July 12 but failed of action in the Senate.

see in the language of the preamble an entering wedge for future big expenditures, publicly labeled Point Four "a permanent policy of giving our money away." [39]

There were other objections. Senator Connally expressed a rather widespread feeling when he questioned the proposed participation of the United States in United Nations technical assistance programs. "I don't see why in the world we need to turn this over and let us put up the money and let the United Nations run it and . . . mess it all up," he commented to a State Department representative appearing before the Foreign Relations Committee.[40] These and similar misgivings played a part in repeated attempts which were made to reduce the funds for the program's first year. Representative Christian A. Herter, Republican of Massachusetts, who had participated actively in rewriting the administration's bill, led a successful move in the House to cut $20 million from the authorization. At one moment in August both houses agreed on an appropriation of $15 million, as contrasted with the administration's original request for $35 million (net) and with an eventual net appropriation, after determined intervention by the President, of $26.9 million.

It was not without significance that the heaviest assaults on both the European Recovery Program and Point Four occurred during consideration of the appropriation bill in July and August—in other words, after the Communist aggression in Korea. In marked contrast to its docility in passing new appropriations for national and collective defense, Congress made zealous efforts to curtail the minimum economic aid expenditures already fixed. In addition to cutting down the major economic assistance programs, it threw out entirely an item of $15 million to support United Nations activities for children, though confirming a $27.45 million contribution to the United Nations Relief and Works Agency for Palestine Refugees. Then, as an alternative to deeper cuts in the E.C.A. program, it sent the $36 billion appropriation bill to the President with in-

[39] New York Times, June 8, 1950.
[40] Act for International Development: Hearings before the Senate Foreign Relations Committee, 81st Congress, 2nd Session (Washington, 1950), 34.

structions to make additional reductions of $550 million on his own account "without impairing national defense."

By its actions and omissions before the Korean aggression, Congress as a whole had demonstrated once again that it did not by any means go all the way with administration views concerning the proper scope and direction of United States foreign economic policy. Resistance to fundamental aspects of the administration program seemed to reflect a genuine and widespread disbelief in the necessity for individual or national sacrifice in the interests of world recovery. By its actions after the Korean aggression, Congress in effect registered disagreement with a still more basic premise of the national policy, namely, the interdependence of economic, military, and moral factors in the world crisis. To some observers, the war in Korea seemed to call for more rather than less emphasis on the rebuilding of solid social and economic foundations in that part of the world which still remained free. Congress appeared to have little of this feeling, and to discount its influence among the American public. It recognized and responded to the military threat in Korea, but the nature of its response revealed a familiar tendency to concentrate on a single, isolated aspect of the problem.

It was easy enough to find fault with the details of administration policies, on economic affairs as well as on the Far East, on East-West relations, and on the United Nations. It was no great task to stultify them by parliamentary obstructions, limiting conditions, and diversionary actions. But it was not so easy to develop sound alternatives, based not on wishful thinking but on rigorous, comprehensive analysis of the world crisis in all its aspects. Until the monumental problems that faced the United States had been more carefully thought through, by administrators, legislators, and ordinary citizens, American policy would continue to be in large part the erratic product of contradictory emotions. In mid-1950, as Soviet Communism passed over to direct military action against the free world, it seemed that many people in the United States—to paraphrase words used at another critical moment in American history—had not yet begun to think.

CHAPTER THREE

STRENGTHENING THE ATLANTIC COMMUNITY

THE CENTRAL core of the free world menaced by Soviet-Communist aggressions comprised the 12 nations which had signed the North Atlantic Treaty on April 4, 1949. These 12 nations, whose territory extended from California to Norway and from Italy to Alaska, encompassed most of the vital centers of Western civilization and the principal resources whose timely and effective mobilization was required for its survival. Among them they possessed an overwhelming preponderance of the world's developed wealth and industrial power, together with the scientific and technological abilities needed for industrial maintenance and growth. Not less important, they were the principal custodians of the liberal, humanistic outlook summed up in the phrase "Western democracy." This was the only outlook that seemed potentially capable of outmatching, on a global scale, the ideological appeal of Soviet Communism. It was the ultimate source of whatever strength and cohesion the free nations possessed and, in turn, depended for its continued efficacy on those nations' remaining free.

Although the North Atlantic Treaty provided the nearest approach to a common rallying point for the free nations of the West, it had definite limitations both as a security pact and as a political symbol. The official "North Atlantic community" as defined by the treaty was not fully coextensive with "the West" in the larger meaning of that term. Confined to Western Europe and North America, it excluded not only the Latin American republics and several nations of the British Commonwealth but also various European states—Ireland, Spain,

Sweden, Switzerland, Germany, Austria, Greece—which belonged essentially to the Western tradition but for one reason or another had declined or been excluded from membership. Each of these nations, except Spain, did participate in one or more of the various Western European organs established since World War II in response to the same general conditions that eventually produced the Atlantic Pact. Such institutions as the Organization for European Economic Cooperation, the Western Union (Brussels Treaty), and the Council of Europe could be considered parts of the same general system, even though they did not directly include the United States or Canada and had no organic connection with the North Atlantic Treaty itself.[1] Variations in the membership of these bodies were one indication of the difficulties involved in finding any single basis for common action among nations whose circumstances and historical development within the main stream of Western civilization had been highly diverse.

This diversity was strongly marked even among the countries which, by accepting the North Atlantic Treaty, had explicitly acknowledged a community of ideals animating the Western European and North American peoples. Their differences in geographical position, historical tradition, political structure, population, language, culture, national wealth, economic development, and military power were the source of innumerable tensions and conflicting aims, which it was the purpose of the North Atlantic governments to reconcile as far as might be necessary to assure the security of the North Atlantic area and secure unified action on the other transcendent issues of the time.

From the moment of its inception it had been apparent that the future of this novel international grouping would be governed by the interplay of conventional national aims with larger purposes which could be sought only through collective measures involving at least a partial sacrifice of individual national autonomy. Each of the 12 nations had not only its absorbing internal problems and disagreements but also a va-

[1] See map in *The United States in World Affairs, 1949*, 107.

riety of particular interests, European and extra-European, which did not readily subordinate themselves to the requirements of the larger entity. Since all but Portugal had responsible democratic governments, the determination of which matters were appropriate for common solution and which ones were not would ultimately depend on the judgment of some 170 million Europeans and an almost equal number of North Americans.

Foremost among the centrifugal tendencies which promised to impede the realization of common North Atlantic aims was the chronically unstable relationship between the United States and its European partners. The concept of an identity of interest between the United States and Western Europe was the cornerstone of the entire structure, in its purely European as well as its transatlantic aspects. Without wholehearted American support it was unlikely that Western Europe could have overcome its initial postwar economic and moral paralysis, or could maintain its independence in the future against the political and military threat from the East. That the United States itself could permanently hold out if Europe fell under Soviet control seemed almost as doubtful. On both sides of the Atlantic the responsible governments had based their postwar policies on the conviction that joint European-American effort was the only road to long-term self-preservation. Yet neither in Europe nor in the United States had the implications of this belief been fully faced and accepted. Neither side was sufficiently impressed with the urgency of the situation or felt sufficient confidence in the other to be willing to stake its future on an all-out partnership.

Enough has already been said about the psychological difficulties of the American-Western European relationship. American impatience with Europe, and European suspicions of America, formed at best a slippery ground for common effort. Many on both sides, moreover, appeared to reject the whole concept of mutual dependence. Though some Americans argued strongly for closer union of the Atlantic nations in a federal structure, a growing section of American opinion clamored for a complete reversal of emphasis which would subordinate American interest in Europe to the supposed requirements of the Far Eastern theater. On the military side, there were those in the United States who disagreed fundamentally with the official policy of trying to recreate sufficient ground forces on the European continent to fill the existing military vacuum and counterbalance the mobilized might of the U.S.S.R. Enthusiasts for strategic bombing were especially dubious about the possibility of building up a European force which could stop the Soviet army anywhere short of the Pyrenees or the English Channel; their tendency was to "write off" Europe in the event of war, and to insist that overwhelming air power directed against the Soviet Union itself—and perhaps against a Soviet-occupied Europe too—was the only key to victory.

Needless to say, the expression of these and similar views in the United States aroused no enthusiasm among Europeans, who wished neither to be overrun by the Soviet army nor to be bombed out of existence as the prelude to an American victory through air power. An alternative idea which also seemed to be gaining popularity in America, the recreation of a German military force, was hardly less distasteful to the French and other peoples who had only recently been liberated from the Nazi Reichswehr. Thus the Communists in Western Europe had many involuntary allies in their task of alerting European opinion to alleged dangers from across the Atlantic. In some quarters, distrust of the United States bred a feeling of hopelessness and defeatism. In others it served to keep alive the wishful belief that Europe, by marshaling its own strength, could somehow "neutralize" itself and escape involvement in a clash of superpowers. Neither attitude was compatible with the most effective functioning of the North Atlantic community as a positive influence in world affairs.

The forces that divided the European members of the association from each other were more varied and equally potent. With or without the Atlantic Pact, a large measure of Western European "unity" in economic, military, and ultimately in political matters was not only an inherent necessity of the postwar world but also an explicit condition of American aid, which was based on the principle of "self-help and mutual cooperation" and was supposedly available only to the extent that the recipient nations in Europe cooperated to maximize its effectiveness. Every step toward unity within Western Europe was enthusiastically acclaimed in the United States; every sign of hesitation was liable to be cited in this country as proof that our aid was being misdirected.

Yet the basic postwar trend toward unity in Western Europe was impeded during the later 1940's by pressures and cross currents of every kind. The admonitions of statesmen and the resolutions of parliaments made slow headway against the weight of custom and the resistance of vested interests. Lacking the geographical detachment which minimized the difficulties in American eyes, Europeans found it far from easy to recast age-old political and economic habits formed in a national mold. Though each Western European government recognized in principle the need for concerted effort and mutual concessions, there were few if any that did not try to combine such cooperation with the maintenance of national policies and relationships carried over from an earlier period.

This tendency was especially conspicuous in the case of the larger and stronger European nations, each of which, like the United States itself, had special preoccupations to which it gave at least equal weight with the general cause of European cooperation. Thus the United Kingdom, as the center of a world-wide system of political and economic relationships dating from the heyday of the British Empire, flatly declined to participate in any European association that could impair its ties with the Commonwealth and the sterling area or weaken its direct relationship with the United States. France combined a vivid enthusiasm for European unity with invincible distrust of Germany. From the French point of view unity was desirable, among other reasons, as a means of keeping a reviving Germany under some kind of permanent international control; but French opinion was likely to balk, somewhat inconsistently, at any procedure tending to bring Germany closer to the equal European status implied in such an arrangement.

The foundation of the German Federal Republic at Bonn in September 1949 had carried the German problem fully into the foreground of Western European and North Atlantic affairs. In view of the continued tension between East and West and the many limitations on full mobilization of the strength of the Atlantic nations, German reserves of manpower and industrial potential were coming more and more to be looked upon in some quarters as the decisive factor in the upbuilding of Western Europe against the Russian menace. The idea that Germany should ever be rearmed had been repeatedly disavowed on the highest authority and in the strongest terms. Yet to a good many observers in the United States and to some in Europe the Federal Republic was coming to represent what Secretary Acheson, in a quite different connection, had called "the missing component in a situation which might otherwise be solved." [2]

That post-Hitler Germany, still divided and occupied by foreign armies, should anywhere be thought of as the potential salvation of the free world was a sufficient indication of Western Europe's precarious mid-century situation. German opinion on the matter was scarely clear-cut as yet; but there were reasons for doubting whether the Germans would show much eagerness to come to the rescue of their former enemies. At the very least, it would be only natural for German representatives to drive a hard bargain and use the opportunity to get rid of the disabilities imposed on their country after its defeat. Plainly, the delicate enterprise of consolidating and maintaining Western Germany's democratization while co-opting it into the Western European fellowship was one that would critically test the quality of North Atlantic statesmanship.

[2] Speech at the National Press Club, Washington, January 12, 1950.

1. Britain, France, and the German Question

Although relations within the North Atlantic community were nominally governed by the principle of the sovereign equality of its members, considerations of national wealth and power exerted a potent influence in North Atlantic affairs. The strongest voice inevitably was that of the United States, which paid the piper and, though with due restraint, usually called the tune. Great Britain and France, as "great" powers in their own right and partners of the United States in the occupation of Western Germany, shared with this country the pains and privileges of leadership. Progress on most matters was fairly rapid when the Western Big Three were in agreement; much less was accomplished when any one of them felt it necessary to resist a course favored by the other two. To that negative extent, at least, North Atlantic interdependence was already a vital reality.

Although each of the Western powers occasionally found itself defending a minority position, that role was assumed almost automatically by France in all matters of German policy and by the United Kingdom in all matters which concerned the future organization of Western Europe. Great Britain, which had pointed the way toward European union in sponsoring the five-power Brussels pact of March 17, 1948, was generally considered to hold a decisive influence over Europe's future. British economic and military power represented not only an indispensable element in any functioning European system, but also the only possible counterweight to the power of a revived Germany. Continental statesmen felt that any European organization from which Britain held aloof was in danger of being dominated by Germany through sheer weight of numbers and industrial might.

Yet it was precisely Great Britain which, for a variety of reasons, offered the most serious resistance to common action in the various organisms created to facilitate Western European cooperation in the economic, political, and military fields.

British intransigence in the Organization for European Economic Cooperation and the Council of Europe, where Foreign Secretary Ernest Bevin held a veto in the all-powerful Committee of Ministers, attracted much more notice than did the very real contributions the United Kingdom had made toward the economic and military recovery of its European neighbors. The British attitude was the despair of European-minded statesmen and occasioned more than one petulant outburst on the part of such European leaders as Paul-Henri Spaak of Belgium, president of the Consultative Assembly or deliberative branch of the Council of Europe.

Both traditional and novel factors helped to explain the cautious aloofness of the United Kingdom Government in matters of European cooperation. Britain, after all, had never considered itself primarily a European power. Its historic policy in Europe had emphasized the prevention, not the creation, of any large political aggregation beyond the Channel and the North Sea. Under the Labor government of Prime Minister Clement R. Attlee, its economy and world position still depended essentially on the web of commercial and financial relations spun out of London through the nineteenth and early twentieth centuries. Great Britain had real obligations, moral as well as political and economic, to the Commonwealth and sterling area countries, and it was not altogether easy to see how they could be reconciled with a narrowly European orientation. Britain's relations with the United States, moreover, were of so specially intimate a character and based on so obvious a mutual dependence that most Britishers thought it unrealistic to condition them on any arbitrary shift in the emphasis of British policy. Besides, for Britain to turn its back on Asia and the East would only create new responsibilities for the United States in those parts of the world.

To these larger considerations were added certain effects of Britain's internal struggle between rival parties representing rival theories of economic management. Winston Churchill and the Conservative opposition, without minimizing the importance of the Commonwealth connection, had embraced the

European cause with as much seeming ardor as the Laborites treated it with chaste reserve. Conviction apart, Europe offered the Conservatives much the same kind of political opportunity that China provided the opposition party in the United States. The Laborite leaders, on their side, showed perhaps more of the doctrinaire qualities of British socialism than they did of the breadth and flexibility needed to deal with their country's changing position. Maintenance of the economic gains secured by the hard work and self-denial of the British people, and protection of the terrain Labor had conquered for socialism, became not only a primary preoccupation but also a strong deterrent to closer union with nonsocialist countries. Partisan interests thus reinforced the influence of geography, history, economics, and ingrained political sentiment in putting the Commonwealth and the United States ahead of Western Europe.

The leaders of the Labor party, relentlessly prodded by the opposition, passionately dedicated to their own program, resentful of the disapprobation which American enthusiasts for free enterprise made no attempt to conceal, and impressed by the drift away from socialism on the European continent, seemed almost to have developed some of the stiff-neckedness of a persecuted sect. By the winter of 1949–1950 their insistence on safeguarding Britain's complete freedom of action had brought European affairs to an impasse from which it seemed that only a political change in the United Kingdom could rescue it. The British general election of February 23, 1950, though fought mainly on the internal issue of socialism, was widely expected to clarify the future trend of British European policy. But such expectations were belied by the vote, which seriously cut into Labor's representation but left it a majority of six in the House of Commons—too little to claim a genuine popular mandate, yet enough to form a cabinet substantially indistinguishable from its predecessor. European issues would, it appeared, remain in suspense pending the outcome of Labor's attempt to continue its program of nationalization with a majority so small that the illness of a single member might destroy its control of the House.

In France the mixture of domestic, foreign, and imperial issues was somewhat different but the resulting situation was perhaps even more precarious. Whereas the British Laborites, Conservatives, and Liberals were all equally firm in their attachment to democratic methods, the overthrow of a French cabinet always involved a certain peril to the democratic process itself. France exemplified with special clarity the political and social struggle between moderate and extremist forces, both rightist and leftist, which was in some degree typical of most of continental Western Europe. Disregarding minor differences, the spectrum of French politics embraced three broad bands of political opinion: on the Right, conservative and to some extent authoritarian forces typified by General Charles de Gaulle's Rally of the French People; on the Left, a sizable Communist and pro-Communist element controlled by men who were firmly committed to the purposes of the Stalinist international; in the center, an ill-assorted group of Radical, Catholic, Socialist, and Independent parties, sometimes referred to collectively as the "Third Force," which had made up the various coalition regimes that had governed France since the Communists were excluded from office in 1947.

Since neither Right nor Left in France could be considered very sympathetic to the existing bases of European cooperation, international as well as domestic interests were involved in the survival of moderate coalition government— all the more so because French politics continued to exert a considerable influence in neighboring countries. The French Communists and their supporters, representing perhaps 30 percent of the electorate, denounced the entire structure of European cooperative relationships as a device for American "enslavement." De Gaulle and his followers, though yielding to none in the vehemence of their anti-Communism, resented France's acceptance of any position in Europe short of out-and-out leadership, and claimed that French interests were being scandalously disregarded in "Anglo-American" strategic planning under the Brussels Treaty and the Atlantic Pact. Although de Gaulle sometimes talked in terms of eventual Franco-German cooperation, the French Left shared and frequently appealed to the anti-German feeling which was common to most Frenchmen and which represented perhaps the greatest external obstacle to the association of Western Germany with the North Atlantic community.

The problem of French government was made incomparably more difficult by the intensity of the domestic social and economic struggle. In no other country was public life so dominated by the fundamental question of how to distribute a rather modest national income between different sections of the population, and between consumption and investment. Wage and price policy, rather than abstract theories of economic organization, were the customary stumbling blocks of postwar French cabinets. Despite the initial success of the Marshall Plan in increasing production and curbing inflation, the average French worker still had real difficulty in keeping body and soul together. Continual pressure for wage increases, cost-of-living bonuses, restoration of collective bargaining, and other devices to mitigate the squeeze between individual income and living costs reflected widespread need as well as efficient labor organization. Significantly, the non-Communist French labor federations, which opposed strikes for political purposes and generally execrated the policies of the Communist-dominated General Confederation of Labor, were ordinarily compelled to join in that body's agitation for social and economic benefits.

The coalition parties, which together commanded a fragile majority in the French National Assembly, differed so widely in their views on this central problem that every cabinet crisis raised the question whether the "Third Force" would not finally break up into its disparate elements, thus opening the door to new elections and a probable reinforcement of extremist tendencies. To find a basis on which the Catholic M.R.P. (*Mouvement Républicain Populaire*), the Socialists, and the Radicals could agree to govern France was always just short of impossible. More than three weeks of negotiations and false starts preceded the acceptance in October 1949 of the cabinet of Georges Bidault, which never surmounted the handicaps resulting from Socialist-Radical disagreements on fiscal policy. The Socialists withdrew in February 1950 in protest against the government's refusal to grant a bonus to low-paid workers, and in June the entire cabinet was brought down by its failure to provide a scheduled increase in civil service salaries. More feverish negotiations ensued before the Socialists agreed to join a new coalition under René Pleven, a moderate who had served as Minister of Defense under Bidault.

Despite these arduous reshuffles, a basic continuity was evident in the familiar personalities and political tendencies which made up each new grouping. In foreign policy this continuity was reflected in the uninterrupted presence of Robert Schuman at the Ministry of Foreign Affairs, where the distinguished M.R.P. statesman labored unceasingly to bridge the gap between the narrowly nationalistic policies of the French past and the broader outlook of the European future. The scope of these efforts was necessarily much influenced by the political problem at home; in particular this induced a marked caution in regard to German affairs, easily understandable in the light of French history but likely to impress outsiders as even more exaggerated than that of Bevin in larger European questions. Schuman's work did, however, give French foreign policy a certain stability and a measure of protection from the sharp, unpredictable winds of French politics.

Germany's relation to the European problem was fundamentally different from that of Britain, France, and the other Western European democracies. Germany had been the principal source of totalitarian aggression in the recent war; it was only thanks to the greater totalitarian threat looming in the East that a portion of the former Reich had come to be looked on as a possible candidate for membership in the new Western European community. Germany, moreover, was no longer a sovereign member of the family of nations, but a conquered country occupied by the armies of four victorious allies. The Federal Republic recently established at Bonn could not as yet pretend to speak authoritatively for the people of Germany. Its jurisdiction in its own territory was limited by the authority of a British-French-American Allied High Commission and other bodies established by the Western powers with the aim of forestalling any recrudescence of militaristic and antidemocratic tendencies. Over the 18 million Germans of the Soviet occupation zone, nominally ruled by a "popular democratic" government on the Soviet-Eastern European model, the West German republic had no authority whatever; and toward the 2.5 million Germans in the Western sectors of Berlin its expressions of solidarity were as yet unaccompanied by political responsibility or control.

In the German mind, the broad issues raised by Soviet-Communist expansionism in Europe interpenetrated with more immediate concerns growing out of Germany's defeat and occupation. It would be difficult to say which order of problems loomed largest for the average German. No people had been more directly exposed to the perils and vicissitudes of the East-West conflict. Years of Soviet occupation, accompanied by Communist tyranny, police terrorism, and even a prolonged attempt at mass starvation of the people of Berlin, had bred a detestation of the Russians and their Communist agents which appeared to be rather general in Eastern as well as Western Germany. German opinion recognized the primary responsibility of the U.S.S.R. for the loss of East Prussia, Silesia, and other territories and the division of what remained at the line of the Iron Curtain. As Germany recovered from the shattering experience of defeat, the redress of these grievances began to loom as the principal long-run objective on which most Germans instinctively felt themselves in agreement.

Dissatisfaction with the U.S.S.R. tended to sway German opinion to the side of the Western powers, which had repeatedly affirmed their intention of bringing about a progressively closer association of the German Federal Republic with the developing unity of Western Europe. Such an association, if freely entered into and accompanied by suitable safeguards, seemed to be in the interest of all parties. Yet there were weighty factors on the German side which militated against any wholehearted acceptance of the Allied invitation. The

West Germans had considerable grievances against the West
as well. They were not sure that political and economic association with Western Europe would hasten the reunification of
their country, or even provide them any real security against
the U.S.S.R. The "strategic concept" on which the North Atlantic Treaty powers were ostensibly basing their plans was
altogether too vague about what would happen to Western
Germany in case of war. The citizens of the Federal Republic
did not feel especially comfortable about the atomic bombs the
Russians as well as the Americans were known to be developing. Debarred from maintaining armed forces of their own,
they lacked even the means for defense against the militarized,
Communist-oriented "People's Police" that was being built up
in Eastern Germany.

Possibly even deeper than these preoccupations was the
rankling sense of humiliation and injustice observable in a
people whose national pride had suffered unprecedented blows
in the defeat of 1945 and subsequently. If the Soviet occupation was detested, that of the United States, Britain, and France
could certainly not be called popular. The Western powers,
too, were held partially responsible for Germany's partition,
and no German could be entirely unmoved by the Kremlin's
intermittent demands for reunification of the country, even
on Russian terms, and speedy withdrawal of the occupation
forces. Those Germans who detected the guileful aims of the
Soviet Government were not on that account less critical of the
Western powers, who, for all their friendly professions, clearly
had no present intention of accepting Western Germany as an
equal partner. To German observers the Western governments
seemed to aim at getting the benefits of German association
while keeping Germany in a permanently subordinate position.
No matter how rapidly allied restrictions on Western Germany
were relaxed, German anticipation remained well in advance
of allied action. For many Germans the removal of allied-
imposed disabilities definitely took precedence over resisting
Soviet-Communist expansionism.

Intermingled with these broad problems were the many internal political, social, and economic issues that formed the substance of West German politics. Germany, too, was the scene of a struggle between adherents of the democratic way of life and others, more numerous here than elsewhere, whose natural tendency and experience inclined them rather to some form of totalitarianism. The democratic outlook of which the Bonn government stood as the official symbol was only one of several competing ideological currents in Germany. Some Germans viewed it with indifference, others with outright contempt. On the Left, the German Communist party made up in virulence for the smallness of its numbers. On the Right, various political, business, and former military groups openly displayed authoritarian and chauvinistic leanings such as had been in vogue during the Nazi regime. The presence in Western Germany of some millions of expellees from the East and other discontented persons offered fertile ground for the spread of extremist attitudes, which might receive further impetus from the economic difficulties and increased unemployment that were likely to occur after American economic aid came to an end.

Within the democratic framework of the Bonn government there was bitter strife between government and opposition parties. The governing coalition, headed by Chancellor Konrad Adenauer of the Christian Democratic Union, stood in general for free enterprise, the preservation of traditional "Christian" values, and cooperation with the West on terms of equality and mutual respect. The large Social Democratic party under Kurt Schumacher was equally antitotalitarian in outlook but insisted strenuously on a more "progressive" social and economic policy, leading ultimately to the "socialization" of industry, banking, and other large-scale economic enterprises. In addition, Schumacher in his role as leader of the opposition missed no opportunity to appeal to nationalist feeling and damn the government for its alleged subservience to the Western powers and its acquiescence in allied policies.

In reality, resistance to all allied policies which implied an inferior position for Germany was the common denominator of

West German politics, on which government, parliamentary opposition, and extraparliamentary groups were virtually united. Every allied arrangement—and there were a great many—which smacked of a limitation of German sovereignty was the object of stubborn pressure until its removal focused attention on a new objective. The Occupation Statute, promulgated simultaneously with the formation of the Bonn regime in September 1949, was resented as the chief remaining symbol of German subordination. Additional bitterness had been generated by some of the detailed restrictions designed to limit Germany's war-making capacity—notably allied arrangements for the control of the Ruhr, the capacity and production ceilings imposed on steel and other branches of industry, and the concurrent dismantling of excess industrial plant for reparations to Germany's victims. Steady relaxation of these policies by the Western occupying powers had helped greatly to accelerate German recovery but failed to eliminate the resentment they had caused in the German mind.

With the virtual abandonment of dismantling in the autumn of 1949, attention had shifted to certain aspects of Western Germany's political status on which decisions could no longer be postponed. Because the problems immediately at issue were of peculiar concern to France, they provided another demonstration of the critical importance of French-German relations in attempting to weld the antagonistic elements of the old Europe into a higher unity.

The most important bilateral issue outstanding between France and Germany concerned the important coal-mining territory of the Saar, an area long in dispute which, after voluntarily joining Hitler's Reich in 1935, had now again been detached from Germany and incorporated into the French economy under an "autonomous" government confirmed by popular election. France, which had unwillingly surrendered its grandiose postwar plans for the severance of the Ruhr and the Rhineland from Germany, doggedly insisted that the Saar, at any rate, must remain permanently under French control. Its claims had been reluctantly recognized—subject to con-

firmation in a German peace treaty—by the United States and
Great Britain, though not by any German authority outside
the Saar itself.

Closely involved with this issue was the problem of Western
Germany's proposed membership in the Council of Europe, a
logical step in the political reincorporation of Germany into
the Western family. France had linked the two questions and
caused the Council of Europe some embarrassment at its
November 1949 meetings by insisting that Germany must not
be invited to join unless a similar invitation was tendered
independently to the French-oriented government of the Saar.
The Bonn government, on the other hand, was by no means
reconciled to the loss of the Saar, whose sentimental importance
to Germans somewhat outweighed its economic value. If adherence to the Council of Europe was to be conditioned on an
implicit renunciation of the Saar, the West German government was not sure it cared to join.

Agitation over this problem during the first weeks of 1950
threatened to nullify the hopes for a better understanding between France and Germany which had of late been expressed
with some insistence on both sides. During the winter lull between sessions of the Council of Europe, opinion at Bonn
became greatly exercised over reports that France, in complete
disregard of German sentiments, was negotiating a series of
agreements with the Saar government which included a formal
recognition of the autonomy of the territory and a 50-year
lease of the Saar mines. German political leaders made a number of bitter statements about the *fait accompli* technique, the
puppet status of the Saar government, the allegedly pro-
German sentiments of the Saar population, Germany's legal
interest in the status of the coal mines, and the necessity of
deferring all decisions on the Saar until a German peace treaty
could be negotiated. Signature of a pending Franco-German
trade agreement was delayed, and a meeting between Adenauer
and Schuman in Bonn on January 15 produced only a reaffirmation of sharply conflicting views on the legal position.

While East German Communists gloated over the discom-

fiture of their rival regime and American officials made un-
availing efforts to quiet the disturbance, the protest movement
in Western Germany failed to subside. Signature of the French-
Saar agreements on March 3 loosed a new flood of criticism at
Bonn, despite the explicit subordination of the coal-mine lease
to the provisions of a future peace treaty. Adenauer declared
that the agreements endangered European unity and would
give impetus to nationalistic tendencies in Germany. The Bonn
government issued a White Book demanding a new plebiscite
in the Saar as a prerequisite to its political separation from
Germany.

On March 25 the Chancellor further implied that under the
circumstances the Federal Republic would attach definite conditions to its adherence to the Council of Europe, among them
the stipulation that the Saar should receive no more than provisional membership until a peace settlement determined its
ultimate status. Since Germany itself was to be offered only
associate membership, with representation confined to the Consultative Assembly, Adenauer also asked that his government
be allowed to accredit an observer to the Committee of Ministers pending early promotion to full membership.

These proposals had no legal basis under the Statute of the
Council of Europe, and were perhaps not taken too seriously
either by Adenauer himself or by the Committee of Ministers,
which assembled in Strasbourg under Schuman's chairmanship
on March 30. With a minimum of debate the 13 Foreign
Ministers decided to extend parallel invitations to the Saar and
Germany, offering them associate membership with representation in the Consultative Assembly only. The Saar would be
allotted three seats in the Assembly; Germany would have 18,
the same number as France, Italy, and the United Kingdom.
Although the offer was scarcely satisfactory to German opinion,
it did represent a significant step toward Germany's international reacceptance. For the first time the Federal Republic was
acknowledged, by a group of governments most of which were
still formally at war with Germany, as politically qualified to

collaborate in the great work of building a free and united Europe.

The Bonn government might procrastinate, but could not afford to renounce these advantages.[3] Meanwhile, pending the time for formal action on the Council's invitation, the weight of discussion in Adenauer's entourage—and to some extent in French quarters as well—was shifting from the details of the French-German quarrel to the concept of a broader association in which such conflicts of national interest might sublimate themselves. Even at the height of the Saar controversy there had been noticeable on both sides a curious partiality to the idea of closer French-German union. A more intimate relationship might offer a means of transcending existing difficulties, pave the way to a more substantial unity throughout Western Europe, and incidentally consolidate the right-of-center political influences which were tending to predominate in both governments. In March, Adenauer himself had broached the idea of a German-French union, beginning with a customs agreement and leading up to a joint economic parliament within the framework of a larger European union. Such notions were in the air in Europe. The sources and strength of this current were difficult to gauge, but at first glance it struck the observer as both more novel and infinitely more promising than sterile debate over problems like the Saar which were insoluble on the old nationalistic basis. It helped to explain the electrical effect with which, only two months later, M. Schuman was to bring forth his plan for building European union upon the merger of the French and German coal and steel industries.[4]

2. Defense of the North Atlantic Area

The differing preoccupations of the United Kingdom, France, and Western Germany within the general framework of West-

[3] Associate membership in the Council of Europe was formally accepted, after appropriate parliamentary action, by the Saar on May 13 and by the Federal Republic on July 13. By November both governments were represented by observers in the Committee of Ministers.

[4] See below, pp. 141 ff.

ern cooperation were fairly typical of the situation prevailing throughout the larger Atlantic world. Unlike the states which had become more or less involuntary participants in the Soviet bloc, the nations associated with the North Atlantic grouping remained largely free to follow their own bent except in those few matters that were expressly regulated by agreement among them—or, in the case of Italy and Germany, by arrangements growing out of their military defeat.

This freedom from arbitrary constraint was part of the essential strength of the Atlantic world, which derived its coherence from a similarity of interests freely recognized by its members. But it also meant that common action was not possible unless the necessity for it really was recognized by the governments and peoples concerned. In practice such recognition often was not readily forthcoming. The growth of the Atlantic community was limited by the same reluctance to face unpleasant situations and draw uncomfortable conclusions that has been noted in other connections earlier in this volume. Very frequently in North Atlantic matters the United States pressed for more vigorous and far-reaching action than its European partners—and some Americans—were willing to accept. Though frequently exaggerated by unfriendly critics, a real tendency to avoid drastic innovations and hope for the best could be discerned in all branches of North Atlantic affairs.

The characteristic gap between promise and performance was perhaps widest in the realm of North Atlantic defense, notwithstanding the vigorous efforts that had been made to develop some kind of local counterpoise in Europe to the overwhelming military power of the Soviet Union. The need to counteract the sense of menace hovering over Western Europe and discourage any thought of military aggression on the part of the Soviet leaders had given rise successively to the Brussels Treaty of Britain, France, and the Benelux countries and the wider North Atlantic framework which brought in directly the United States and Canada together with Italy, Norway, Denmark, Iceland, and Portugal. Having recognized their joint peril and undertaken to react in common against a threat to any one of them, these governments had proceeded in the autumn of 1949 to establish a Council and an elaborate network of committees and planning groups, with the general task of coordinating their military and economic preparations to deal with any aggression that might occur despite their emphatic avowal of their peaceful intentions.[5]

Shortly afterward Congress had passed the Mutual Defense Assistance Act of 1949, allocating $1 billion for the procurement of United States military supplies and equipment for North Atlantic Treaty countries in the fiscal year 1949–1950 on condition that (1) each recipient country concluded an appropriate bilateral Mutual Defense Assistance agreement with the United States, and (2) the appropriate treaty organs worked out and the President of the United States approved "recommendations for an integrated defense of the North Atlantic area." These conditions were fulfilled on January 27, 1950, when eight bilateral aid agreements were signed in Washington and the President made known his approval of the "strategic concept" previously agreed upon by the North Atlantic Defense and Foreign ministers. By April the first consignments of airplanes and other armaments were safely reaching their European destinations, despite threats of Communist sabotage in France and Italy. At the end of June approximately 134,000 tons of rifles, combat vehicles, antiaircraft guns, artillery, and other equipment were in the hands of their European consignees.[6]

This record of cooperative accomplishment, though certainly without precedent in peacetime, did not by any means represent a solution of the grave military-political problem facing the North Atlantic nations. American officials, amid expressions of satisfaction over the progress already made, did not pretend that it constituted more than a good beginning toward the

[5] The various actions taken in implementation of the North Atlantic Treaty in 1949 and early 1950 are discussed in *The United States in World Affairs, 1949,* 134-143; see also *First Semiannual Report on the Mutual Defense Assistance Program: Message from the President,* House Document 613, 81st Congress, 2nd Session (Department of State Publication 3878, Washington, 1950).

[6] U.S. Department of Defense, *Semiannual Report of the Secretary of Defense . . . January 1 to June 30, 1950* (Washington, 1950), 11.

establishment of a system of defenses that could effectually discourage a Soviet attack. Even in the strictly military sphere, President Truman told Congress in his *First Semiannual Report* on the Mutual Defense Assistance Program, "Planning to date . . . can obviously represent no more than the first rough cut at a thoroughly realistic defense program. . . . The next months must therefore mark not only the thorough review and refinement of the first military plans but also the progressive solution . . . of the urgent production and economic problems upon which the success of these plans is conditioned." [7]

The basic difficulty of the Atlantic nations arose from the fact that they were attempting, with limited means and without sacrifice of other vital objectives, to counterbalance a military machine which completely dwarfed their own defense establishments and, moreover, was backed up by all the immense power and resources of the Soviet Union. Even if rearmament were carried forward at a maximum rate, the armed strength of the Atlantic powers in Western Europe would be no match for the U.S.S.R. and its satellites if war should come at any time within the next several years. In the crucial matter of ground forces, the dozen Western European divisions and the two American divisions in Germany were outnumbered by six or eight to one. Such superiority as the West possessed in naval and air power scarcely compensated for this disadvantage in terms of a realistic politico-military strategy. Naval power would be unable to bring decisive pressure against the U.S.S.R.; its main usefulness would probably lie in keeping the Atlantic sea lanes open for the transport of American supplies and troops to Europe. For the time being the North Atlantic defense planners were compelled to depend heavily on the potentialities of strategic bombardment directed against the sources of Soviet power. The prospect of such bombardment might help to dissuade the Soviet leaders from precipitating war. If war should come, it might or might not cause a breakdown within the U.S.S.R. itself, but it would hardly save Western Europe from being overrun in the meantime. And with

[7] *Op. cit.*, 38.

Europe in Soviet hands, the balance of strategic advantage would in all likelihood have shifted decisively against the United States and the free world. Meanwhile Western Europeans could never feel secure while only the atomic bomb stood between them and the horrors of a Soviet occupation.

If the Western nations were unwilling to live with the risks inherent in this situation, strenuous efforts to fill the "military vacuum" in Western Europe were clearly indicated. There was no possibility, and perhaps no necessity, to match the Russian ground forces in numerical strength. Their quantitative superiority would have to be offset mainly by superior organization and equipment. It would, however, be essential, as an absolute minimum, to build up a Western European force that would be capable of holding the Russians in check while the large armies needed to meet them on equal terms were being raised and transported. Until such a force was in existence, the defense of Western Europe would have to continue relying largely on the "deterrent effect" of Western defense preparations—including the atomic bomb—on the ambitions of any would-be aggressor. Knowledge of the Atlantic powers' determination and growing strength would, it was hoped, keep the Russians in a state of passivity through the period of maximum danger.

Although this strategy called for the most rapid development of an effective defense force in Western Europe, the idea that the Kremlin could be temporarily checked by militarily insufficient means lessened somewhat the incentive to undertake an all-out defense effort. There was, moreover, a still graver obstacle in the latent conflict between economic and military requirements in Western Europe. At bottom the Atlantic nations had still to face some of the problems involved in allocating limited resources to a variety of essential purposes. Any significant expansion of their military establishments, either in manpower or in equipment, would have an inflationary tendency and would cut into the resources available for economic recovery and direct consumption. The probable consequences would be lower living standards, diminished social expenditure, increased internal strains, and new opportunities for political subversion. In passing the Mutual Defense Assistance Act, Congress had declared that "economic recovery is essential to international peace and security and must be given clear priority." This principle, though it implied definite limits on the scale of the rearmament effort, was not unwelcome to Europeans and formed the basis of all mutual defense planning until the Korean aggression showed the necessity for a radical reassessment of North Atlantic defense policies.

Limitations on the means available for defense put a premium on the most effective utilization of whatever means were available. The necessity for the closest coordination of defense policies, plans, and operations was a basic principle of the North Atlantic Treaty organization, reflected in the "self-help and mutual aid" provisions of the treaty and reinforced by congressional insistence that the defense of the North Atlantic area be planned and carried out on a genuinely "integrated" basis. By mid-1949 the military authorities had already approached agreement on a broad international allocation of responsibilities, based on the principle of national specialization in the particular military functions for which each member was deemed best suited.

The "strategic concept" produced in the winter of 1949–1950 formalized this idea of a rough division of labor, but seemed to envisage only a limited measure of the kind of "integration" Congress presumably desired. Real integration would involve central control over the size, composition, and deployment of each nation's armed forces, and ultimately, perhaps, of its entire military potential. It would require each nation to relinquish the idea of finding national security for itself alone, and to seek it in the security of the North Atlantic group as a whole. This was a political and psychological leap which few of the North Atlantic governments seemed likely to make without long preparation or an impelling emergency.

That the United States itself was still far from accepting the full consequences of the integrationist doctrine was evident from the trend of United States national military policy, which

THE NORTH ATLANTIC TREATY ORGANIZATION, 1950

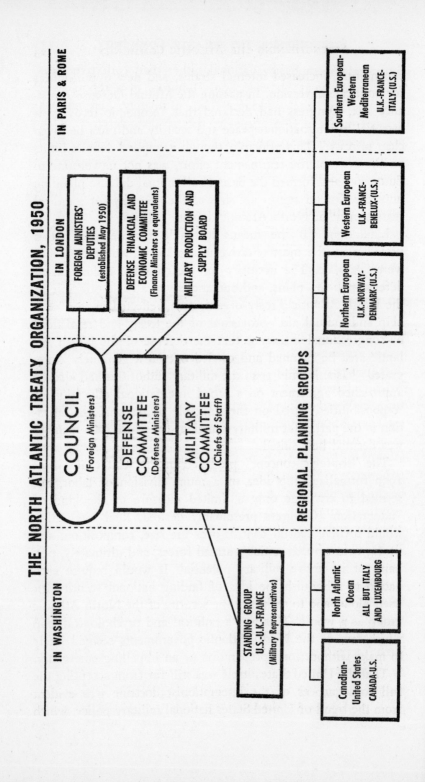

IN WASHINGTON

IN LONDON

IN PARIS & ROME

COUNCIL
(Foreign Ministers)

FOREIGN MINISTERS'
DEPUTIES
(established May 1950)

DEFENSE
COMMITTEE
(Defense Ministers)

DEFENSE FINANCIAL AND
ECONOMIC COMMITTEE
(Finance Ministers or equivalents)

MILITARY
COMMITTEE
(Chiefs of Staff)

MILITARY PRODUCTION AND
SUPPLY BOARD

STANDING GROUP
U.S.-U.K.-FRANCE
(Military Representatives)

REGIONAL PLANNING GROUPS

Canadian-
United States
CANADA-U.S.

North Atlantic
Ocean
ALL BUT ITALY
AND LUXEMBOURG

Northern European
U.K.-NORWAY-
DENMARK-(U.S.)

Western European
U.K.-FRANCE-
BENELUX-(U.S.)

Southern European-
Western
Mediterranean
U.K.-FRANCE-
ITALY-(U.S.)

continued to emphasize national rather than collective measures. Secretary of Defense Louis Johnson, in a report dated
December 30, 1949, declared that "ultimately" our national
defense might be "so geared to the national defenses of the
other member nations that we will be forced to stand or fall
collectively." [8] For the present, however, American defense
planning continued to reflect the concept of "balanced" national forces which Secretary Johnson had devised as a basis
for the unification of the American defense services. Economy
and fair apportionment of the defense dollar, rather than
adaptation to an integrated North Atlantic strategy, were the
yardsticks applied to the $13.5 billion defense budget for
fiscal year 1950–1951, which underwent a modest increase in
the course of the spring after General of the Army Dwight
D. Eisenhower had publicly voiced his concern over the extent
to which the United States had unilaterally disarmed itself.

The revelation that Russia possessed the atomic bomb produced no perceptible change in the over-all strategy of North
Atlantic defense, still based essentially on the idea of a holding
force in Western Europe combined with strategic bombing by
the United States. Inevitably, however, this modification in the
atomic balance of power tended to neutralize the principal
asset of the North Atlantic countries and thus gave even greater
importance to the building up of more adequate ground forces
on the European continent. A series of high-level meetings during the spring was devoted to further exploration of this
problem and to contemplation of the gap between requirements and immediate capabilities.

At each level the basic issue was the same: how to provide
an adequate defense at a price which the North Atlantic partners would be able and willing to pay, and without necessitat-
ing such unpopular courses as a complete merger of defense
establishments or the inclusion of Western Germany in collective defense planning. In general the United States appeared
more impressed with the military requirements of the situation

[8] U.S. Department of Defense, *Second Report of the Secretary of Defense . . .
for the Fiscal Year 1949* (Washington, 1950), 25.

than did the European members; the latter, on the contrary, seemed more impressed with the many obstacles to mobilization of the size and character officially advocated by this country.

This difference of outlook made it easier to agree on general formulas than on specific courses of action. To the outsider it sometimes seemed that each new meeting in the North Atlantic Treaty Organization produced the same accord that had already been reached a dozen times before. Thus the Military Committee (Chiefs of Staff) of the North Atlantic nations met at the Hague on March 28 and drew up an "integrated defense plan" based on the "strategic concept" already agreed upon. On April 1 this plan was approved in its turn by the Defense Committee (Defense Ministers), who announced that it called for "an integrated defense of the entire North Atlantic area, as distinguished from individual national defense." The ministers also took note of the importance of "adequate financing to carry out the plan and the need for careful balancing of the respective national economies in the light of the present world situation."

The difficulty concealed behind this abstract language was frankly described by General Omar N. Bradley, chairman of the United States Joint Chiefs of Staff, in a speech at Chicago on April 14. The total forces envisaged by the professional men at the Hague, General Bradley said, "were of such dimensions that the 12 governments . . . might consider them beyond our reach." Precisely what forces were under consideration was not disclosed. There was talk of a long-range goal of 36 Western European divisions by 1955—a figure that certainly fell far short of the ground force strength which would be available to the Soviet Union in Europe, both then and throughout the intervening years. Determination of the exact requirements would be influenced by a variety of factors, both technical and strategic; for example, deficient numbers might be compensated to some extent by the choice of a shorter defense line, or by superior training and equipment. But it was already becoming clear that the type of forces the military planners would consider adequate could not be created unless the 12 nations were willing to reexamine seriously their economic and political as well as their military policies.

Such difficulties often had the effect in Europe of turning attention momentarily away from the difficult enterprise in hand and focusing it on other, equally important but perhaps neglected aspects of the Atlantic relationship. There was some feeling among some of the Atlantic governments that the strictly military side of the alliance had been overemphasized, and that more should be done toward developing the latent political and moral forces residing in this combination of free nations. A contributing factor was the widespread opinion, sedulously encouraged by Communist propaganda, that responsibility for the East-West tension did not lie entirely with the Russians and that things might be better if the United States were not so insistent on collective military measures whose defensive character might easily be misunderstood in Moscow.

The North Atlantic community had, after all, been conceived as a political association, not a mere military alliance; unless it was capable of inspiring allegiance as a political symbol, there was little chance that it could do its detailed military work effectively. Preparations for meeting aggression on the military level were unpopular and politically difficult in the best of circumstances; they would be meaningless unless related to the broad purposes of the organization, which had emphasized the safeguarding of peace through the United Nations and the promotion of "stability and well-being" in the North Atlantic area. In any case, no satisfactory adjustment was likely until the leading North Atlantic governments coordinated their policies better and reached understanding on certain crucial political questions—among them the future of Germany and the attitude to be adopted toward France's war against Communism in Indochina, which was draining the defenses of Western Europe and at the same time antagonizing potential friends of the democracies in Asia.

Characteristically, it fell to the French Government to crystallize some of these feelings in a striking proposal. In a speech at Lyons on April 16, Premier Bidault called on the Atlantic nations to establish what he called an "Atlantic High Council for Peace." The first duty of this body, he said, would be to coordinate Atlantic military and economic requirements and thus combat the twin dangers of "aggression and depression." A logical outgrowth of the Brussels Treaty and the Organization for European Economic Cooperation, such an executive organ would deprive the opposing (Soviet-Communist) forces of their present monopoly of the word "peace." Foreign Minister Schuman intimated a few days later that France would favor giving the proposed council actual coordinating powers over the work of the North Atlantic Treaty Organization, the Western Union, the O.E.E.C., and the Council of Europe.

This project, which would have affected the position of several governments not included in the Atlantic Pact, had no immediate sequel; indeed, it was soon crowded out of view by M. Schuman's even more striking plan for a European coal and steel pool, which he advanced on May 9 on the eve of discussions among the Western Foreign Ministers in London. The earlier proposals, however, pointed up some of the underlying issues of the Atlantic association and established a kind of standard for measuring the achievements of the Atlantic Foreign Ministers at their May meeting.

The meetings of the North Atlantic Council were customarily preceded by separate discussions among the Foreign Ministers of Great Britain, France, and the United States, who met together in the British capital on May 11-13 to confer on various matters both within and outside the scope of the North Atlantic Treaty. Their most important decisions had to do with the continuing East-West struggle over Germany, and may be left to the next chapter since they involved no closer approach to the problem of associating Western Germany in the defense of Western Europe. On the general problem of defense economics Bevin, Schuman, and Acheson reaffirmed the familiar conviction that the issue was a two-sided one. Their aim of "reducing the risks of war and establishing the con-

ditions of a lasting peace," they said, required "a closer coordination in the employment of their joint resources to
underpin their economies in such a manner as to permit the
full maintenance of their social and material standards as well
as the adequate development of the necessary defense measures." [9] The language was involved, but the aim was clear.

The same problem of balancing military and civilian requirements appeared to be the chief concern of the 12 North
Atlantic Foreign Ministers at their four-day London meeting
under Acheson's chairmanship on May 15-18. No agreement
was announced concerning new forces to be raised or equipped,
concerning coordination or unification of command, or concerning a possible reexamination of the German problem.
Those in a position to know intimated that the United States
had been virtually alone in urging positive action along these
lines. Instead the ministers' communiqué laid main emphasis
on the theme that their countries' combined resources, "if
properly coordinated and applied," were sufficient to ensure
"the progressive and speedy development of adequate military
defense without impairing . . . social and economic progress."
As one seemingly obvious means to this end, the subordinate
North Atlantic bodies were advised that "the problem of adequate military forces and the necessary financial costs should
be examined as one and not as separate problems."

All ministers agreed once again that adequate defense could
be achieved only through "the most economical and effective
utilization" of the available forces and material. Accordingly,
they undertook to urge their governments "to concentrate on
the creation of *balanced collective forces* in the progressive
build-up of the defense of the North Atlantic area"—in other
words, to abandon the attempt to build up self-sufficient national defense establishments, and gear their expansion entirely
to the collective requirements established by the appropriate
treaty authority. If the over-all defense required large French
ground forces, for example, France should concentrate on sup-

[9] Communiqué, May 13, in *New York Times,* May 14, 1950. Acheson had previously conferred with Schuman in Paris on Indochina and other matters.

plying ground forces and not submarines or bombing planes. The principle was scarcely new, but even now its enunciation was accompanied by a significant reservation. Each government was, at the same time, expected to take "fully into consideration the requirements for national forces which arise out of commitments external to the North Atlantic area." [10] Since nearly every North Atlantic government had such external commitments, balanced collective forces for the North Atlantic area were still subordinated to individual requirements in the wider field where the 12 governments had accepted no collective responsibilities.

On the practical side, the ministers decided to appoint fulltime deputies to keep the situation under review and promote coordination among the various treaty organs and the programs they developed. A special Planning Board for Ocean Shipping was set up to deal with the shipping aspects of defense planning. Much less was accomplished along the lines of political coordination and spiritual mobilization. Here the ministers confined themselves to a few resounding phrases and a carefully worded statement to the effect that they planned to ". . . exchange views on political matters of common interest within the scope of the Treaty; . . . promote and coordinate public information in furtherance of the objectives of the Treaty while leaving responsibility for national programs to each country; [and] . . . consider what further action should be taken under Article 2 of the Treaty, taking into account the work of existing agencies in this field." [11]

This cautious statement, reflecting the widely divergent political outlooks of some of the North Atlantic governments, emphasized the psychological disadvantage under which they

[10] Communiqué, May 19, in *Department of State Bulletin*, XXII, May 29, 1950, 830 (emphasis supplied).
[11] Resolution on Central Machinery, May 19, *ibid.*, 831. Article 2 of the North Atlantic Treaty reads: "The Parties will contribute toward the further development of peaceful and friendly international relations by strengthening their free institutions, by bringing about a better understanding of the principles upon which these institutions are founded, and by promoting conditions of stability and well-being. They will seek to eliminate conflict in their international economic policies and will encourage economic collaboration between any or all of them."

labored in relation to the Soviet bloc and the world Communist apparatus. While the North Atlantic Council worked to establish realistic conditions for peace with freedom, the latter were throwing all their resources into a spurious but powerful "peace offensive," obviously designed to undercut the North Atlantic governments and attract at least passive support from the maximum number of Western Europeans. To this superbly coordinated propaganda drive (to be discussed in the next chapter), the West had little to reply, except for a few inspired stories in American newspapers about wonderful new weapons which allegedly would enable Western Europe to stop the Red Army in its tracks.[12] Though the London meeting might have carried forward the slow work of breaking down the barriers to cooperative effort, the 12 governments were evidently far from any accord on how to breathe life into the principles most of them professed.

A more immediate concern for the government of the United States was to secure congressional sanction for the second year of the Mutual Defense Assistance Program. "We have not yet fully determined the size and the nature of the forces and equipment necessary," said the President's message of June 1, in which he asked for $1 billion in new military assistance funds for Western Europe in the fiscal year 1950–1951. "But, one thing is already plain. The military establishments of Western Europe are below the minimum level consistent with security. Those countries must build up their forces as swiftly as their resources permit, assisted by such help as we can afford."

Secretary Acheson, testifying before the Senate Armed Services and Foreign Relations committees on June 2, emphasized the North Atlantic governments' conviction that the defense of the Atlantic area was a "real and attainable objective." General Bradley cautiously testified to the progress achieved in the past year: ". . . It now appears possible that these European nations, with the help that the United States has given them, and the strength derived from our collective-security planning, will—if given time—be able to defend and hold Western

[12] E.g., André Visson, "Protection for Europe," *Washington Post*, May 21, 1950.

Europe, if our present rate of progress continues. . . ." But more important than its effect in defensive war, in General Bradley's opinion, was the possibility that the continued strengthening of North Atlantic military potential "may result in preventing any aggression whatsoever." [13]

Neither the financial nor certain novel administrative aspects of the military aid bill encountered anything like the congressional resistance the entire program had met the year before. In this respect it fared considerably better than the European Recovery Program and Point Four. The Senate committees concluded that "The only alternative to military assistance is the abandonment of freedom, and the confession of weakness which the Soviet Union would not be slow to interpret as an invitation to aggression." [14] The outbreak of hostilities in Korea on June 25 crumbled whatever floor opposition might have formed against the measure. Approved by the Senate on June 30 by 66-0, it passed the House by 361-1 on July 19 and received the President's signature a week later.[15] No cuts were inflicted in the appropriation process.

Meanwhile, the President had warned Congress that this bill was not the last word. The Communist aggression in Korea, he said, had shown that the free nations of the world would have to "step up their common security program . . . and divert additional economic resources to defense purposes." As soon as possible he would lay before Congress a request for such additional military assistance as might be found necessary.

In effect Korea had "called the bluff" on which the North Atlantic defense system was based. By showing that the Russians were willing to take considerably greater risks than had been assumed, it indicated that an adequate "deterrent" force

13 *Mutual Defense Assistance Program, 1950: Hearings* [on S. 3809] before the Senate Foreign Relations and Armed Services Committees, 81st Congress, 2nd Session (Washington, 1950), 4, 73.

14 Senate Report 1853, 81st Congress, 2nd Session, June 21, 1950 (Washington, 1950), 26.

15 The amended act (Public Law 621, 81st Congress, approved July 26, 1950) also authorized $131.5 million in military assistance funds for Greece, Turkey, and Iran; $16 million for Korea and the Philippines; $75 million for the general area of China; a carryover of some $214 million in unobligated funds; and release of an additional $250 million in excess military equipment.

in Western Europe would probably have to be much larger than any of the Atlantic powers had been willing to contemplate thus far. It thus provided the incentive for a considerably increased and more closely coordinated mobilization effort on the part of the North Atlantic governments, without, however, resolving the dilemma of military versus economic expenditure or removing the political barriers to the use of German armed forces. The attempt to devise a new synthesis of these requirements, military, political, and economic, was to occupy the second half of 1950.

3. Economic Integration and the Schuman Plan

The emphasis on economic considerations in North Atlantic defense planning showed a realistic awareness of the interrelation of military, economic, and political-psychological factors in the total situation of the Western nations. Although the assumption that an adequate level of rearmament could be achieved without impairing economic progress may seem naive in retrospect, it was readily understandable in the light of what was known about Soviet intentions before the Korean war. To most observers armed conflict with the Soviet Union did not then seem any more imminent than it had at most times in the preceding two years; the task of combating Soviet attacks on the social and ideological level seemed much more pressing than that of preparing for a war which no one wanted and perhaps would never occur.

André Philip, a French Socialist and leading crusader for European unity, summed up a widespread feeling on the eve of the Korean hostilities. "What menaces our existence today," he wrote, "is not the immediate danger of war; I have less fear of the atom bomb and the hydrogen bomb than of the misery of the workers—a misery which could erupt into political and social chaos." [16] Even the United States, though seemingly obsessed with a greater sense of urgency than most European

[16] André Philip, "France Proves She is Still a Power," New York Times Magazine, June 25, 1950, 19.

governments, did not want to start a rearmament program of a size that would interfere with the scheduled wind-up of the European Recovery Program in 1952. Nor did it overlook the fact that a stronger economy and a contented population were prime requisites in the restoration of Western Europe's defense potential.

There could be no doubt that Western Europe, by the spring of 1950, was more nearly equipped to stand its ground in the world than at any time since the end of the war. Statistics compiled by the Economic Cooperation Administration showed that industrial production in the 18 Marshall Plan countries in the first quarter of 1950 had climbed to 123 percent of the 1938 level (149 percent in Great Britain, 121 percent in France, and 82 percent in Western Germany, where recovery had begun more slowly). Agricultural production was up to 97 percent of the prewar average, although a 10 percent population growth in the interim had contributed to keep individual consumption substantially below prewar standards. Living costs had continued to rise in some countries, partly as a result of the general currency devaluation in the fall of 1949, but no serious new inflationary tendencies had developed. Although unemployment was causing concern in Western Germany, Italy, and Belgium, employment elsewhere in Western Europe was generally at a high level.

The upward tendency in Western European trade had been equally gratifying. The volume of exports from Western Europe in the first quarter of 1950 was 18 percent above the prewar level. Intra-European trade had increased by almost one-third over the preceding year, and was up to 114 percent of 1938. These accomplishments, in turn, were helping to reduce Western Europe's dependence on the United States and thus lessen the size of the critical "dollar gap." Increased production at home and increased trade among themselves had enabled the Marshall Plan countries to absorb cuts in dollar aid and begin reducing their direct imports from the United States; meanwhile currency devaluation and other factors had enabled them to effect a slight increase in both direct and "invisible" exports to the United States, and to take advantage of increased opportunities for trade with sterling area and Latin American countries.

With the slackening of the world demand for American goods and of the world scramble for dollars, a more normal pattern of world trade was beginning to make its appearance. As a result, the trade deficit of the Marshall Plan countries and their overseas territories with the United States declined from $904 million in the first quarter of 1949 to $494 million in the first quarter of 1950. Meanwhile the United Kingdom and several other countries in the group improved their foreign exchange position and considerably increased their gold and dollar reserves.[17]

These favorable developments, although they justified a period of optimism before the outbreak of war in Korea renewed the inflationary threat and introduced a host of new uncertainties, were not to be confused with a total solution of Western Europe's economic problems. What the statistics revealed was a series of trends which, *if maintained over the next couple of years,* might enable the Marshall Plan countries to carry on an expanded trade with each other and with the rest of the world without depending on further extraordinary dollar assistance. In fact, the various indicators of progress continued to rise during the second quarter of 1950; but much strenuous effort would still be needed under the best of circumstances. E.C.A. calculated that to balance their international accounts at "tolerable" levels the Marshall Plan countries would still have to increase the volume of their commodity exports to the rest of the world by 38 percent, and to the United States and Canada by 65 percent, during the period 1950–1953. This would require drastic action in North America as well as in Europe.[18]

[17] *Eighth Report to Congress of the Economic Cooperation Administration, for the quarter ended March 31, 1950* (Washington, 1950), 3-8, 21-37.
[18] *Ibid.,* 15. As one step in this direction the Foreign Ministers of the U.S. U.K., France, and Canada agreed in London that the two North American countries should establish an informal working relationship with the O.E.E.C. See their communiqué of May 18 in *Department of State Bulletin,* XXII, May 29, 1950, 827.

In reality the North Atlantic-Western European community faced two separate problems. One was to bring about a sufficient improvement in Western Europe's balance-of-payments position so that E.R.P. could be wound up on schedule without serious economic or political disturbances. The other was to promote the kind of continued economic growth and progress that would help make Western Europe a firm bastion of the free world. This latter process, an inherent part of the United States program of creating "situations of strength" abroad, was of somewhat larger scope and could not be terminated as of mid-1952 or any other specific date. Progress toward equilibrium in the balance of payments reflected progress toward this other, more basic goal as well. But even if some sort of payments equilibrium were attained by 1952, Europe would still be far from having regained its full weight in the world political-military balance. All-out production for export, coupled with a high rate of domestic investment, was essential to close the dollar gap, but would mean inadequate housing and limited consumption of food, clothing, and other necessaries for a long time to come. The political perils of this situation might be kept within bounds while prosperity was increasing, but might be difficult to control if any large-scale rearmament effort were to be superimposed upon the present fragile economic structure.

Although the two problems were logically distinct, the means of dealing with them were largely identical. Generally speaking, measures to increase the over-all strength and productivity of the Western European economy would help to alleviate the balance-of-payments problem, and vice versa. Western Europe's fundamental task throughout the postwar years had been a two-sided one. Every country had been endeavoring to increase the productivity of its workers in industry and agriculture by modernizing, rationalizing, and expanding its stock of capital equipment and applying up-to-date technical "know-how." And, equally important, the same process had been carried forward internationally as well as nationally. Optimum use of Western Europe's limited assets required that they be regarded as part of a common stock, to be utilized in whatever way was most efficient for the recovery of the entire area. Organization of the Western European economy according to criteria of general efficiency, rather than national or group interest, offered Western Europe's best chance to overcome its postwar economic handicaps. Only in this way, many authorities believed, could it relieve itself of excessive dependence on the United States, make the most of the European internal market, and equip itself to play its full part in world trade. This was the root meaning of the economic "integration" preached by E.C.A. and advocated, under that and various other names, by men of high position both in the United States and in Western Europe.

In theory such a reorganization of the European economy might have been promoted in either of two ways: (1) through direct governmental intervention, based on an agreed international plan, or (2) by removal of artificial restraints of all kinds, in order to let free competition determine which enterprises in which countries were best qualified to survive and grow. In practice, however, the first method would have been unworkable because it ran counter to the dominant economic philosophy both in the United States and in most of the participating countries. Except in Great Britain and some of the Scandinavian countries, the over-all trend of the late 1940's was away from government planning and *dirigisme,* although not necessarily favorable to the vigorous competition implied in the alternative method. American quarters strongly advocated free competition within Europe, as long as it did not involve discrimination against this country. The E.C.A., being itself highly partial to free enterprise and competition, consistently used its great influence in the O.E.E.C. and with the individual governments to encourage them to cast aside their economic crutches—exchange controls, import quotas, tariff barriers, cartels, etc.—and join together in the quest for a prosperous, united Europe based on free competition.

The drive toward economic unity through the coordinating mechanism of the O.E.E.C. had both its technical and its general, intangible aspects. The O.E.E.C. itself, as the representative of the 18 governments concerned and their principal point of contact with the United States, was a sensitive barometer of European trends and a powerful influence toward intergovernmental cooperation. Those who favored European cooperation in principle also favored strengthening and tightening the organization of the O.E.E.C., and associating it more closely with kindred European bodies in the political and defense fields.

During the winter of 1949–1950, a strong movement arose to enhance the political influence of the O.E.E.C. by nominating a prominent European figure to serve in the capacity of director-general. Paul-Henri Spaak of Belgium, president of the Consultative Assembly at Strasbourg and a leading advocate of European unity, was an obvious candidate and was favored by the United States. This plan, however, was unacceptable to some nations precisely because it promised to exalt the O.E.E.C. further at the expense of individual governments. The British, moreover, resented Spaak's past intimations that they had been "dragging their feet" in the matter of European union. As a compromise, the O.E.E.C. Council decided late in January to create the less influential post of "political conciliator" to deal with problems falling outside the technical realm. Dirk U. Stikker, Foreign Minister of the Netherlands, whose government pursued a middle course in economic policy, was unanimously chosen for this function.

On the technical side, O.E.E.C. and E.C.A. laid great emphasis on measures tending to bring about the kind of "integration" Mr. Hoffman had demanded in his famous speech to the O.E.E.C. Council on October 31, 1949: ". . . the formation of a single large market within which quantitative restrictions on the movement of goods, monetary barriers to the flow of payments, and, eventually, all tariffs are permanently swept away." [19] Progressive removal of import quotas, and progressive improvements in the mechanism for financing trade among the participating countries, had been primary preoccupations of both organizations throughout most of their history. Tariff

[19] *The United States in World Affairs, 1949,* 131-132.

barriers had been reserved for later attack after import quotas and other restrictions of an emergency character had been reduced.

The campaign for a progressive reduction and eventual elimination of import quotas had begun in earnest in July 1949, when the O.E.E.C. requested its member governments to furnish lists of commodities on which they were prepared to drop controls. Efforts along this line were intensified after Hoffman's speech. On November 2, 1949, each participating country was requested to eliminate quotas on at least 50 percent of its private imports (as of 1948) from other participants. On January 31, 1950, the O.E.E.C. Council decided to raise this figure by stages to 60 and then to 75 percent, and to require justification for all quotas remaining in effect after the beginning of 1951. Participating countries were also urged to drop restrictions on "invisible" transactions. Although the programs were so set up as to make the first steps relatively easy and the initial targets were generally met, increasing resistance was encountered as the sights were raised and the reductions began to affect enterprises that were protected for political reasons. Moreover, despite considerable progress, the removal of quotas seemed to some extent to encourage other restrictive devices, including tariff and customs barriers and cartel-like arrangements among private producers.

The financing of intra-European trade was the second major aspect of O.E.E.C.-E.C.A. efforts along these lines. Here the long-run objective was to devise a banking mechanism which would (1) promote multilateral trade and currency convertibility, by making it possible for individual countries to offset their debits and credits with all other members of the group instead of settling them bilaterally; and (2) provide additional means of financing trade movements. The Intra-European Payments and Compensation Agreements for 1948–1949 and 1949–1950, under which European creditor countries made grants of "drawing rights" to their European debtors on a bilateral basis and received matching "conditional" dollar aid from the United States, represented a partial approach to this goal. For the period beginning July 1, 1950 a new system was contemplated, to be known as the European Payments Union (E.P.U.). Its essential feature was a multilateral cancellation of trade debits and credits which would make each country a net debtor or creditor of the whole group rather than of the individual members. Highly complex arrangements were provided for the settlement of these balances, partly in gold or dollars and partly in credits, with the aim of encouraging countries to balance their trade with the rest of the group. To help finance the Union, E.C.A. agreed to provide it with some $350 million for fiscal year 1950–1951. Although the scheme required dollar support in the early stages, it might prove suitable to continued operation after the recovery program ended.

The chief difficulty in setting up the successive payments mechanisms had always been the reluctance of the British to accept any scheme that could lessen the importance of sterling as an international currency or involve them in a loss of gold or dollars. Sir Stafford Cripps, as Chancellor of the Exchequer, had held out long and inflexibly against the multilateral features of the 1949–1950 payments agreement and played a somewhat similar role in the negotiations for the E.P.U., in which E.C.A. representatives took their customary direct and prominent part. For several weeks it was uncertain whether the United Kingdom would be willing to participate at all; later it appeared that Belgium might abandon the project because of dissatisfaction with the terms on which Britain had consented to come in. As usual, compromises were reached after long and exasperating delays. In the interest of making sterling convertible with other European currencies, E.C.A. undertook to reimburse the United Kingdom for any loss of dollars resulting from the arrangement. On July 7 the O.E.E.C. Council approved the scheme in outline, tying it in with the general trade liberalization policy by a provision designed to bar all trade discrimination among member countries. The detailed agreement was not signed until September 19 but was made retroactive to July 1.[20]

Programs for liberalizing trade and promoting economic integration on a universal basis within Western Europe had the disadvantage that they could be held up by any key country which felt that its economy would be adversely affected. This difficulty was less pronounced in various projects or proposals for reaching similar goals in a more selective fashion. Some progress had been made since the war in the direction of smaller customs or economic unions, such as those between the Benelux countries and between France and Italy; and intermediate groupings such as "Finebel" (France, Italy, Netherlands, Belgium, Luxembourg) and "Uniscan" (United Kingdom and Scandinavia) enjoyed an intermittent vogue as a possible means of meeting the special needs of countries whose situation and economic policies did not fit readily into a universal grouping. An alternative method, which also was claiming increased attention in early 1950, was the "functional" approach whereby the European economy would be unified industry by industry instead of all at once or region by region.

The striking proposal which M. Schuman enunciated on behalf of the French Government on May 9, and which monopolized the limelight for weeks thereafter, owed something to both kinds of thinking. The core of the "Schuman Plan," unquestionably the most important and constructive idea to be produced in the free world in 1950, was the placing of the coal and steel production of France and Germany under "a common high authority in an organization open to the other European countries." In selecting coal and steel, the French Foreign Minister chose two basic industries whose organization would be likely to have decisive influence on the future of the whole European economy. In focusing on France and Germany, the two leading coal and steel producers on the European continent, he suggested a method by which the risks

[20] A full account of the negotiation and operation of the E.P.U. appears in a forthcoming volume by William Diebold, Jr., to be published under the auspices of the Council on Foreign Relations.

involved in restoring Germany's economic and military potential might be minimized; for such a pooling of production, he said, would make any war between France and Germany "not only *unthinkable,* but materially impossible." In inviting the participation of other European nations, M. Schuman opened the door to eventual federation based on common economic interests, and incidentally brought to a head the sore question of Great Britain's relationship to the organization of Europe.

The idea of some kind of international administration of Europe's basic industries was by no means new, but the French plan was put forward with a suddenness and lack of preparation which left many people wondering about its real aims and implications. The "high authority," according to M. Schuman, was to be composed of "independent personalities designated on a parity basis by the governments," and its decisions would be binding on France, Germany, and whatever other countries decided to join. Its purpose would not be to restrict competition and maintain profits like an international cartel, but to merge markets and expand production. Specifically, it would have authority to modernize coal and steel production and improve its quality, to supply coal and steel on equal terms to the markets of the participating countries, to increase exports to other countries, and to improve and equalize the living conditions of the industrial workers in the participating countries. Customs duties and freight rate differentials on the movement of coal and steel within the affected areas would be suspended immediately, as a first step toward the gradual rationalization of production and the equalization of costs and prices on an area-wide basis.[21]

Like President Truman's "bold new program," the Schuman Plan was dramatic enough to captivate some people immediately, had enough unexplored angles to tempt some who were ambitious for private advantage, and yet looked innocent enough on the surface to spur the cautious and the skeptical

[21] Declaration of the French Minister for Foreign Affairs, May 9: French text in *La Documentation française: Notes et études documentaires,* No. 1,339, June 13, 1950; English text issued by the French Press and Information Service, New York.

into a prolonged search for Machiavellian motives and hidden meanings. It was known that the plan originated in the offices of Jean Monnet, author of France's own long-term economic reconstruction plan. But what factors led to its being produced at this precise moment, on the eve of the Big Three and North Atlantic Foreign Ministers' meetings, and what induced the French to solicit just such a tête-à-tête with Germany as they had hitherto consistently sought to avoid, remained largely speculative.[22] The reception of the plan in France itself was very mixed, although it was inherently less unpopular than any project for German rearmament would have been; it certainly did not crystallize French opinion in favor of a reconciliation with Germany.

With the stated objectives of the plan, however, it was difficult for any outsider to quarrel, especially after Chancellor Adenauer had warmly endorsed them on behalf of the West German government. Objections in other German quarters, notably in the Social Democratic party, were unnoticed for the moment. Secretary Acheson called the proposal "a major contribution toward the resolution of the pressing political and economic problems of Europe." President Truman termed it "an act of constructive statesmanship . . . in the great French tradition," and expressed gratification over the fact that it contemplated leaving the coal and steel industries open to "the full benefits of the competitive process." [23]

But the feature that specially commended the plan to the President was the one perhaps least calculated to win the approbation of the British Labor Government, which spoke for the country with the largest individual share of Europe's coal and steel production. Labor had already nationalized the coal mines of the United Kingdom, and looked to the nationalization of steel as its next big task. Although M. Schuman had said that the setting up of his high authority "in no way prejudices property rights in the enterprises concerned," it was

[22] Some of these questions are explored in William Diebold, Jr., "Imponderables of the Schuman Plan," *Foreign Affairs*, XXIX, October 1950, 114-129.
[23] Statements released May 19, in *Department of State Bulletin*, XXII, May 29, 1950, 828.

difficult to see how common policies could be developed which would satisfy both the British socialists and the Franco-German coal and steel interests. The future of the continental coal and steel industries was of the greatest importance to the United Kingdom, whose production and export drives depended largely on continued British preeminence in those fields. Participation in a supranational regulatory authority did not strike the British leaders as the best way to safeguard British social or commercial interests in an increasingly competitive world. Thus the British found themselves once again in the position of opposing what looked like a fruitful and constructive proposal for the benefit of Europe as a whole—one toward which other governments felt unable to hold aloof even if skeptical of the outcome.

The preliminary negotiations on the Schuman Plan took a course which placed British reservations in the most glaring light. On May 25, after a fortnight of intense preparatory discussion, the French Government formally invited the interested European governments to join with it in negotiations to set up a coal-steel pool. At the same time it made the unusual request that those governments which planned to participate should immediately indicate their acceptance of the general principles of the plan, including the high authority with power to make binding decisions. This condition was accepted by Western Germany, with the approval of the Allied High Commission, by the Benelux governments (with slight reservations by the Netherlands), and by Italy. It was politely rejected by the United Kingdom. Although the British emphasized that all they were rejecting was the proposed method of starting negotiations, it was evident that the real objections centered on the idea of a supranational authority with absolute power over key British industries.[24]

Foreign Secretary Bevin was ill in hospital during these exchanges, but other British official spokesmen, while declining

[24] *Anglo-French Discussions regarding French Proposals for the Western European Coal, Iron and Steel Industries, May-June, 1950,* Miscellaneous No. 9 (1950), Cmd. 7970 (London, 1950); French version in *La Documentation française: Notes et études documentaires,* No. 1,339, June 13, 1950.

to join the scheme at this stage, had praised the French initiative in the most friendly and sympathetic terms. Now, however, an unfortunate coincidence occurred which cast doubt on the sincerity of these professions and made the prospects of effective British-Continental cooperation look darker than ever. The national executive committee of the Labor party, which included Prime Minister Attlee and a half-dozen other cabinet members, chose this moment (June 13) to release a pamphlet on *European Unity* which summed up in fairly blunt terms the views of the Labor party's doctrinaire isolationist wing. Though not directed against the Schuman Plan as such, this document took sharp issue with any idea of an economic or political union between socialist Britain and nonsocialist continental states. The objective in Europe, it insisted, was not a complete union or a supranational authority, but harmonization and coordination of national policies through cooperation between governments. The Labor party could never accept any commitments that interfered with the pursuit of "democratic socialism," and Great Britain would have to continue working "at least as closely with the Commonwealth and U.S.A. as with Western Europe." [25]

In effect, despite Mr. Attlee's embarrassed attempt to distinguish between a party pronouncement and a government document, this was merely an unusually downright if not wholly consistent statement of principles that appeared to have guided the Labor government in its European policy all along. In the circumstances, however, it was bound to cause a sensation disproportionate to its real significance. Expressions of rage and disillusionment were heard in the United States, on the Continent, and in the more European-minded section of British opinion. British opposition leaders demanded a full parliamentary debate, in which they avoided taking a final position on the plan itself but insisted that both national and internationalist interests should have impelled the government to join in the negotiations. A motion to accept the French

[25] Labour Party, *European Unity* (London, Labour Publications Department, 1950), *passim.*

invitation, though with reservations, was defeated on June 27 by one of those slender Laborite majorities which had become familiar since the indecisive general election in February. As usual, the British stand incurred widespread criticism and resulted in lessened appreciation abroad for Britain's solid contributions in the sphere of economic recovery and collective defense.

The delicate balance between British opponents and proponents of the Schuman Plan resembled in certain respects the situation in the two other principal coal- and steel-producing countries, France and Germany. In France, where the plan was generally acceptable to the parties of the governing coalition, it was rejected both by the Communists and by the Gaullists and the extreme Right. In Germany the position was that of Great Britain in reverse: the Social Democratic party, which was in opposition, viewed the plan with considerable mistrust, whereas the conservative coalition led by Dr. Adenauer had accepted with alacrity, though the attitude of Adenauer's industrialist supporters was less clear. In all three countries the political balance was somewhat precarious. A political overturn in any one of them might have unforeseeable effects on the Schuman Plan and, for that matter, on the whole evolution of Western Europe.

Meanwhile initial preparations to implement the Schuman project were going ahead with a dispatch that contrasted with the slower progress of bodies like the O.E.E.C. and the North Atlantic Treaty Organization, which had already come to grips with stubborn realities. Delegates of France, Germany, the Benelux countries, and Italy met in Paris on June 20, and remained in session five days while French spokesmen explained their conception of the draft treaty which would establish the new high authority. Some of the technicalities were spelled out more fully in a French "working paper" which was offered as a basis of discussions, and which proposed three interesting political features: a court of arbitration to deal with disputes between the high authority and governments; a joint assembly, elected by the parliaments of the participating states, which would meet once a year to review the work of the high authority and could turn it out of office if dissatisfied; and a panel of consultative committees to represent the interests of employers, workers, and consumers.

The immediate objective of the high authority was defined by the working paper as the promotion of "a policy of economic expansion, full employment and higher living standards for the workers"; as to the long-range objective, "looking beyond coal and steel, it would lay the first foundations of a European community." [26] "We feel we are not permitted to fail," M. Schuman declared in his address of welcome, which stressed both the unprecedented nature of the undertaking and France's intention of leaving the door open for Great Britain to join or at least cooperate with the six governments.

On June 24, as the French working paper was being distributed at the Quai d'Orsay, the Bidault government resigned in consequence of an adverse vote on a domestic matter in the National Assembly. In Belgium the day before, a new cabinet had decided to risk revolution by inviting King Leopold III to return from his Swiss exile. Next day came the news of the Communist attack across the 38th parallel in Korea.

To some extent these events symbolized the provisional character of the Schuman Plan and everything that had been accomplished or projected in the North Atlantic community in the preceding months. Despite hard work by everybody concerned, the Western European-North Atlantic association still was more an ideal than a solidly based reality. Jealousies, rivalries, and conflicts of aim and interest, between and within nations, belied the smooth professions of solidarity that emanated from every ministerial meeting. True, Europe thus far had escaped catastrophe. Its progress in many respects was startling; but it was not yet out of the woods. Its material foundations were still weak, its peoples were divided and confused, uncertain about their transatlantic allies, and skeptical about their own future.

[26] French Press and Information Service, New York, "Summary of the French Working Paper on the Coal-Steel Pool," Document 16, July 5, 1950.

Contrasted with the past, Europe's over-all situation had its decidedly hopeful aspects. The consciousness of solidarity among the Atlantic nations had certainly gained over the sense of disparity; and political conflicts, as the Belgian experience was to demonstrate, were not necessarily insoluble provided all parties kept their heads and retained a sense of proportion. In terms of the present and the foreseeable future, however, the incoherent state of Europe justified profound concern. The aggression in Korea cast a new light on the thinking of the Kremlin, and on the Atlantic nations' military, economic, and psychological unpreparedness to face a showdown with the Communist world. Future deliberations in the North Atlantic community would revolve about the same fundamental tensions—America versus Europe, Britain versus the Continent, national government versus international collectivity, socialism versus free enterprise, rearmament versus recovery. But they would have to proceed at a new tempo and, if the free world was to survive, with a new determination to fix on the essentials and pursue them with consistency and resolution.

CHAPTER FOUR

THE WORLD AT THE CROSSROADS

THE SPRING of 1950 marked the culmination of that peculiar phase of postwar international relations known as the "cold war," the distinctive feature of which had been unlimited hostility between East and West combined with an absence of overt military action by the principals on either side. The cold war was a life-and-death struggle fought with words and diplomatic maneuvers more than with tanks and guns. The element of physical force loomed large in the calculations of both camps, but for the moment its all-out application was held in abeyance both by the Russians and by the powers that were seeking to counter Soviet expansionism. As yet the clash of arms had been heard only on a reduced scale and in remote theaters like Greece, China, and Indochina.

On June 25 the Communist aggression against the Republic of Korea abruptly transformed this limited conflict into something decidedly more dangerous and qualitatively different. Communism, as President Truman said two days later, "has passed beyond the use of subversion to conquer independent nations and will now use armed invasion and war." It is, of course, quite possible that in sanctioning the Korean aggression the Soviet leaders failed to foresee that it would result in completely transforming the international situation. Although it is unlikely that the attack was undertaken without their knowledge, Korea was an area that they had some reason to regard as beyond the range of effective protection by the instrumentalities of the free world. Yet they must have realized that so flagrant a defiance of international law and morality was bound to intensify the general world crisis and lessen the long-run chances of a peaceful outcome.

The events recounted in this chapter form an essential part of the background of the Korean attack, but provide no sure clue to its aims and significance. Like so much of recent Soviet history, the specific considerations which impelled the Politburo to embark upon, and persevere in, this perilous adventure are hidden from the Western observer. Soviet actions are rarely explainable in terms of any single objective, apart from the all-encompassing objective of eventual world revolution, and it would be misleading to attribute the Korean attack exclusively to any one motive such as the discrediting of the United States or the United Nations, the acquisition of a base for future action against Japan, the disruption of the free nations' plans for remedying outstanding weaknesses in the Far East, or the destruction of the Western European economy under the burden of an expanded rearmament effort. Some or all of these desiderata may have played a part in Soviet calculations, but no one of them by itself is sufficient explanation.

Two general statements seem warranted in the light of subsequent developments. First, the Soviet leaders appear to have concluded during the spring of 1950 that it was possible, if not essential, to accelerate the tempo of their offensive against the free world. Their methods of previous years, though certainly not unrewarding, had produced a gradual stiffening of resistance which might have unfavorable consequences if allowed to continue without interruption. We do not know to what extent their actions were governed by the vicissitudes of their experimentation with atomic weapons, nor how far they were impressed by American decisions relating to the hydrogen bomb, the failure of proposals for new international negotiations on atomic energy control, or the unyielding attitude of American diplomacy in various areas of contact throughout the spring. One may suspect that their hopes of an economic crisis in the United States had been disappointed and that a spontaneous collapse of the capitalist world no longer could be considered imminent. Such observations, coupled with the gradual increase in Western military preparedness, may have helped to persuade them that they could not afford to wait.

Second, while recognizing that opposition to their plans was hardening in some respects, the Soviet leaders would seem to have relied heavily on the disruptive influences that were also operating in the life of the free world. The United States was experiencing something of an internal convulsion as a result of the McCarthy charges and the general dispute over Far Eastern policy. The refusal of important elements in this country to accept the Communist victory in China had set the United States in opposition to some of its allies and accentuated the latent distrust of American aims in both Asia and Europe. If the United States failed to react in Korea, its reputation as a protector of weaker nations would be seriously impaired and the will to resist in other countries would be undermined. If it did react, there would be opportunities to encourage the divisive tendencies that were already evident in relations between Asia and the West and among the Western nations themselves. Perhaps the Kremlin already foresaw that heavy involvement of the United States in the Far East would seriously strain its relations with its European allies.

Whatever the precise expectations of the Soviet leaders in sanctioning the Korean attack, their handling of it was entirely consistent with the main outlines of their political strategy before June 25. Reduced to its simplest terms, this strategy appeared to aim at the destruction of the free world through the moral and physical isolation of its strongest member, the United States. To permit the further consolidation of the free world under American leadership would seriously imperil the cause of world revolution in the next few years and might even encourage a "capitalist crusade" against the U.S.S.R. —or so, at any rate, the Soviet leaders may have reasoned. Isolation of the United States, on the other hand, would mean the collapse of the entire structure of world security, political, military, and economic—United Nations, Atlantic Pact, European Recovery Program, Point Four, and the rest. Once the "reactionary" influence of the United States was neutralized, the revolution would encounter no insuperable obstacles in the rest of Europe and Asia.

Within this broad strategy of pressing its own advantages and alienating the United States from its friends, Soviet action through the months before Korea showed all its familiar diversity, elasticity, persistency, and cynicism. While awaiting the consolidation of the new regime in China and the maturing of the free nations' disagreements over Far Eastern policy, Moscow continued to hammer pertinaciously at various European issues and kept the German pot boiling against the day when the campaign for Germany could be reopened in full vigor. As the major element of its political warfare in Europe it intensified with great effect the "peace" propaganda specifically aimed at the United States and the atomic bomb. It offered continuing encouragement to the many persons, important and unimportant, who still believed in its readiness for peaceful and fair adjustment of world problems. Concurrently, knowing that the official position of the Western powers was unlikely to be shaken by such means, it laid the foundations for open war in the Far East.

Analysis of the complex interplay of world events in this period resembles that of an orchestral score, each line of which proceeds according to its own logic but lacks full significance until considered in relation to the whole of which it forms a part. Of the thematic elements which made up the troubled international counterpoint of early 1950, we have thus far considered only the varied efforts of the Western governments to strengthen the North Atlantic community—efforts which culminated in May in the enunciation of the Schuman Plan, the London meeting of the Big Three Foreign Ministers, and the second full-dress session of the North Atlantic Council. This chapter will be concerned with four others: (1) the attempts of the U.S.S.R. and the world Communist movement to hinder this consolidation in the free world by intensifying their deceptive "peace" campaign; (2) specific issues in Europe which continued throughout the spring to generate dangerous friction between the two camps; (3) the progress of Western programs to counter the advance of Communism in the Far East; and (4) the failure of efforts to end the "cold war" by compromise and mediation instead of violence.

1. The Soviet "Peace" Offensive

No weapon in the Soviet ideological arsenal has been employed more consistently and effectively since 1917 than the idea of "peace," which Stalin has more than once proclaimed to be "the basis of Soviet foreign policy." Most articles of the Leninist-Stalinist creed appeal primarily to particular social classes and suppressed groups. Peace, on the contrary, represents a goal which in the twentieth century has become practically universal and focuses more and more strongly the emotions of mankind. In the hands of skilled and unscrupulous propagandists, both Nazi and Communist, it has provided a potent means of dissolving antagonisms, winning friends, blackening enemies, confusing issues, and distracting attention from the real purposes of those who use it.

From the beginning of its history the Soviet Union was peculiarly well placed to exploit the potentialities of "peace" propaganda, because of solid political interests as well as superior skill in psychological methods of attack. The founders of the Soviet Union certainly did not believe in the possibility of permanent peace with the capitalist world, nor did they look on war as necessarily reprehensible in itself. "If war is waged by the exploiting class with the object of strengthening its class rule," Lenin wrote in 1918, "such a war is a criminal war. . . . If war is waged by the proletariat after it has conquered the bourgeoisie in its own country, and is waged with the object of strengthening and extending socialism, such a war is legitimate and 'holy.' " [1]

---

[1] V. I. Lenin, "Left-Wing Childishness and Petty-Bourgeois Mentality," *Selected Works* (New York, International Publishers, 1943), VII, 357. For recent American and Soviet comments on this doctrine see the speech of Warren R. Austin in the First Committee of the U.N. General Assembly, October 26 (*Department of State Bulletin*, XXIII, November 13, 1950, 767-768), and Vyshinsky's rejoinder of October 28 (U.N. Document A/C.1/SR.380, p. 223).

Nevertheless the internal preoccupations and international isolation of the U.S.S.R. between the two wars excluded any early resort to a war of revolution, while putting a premium on peaceful relations with the surrounding capitalist world until such time as the "inherent" contradictions of capitalist society created new opportunities for the advance of socialism. Without renouncing its ultimate revolutionary aims or its determination to expose the "hypocrisy" of peaceful professions by the capitalist powers, the Soviet Government under Stalin set itself to pursue "a policy of peace and of strengthening trade relations with all countries." This policy, as the Comintern declared at its Sixth World Congress in 1928, "rallies all the allies of the proletarian dictatorship around its banner and provides the best basis for taking advantage of the antagonisms among the imperialist states. The aim . . . is to guard the international revolution and . . . to put off the conflict with imperialism for as long as possible." Yet such methods were considered in no way inconsistent with "preparations for defense and for revolutionary war." "Revolutionary war of the proletarian dictatorship," the Comintern averred, "is but a continuation of revolutionary peace policy 'by other means.' " [2]

The conclusion of the Second World War did not lessen the appositeness of a "peace" policy based on such reasoning. The experiences of the war had strengthened mass longing for a genuine and durable peace, especially in those countries that had suffered most in 1939–1945. It is not altogether easy for Americans to grasp the full extent of this feeling, born of the psychological ravages of two world wars, successive occupations and liberations, repeated economic crises, and a general breakdown of traditions and cultural standards. The resultant profound weariness and revulsion against war created an ideal climate for the prosecution of Soviet aims. By establishing itself as the champion of these peaceful aspirations and branding its principal adversaries as "warmongers," the Soviet Union could count on generating widespread sympathy for its own

[2] *International Press Correspondence*, No. 84, November 28, 1928, 1590.

actions, and widespread misunderstanding and condemnation of those of its recent allies. Superficially, such a strategy might seem to rest on a low estimate of average human intelligence. Actually it revealed considerable psychological discernment and a shrewd appreciation of factors that were sometimes overlooked in anti-Soviet quarters.

Leadership of this deceptive "struggle against a new war" formed the groundwork of all Soviet political activity from 1946 onward and engaged every part of the Communist political apparatus. To prove the good intentions of the U.S.S.R. and place the burden for deteriorating relations on the West, Stalin accorded interviews expatiating upon the possibilities for "peaceful coexistence" of capitalism and socialism—provided capitalism wished to "cooperate." [3] Each year hundreds of speeches by Soviet dignitaries, and thousands of articles, news items, and cartoons in Soviet and Communist publications, "tore the mask" from the "advocates of aggression" and the "fomenters of a new war," otherwise identified as "Anglo-American ruling circles." Soviet tactics in the United Nations were shaped to secure the dissemination of this propaganda on a world scale. Evidence of warlike actions or attitudes in the Western world was sedulously collected, distorted, rearranged, and sprayed in an unending stream over the heads of the international public.

Every Soviet satellite government and every Communist party and front organization prosecuted this activity with the utmost vigor. The more the international tension grew, the more loudly the Communist propaganda machine denounced the "warmongers" and the more confidently it prophesied the frustration of their plans. The entire campaign seemed aimed at building up in the popular mind a subconscious identification of the United States with war and of the U.S.S.R. with peace, thus encouraging a kind of automatic reflex in the response to new international developments. As an integral

[3] See especially Stalin's interviews with Elliott Roosevelt (*Look*, February 4, 1947) and Harold Stassen (*New York Times*, May 4, 1947), both frequently cited by Soviet commentators.

part of its technique the Kremlin deliberately generated "war scares" and exploited the resultant fear to increase the sentiment for peace at any price.

In 1948–1949 the peace movement acquired formal status with the holding of international "peace congresses" in Wroclaw (Breslau), Paris, London, Moscow, Mexico City, and other capitals and the establishment of a permanent World Peace Committee made up of delegates from 54 countries as well as representatives of the World Federation of Trade Unions, the Women's International Democratic Federation, and other Communist-controlled organizations. Under the characteristically militant name of "Partisans of Peace," this body coordinated the activities of thousands of national and local "peace" committees throughout the world and ensured that the peaceful aspirations of their adherents were expressed in strict conformity with the Communist party line. Men of distinction in various walks of life lent their active participation to the movement, among them Frédéric Joliot-Curie, the French atomic scientist, Pablo Picasso, the exiled Spanish painter, and the Reverend Hewlett Johnson, "Red" Dean of Canterbury. Their presence, and the ostensible innocence of its aims, made the Partisans for Peace organization a natural magnet for the indiscriminately well-intentioned and a source of periodic embarrassment to the democratic governments whose hospitality it went out of its way to abuse.[4]

The purposes of this "peace" movement included not only the mobilization of pro-Soviet world opinion, not only obstreperous condemnation of the Atlantic Pact and related moves by the Western governments, but also definite, practical obstruction of Western acts and policies. Whether they realized it or not, those who flocked to the Soviet "peace" banner were expected to subordinate all other loyalties to the cause of "peace" as expounded from the Kremlin. Thus the newspaper

---

[4] A brief factual account of the "Partisans for Peace" movement appears in *Department of State Bulletin*, XXII, March 13, 1950, 400-402. Abundant details are published regularly in the Soviet and Communist publications *New Times, USSR Information Bulletin,* and *For a Lasting Peace, For a People's Democracy!*

of the eight-party Communist Information Bureau (Cominform), itself significantly entitled *For a Lasting Peace, For a People's Democracy!*, proclaimed in its issue of February 10, 1950 that the world peace movement was entering a new, higher stage in which declarations and "pacifist phrasemongering" must give way to "concrete patriotic actions against war." Among the kinds of action cited were pressure on workers to refuse to manufacture lethal weapons or handle those delivered under the American military aid program; agitation to terminate the French campaign in Indochina; ouster of the "reactionary" French and Italian governments, as a preliminary to repudiation of the North Atlantic Treaty; and active support of the Soviet proposals (already once rejected by the United Nations General Assembly in 1949) to prohibit atomic weapons and conclude a "peace pact" of unspecified nature among the five great powers.

All of these tasks were directly related to Soviet foreign policy objectives, but some were easier to accomplish than others. Threatened Communist interference with arm shipments under the military aid program failed to materialize, although it caused the Western governments some apprehension and occasioned large concentrations of police and military at certain points in March and April. Agitation against the atomic bomb, on the other hand, required no great nerve and proved eminently successful. A simple but highly effective technique, that of the signed petition, was used to elicit mass expressions of support for a thesis on the atomic bomb and other weapons of mass destruction which looked wholly innocuous, but which actually was aimed directly at undercutting the position of the Western powers in their controversy with the U.S.S.R. Throughout the spring and summer of 1950 this loudly advertised "signatures for peace" campaign provided camouflage for Moscow's increasingly bold and aggressive actions in the domain of world policy.

The so-called "Stockholm Peace Appeal," which formed the basis of this campaign, originated at the third session of the

Permanent Committee of the World Peace Congress, held in the Swedish capital on March 15-19, 1950. It read: [5]

We demand the unconditional prohibition of the atomic weapon as a weapon of intimidation and mass extermination of human beings. We demand the institution of strict international control to enforce this. We shall consider as a war criminal that government which first employs the atomic weapon against any country.

We call upon all people of good will throughout the world to sign this appeal.

"It is not difficult to see why this appeal has spread through the world like wildfire," wrote a Soviet commentator. "[It] touches upon questions which truly agitate the minds of all the people on the globe." [6] In fact, it would have been difficult to mislead simple people and confuse issues more completely than was done by this text, which seemed to reflect so clearly the fears and hopes of humanity at large. The pitfalls were obvious to anyone who had followed the international negotiations on atomic energy control. "Unconditional prohibition of the atomic weapon," in Soviet language, meant unilateral renunciation by the Western powers of the one arm in which they still held a possibly decisive margin of superiority over the U.S.S.R. "Strict international control" meant acceptance of the Soviet plan which had been found untrustworthy and impractical by a majority of the United Nations. Branding the use of the atomic weapon as "criminal"—a favorite Soviet theme—recalled the Soviet contention at the last session of the General Assembly that atomic bombardment was "incompatible with the conscience and honor of nations and with membership in the United Nations organization." [7] Such stigmatizing of the atomic weapon as immoral was logically fallacious in so far as it implied that other forms of violence and cruelty abroad in the world were less reprehensible; but it undoubtedly encouraged the popular revulsion against atomic warfare and

[5] USSR Information Bulletin, X, April 28, 1950, 234.
[6] M. Mikhailov, "The Appeal for Peace Is a Call to Struggle for Peace," ibid., 233.
[7] The United States in World Affairs, 1949, 305.

thus tended to build up the psychological obstacles to the use of the atomic bomb by the United States.

For the average man in the spring of 1950 was in no mood to hesitate over logical subleties. A clear-cut declaration against the atomic bomb, irrespective of origin and implications, offered a ready way of discharging anxieties that had been building up for months. If the Western governments were unsympathetic to the petition, that seemed all the more reason to make it clear that their peoples were against atomic warfare under all circumstances. Said the Dean of Canterbury, "1,000,000 signatures to the peace petition will cause annoyance among the warmongers; 10,000,000 will cause alarm in their ranks; 100,000,000 signatures will wreck all their plans and save the world." [8]

By this standard the world was already saved by the beginning of June, when officials of the World Peace Congress announced that over 100 million signatures had been gathered in the first six weeks of the campaign. By August, after the entire adult population of the Soviet Union had enrolled itself, the total of "mainly adult" signers had grown to 273,470,566 and the sponsors were claiming the implicit support of 600 million men, women, and children, or nearly a quarter of the world's population. [9]

Even if genuine, these figures had obviously to be interpreted with caution. It was significant that more than 85 percent of the signatures came from the U.S.S.R. and the countries it controlled, where signature was practically obligatory. Elsewhere the figures were roughly proportionate to, but considerably larger than, the number of local Communist voters, a fact which emphasized the close dependence of the entire movement on its Communist foundations. In Western Europe a total of 31.9 million signatures was rolled up, including 14.6 million in Italy, 12 million in France, and 2 million in Western Germany. Preliminary claims for other areas included 5.68 million in Korea, 2.2 million in Latin America, 1.35 mil-

[8] *USSR Information Bulletin,* X, May 12, 1950, 264.
[9] *Ibid.,* June 9, 1950, 336; September 8, 1950, 520.

lion in the United States, 1.35 million in Japan, 1 million in Burma, 519,000 in French Africa, and 477,000 in the British Commonwealth.[10]

The actual totals were less impressive than the air of sanctity with which the sponsors managed to surround the campaign and the skill with which they kept it in the foreground of public attention. Churchmen, cabinet ministers, and others in Western Europe who had nothing in common with the originators of the movement were placed before the embarrassing alternatives of signing a Communist document or letting themselves be classed among the enemies of "peace." Many who avoided the trap were still impressed by the underlying idea, and predisposed in favor of any and all efforts to end the atomic deadlock and restore contact among the great powers. Soviet statesmen and propagandists did their best to heighten this mood by underlining the peaceful aims of Soviet policy and vilifying the "aggressive" plans of the Western powers.

Inevitably, this activity had its effect in confusion of the public mind and in lessened confidence in the North Atlantic governments. Thus it helped to create a favorable atmosphere for the series of Soviet-directed political moves in Europe that preceded the Communist aggression in the Far East at the end of June.

2. East-West Struggle in Europe

Direct relations between East and West in 1950 revolved for the most part around stale, perennially unsolved issues left over from the days when peacetime cooperation among the great powers had still seemed practicable. Events of the past few years had removed many East-West controversies from the realm of constructive negotiation. The Soviet boycott

[10] Some of these figures had risen considerably by November, by which time the claimed over-all total had been increased to more than 500 million through the addition of new signatures in China (preliminary total 223.5 million), Italy (16.9 million), France (15 million), Japan (6 million), Vietnam (3.9 million), Burma (3 million), the U.S. (2.5 million), and elsewhere. See *New Times*, No. 45, November 7, 1950, 14 and 16; No. 46, November 15, 1950, 3; No. 47, November 22, 1950, 5.

of United Nations bodies sufficed by itself to prevent serious discussion of the great questions raised by the advent of a Communist China. Great-power "collaboration" in the former enemy states of southeastern Europe had long since broken down; the Western governments, faced with an implacable assault on their direct interests and on general human rights and freedoms in the area, could only complain to the United Nations or consider suspending diplomatic relations, as the United States had done with Bulgaria in February 1950.[11] American determination to assist Marshal Tito's fight for survival in Yugoslavia, underlined by two Export-Import Bank credits in amounts of $20 million each,[12] was hardly a matter for direct discussion with a government that was tirelessly working for Tito's overthrow. What remained were the chronically dangerous East-West confrontation in Germany and Austria; miscellaneous frictions arising out of the Italian Peace Treaty, the Japanese surrender, and other diplomatic arrangements; and, above and beyond these, the explosive situation inherent in the coexistence of such radically hostile powers on the same planet.[13]

The manner in which specific East-West issues continued to be raised, dropped, shelved, and revived was superficially confusing but fully corresponded with the Soviet tactic of holding the initiative, probing constantly for weak spots, wearing down psychological resistance, and making the most of the confusion produced by its own and other people's propaganda. Symbolically enough, the year began with a flare-up in the heart of

[11] *Department of State Bulletin*, XXII, March 6, 1950, 351-356, 381.
[12] *The United States in World Affairs, 1949*, 256-257; *Department of State Bulletin*, XXII, March 20, 1950, 445.
[13] In a subordinate category were the occasional exchanges of diplomatic communications between Washington and Moscow on such matters as the captive status of some 2,000 presumptive U.S. citizens or spouses of citizens in the U.S.S.R. (*Department of State Bulletin*, XXII, March 20, 1950, 433-441); the unfavorable exchange rate imposed on foreign diplomatic establishments in the U.S.S.R. (*ibid.*, April 10, 1950, 561); and the delayed return of U.S. vessels made available to the U.S.S.R. under wartime lend-lease (*ibid.*, May 22, 1950, 818). Arrangements to resume negotiations for a lend-lease settlement were made late in the year (*ibid.*, XXIII, November 20, 1950, 817-818; XXIV, January 15, 1951, 93-94; *New York Times*, January 6, 1951).

Europe, as the East German Communists revamped their apparatus for political agitation and the four commandants in Berlin renewed their endemic quarrel. A Russian-imposed "little blockade" of traffic to and from Berlin's Western sectors served to remind the Western governments that, despite the victory of the airlift in 1948–1949, their position in the former Reich capital could still be made difficult whenever it suited their Soviet co-occupants. This controversy, complicated by recriminations over the execution of the 1949–1950 trade agreement between West and East Germany, dragged on through February, forcing the American authorities at Frankfort to make preparations to revive the airlift but never quite reaching the proportions of a real crisis.

Kept tense by this and similar incidents, East-West relations during the first three months of 1950 could be described as thoroughly bad but not acutely dangerous. This was the period of maximum effervescence in the Western world over the question of atomic energy control and possible East-West reconciliation. In April, after authoritative American statements had made it clear that American policy remained unchanged, relations took a sharp turn for the worse. As the "peace" offensive continued with rising intensity, the U.S.S.R. appeared also to be increasing its political pressure all along the line. This tightening of the screws—on Germany, Austria, Italy, Turkey, Scandinavia, even Iran and Afghanistan—was one of the two salient aspects of Soviet policy during the second quarter of the year. The other, to be considered later in this chapter, was the continuing encouragement of attempts to mediate the East-West quarrel on Soviet terms.

A tragic accident gave the first danger signal. On April 8 an unarmed United States Navy aircraft disappeared over the Baltic on what was officially described as a "routine training flight" from Wiesbaden, Germany, to Copenhagen. Three days later the Soviet Government protested that a "four-engined military plane"—obviously the same machine—had penetrated Soviet territory in Latvia to a distance of 21 kilometers, disregarded a summons to land, fired (!) on pursuing Soviet aircraft, then turned out to sea and disappeared. The facts, as stated by American and Soviet quarters, flatly contradicted each other. The U.S.S.R. claimed a "gross violation" of its frontier and an "unheard-of violation" of international law. The United States, after investigation, denied that there had been any violation of Soviet territory or waters, charged that "Soviet military aircraft fired upon an unarmed American plane over the open sea," and demanded appropriate indemnity and disciplinary action. The Kremlin, in turn, angrily rejected these contentions and added the charge that the plane had been sent to "photograph Soviet defense installations." [14]

Earlier occurrences of the same sort had taught Americans patience. The incident was not allowed to get out of hand, but it went far to recreate the atmosphere of foreboding in which the Western world had lived in the days of the blockade and the airlift. It also sharpened the effect of a number of Soviet diplomatic gestures which were undertaken at about the same time. Thus on April 19 the Soviet Navy journal *Red Fleet* recalled Russia's long-standing demand to share with Turkey in the control of the straits between the Black Sea and the Mediterranean.[15] Showing a lively interest in questions of maritime rights, Soviet spokesmen also redefined their claims respecting territorial waters in the Baltic, and the Soviet legal journal published an ominous article underlining the Kremlin's interest in the status of the Baltic straits between Denmark and Sweden.[16] Roughly in the same pattern was a note to seven governments interested in the Antarctic, recalling Russian explorations in that area and roundly claiming the right to participate in any decisions about its future.[17]

These were general claims which might be worked upon as occasion offered. Trieste, Austria, and Germany provided opportunity for immediate, positive action—or obstruction—based

[14] *Department of State Bulletin*, XXIII, May 1, 1950, 667-668; May 15, 1950, 753-754.
[15] U.S. comment *ibid.*, XXII, May 1, 1950, 687.
[16] Yu. U., "The Regime of the Baltic Straits in International Law," *Sovetskoye gosudarstvo i pravo*, No. 5, May 1950 (*Current Digest of the Soviet Press*, II, No. 31, September 16, 1950, 7-8).
[17] Soviet note, June 7, in *USSR Information Bulletin*, X, June 23, 1950, 380.

on well-established positions. The Trieste question had specially intriguing potentialities for the Soviet Union because the status of the Free Territory, established by the Italian Peace Treaty in 1947, was in dispute not only between East and West but also between Italy and Yugoslavia, Moscow's former satellite. The Western powers still held to the position they had adopted in 1948 that the peace treaty had proved unworkable and should be revised in order to return Trieste to Italian administration.[18] But Yugoslavia still ruled the southern part of the Free Territory, and its insistence on maintaining its own position had proved a major stumbling block in the way of Western efforts to improve relations between the two Adriatic countries.

The U.S.S.R., which had originally supported Yugoslavia's claims in Trieste, had no reason to depart from the strict letter of the treaty now that it had washed its hands of the Tito regime. Many of the treaty provisions had become all but inapplicable in the last two years; but the Soviet Union, as one of the four great powers responsible for the treaty's execution, had a formal right to protest any deviation from its terms for whatever reason. On April 20, amid rumors of a new attempt to solve the matter by direct negotiation between Italy and Yugoslavia, it addressed sharp notes to the United States, Britain, and France, accusing them of "rude violations" of their treaty obligations and demanding implementation of the arrangements for establishing a governmental administration and withdrawing military forces from the Free Territory.[19]

Although the Russians on this occasion were in a somewhat stronger legal position than usual,[20] it was unlikely that their intervention would have much influence on the actual situation in Trieste. What it did do was to provide them with an excuse

---

[18] The United States in World Affairs, 1948–1949, 46, 443-444.

[19] USSR Information Bulletin, X, April 28, 1950, 237-239.

[20] In rejecting the Soviet allegations on June 16 the U.S. made no claim that the relevant treaty provisions were being carried out but contended that the responsibility "lies squarely upon the Soviet Government whose conduct following the conclusion of the Treaty rendered the settlement envisaged therein impossible of execution" (Department of State Bulletin, XXII, June 26, 1950, 1054). Similar replies were returned by the U.K. and France, and the U.S.S.R. then reaffirmed its own position in notes of July 8 (USSR Information Bulletin, X, July 28, 1950, 446).

for further delaying the three-year-old negotiations for a treaty with Austria, an intrinsically more important matter on which the Soviets had long been lavishing their talent for diplomatic sabotage. The question had an important bearing on their general position in Europe, since until a treaty was signed they were entitled to maintain armed forces not only in Austria itself but also in Hungary and Rumania, where they could be used to overawe the local populations and also to threaten Yugoslavia.

Most of the genuine legal and technical obstacles to an Austrian treaty had been disposed of by the Big Four Foreign Ministers and their deputies in the course of 1949, with the result that Soviet obstruction now took the form of raising extraneous issues and insisting that they be settled before negotiations were continued. From November 1949 to April 1950 the deputies were unable to make any progress because the Soviet representative insisted on awaiting the outcome of certain bilateral economic negotiations between the Soviet and Austrian governments—negotiations which the Kremlin appeared to be deliberately keeping from completion. In April the Soviets shifted ground and began to accuse the Austrian Government of failing to carry out its denazification and demilitarization obligations, thus hinting that it might be necessary to reconsider parts of the treaty already agreed upon. And in May they achieved a pinnacle of irrelevance by announcing that further progress on the Austrian treaty would depend on a satisfactory response to their note on Trieste.[21]

The cynicism of this procedure in no way lessened its inconvenience from the Western and Austrian point of view. What it meant was that Austria's rights and interests would be disregarded until the Western powers saw fit to carry out the provisions of the Italian Peace Treaty—provisions which they had already decided were unworkable and which were even more unacceptable now than they had been two years earlier. Per-

[21] *Department of State Bulletin*, XXII, January 30, 1950, 162; March 6, 1950, 379; May 8, 1950, 731; May 15, 1950, 777; May 22, 1950, 818; June 5, 1950, 921-922; June 26, 1950, 1054; *USSR Information Bulletin*, X, May 26, 1950, 305; June 9, 1950, 341-342.

haps never before had the Kremlin maneuvered its opponents into quite such an uncomfortable political and legal quandary. They could not retreat from their position on Trieste without creating new opportunities for Stalinist intrigue at the head of the Adriatic, mortally offending Italy, their ally in the Atlantic Pact, and embarrassing Yugoslavia in its battle for independence. On the other hand, so long as they refused to compromise on Trieste they could not prevent the Russians from censuring their disregard of treaty commitments, nor could they do much to alleviate occupied Austria's economic and political plight. Withdrawal of the occupation troops would have been unthinkable while the Russians remained in the eastern half of the country. Austria had suggested a number of methods by which the occupation burden might be reduced, but for the moment the Big Three felt unable to do anything more specific than announce that civilian High Commissioners would be appointed to replace the military authorities in the three Western occupation zones.[22]

While multiplying diplomatic embarrassments for the Western powers in Trieste and Austria, the Kremlin had been laying the foundations of a much graver crisis in Germany. Moscow, which rightly saw in Germany's position and resources the key to mastery in Europe, was anything but reconciled to the existing state of affairs in the former Reich. It wholly rejected the Bonn government, symbol of Western Germany's provisional attachment to the Atlantic world. While using its own puppet "German Democratic Republic" as a vehicle of political control in Eastern Germany, it clearly held to the long-range objective of reuniting the Eastern and Western zones under conditions favorable to Communist control of the entire country. Thus its propaganda and political activity were directed primarily to discrediting the Bonn regime as a supine, antinational instrument of Western aims, and using the East Ger-

---

[22] Declaration on Austria by Acheson, Bevin, and Schuman (London, May 19), in *Department of State Bulletin*, XXIII, July 10, 1950, 74. On June 12 the three governments formally advised the U.S.S.R. of this decision and invited it to follow their example (*ibid.*).

man regime to play upon German national sentiment with the aim of directing it into anti-Western and pro-Soviet channels.

In this endeavor the Kremlin and its agents were handicapped not only by the heritage of anti-Russian feeling in Germany but also by the fact that many of their own postwar policies had been clearly detrimental to German national interests. Notable in this respect were the Soviet (and Polish) annexations of former German territory, the stripping of the East German economy, and the retention of hundreds of thousands of German war prisoners in the U.S.S.R., presumably for forced labor. But the Kremlin also possessed important psychological and practical advantages in Germany. If it had little hope of making itself generally beloved, it could at least make itself generally feared. Its heavy military concentrations in Eastern Germany, its tight control of the East zone population, its ability to invoke mass demonstrations by the regimented membership of the Communist-controlled "front" organizations, its sponsorship of a large, partially militarized German "People's Police"—all this had considerable effect on German thinking. If it did not win many active partisans for the Kremlin, it at least predisposed a good many Germans against making irrevocable commitments to the West.

In Germany as elsewhere the Western powers were prevented from playing the Soviet game on equal terms, not only by their military weakness and by disagreements among themselves but also by their commitment to an ethical, democratic standard of political action. Confronted by an attack that addressed itself without scruple to the most primitive human instincts, their only recourse was to try to repel it by mobilizing the forces of reason which they believed to be inherent in communities of free men. Thus their ordinary response to Eastern criticism of Western policies was to cite the record of Soviet actions and show that they themselves had often stood out as the defenders of German interests. To Eastern proposals for the reunification of Germany and the withdrawal of occupation troops their reply was to reiterate their insistence that reunification must be on a federal basis with full democratic guarantees.

To Eastern attempts to discredit the Bonn government, they replied by successive concessions to Bonn, designed to strengthen the West German regime and bring it into closer association with the West. To the implicit threat of forcible action, against West Berlin or against West Germany itself, they replied not by rearming Germans or increasing their own military contingents, but by repeatedly declaring their solidarity with the threatened populace and their determination to stand by it under all circumstances. Such gestures, too, were by no means without effect; but their impact in Germany was tempered by awareness that the West was militarily unprepared to defend Germany, and politically unprepared as yet to treat Germany as an equal or even leave it full control of its own internal life.[23]

Through the spring of 1950 the complicated psychological battle went forward with growing intensity, paced as usual by the Soviet-Communist apparatus in the East. As the season advanced there were some indications that Moscow might be working toward a first-class crisis, comparable to the Berlin blockade of 1948. Once again, it seemed, Stalin planned to assail the Western powers at their most vulnerable spot, deep within the Soviet zone. Just as in 1948, Moscow could count on German opinion to draw the correct conclusions from Western actions. Any sign of faltering would probably convince the people of Western Germany—and Western Europe, for that matter—that American support was not to be relied upon in an emergency. Even if there were no faltering, a crisis in Germany would accentuate the discomfort of American policy, already torn between the conflicting demands of the European and Far Eastern theaters.

Whitsunday, May 28, was the date chosen by the East German Communist forces for a decisive trial of strength. As early

[23] For an authoritative statement of U.S. policy in Germany, illustrating both the positive aspects and the handicaps of the Western position, cf. the speech of U.S. High Commissioner John J. McCloy at Amerikahaus, Stuttgart, February 6 (*ibid.*, XXII, February 20, 1950, 275-279).

as February it became known that 500,000 or 600,000 members
of the Communist-dominated Free German Youth had scheduled for that date a "march on Berlin" and a monster rally,
which could easily lead to violence if they defied the ban of
the West Berlin authorities and attempted to invade the Western sectors of the city. All through the spring tension built up,
aided by the inflammatory statements of East German leaders
and the extraordinary precautions of the West Berlin government and the Western military commandants. Firmness and
resolution were the keynote on the Western side, which refused to be shaken either by threats or by assurances that the
demonstrations would be peaceful. "The Communists will not
succeed in taking over the city," said American High Commissioner John J. McCloy on April 4. ". . . The free men and
women of the city will not permit it and we will not permit it.
The British, the French, and the Americans are fully determined and fully united. We shall stay in Berlin." But this very
air of resoluteness contributed to a feeling that days of acute
danger were not far off.

The threat to Berlin naturally involved a threat to the whole
position of the Western powers in Germany, and also to that
of the federal government they had sponsored at Bonn. The
issue of that government's status and prerogatives thus assumed an unusually critical character in the weeks before the
expected storm. As always, however, the Western powers were
hindered from making full use of Bonn's political potentialities by the duality of their own objectives in Germany and their
feeling that the Federal Republic must be kept under a tight
rein. An attempt by Bonn to seize the psychological initiative
by proposing a free election throughout Germany won the endorsement of McCloy and the State Department, and forced
the East German regime to assume the onus of rejecting the
offer.[24] In more practical matters of internal legislation and administration, however, the Western powers continued to exer-

[24] A comparable proposal for free city-wide elections in Berlin was put forward
in April by the West Berlin City Assembly and endorsed by the Western commandants, but dropped after Soviet authorities insisted on various unacceptable
conditions such as the prior withdrawal of all occupation forces.

cise their own authority with comparatively little regard for German sensibilities. Nor did they respond with any enthusiasm to Chancellor Adenauer's repeated requests for revision of the Occupation Statute and some kind of Allied "security guarantee" which would compensate for Western Germany's disarmed and defenseless state.

But the Russians, too, were still plagued by the legacy of World War II. At the very moment when Communist fervor in Germany was reaching its highest pitch, they poured a cold douche over the entire German people by foreclosing virtually all hope for the many men who had not yet returned from Soviet prisoner-of-war camps. With what seemed incredible ineptitude, the TASS agency announced on May 4 that the repatriation of German prisoners, except for a few thousand war criminals and suspects, had been completed. Over 1.9 million Germans had been repatriated, said TASS; but in 1945 the agency had announced a total of 3.5 million in Soviet custody. Thus a good million and half remained unaccounted for, with a strong presumption that they had died of hardship and exposure.

The effect in Germany, especially on the East German Communist leaders, was almost catastrophic. Hasty efforts were made to find some way of repairing the damage, without, of course, exacting real sacrifices from the Soviet Union. The field of reparations was already so confused as to offer a good basis for mock concessions. Within a week the East German government had decided to sound the Kremlin about a reduction of reparations deliveries. On May 16 Stalin magnanimously replied that the Soviet Government was prepared to forgive Eastern Germany half its remaining reparations debt. From 1951 through 1965 the "Democratic Republic" would have to pay only $3.2 billion instead of $6.3 billion; taking into account the $3.7 billion already paid, its total reparations would thus come to only $6.9 billion instead of $10 billion. Foreign analysts found these figures wholly fanciful and estimated that they greatly understated the wealth already lost to the German economy. The East German People's Chamber, however, dutifully voiced its "joy and gratitude," leaving it to speculation how far the shattering effect of the TASS announcement had been counteracted.

Soviet mishandling of the prisoner-of-war issue, coinciding with the enunciation of the Schuman Plan in Paris, created a favorable opportunity for the three Western Foreign Ministers, who devoted much of their time to German problems at their London meeting on May 11-13. Though unable to agree on the great question of West German rearmament or on fundamental changes in the status of the Federal Republic, they announced a number of decisions calculated to maintain Bonn's prestige, neutralize Soviet-inspired propaganda, and encourage a firm stand against Communist encroachments. The theme of their meeting was stated by Secretary Acheson on the eve of the conference when he reminded a London audience of the "peculiar need for closer and more organic contact of Germany with its Western neighbors." "The reestablishment of Germany in the family of Western civilization," he said, "must be a cooperative enterprise, in which the risks and responsibilities are shared by all. No harder enterprise . . . has ever been undertaken jointly by a group of nations. . . . But it is a problem dictated to us by the demands of the times." [25]

The agreed views of the three Western governments in this matter were formalized on May 14 in an official declaration reaffirming their desire that Germany should "reenter progressively the community of free peoples of Europe," but also their conviction that realization of the German desire for a relaxation of controls and restoration of sovereignty depended on the success of the Germans themselves in creating an atmosphere of security for the Allies and democracy and individual freedom for the German people. The allied occupation, they said, was the result of the division of Germany and the international position, and would have to continue until this situation was modified; similarly, a treaty of peace would remain impossible as long as present Soviet policies persisted. How-

[25] Address before the Society of Pilgrims, London, May 10, 1950.

ever, the Western powers promised to set up a study group to
prepare for a review of the Occupation Statute and recommend
ways of attenuating the inconveniences of the existing situation. Furthermore, they declared once again that the "peaceful reunification of Germany" was "the ultimate object of their
policy," and renewed their offer of June 1949 to admit the
states of the Soviet zone to the benefits of the federal constitution and the Occupation Statute.[26]

This last proposal was obviously put forward not with any
expectation of Soviet acceptance but as a psychological counter
to the agitation for "unity" on a Communist basis. As a striking follow-up the three ministers endorsed the Bonn project
for free all-German elections and an all-German democratic
constitution, and drew up for presentation to the Soviet Control Commission in Germany a statement of the principles—
consistent with Western but wholly alien to Soviet practice—
which they believed should govern the process. Once an
all-German government was formed on this basis, they emphasized, the Big Four "should immediately address themselves to
a peace settlement." [27] This was carrying the war to the enemy
with a vengeance.

Moreover, the ministers seized the opportunity to penetrate
other chinks in the Soviet-Communist armor. A special statement on the prisoner-of-war issue called attention to the
U.S.S.R.'s persistent disregard of prior commitments and international obligations in this respect, and promised to take "all
possible steps" to obtain information and "bring about repatriation in the largest possible number of cases." [28] Agreement
was also reached on a stiff formal protest to the Soviet Government against the remilitarization of Eastern Germany in the

[26] *Department of State Bulletin*, XXII, May 22, 1950, 787-788; cf. *The United States in World Affairs, 1949*, 41, 176.
[27] *Department of State Bulletin*, XXII, June 5, 1950, 884-885.
[28] *Ibid.*, June 19, 1950, 1018. On July 14 the three governments addressed notes to the U.S.S.R. asking it, among other things, to agree to an impartial inter-national investigation in the Soviet Union of the fate of prisoners known to have been in Soviet custody (*ibid.*, XXIII, July 24, 1950, 132-133; September 11, 1950, 435-436). The U.S.S.R. replied negatively on October 2 (*New York Times*, October 3, 1950). Meanwhile, in August, the issue had been carried to the United Nations (below, pp. 383-384).

guise of a police force.[29] Lastly, the Foreign Ministers strongly reaffirmed their governments' determination to uphold their rights in Berlin and protect the democratic rights of its inhabitants, while striving to ameliorate economic conditions in the former capital and pressing for its reunification through free elections.[30]

Thus the Western powers served notice once again that they would not be intimidated by any maneuvers attempted under cover of Berlin's approaching youth congress. But even as the ministers conferred, the Whitsuntide rally was beginning to look less menacing. For some reason the heat appeared to have been taken off. So greatly built up in advance, the demonstrations which occurred in East Berlin at the end of May were large but decidedly anticlimactic. No organized invasion of the Western sectors was attempted, and individual youths who drifted over from curiosity or hunger showed none of the fiery spirit ascribed to them by the official Communist propaganda.

In other respects, too, the emphasis of Soviet policy in Germany seemed to be undergoing one of its periodic displacements. Instead of treating the East German regime as the standard-bearer of all-German nationalism, the Kremlin was beginning to show renewed interest in welding it more closely into the existing Soviet bloc. On June 7 the "Democratic Republic" was compelled to announce a series of agreements with Poland, one of which provided for a 60 percent increase in mutual trade while another acknowledged the finality of Germany's territorial losses in the East by formally recognizing the Oder-Neisse line as the permanent Polish-German frontier.[31] On June 23 similar agreements with Czechoslovakia were announced; these included a renunciation of all German claims to the Sudentenland, including the right of German expellees to be resettled in that area. A third series of agreements, with

<hr />

[29] U.S. note of May 23, *Department of State Bulletin*, XXII, June 5, 1950, 918-919.
[30] Tripartite statement, London, May 13 (*ibid.*, June 26, 1950, 1039).
[31] Texts in *Europa-Archiv*, V, September 5, 1950, 3329-3331. The U.S. position of refusal to recognize the postwar Polish-German boundary was reaffirmed in *Department of State Bulletin*, XXII, June 19, 1950, 1016-1017.

Hungary, was made known a day later. These arrangements involved a humiliating sacrifice of generally accepted national aims. More far-reaching than any of the territorial concessions required of the Federal Republic in the West, they could not fail to reflect adversely on the Eastern government's status within Germany. For the moment, however, the "German Democratic Republic" seemed destined to turn its eyes eastward, shelving its "national" function in order to make its contribution to the solidity of Soviet-controlled Eastern Europe.

3. East Asia on the Eve

In Asia the conditions of the East-West struggle were more fluid, and consequently more favorable to Soviet gains. Whereas in Europe the U.S.S.R. was reduced to endless battering against positions more or less firmly held by the West, in southern and especially eastern Asia it was ringed by loosely knit, inherently unstable societies already quivering under the impact of revolutionary change. Rudimentary conditions of life, lack of political sophistication, and a complex intermingling of anti-imperialist, nationalistic, and reformist impulses offered an extraordinarily favorable climate for purposeful revolutionary activity, geared to the vague but powerful aspirations of an awakening continent.

With the Communist conquest of China the revolutionary cause gained the further advantage of being able to work through a purely Asian power, one whose problems and experience mirrored those of other Asian nations and were capable of arousing their sympathy and emulation. By making Communist China the executant of its designs in the Far East, the Soviet Union could benefit by Asian admiration for Mao Tse-tung's achievement while escaping the odium that went with direct Soviet intervention. Eight million Chinese scattered over Southeast Asia, and generally loyal to Peking, could be useful auxiliaries of the Far Eastern revolution. To be sure, these arrangements would work in the long run only if Peking remained unequivocally loyal to Moscow, and there were recurrent indications—such as the two-month interval between Mao's arrival in Moscow in December 1949 and the signature of the Sino-Soviet friendship treaty on February 14, 1950—that the two governments might not see eye to eye in all respects. For the present, however, Communist China was clearly more interested in consolidating a position in the Far East than in resisting Moscow's steady encroachments on its own sovereignty. By the time Moscow's yoke began to chafe, it might be too late to shake it off.

Communist ambitions in Asia were also favored by the piecemeal, uncoordinated, and essentially unimaginative way in which the West had set about trying to remedy a position that was strategically and politically weak to begin with. From the Near East around to Korea and Japan, the Western powers appeared solicitous in a general way for the independence, or at least the integrity, of the countries bordering the Sino-Soviet realm. Their resistance in each threatened sector, however, tended to base itself not on the newly awakened popular forces but on the idea of conserving as much as possible of the established political and social order. This bias not infrequently had the effect of placing them in opposition not only to Communism but also to the progressive tendencies which Communism was trying to use for its own purposes. Mutual suspicion and intolerance, the heritage of the age of imperialism, still poisoned the relations of Europeans and Asians; and each Western country had its own opinions, aims, and sympathies which prevented a unified Western approach to any single Asian problem.

Under the pressure of a common peril, the Western nations were making some progress toward overcoming these differences; but the progress was painfully slow, and subject to constant interruption. Provisional settlements in Palestine in 1948–1949 and in Indonesia during 1949 had partially disinfected two major sources of irritation, but meanwhile the Communist conquest of China had raised new issues that were even more explosive and seemingly were incapable of adjustment through the processes of the United Nations. The West-

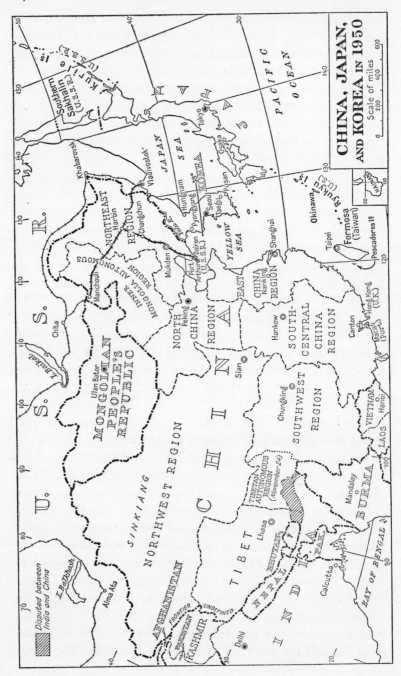

CHINA, JAPAN, AND KOREA IN 1950

Scale of miles
0   200   400   600

ern powers were fortunate that at least one theater of the cold war, the Middle East, remained relatively quiet while they struggled to take in the implications of the Chinese revolution. In the Far East they found themselves in the uncomfortable position of trying to erect a ring of outer defenses against a power concerning whose nature and treatment they completely disagreed. Activities on the periphery of China had at best a provisional value while the China problem itself remained unsolved.

Since there was no early prospect of bridging the Western disagreements over China policy, Western action with reference to the central problem of the Far East was limited to helpless waiting—waiting to see whether the Communists would attack Chiang Kai-shek on Formosa, try to enforce their claim to sovereignty over Tibet, go to the aid of Ho Chi Minh in Indochina, take over Hong Kong, or confine themselves to stamping out guerrilla resistance and consolidating their internal position; whether they would eventually condescend to act on Britain's offer to establish diplomatic relations; whether they would show any disposition to resist the growing Soviet control of their affairs; above all, whether they or the Kremlin planned any fresh move in the campaign to oust the Nationalist regime from the United Nations and seat a delegation from Peking in the Security Council.

With respect to other areas in the Far East the picture was less frustrating. In Southeast Asia, in Japan, and in Korea the free nations appeared to be reconciling some of their differences and moving with a new determination to create "situations of strength" instead of the weakness that invited malevolent adventures. But these gains would count for little if Soviet or Chinese Communism were to interfere decisively before the results materialized.

NOTE ON MAP OPPOSITE: This map shows the new administrative regions established by the Chinese Communists on an intermediate level between the central government and the provinces. Formosa is nominally included in the East China Region. Also indicated are the Chinese Changchun Railway and other Soviet interests in the Northeast Region (Manchuria) under the treaty of February 14, 1950.

In Southeast Asia the spring of 1950 was chiefly notable for the open acceptance by the United States of a part of the responsibility for halting the internal disintegration which armed Communism was doing everything to stimulate. Outside of the Philippines, American aid had hitherto been available in Southeast Asia only as a by-product of Marshall aid to Great Britain, France, and the Netherlands. A conviction that the situation could not be saved without more decisive American action had been growing for months and was crystallized by Ambassador Jessup's tour of the area early in the year. The first results were the decision to support the French-sponsored Bao Dai regime in Vietnam (Indochina) and the grant of a $100 million Export-Import Bank credit to the new United States of Indonesia. Gradually, through the spring and summer, a more general program of economic and military assistance unfolded itself, based mainly on the limited funds appropriated by Congress for use in the "general area" of China. Priority was given to Indochina as the country in which Communist activities were already most menacing. The nature of the program varied from country to country, but its most conspicious features were adaptability to local situations, limited scope, and an attempt to maintain political neutrality as between the various European and non-Communist native interests in each.

The groundwork for a modest program of economic and technical assistance based on the Point Four concept was laid by an investigating mission which returned to Washington in May with initial recommendations that were said to total roughly $60 million, including $23 million for Indochina, $11 million each for Indonesia, Thailand, and Burma, and $5 million for Malaya. The conduct of the enterprise was entrusted to the Economic Cooperation Administration, which immediately set about planning concrete programs for the first four of those countries. A formal agreement for the administration of economic aid to the Associated States of Indochina was reached late in May, and an American representative was designated to work there with the governments of Cambodia, Laos, and Vietnam, the French High Commissioner, and any joint French-Indochinese body that might be set up.[32]

Because of its direct accessibility to Chinese Communist interference, Indochina also received first priority for military assistance among the countries where Communist-led groups were in armed revolt against the established authorities. Secretary Acheson, after conferring with the French Foreign Minister in Paris on May 8, announced that in the opinion of the United States the situation in Indochina was sufficiently menacing to warrant the granting of military equipment as well as economic aid to the Associated States and France. Taking indirect note of the criticism directed against the Bao Dai regime as a French puppet government, he added that American assistance could and should contribute both to the restoration of security and to the development of "genuine nationalism." Unofficially it was reported that Indochina would receive half of a projected military aid allocation of $30 million, with another $10 million going to Thailand and $5 million to Indonesia.[33] Burma and Malaya, though more immediately threatened by Communist insurgents, were evidently viewed as a British rather than an American responsibility.

Meanwhile some tentative effort was being made to arrive at a better over-all coordination of allied policies in Southeast Asia. At their London meeting in May the three Foreign Ministers declared themselves in agreement both as to the seriousness of the situation there and as to the necessity of encouraging and supporting the new governments in the area. Remarking that Southeast Asia as a whole was economically underdeveloped, they urged "all governments in the region" to collaborate in intensifying "measures . . . to raise the general standard of

[32] Department of State Bulletin, XXII, May 22, 1950, 791; May 29, 1950, 869; June 12, 1950, 977; Ninth Report to Congress of the Economic Cooperation Administration (Washington, 1950), 93-105; Lawrence S. Finkelstein, "U.S. at Impasse in Southeast Asia," Far Eastern Survey, XIX, September 27, 1950, 169-170.
[33] Department of State Bulletin, May 22, 1950, 821; Finkelstein, loc. cit. The Philippines were already receiving military aid under a separate disposition of the Mutual Defense Assistance Act.

living." [34] The British Commonwealth countries were already working toward this end along the lines projected at the Colombo conference in January. A special meeting at Sydney, Australia in mid-May outlined a three-year technical assistance plan for South and Southeast Asia, designed to cost £8 million ($22.4 million), and Acheson assured the British Foreign Secretary that the United States would try to coordinate its efforts with those of the Commonwealth "in order that our actions will be mutually supporting." [35]

All of this represented a small, late start, but still a start, toward assuring "these newly independent peoples . . . a period of peace and quiet in which they can concentrate on the difficult problems of establishing their political and economic institutions." [36] Allied policies toward Southeast Asia in the spring of 1950 had attained about the same degree of adequacy and coordination as Allied policies in Europe three years earlier, before the inauguration of the $375 million Greek-Turkish aid program and the Marshall Plan. But the over-all situation in Southeast Asia in 1950 contained perhaps fewer hopeful elements than that of Europe in 1947. The great question was whether such modest efforts, begun so late and under such handicaps, would be given time to bear fruit or would be nipped in the bud by military pressure and internal subversion on behalf of Soviet Communism.

There could be little doubt that the loss of Southeast Asia, with its rich resources, large populations, and proximity to vital centers of the British Commonwealth, would be so damaging to the free world as to justify much stronger efforts to hold it. From the point of view of global strategy, however, there was some reason to regard it as a secondary area compared with certain other parts of the Far East, notably Japan and the islands of the former Japanese empire. Many of these had already been parceled out among the United States, the U.S.S.R., and China, whose Nationalist government was now confined

[34] Communiqué, May 13, in *New York Times*, May 14, 1950.
[35] Report to members of Congress, Washington, May 31, 1950.
[36] *Ibid.*

to the island of Formosa. Japan itself for the present was firmly within the orbit of American military power, an integral part of the "defensive perimeter" which Secretary Acheson had described in his speech of January 12. Whatever arrangements might be made for Japan's future, he had said, its defense "must and shall be maintained."

American interest in the future of Japan was fully matched by that of the Soviet and Chinese Communist governments, whose alliance treaty of February 14, 1950 was specifically directed against "the rebirth of Japanese imperialism and a repetition of aggression on the part of Japan or any other state which should unite in any form with Japan in acts of aggression." Historically Japan had figured as an inveterate foe of both countries, and its strategic position would continue to constitute an implicit threat to their security as long as nations continued to think of each other in military terms. Under Communist control, on the other hand, Japan's alert population and highly developed industry would be priceless assets to the revolutionary cause. These dual potentialities undoubtedly weighed heavily with the Communist leaders in Moscow and Peking as they shaped their course in Korea and other areas of the Far East.

For the moment Communist China was excluded from any voice in Japanese affairs, while the U.S.S.R. and the United States still confronted each other on terms of an ostensible common interest growing out of their joint participation in the final stages of Japan's overthrow. The Russians, though lacking any real influence on the administration of Japan as conducted by General MacArthur in the name of the Allied Powers, continued to participate in the 13-nation Far Eastern Commission and the advisory Allied Council even after the breakdown of four-power government in Germany had destroyed the last semblance of great-power collaboration in Europe.

Having no power to affect the decisions of the Supreme Commander (SCAP), the Soviet Government used its position mainly for propaganda and miscellaneous obstruction of the occupation policy. Within Japan these efforts were generally supported by the sizable Japanese Communist party, whose activities in the labor movement and the civil service harassed but did not seriously threaten the occupation and the conservative Japanese government of Premier Shigeru Yoshida. As yet Soviet-Communist tactics in Japan had possessed little more than nuisance value. Still to be answered was the question what would happen after the American occupation ended, and whether in the meantime a more decisive resistance would eventually be offered to an American policy which was based more and more openly on the concept of turning Japan into an advanced bastion of the free world's defense against Soviet-Communist expansionism.

One of the fragile East-West links in Japan was further weakened in December 1949 and January 1950 when the Soviet representative conducted a series of walk-outs from the meetings of the Allied Council in Tokyo. This maneuver, which roughly coincided in timing with the Soviet walk-outs from United Nations bodies over the question of Chinese representation, was ostensibly concerned with a different issue, that of the U.S.S.R.'s failure to repatriate an estimated 377,000 Japanese, mostly prisoners of war, held in Soviet-controlled territories. When this issue was formally raised by the United States and later by Australia, the Soviet representatives in Tokyo simply refused to discuss it.[37] Instead the Soviet Government suddenly lodged a sensational demand for the trial as war criminals of the Emperor Hirohito and other Japanese nationals on the ground that they had shared responsibility for alleged preparations to conduct bacteriological warfare. Whether or not this move was intended, as the State Department claimed, to distract attention from the prisoner issue, the attack on the Emperor struck at the very roots of the American

[37] The United States in World Affairs, 1949, 454; Department of State Bulletin, XXII, January 2, 1950, 24-28; January 16, 1950, 102-103. The TASS agency reported on April 21 that Japanese repatriation had been completed except for 2,467 war criminals, suspects, and ill persons (USSR Information Bulletin, X, May 12, 1950, 272). For later developments, including consideration by the United Nations, cf. Department of State Bulletin, XXIII, August 14, 1950, 256-257; September 11, 1950, 433-435; and pp. 383-384, below.

occupation policy, illuminating luridly enough the absence of any area of basic Soviet-American agreement on the treatment of the vanquished aggressor.[38]

Other Soviet-American exchanges during the spring served to emphasize this point. When the Soviet Government protested against SCAP's provisions for parole of convicted Japanese war criminals, the State Department sharply replied that the objection was out of order and that the Supreme Command's policies were "in accordance with the practice in enlightened and democratic countries."[39] When the Soviet representative in Tokyo complained obliquely about the reconstruction by the United States of former Japanese air and naval bases, General MacArthur retorted (May 4) that he could only regard the inquiry as "a vehicle of propaganda or a provocative impertinence." Japan itself was fully disarmed, he added, but the occupation forces would continue to maintain their bases and installations "in a condition of such adequacy and preparedness as will ensure the fullest security, operational efficiency, and complete readiness for any eventuality."[40]

On another front, General MacArthur insistently renewed his suggestions to the Japanese that the Japanese Communist party had behaved in such a manner as to forfeit its right to the protection of the laws. In June, after a new wave of Communist-inspired disorders had resulted in the beating of five American soldiers, he ordered the Japanese Government first to bar the party's central committee from public life, then to purge the editors of its official newspaper, and finally to suspend the paper for 30 days. A Soviet protest was rejected by SCAP on June 25, the day of the Korean aggression, as offering "no bases for rational discussion."

Meanwhile international discussions of the problem of a

[38] *USSR Information Bulletin,* X, February 24, 1950, 112-113, and June 9, 1950, 340; *Department of State Bulletin,* XXII, February 13, 1950, 244. The Soviet demand was renewed on December 15 at the height of the world diplomatic crisis (*New York Times,* December 16, 1950).
[39] *Department of State Bulletin,* XXIII, July 10, 1950, 60-61.
[40] *USSR Information Bulletin,* X, May 12, 1950, 272; Royal Institute of International Affairs, *Chronology of International Events and Documents,* VI, May 4-17, 1950, 303.

peace treaty for Japan confirmed the trend toward shutting out the Soviet Union from any effective influence on Japanese affairs. In the absence of any basis for agreement between the U.S.S.R., Communist China, and the West, both Japanese and non-Communist allied opinion was gravitating toward the idea of a separate peace treaty between Japan and the non-Communist powers. The Japanese Government under Premier Yoshida was committed to such a policy, and received a measure of public endorsement in elections to the upper house of the Diet on June 4. British Commonwealth representatives had been actively working toward a community of views on the matter since the Colombo conference in January. In the United States, President Truman said on May 18 that he hoped a treaty was not too far distant, and the State Department announced that John Foster Dulles was giving special attention to "problems concerning a Japanese peace settlement." Early in June Defense Secretary Johnson and General Bradley, followed by Mr. Dulles, left for brief visits to the Far East during which the matter was intensively canvassed with General MacArthur.

Although many differences among the non-Communist nations and between them and Japan remained to be adjusted, the trend was hardly one that Moscow would regard with equanimity. Apart from its imperfect juridical basis, any peace treaty on which the non-Soviet world could agree would almost certainly provide in some fashion for continued American protection of Japan against the hazards of its position on the fringe of Communist Asia. Either Japan itself would have to be rearmed, contrary to the firmly established policies of both the allied and Japanese governments, or the United States would have to assume major responsibility for its defense. The most advanced industrial nation of the Far East might thus be withheld from Soviet influence for an indefinite time to come.

A similar progress toward consolidation on a non-Communist basis was discernible in the Republic of Korea, a country situated on the very doorstep of the Communist world and in which the United States had retained primary responsibility for frustrating Communist aims. Morally and legally the Republican government was a ward of the United Nations, whose General Assembly recognized it as the sole legal government of the country pending fulfillment of the resolutions calling for the reestablishment of a free, united, and independent Korea. Only the United States, however, was in a position to furnish the Republic with the support it needed to survive in the face of the militantly aggressive Communist regime installed north of the 38th parallel.

In Korea no less than in Southeast Asia, the essential problem was to ward off Communist armed attacks while remedying the serious internal weaknesses that made the country a tempting victim. Just as in Southeast Asia, moreover, American policy seemed to rest on the hope that no all-out attack would occur while the process of internal reconstruction was going on—in other words, that the adversary would remain quiet while the projected victim gathered strength. The United States had no plans for helping the Republic withstand a major military assault, still less for underwriting its leaders' evident ambition to reannex Northern Korea by force of arms.[41] Korea was not even within the "defensive perimeter" whose defense Secretary Acheson had said the United States "considered essential under all circumstances." Its 100,000-man army, aided by the counsel of an American Military Advisory Group but lacking tanks, artillery, and aircraft, was designed to maintain internal order and deal with guerrilla outbreaks, not to fight a modern war. The modest $10.2 million allotted to Korea under the 1949–1950 military aid program was intended not for rearmament but merely to maintain and supplement the small

[41] Brig. Gen. W. L. Roberts, Chief of the U.S. Military Advisory Group, told members of the U.N. Commission on Korea in January 1950 that the U.S. Government "had informed the Government of the Republic that the launching of any attack from South Korea would be immediately followed by the termination of all aid, both military and economic, from the United States. Further, he stated that the armament left . . . by the United States forces when they withdrew had been limited to defensive weapons, including small calibre artillery, but without tanks and without airplanes, and that this had been done in order to make it impossible for South Korea even to contemplate launching a war for the unification of the country." *Report of the United Nations Commission on Korea* (U.N. General Assembly, *Official Records, Fifth Session,* Supplement 16, Lake Success, 1950), 10.

arms and equipment left by United States forces when they withdrew in mid-1949.[42]

The large-scale invasion launched on June 25 by Communist forces from North Korea showed that American policy had rested on an unduly hopeful estimate of Communist intentions. Up to that moment, however, there had been grounds for moderate optimism concerning the Republic's effort to establish a viable life within the artificial confines of the 38th parallel. By early 1950 guerrilla resistance had been virtually extirpated, and vigorous enforcement of South Korea's stringent internal security law had brought a considerable improvement in internal stability.

The obverse of this picture was the continuance of high-handed and undemocratic procedures by an inexperienced government which felt itself living virtually under siege conditions. President Syngman Rhee's frequent disregard for consitutional restraints, coupled with the generally authoritarian outlook of his government and its leaning toward methods associated with the totalitarian police state, gave the regime a somewhat dubious world reputation and occasioned sharp hints from the United States that greater regard should be paid to personal liberties and constitutional obligations as well as sound financial policy.[43] The general trend, however, was progressive. The National Assembly exhibited a courageous resistance to executive despotism, and the new general elections held on May 30, which brought out 90 percent of the electorate and engaged the interest of moderate elements who had boycotted

[42] The nature and extent of U.S. military aid to the Republic of Korea are detailed in *Background Information on Korea,* House Report 2495, 81st Congress, 2nd Session, July 11, 1950 (Washington, 1950), 33-35. The mission of the Korean "internal security force" is there defined (p. 34) as follows: "(a) To preserve internal security; (b) To prevent border raids and incursions from north of the thirty-eighth parallel; and, as a byproduct; (c) To deter armed attack or other aggression by the forces from North Korea." Some further background data are presented in "The Fight Against Aggression in Korea," *Foreign Affairs Outlines: Building the Peace,* No. 24, Autumn 1950 (Department of State Publication 3971, Washington, 1950), and on pp. 91-93, above.

[43] See especially the remarks of Ambassador-at-Large Jessup to the Korean Assembly, reported in *New York Times,* January 13, 1950, and the State Department aide-mémoire of April 3, in *Department of State Bulletin,* XXII, April 17, 1950, 602.

the previous election of 1948, resulted in the return of a much more representative legislative body which convened on June 19 "in a hopeful atmosphere conducive to continued progress." [44]

Economic and social conditions were also improving, albeit slowly. Thanks to heavy fertilizer imports by the Economic Cooperation Administration, by the spring of 1950 South Korea was attaining self-sufficiency in foodstuffs for the first time. Individual living standards remained abysmally low, but industrial production was climbing, inflation was under vigorous attack, and land reform was at last well under way.[45] Although they required plenty of time to consolidate themselves, the elements of recovery were definitely present. John Foster Dulles, addressing the National Assembly on June 19, voiced the confidence inspired by brief direct observation of the South Korean scene: [46]

As you establish here in South Korea a wholesome society of steadily expanding well-being, you will set up peaceful influences which will disintegrate the hold of Soviet communism on your fellows to the north and irresistibly draw them into unity with you. Never, for a minute, do we concede that Soviet Communists will hold permanently their unwilling captives. No iron curtain can indefinitely block off the attracting force of what you do if you persist in the way you have been going.

To the rulers of the "Democratic People's Republic" in North Korea, such prospects were as unwelcome as was the progress of the Bonn government to the Communist leaders of Eastern Germany. Both regimes were bound to resist the trend, and the similarity of their methods indicated a common inspiration. But whereas the East German Communists still confined themselves to nonviolent forms of attack on the Federal Republic, their North Korean fellows under Kim Il Sung were

[44] Cablegram from the U.N. Commission on Korea, June 26 (U.N. Document S/1505, June 26, 1950). The basic document on internal conditions in Korea before the Communist attack is the U.N. Commission's *Report* cited in note 41 above.
[45] *Eighth Report to Congress of the Economic Cooperation Administration*, 79-87; *Ninth Report*, 91-93.
[46] *Department of State Bulletin*, XXIII, July 3, 1950, 13.

already preparing to wage open warfare on the rival regime at Seoul.

Foiled in its attempt to disrupt the internal life of South Korea by subversion and guerrilla action, the Pyongyang regime appeared to be falling back on an intensified psychological and propaganda offensive. A renewed "struggle for national unity" was heralded by the Pyongyang radio at the beginning of June. References were made to an appeal for "peace and unification" which allegedly bore the signatures of 5.3 million North Koreans. On June 7 a proposal was broadcast for unification of the country by August 15, through general elections and the formation of a unified legislative organ. Despite its scathing references to the "traitors" in the Rhee government and the malign influence of the United Nations Commission on Korea, the tone of the proposal was unusually moderate. Subsequently it was altered to provide for merging of the existing North and South Korean assemblies into a single legislative body, still with August 15 as the final deadline for peaceful unification.[47]

This offer elicited virtually no response in South Korea. South Korean quarters were more interested in the accompanying military activities which had been observed just north of the 38th parallel. As early as May 10 Republican authorities made known that elements of the North Korean regular army, which was estimated to total 183,000 men equipped with planes and tanks, were moving in force toward the dividing line. Meanwhile guerrillas and "People's National Defense" forces stationed along the parallel were increasing their activity. The significance of this information was not clear. South Koreans claimed that there was "imminent danger of invasion from the North"; American observers questioned this interpretation.[48] But the real meaning of the movement became obvious on June 25, when North Korean units crossed the parallel in force. The United Nations Commission was impelled to conclude that

[47] U.N. Document S/1505; *Report of the United Nations Commission on Korea,* cited, 10-11, 18-19, 35-40.
[48] *Ibid.,* 28-29.

"the radio propaganda offensive calling for early unification by peaceful means seems to have been intended solely for its screening effect," and "had no other purpose than to divert the attention of the Government of the Republic of Korea from all thought of aggression from the North." [49] In any case it was clear that military preparations and political maneuvers had been used as interdependent elements in a single over-all strategy aimed at disrupting the progress of one outpost of the free world.

4. Failure of a Mission

The threat of war which was inherent in East-West relations during this troubled period was a source of concern to most of civilized humanity, and particularly to those non-Communists whose situation enabled them to visualize most clearly the horrors of another international conflagration. World Communism tried with considerable skill to ride the wave of antiwar feeling and direct its force against the United States and our associates; but many who saw through this tactic remained obsessed by the actual perils to civilization and felt a compelling obligation to fight the drift toward war.

The framers of United States foreign policy, though daily accused by this country's enemies of the most atrocious militarism and saber-rattling, unquestionably shared to the full this deep concern for peace. Their aim, however, was to safeguard peace not through further concessions to the Stalinist appetite but by repairing the many weaknesses of the free world. Only so, they argued, could the free nations hope to deal with the Soviet world on terms that would assure a peace founded on reality, not on the treacherous crust of Soviet forbearance.

Others, without impugning the sincerity of this position, found it unduly rigid and called for what seemed a bolder, more imaginative approach, a real effort to arrive at a settlement of East-West differences by negotiation before it was too late. A strong current of opinion in favor of East-West negoti-

[49] *Ibid.,* 11.

ations had developed in the United States under the stimulus of the hydrogen bomb announcement, only to lose its impetus against the administration's unshakable refusal to open conversations which promised no constructive outcome. Elsewhere the desire for an East-West détente, and the belief in its possibility, remained strong, nowhere more so than at the headquarters of the United Nations in Lake Success. Throughout the spring, while East and West scowled at each other all around the globe and each new meeting of a United Nations body witnessed a repetition of the solemn farce of Soviet withdrawal, officials of the world organization labored to find a basis on which normal international life could resume.

The chief promoter of these efforts and the most prominent international advocate of an East-West settlement was Trygve Lie, the Norwegian Secretary-General of the United Nations. As the executive head of the world organization and as an individual nominally possessing the confidence of both sides, Lie was exceptionally well placed to serve as an intermediary between them. His frequently expressed abhorrence of what he called the "ideological struggle" among the great powers, his insistence on the necessity for great-power collaboration, and his constant urging of negotiation and compromise, had given him considerable prestige with a section of the international public. American officials felt that his concern for neutrality in the political battles raging about his feet was a trifle naive and frequently carried him into actions unduly favorable to the Soviet Union; but neither they nor, as yet, the Russians seriously questioned his sincerity or good faith.

The crisis in the United Nations that resulted from the withdrawal of the Soviet bloc created an opportunity, if not an obligation, to intensify the conciliatory efforts with which the office of Secretary-General had become identified. The symbolic role of Trygve Lie as the representative of *all* the United Nations was magnified by the withdrawal of one party. To bring about the return of the Communist states would be a signal service to the United Nations and to the cause of peace; to leave the breach unhealed would be to court the danger of a third world war and admit the futility of striving for a peaceful, all-embracing world order. Quite obviously, however, the breach would not be healed as long as all parties adhered to their present positions. A new start implied negotiation and compromise, and would require concessions not only by the Soviet Union but also—perhaps especially—by the governments whose policies had precipitated the Soviet walk-out. The possibility of obtaining the requisite concessions was a matter of judgment. At any rate, the Secretary-General undertook to try.

Two lines of action seemed to Mr. Lie to offer the best hope of progressively relieving the tension. One was a settlement of the acute question of China's representation in the United Nations, on which the Soviet Government was adamant while the non-Communist governments were divided. The other was a renewal of direct contact among the great powers and a more vigorous use of the instrumentalities available for negotiation and compromise—not for "appeasement," Mr. Lie emphasized, but for *"negotiation*—which requires honest give-and-take by both sides." "I do not believe in political miracles," he told a Washington audience on March 21. "It will take a long series of steps to reduce the tensions of the conflict and bring the great powers together. Equally, I do not think the world can safely delay taking the first steps on this road of negotiation and conciliation. The danger of an indefinite continuation of the cold war in this age of the atom bomb, the hydrogen bomb, and bacteriological weapons is too great. . . . What we need, what the world needs, is a twenty year program to win peace through the United Nations."

The difficulty was that no 20-year program could possibly get under way before the China issue was settled; and Mr. Lie had made no attempt to conceal the fact that he thought it should be settled by admitting Communist China to the United Nations. This view, he protested, was not the result of the present Soviet boycott. "It is a serious matter to have the Soviet Union staying away from United Nations meetings, but that is not the first consideration. The first consideration is the people of China. . . . They have a right to be represented in the United Nations by whatever government has the power to 'employ the resources and direct the people of the State in fulfillment of the obligations of membership' [50] in the United Nations. I repeat—whatever government is thus qualified, regardless of its ideology." Already, he pointed out, the "People's Republic Government in Peking" had been accorded diplomatic recognition by 26 governments, including 15 members of the United Nations. His plain implication was that other governments which continued to recognize "the Nationalist Government now on the island of Formosa"—headed, of course, by the United States—should withdraw their opposition to Communist China's admission to the world body even if they did not see fit to accredit representatives to Peking.

This position, which coincided with the views of the U.S.S.R., Great Britain, and various Asian and European governments, was in flat conflict with the present attitude of the United States as well as Nationalist China (still one of the permanent members of the Security Council), France, and most of the Latin American countries. The United States, Secretary Acheson had made known, would not absolutely veto Communist China's admission to the Security Council in place of Nationalist China; but this government was clearly determined to resist that development as long as possible, especially now that the Soviet Union had resorted to blackmail in order to enforce its views. Under the circumstances the State Department was inclined to resent suggestions like that of the Secretary-General. They made its own position more difficult to sustain, and seemed to encourage the idea that the United States, rather than the U.S.S.R., was obstructing the will of the United Nations and the quest for peace.

Put forward in this context, the specific elements of Lie's "peace program" were unlikely to arouse much enthusiasm in Washington, the more so as they turned out to be no more successful than other efforts of the kind in getting at the root of

[50] Quoted from a memorandum on the legal aspects of U.N. representation, made public by the Secretary-General on March 8, 1950.

the difficulty. Only one definitely new feature distinguished the ten-point program which Lie was to lay before the major governments in the coming weeks. This was a proposal to inaugurate special "periodic meetings" of the Security Council, to be attended "by foreign ministers, or heads or other members of Governments," which should be used "for consultation—much of it in private—for efforts to gain ground toward agreement on questions at issue, to clear up misunderstandings, to prepare for new initiatives that may improve the chances for definite agreement at later meetings." [51]

Assuming that all of the great powers really desired fair and firm agreements, this might be a fruitful device for getting them together on a high level. The balance of Lie's program, however, merely enumerated the critical fields in which agreement was desirable, thus recalling attention to the profound divergences which had frustrated all attempts to agree in the past. Except for the important question of the veto, he touched upon all the principal sore spots in East-West relations within the world organization—atomic energy, conventional armaments, United Nations armed forces, membership—and urged a new and more determined approach to agreement on each. For good measure, he asked also for more emphasis on economic development, more vigorous use of the specialized agencies, and more energetic promotion of the observance of human rights, the advancement of colonial peoples, and the development of world law.[52]

All of these were matters in which the previous record of the United Nations undoubtedly left a good deal to be desired —not, however, because their importance had been overlooked, but because they reflected the incompatible aims of the Soviet

[51] Article 28, paragraph 2 of the U.N. Charter reads: "The Security Council shall hold periodic meetings at which each of its members may, if it so desires, be represented by a member of the government or by some specially designated representative." No such meeting had taken place, although under the Security Council's rules of procedure they were supposed to be held semiannually.

[52] "Memorandum of Points for Consideration in the Development of a 20-Year Program for Achieving Peace Through the United Nations," *New York Times,* June 7, 1950. The problem of peace settlements for Austria, Germany, and Japan was deliberately excluded as falling outside the purview of the United Nations.

and non-Soviet governments. The areas of disagreement pin-
pointed by the Secretary-General were symptoms, not causes, of
the world's sickness.

In April Mr. Lie announced that he planned to discuss his
still unpublished program with the heads of some of the major
governments. On April 20 he had a "good talk" with President
Truman at the White House; two days later he left for Paris,
London, and possibly Moscow. His trip coincided with a burst
of activity in other United Nations quarters, all attuned to the
same theme that the cold war must be ended and contact between East and West restored before the prospects for world
peace faded altogether. The heads of the United Nations specialized agencies met with Mr. Lie in Paris on May 4 and
unanimously affirmed that "The peace and well-being of all
peoples demand from their governments a great and sustained
new effort by the nations of the world to achieve a constructive
and durable peace." Gunnar Myrdal, left-wing head of the
Economic Commission for Europe, undertook a trip to Moscow
in the hope of breaking the East-West trade impasse, and reported some success in inducing the Russians to consider an
East-West grain deal.

After conferring with the French and British Foreign Ministers, Mr. Lie proceeded to Moscow and on May 15 was received in the Kremlin by Stalin, Deputy Premier V. M. Molotov, and Foreign Minister A. Y. Vyshinsky. Asked whether he
was satisfied with his Moscow conversations, he told the press
that he had "no reason to be dissatisfied," but that final judgment must be deferred for at least two or three months. On
the return journey he held further discussions with the top men
in the French and British cabinets and talked once again to the
President and Acheson at the end of the month. To a press
conference at Lake Success he declared: "My trip has confirmed
my belief that no government wants war."

It was not the Secretary-General's fault that these activities
coincided with and to some extent supplemented Moscow's
own "signatures for peace" campaign. Nevertheless the whole
tone of the proceedings, in conjunction with the Secretary-

General's known views on the China problem, implied a certain measure of reproof to the United States and earned him the condemnation of various American congressmen as well as the commendation of Professor Albert Einstein and other well-known peace advocates.

On June 6 Mr. Lie released his memorandum and a report of his mission to the 59 United Nations member governments. In so doing he came back to his original starting point by declaring that settlement of the China problem was the precondition for progress in other directions. His conversations, he said, had given him "a firm conviction that the United Nations remains a primary factor in the foreign policy of each of these governments and that the reopening of genuine negotiations may [sic] be possible." But, he added, "It is evident that no significant progress can be made while the members of the United Nations remain sharply divided on the question of the representation of one of the permanent members of the Security Council—the Republic of China. It is necessary that this question be settled." In other words, the position was essentially unchanged. The Soviet Union refused to call off its boycott unless the United States and other nations reversed their attitude toward the Chinese Communists.

That the United States would not modify its own position on such terms was obvious. Secretary Acheson reaffirmed it the next day. "The present situation in the United Nations," he said, "does not arise from our position on the question of Chinese representation but from the refusal of the Soviet Union to accept decisions taken by parliamentary majorities in the various organs of the United Nations. . . . Our position of supporting the Nationalist Government and of opposing the seating of the Chinese Communists continues unchanged. But, we will accept the decision of any organ of the United Nations made by the necessary majority, and we will not walk out" as the Soviet Government had done.

As to the ten-point program, Acheson said, "The United States has always been ready to negotiate with other Members of the United Nations on any matter in the appropriate forum.

We are willing to consider any possibilities put forward by
Mr. Lie or by any other Member of the United Nations which
are believed to be practical." Meanwhile, however, "We can't
afford to wait and merely hope that [Soviet] policies will
change. We must carry forward in our own determination to
create situations of strength in the free world, because this is
the only basis on which lasting agreement with the Soviet Government is possible."

In short, United States policy was also unchanged, as the
President and the Secretary indicated at greater length in
formal speeches during the short time that remained before
the Communist attack in Korea.[53] The French and British governments also gave no sign of having altered their positions,
despite the clear-cut British preference for seating Communist
China in the United Nations.[54] On European questions the
results of the Lie mission appeared if anything to have confirmed the Western determination to hold the diplomatic offensive seized by the three Foreign Ministers at their May conference. Several actions on Germany, Trieste, and Austria which
grew out of that meeting [55] happened to synchronize with the
conclusion of Lie's mission, thus deepening the impression that
if the mission had failed in its purpose, it had not at any rate
dampened the resolution of the Western governments.

Whether the Lie mission had any greater effect on the calculations of the Kremlin must remain speculative. The publication and rejection of his memorandum preceded by less than
three weeks the attack on the Republic of Korea; but, as has
been seen, military preparations for that event had been under
way even before Lie's visit to the Kremlin. The absence of
Communist-fomented disturbances in Berlin on May 28 could
conceivably have owed something to his pacificatory influence,
but could be more plausibly attributed to the firm stand of the
West and Moscow's need to concentrate on impending develop-

[53] Speeches by the President at St. Louis (June 10) and by the Secretary of
State at Dallas (June 13) and at Harvard University (June 22).
[54] See especially the statement of Foreign Secretary Bevin in the House of
Commons on May 24.
[55] Cf. above, notes 20, 22, and 28.

ments in the Far East. Mr. Lie's efforts, by focusing world attention on the search for peace, innocently provided a screen for the aggressive designs that were maturing in Korea. Moscow gave him a warm reception, but, far from taking him into its real confidence, permitted him to become the international dupe of the year. Nor is it likely that the American rejection of the Lie program had any decisive effect on the Kremlin's planning. At most it might have confirmed decisions already made but temporarily held in abeyance.

None the less, this abortive mission marked a decisive turning point in international relations, as the Secretary-General seemed aware when he told a Paris press conference (May 3) that the world stood "at the crossroads." The choice, he said, was either peace through the United Nations or a permanent splitting of the world into two camps—a course that in his opinion must inevitably lead "sooner or later" to a third world war. Whether or not this analysis was correct, his journey was a valiant attempt to solve the world crisis through an appeal to reason and mutual tolerance. It was doomed to fail because five years of cold war had convinced the Western governments that those qualities were alien to the Stalinist outlook and afforded no basis for lasting accommodation with the Soviet Union. American concessions on the specific issue of Chinese representation, the merits of which were at least arguable, might have avoided certain future difficulties and made it easier to maintain the unity of the free world on more vital issues. But it is unlikely that they would have altered the intentions of men whose whole aim was to destroy the free world itself. Secretary Acheson summed up the problem at Dallas on June 13. "The one difference which is just about impossible to negotiate," he said, "is someone's desire to eliminate your existence altogether." [56]

[56] In his address to the U.N. General Assembly on September 20, Acheson credited this aphorism to Dr. Charles Malik of Lebanon.

CHAPTER FIVE

CRISIS IN THE FAR EAST

ON JUNE 25, 1950, at 4:00 A.M. Korean time, troops of the North Korean "Democratic People's Republic" struck southward across the 38th parallel in an unprovoked surprise attack on the territory of the lawfully established Republic of Korea. Supported by Soviet-made tanks and aircraft, equipped with ample heavy artillery, and aided by seaborne landings on the Korean east coast, the operation was clearly the fruit of careful and long-continued advance planning. Although the North Korean radio and later the Soviet Government described it as a counterattack aimed at repelling an attempted invasion by Korean Republic forces, the falsity of this claim was perfectly obvious to observers on the spot. Investigation fully confirmed the preliminary conclusion of the seven-nation United Nations Commission on Korea: "first, that judging from actual progress of operations Northern regime is carrying out well-planned, concerted, and full-scale invasion of South Korea, second, that South Korean forces were deployed on wholly defensive basis in all sectors of the parallel, and, third that they were taken completely by surprise as they had no reason to believe from intelligence sources that invasion was imminent." [1]

News of the invasion flashed around the world, shattering

[1] Cablegram from the U.N. Commission on Korea (Australia, China, El Salvador, France, India, Philippines, Turkey), U.N. Document S/1507, June 26, 1950; see also the First Report to the Security Council by the U.S. Government under the resolution of July 7, U.N. Document S/1626, July 25, 1950. For the Soviet version cf. especially Y. A. Malik's statement to the Security Council on August 11, U.N. Document S/P.V. 486, August 11, 1950. Various "documents" of uncertain authenticity supporting the Soviet claim have been published in the periodical *Soviet Russia Today*.

the quiet of a June weekend. What did it mean? Was it simply another Communist probing operation, aimed at testing the defenses of the Korean Republic and the resolution of its supporters? Was Moscow behind the move, or had the hotheads in Pyongyang gotten out of hand and launched an invasion on their own initiative? If so, would the Kremlin repudiate or support them? Would Korea become another Greece, scene of a long-drawn fratricidal strife which constantly threatened to involve the great powers? Was the invasion aimed at destroying American prestige in Asia by showing that the United States was incapable of protecting countries that depended on it? Or was June 25 the actual beginning of World War III, to be followed by other aggressions in the Far East and Europe, perhaps by atomic bomb attacks on New York and Washington?

Months afterward, some of these questions were still unanswered. Some of them might never be answered satisfactorily. No one in the West could say definitely by whom or for what purposes the Korean invasion had been ordered, nor how far the U.S.S.R. was prepared to press this latest and most serious attack on the foundations of international morality and the free world. But the Soviet Government's demeanor soon made it clear that Moscow, while disclaiming responsibility, had at least provisionally made the North Koreans' cause its own and was determined to squeeze the last drop of political advantage from whatever steps the free nations might take, whether forward or backward. So long as the North Koreans were left to carry the whole burden of the fighting, it was still possible to view the affair as a localized operation in which, as it presently appeared, the Kremlin had seriously underrated the resistance potential of the free nations. By late November, after Communist China had intervened on a grand scale, it began to look more like part of a vast strategic conception whose origins might go back to President Mao Tse-tung's sojourn in Moscow at the beginning of the year.

What was immediately apparent was that the Korean aggression confronted the free world, the United Nations, and above all the United States with the most difficult and perilous decisions they had yet been forced to make. Resistance or non-resistance might prove equally disastrous. The South Korean armed forces themselves were in no condition to repel an all-out attack by an army which was thoroughly trained, skillfully led, and greatly superior in numbers and equipment, and which had the whole might of continental China and the Soviet Union at its back. The United Nations, under whose auspices the Republic of Korea had been set up, had no military forces of its own because of long-standing disagreements among the great powers represented on the Military Staff Committee. The United States had decided months before that its contribution to Korean defense must be confined to the provision of limited equipment and advice.

The last American units had actually been withdrawn from Korea in mid-1949, leaving the Republic, as Secretary Acheson had intimated in his speech of January 12, to depend for its defense on its own efforts backed by "the commitments of the entire civilized world under the Charter of the United Nations." The nearest American troops still available were the men of the occupation force in Japan, most of whom were untrained for combat. Of the other free nations only France and Britain maintained substantial military forces in the Far East, and these were fully engaged in Indochina, Malaya, and Hong Kong. To bring in assistance from other areas not only would take time but also would deplete the strength of the free world in other vital sectors of what might soon become a global battlefront. The outbreak of hostilities in one remote corner of Asia revealed the dangerous inadequacy of the free nations' military strength all round the world.

The responsibility for this state of affairs could not be fixed with precision. It was certainly ironical, and probably not accidental, that Soviet Communism had attacked in an area where the free nations recognized a positive moral commitment but were utterly without means to back it up. In the United States the quest for scapegoats enlivened the political scene throughout the summer. Opposition charges flew thick and fast, and conflicting versions of the past disagreements between the Defense and State Departments clouded a picture that was obscure to begin with. The essential elements of the situation, however, were reasonably clear. From a strictly military point of view, Korea lay outside the area whose defense was considered vital to the security of the United States; maintenance of a permanent force there would have been an unwarrantable dispersal of our limited military strength. Yet from a political standpoint Korea, like every other country threatened by Soviet Communism, represented a responsibility which could not be evaded without damaging the whole political and moral fabric of the free world. If Korea were abandoned, what other small country could feel secure? In Korea, as elsewhere, military capabilities had simply failed to keep pace with the political requirements imposed by the very nature of Stalinist imperialism.

Faced with this dilemma, the United States and the United Nations were to take the broader view and aim at complete fulfillment of the basic responsibility for repelling aggression and maintaining international peace and security. In so doing they accepted grave military risks but ensured, for the moment at least, the survival of the United Nations and the principles it represented. A great American soldier was to assume responsibility for directing, in the name of all the United Nations, the military effort undertaken in accordance with the requirements of the Charter. Yet the very preeminence of the United States in this enterprise, natural and inevitable as it was, involved a risk of future difficulties. Korea could not be isolated from other areas of the Far East concerning which deep disagreements prevailed within the free world. The Far Eastern policy of the United States had thus far met with little sympathy among this country's friends and allies; and the intensification of the Far Eastern crisis, by precipitating the United States into a position of active leadership, was to accentuate these differences almost beyond endurance. In the very first days of the Korean conflict the United States on its own responsibility took other actions relating to the Far East which were to generate profound disharmony in the months ahead. Thus the Communist aggression, while it produced an encouraging display of solidarity on the vital issue of Korea, simultaneously opened the seams of Allied disunity in other respects and encouraged tendencies that were making for the isolation of the United States and the ultimate disintegration of the free world.

In its larger aspect, the Korean aggression compelled the United States and its allies to undertake a radical revision of the political and military estimates on which they had so far operated. A myriad of new problems arose which must be reserved for detailed consideration in later chapters. The fundamental task of American diplomacy, however, was identical both in the Far Eastern crisis itself and in the world-wide race to regain military strength. This was the task of maintaining the solidarity of the free nations in the face of disruptive influences of unprecedented force. To the United States the outbreak of war in the Far East brought three strong temptations, any one of which might ultimately prove fatal to the non-Soviet world as a whole. One was to take the bit in our teeth and plunge ahead, irrespective of consequences or of the temper of other nations. The second was to entangle ourselves in the Far East while disregarding the other, equally vital elements in the world strategic situation. The third was to overconcentrate on rebuilding military power and neglect the economic, social, and spiritual defenses at which the corrosion of Communism was already eating away day in and day out. These were the capital mistakes which Moscow obviously wanted the United States to make. The success of American policy from June 1950 onward would depend on how skillfully they were avoided.

1. New Birth for the United Nations

The attack in Korea took the United States and the United Nations completely unawares. President Truman was enjoying a "back-porch vacation" in Independence, Missouri; Warren R. Austin, United States Representative to the United Nations,

was in Vermont; John Foster Dulles was in Japan on his way
back from a trip which had taken him as far as the 38th parallel
in Korea; Trygve Lie was planning another visit to Europe in
furtherance of his peace efforts. Yet the machinery of international relations functioned with remarkable efficiency. First
official word of the North Korean attack reached the State Department Saturday evening, June 24, at 9:26 Washington time.
By three o'clock Sunday morning the momentous decision had
been reached to lay the matter before the Security Council, not
as a mere "dispute" endangering international peace and security, but under the more drastic Charter provisions dealing
with "threats to the peace, breaches of the peace, and acts of
aggression." Ernest A. Gross, Deputy Representative to the
United Nations, immediately telephoned Mr. Lie to request an
emergency meeting of the Security Council. At 2:32 Sunday
afternoon the Council came to order at Lake Success, only the
Soviet delegate being absent as usual.[2]

There could be little doubt that the Security Council, as the
United Nations organ primarily responsible for the maintenance of international peace and security, had the right and
obligation to deal with the Korean situation. Although the
Charter debarred the United Nations from intervening in matters which were "essentially within the domestic jurisdiction of
any state," this principle was hardly applicable to Korea and in
any case did not affect enforcement measures taken in consequence of a breach of the peace.[3] Even the Soviet Government,
though it was to take the position that the Korean strife was
essentially a "civil war" provoked by the "Syngman Rhee
clique," made no great effort to contest the Council's jurisdiction.

A more serious legal difficulty arose from the absence of the
Soviet Union from the Council table. As a permanent member
of the Security Council, the U.S.S.R. claimed that decisions

[2] Most of the essential documentation on the early phases of the Korean crisis is
available in *United States Policy in the Korean Crisis* (Department of State
Publication 3922, Washington, 1950) and in *Korea and the United Nations: A
United Nations Bulletin Reprint* (U.N. Publication 1950.I.3, Lake Success, 1950).
[3] Article 2, paragraph 7, of the United Nations Charter.

made in its absence—and in the absence of Communist China —were invalid.[4] This matter had, however, already been thrashed out to the satisfaction of the other members of the Council. Communist China plainly had no claim to supplant Nationalist China as a permanent member unless and until the Security Council itself made a formal determination to that effect. As to the U.S.S.R., there had been many occasions when permanent members, including the Soviet Union, had abstained from voting on substantive matters without any question being raised as to the legality of the action taken. Absence, in the opinion of most of the non-Communist states, was analogous to abstention. Furthermore, the Charter provided that "The Security Council shall be so organized as to be able to function continuously," and stipulated that "Each member of the Security Council shall for this purpose be represented at all times at the seat of the Organization." [5] The U.S.S.R. could hardly violate this basic provision and expect to claim the benefits of other sections of the Charter.

Actually it was the almost providential absence of the U.S.S.R. that enabled the Council to rise to the occasion and discharge its responsibilities, avoiding the protracted wrangles and eventual veto which would certainly have occurred had Mr. Malik put in an appearance. Every delegate present that Sunday afternoon was conscious of the gravity of the situation and the momentous consequences that would flow from their collective decision. For the first time in its history the United Nations faced an open aggression by a force that presumably had behind it all the armed power of the Soviet bloc. No one could foresee the consequences of resistance, but the consequences of acquiescence were all too plain. Failure to act now would undermine the authority of the United Nations for all time to come and destroy the last hope for peace through inter-

[4] This contention was based on article 27, paragraph 3, of the Charter, which reads in part: "Decisions of the Security Council on all other [except procedural] matters shall be made by an affirmative vote of seven members including the concurring votes of the permanent members. . . ."

[5] Article 28, paragraph 1. The U.S. position, accepted by the other members of the Council, was set forth in a State Department release of June 30 (*United States Policy in the Korean Crisis*, 61-63).

national action. Trygve Lie, whose recent activities gave him some right to view the aggression as a personal affront, summed up the general feeling. "The present situation is a serious one and is a threat to international peace," he told the Council. ". . . I consider it the clear duty of the Security Council to take steps necessary to re-establish peace in that area." Some of the delegates were without instructions from their governments, but very few were in any uncertainty about the proper course to take. The only question had been whether the United States itself would grasp the significance of the occasion and provide the necessary leadership.

In this crisis the United States was not found wanting. Mr. Gross briefly addressed the Council, calling attention to the gravity with which his government viewed this "invasion upon a State which the United Nations itself . . . has brought into being." He then tabled a draft resolution designed to provide the basis for any specific action that might subsequently be decided upon. Adopted with only minor amendments, this historic document unequivocally stated that "the armed attack upon the Republic of Korea by forces from North Korea . . . constitutes a breach of the peace." Thus the way was opened for the application of any sanctions determined by the Council under Chapter VII of the Charter.

As immediate measures, the resolution of June 25 (1) called for the immediate cessation of hostilities, and called upon the North Korean authorities to withdraw forthwith their armed forces to the 38th parallel; (2) requested the United Nations Commission on Korea to submit its recommendations and verify the execution of the resolution; and (3) called upon all United Nations members "to render every assistance to the United Nations in the execution of this resolution and to refrain from giving assistance to the North Korean authorities." The resolution was adopted by nine votes in favor to none against.[6] Yugoslavia, half way along the slippery path from membership in

[6] China, Cuba, Ecuador, Egypt, France, India, Norway, the United Kingdom, and the United States voted for the resolution.

the Soviet bloc to association with the West, asked for more detailed investigation of the facts and abstained from voting.

The United Nations had spoken, but it was doubtful that the aggressor would obey. Thus the question remained what concretely could be done to aid the victim and assert the authority of the United Nations. Hastening back to Washington, President Truman conferred late into the evening with his top military and diplomatic advisers. There was the usual underlying conflict between military and political exigencies: on the military side, the absolute insufficiency of trained forces and equipment, and the danger of assuming commitments in an area of secondary strategic import; on the political side, the imperative need to uphold the reputation of the United States as a nation that honored its obligations and stood for law and against aggression. These latter considerations were decisive, for the President and for his civilian and military advisers. Whatever the risks, the United States could not afford to abandon the small Far Eastern nation in its hour of crisis. The Korean National Assembly was even then preparing an appeal to the President and Congress for "timely and effective aid in order to prevent this act of destruction of world peace." Such aid as the United States could give—and it would be very limited at first—would not be withheld.

In the American view, the Security Council resolution of June 25 constituted an authorization of immediate assistance to the Korean Republic. Next day, accordingly, as the North Korean attackers pressed ahead without remission, the President announced that the United States not only would "vigorously support the effort of the Council to terminate this serious breach of the peace," but was already giving a practical demonstration of its attitude by concretely assisting the Republic of Korea. This assistance, he said, was taking the form of "cooperative action of American personnel in Korea, [and] steps taken to expedite and augment assistance of the type being furnished under the Mutual Defense Assistance Program." One day later, at noon on June 27, the President announced:

"I have ordered United States air and sea forces to give the Korean Government troops cover and support."

It was at this point that the latent divergence between United States and United Nations attitudes on the Far East first began to reassert itself. In making known the actions taken in Korea in the name of the Security Council resolution of June 25, the President also announced a series of actions which were unrelated to that resolution and, in fact, conflicted with the known views of some governments that had voted for it. "Communism," said the President, "has passed beyond the use of subversion to conquer independent nations and will now use armed invasion and war. It has defied the orders of the Security Council." In these circumstances, he continued, he had been impelled to take certain actions affecting not only Korea but also Formosa, the Philippines, and Indochina. Formosa was, in effect, to be protected from Communist attack. American forces in the Philippines were to be strengthened, and military assistance to the Philippine Government accelerated. Military assistance to the forces of France and the Associated States in Indochina would likewise be accelerated, and an American military mission would be dispatched to provide close working relations with them.

Apart from its lack of relevance to the immediate problem before the United Nations, the intensification of the military aid program in Southeast Asia was a logical American reaction to the new situation in the Far East. The decisions regarding Formosa, concerning which the United States had thus far maintained a strict "hands-off" policy despite the invasion preparations that were going forward on the Chinese mainland, seemed to require fuller explanation. Under the circumstances now existing, the President asserted, "the occupation of Formosa by Communist forces would be a direct threat to the security of the Pacific area and to United States forces performing their lawful and necessary functions in that area. Accordingly I have ordered the Seventh Fleet to prevent any attack on Formosa. As a corollary of this action I am calling upon the Chinese Government on Formosa to cease all air and sea operations against the mainland. The Seventh Fleet will see that this is done. The determination of the future status of Formosa must await the restoration of security in the Pacific, a peace settlement with Japan, or consideration by the United Nations."

Whatever reasoning underlay this remarkable decision, it was to be a source of inexhaustible complications in the months to come. At one stroke the United States, on grounds of military necessity, had abandoned the policy of nonintervention in China's civil war—authoritatively reaffirmed as recently as January 5—and assumed responsibility for forestalling any action in the one theater of that war where a decisive action remained to be fought. "Neutralization" of Formosa occasioned some criticism by the Nationalist Government, on the somewhat dubious ground that it was thereby prevented from carrying out raids against the Communist-held mainland. The net effect, however, was to guarantee the continuance of Chiang Kai-shek's regime and thus postpone indefinitely the settlement of questions that had already split the United Nations and caused considerable disharmony within the free world. By the ineluctable logic of events the United States would find itself compelled to oppose the Chinese Communists even on matters where it had thus far remained uncommitted, thus aggravating the division among the free nations and permitting the Peking regime to concentrate all its venom on this country alone.

The evaluation of the actual military threat from a Communist-held Formosa belonged to the arcana of military science and was thus largely exempt from critical examination. It was easy to foresee, however, that not many United Nations members would accept the conclusion that action to repel aggression in Korea required action against a supposedly Chinese island a thousand miles away. The Chinese Communists had not attacked in Korea; some governments were not even convinced as yet that Mao Tse-tung took his orders from the Kremlin, despite the suspicious uniformity of North Korean, Soviet, and Chinese Communist propaganda on all Far Eastern matters.

This blanketing of Moscow, Pyongyang, and Peking under the rubric of "Communism" implied a view of Far Eastern affairs that few nations except the United States were ready to accept without considerable reservations.

To people whose thoughts habitually ran in an anti-American groove, the American action looked very much like a manifestation of the reckless "imperialism" they had conditioned themselves to expect. The United States, according to this view, was taking advantage of the Korean crisis to lay hands on Formosa for its own purposes. It was notable in this connection that the President did not even reaffirm China's right to the possession of Formosa, recognition of which had been the basis of all previous American actions with respect to that island.[7] Determination of its future status, he now declared, must await "the restoration of security in the Pacific, a peace settlement with Japan, or consideration by the United Nations." Was the door being opened for some departure from the purposes affirmed at Cairo and Potsdam?

This recognition of foreign objections is not intended to imply that the decision to neutralize Formosa lacked strategic justification. Very few laymen are competent to pronounce final judgment in this matter, on which even specialists are by no means in agreement. Nor is it possible to give due weight to all the conflicting pressures and opinions, professional and political, that must have been brought to bear upon the President during this critical period. As always, vital decisions had to be based on the best estimate of all the factors in the situation that was available at the moment. In view of later events it seems unquestionable that the United States incurred considerable political disadvantages by its decision unilaterally to underwrite the Nationalist position on Formosa. Future historians may be able to determine whether or not these disadvantages were overbalanced by the increased security of our military forces in the Pacific.

The President was doomed to disappointment if he hoped

[7] Cf. especially the statements of the President and Acheson on January 5, in *Department of State Bulletin*, XXII, January 16, 1950, 79-81.

that a new departure in Formosa would contribute to unity on the home front. The Korean aggression altered the subject matter of the political attacks on the administration's Far Eastern policy, but did not perceptibly lessen their intensity. Various new targets for criticism were discovered, notably the Central Intelligence Agency for its failure to predict the North Korean attack, and Secretary of Defense Johnson for various confident assertions of American readiness to meet aggressions launched "at four o'clock in the morning." But the old pressures were maintained. Senator McCarthy went on campaigning against the State Department, and those who had demanded the dimissal of Secretary Acheson because of his Formosa policy now clamored for his removal on the ground that the policy had been reversed.[8]

The problems raised by the new turn in United States policy did not figure extensively in the Security Council when it met on the afternoon of June 27 to consider the deteriorating situation in Korea. Several delegates, including those of France, the United Kingdom, and Nationalist China, applauded the United States for its forthright response to what Great Britain's delegate termed an "unparalleled affront" to the Security Council and the United Nations. The great fact that this country intended to resist aggression for the moment overshadowed everything else.

Nevertheless this second meeting on Korea produced clear evidence of divergent tendencies within the Council, which were to become more marked as the crisis deepened. Some governments fully accepted the United States view that, as Senator Austin said, the United Nations was facing "the gravest crisis in its existence" and the Security Council had a "plain duty . . . to invoke stringent sanctions to restore international peace." Others, without disputing the gravity of the crisis, inclined to caution. "The people of the world are weary of war and rumors of war," said Sir Benegal N. Rau of India, the Council's president, "and we must try our best not to fail them. . . . Even when things appear to be at their worst, there is no need

[8] For Acheson's original interpretation of the Formosa policy, cf. above, pp. 52-53.

for despair." This attitude of determined hopefulness, of reluctance to face what the United States considered stark realities, was to weigh heavily in the future deliberations of the United Nations and provide a continuing check on the more energetic tendencies of American policy.

The immediate task of the Council was to take note of the North Koreans' total disregard for its cease-fire and withdrawal order, and consider how to enforce obedience to its mandate. Reports from the United Nations Commission left no doubt that the attack was going ahead in full force, and that the departure of the Republican government from its capital at Seoul was imminent. In the meantime that government had formally appealed for United Nations as well as United States help. A new resolution was tabled by Mr. Austin to supplement the resolution of June 25. The former resolution had determined the existence of a breach of the peace and called for the restoration of the status quo; this one, according to Mr. Austin, was the "logical next step." It recommended "that the Members of the United Nations furnish such assistance to the Republic of Korea as may be necessary to repel the armed attack and to restore international peace and security in the area."

Communists and other cynics might argue that the new resolution was needed to put the blessing of the United Nations on measures already taken by the United States in the first two days of the crisis. It was a fact that the second resolution was much more explicit than the first in its authorization of concrete aid to the Korean Republic. American diplomats, however, were convinced that the resolution of June 25, with its finding of a breach of the peace, amply warranted the taking of positive steps to repel the aggression. No friendly government questioned this view. Even if the language of the June 25 resolution was somewhat vague, this was a case in which the urgent plight of the victim and the spirit of the Charter took precedence over narrow legalistic interpretation of its individual articles.

Logically, as Mr. Austin said, the resolution of June 27 was the inevitable sequel of the Council's previous action; but it failed to elicit an equal measure of support. Three of the ten nations represented found reasons to withhold immediate approval. The delegate of Yugoslavia urged the Council to eschew a course which, he said, threatened to aggravate the tension between the two power blocs and "may lead us straight into a new world war." He proposed instead that an attempt be made to mediate the conflict. The delegates of Egypt and India pleaded lack of instructions, and the Council recessed until late evening while they vainly tried to establish contact with their governments. Eventually the resolution was adopted by a vote of 7 to 1, with Yugoslavia opposed, Egypt and India not voting, and the U.S.S.R. absent as usual.

The fact that two governments lacked instructions on a matter of such urgency was in itself indicative of serious reservations about the United Nations action, not only in Egypt and India but in many other parts of the Arab-Asian world. The Korean crisis was to emphasize more strongly than ever the special situation of the Arab-Asian countries and their extreme reluctance to commit themselves to a firm position in the East-West struggle. All of these countries, from the Levant States to Indonesia, shared certain basic attitudes that militated against active opposition to Soviet Communism—preoccupation with grievous local problems, distrust of the "imperialist" West, and a sense of remoteness from the Communist menace, fortified in some instances by an overly optimistic appraisal of Communist society and the aims of the Communist leaders.

These were the attitudes on which Soviet political warfare was to concentrate as Moscow's attempt to split the free world gathered momentum. They were also the attitudes that stood out in Egypt's and India's belated reports to the Security Council when it met for the third time on June 30. Egypt would have abstained from voting on the resolution of June 27, said its delegate, (1) because the Korean conflict was "only" a new phase of the already threatening divergences between the Western and Eastern blocs, and (2) because the United Nations had failed in the past to put an end to other aggressions and violations directed against United Nations members—a thinly disguised expression of the resentment over Palestine that still smoldered in the nations of the Arab bloc.[9] For the Arab governments Zionism, not Stalinism, was still the enemy.

India's reply, already made public in New Delhi, had the more statesmanlike but also more equivocal ring associated with the outlook of Prime Minister Jawaharlal Nehru. India, Sir B. N. Rau reported, "accepted" the second resolution, as it had voted for the first, because it was "opposed to any attempt to settle international disputes by resort to aggression." Its general foreign policy, however, was unchanged. "This policy is based on the promotion of world peace and the development of friendly relations with all countries. It remains an independent policy which will continue to be determined solely by India's ideals and objectives. The Government of India earnestly hope that even at this stage it may be possible to put an end to the fighting and to settle the dispute by mediation." In other words, India believed it possible to condemn an act of open aggression by the Eastern bloc but still avoid taking sides in the over-all East-West conflict.

The practical response of United Nations members to the resolution of June 27 underlined once again the existence of differing attitudes within the free world. Though it was obvious that only the United States could give the beleaguered Republic much immediate help, assistance from other United Nations members was important not only to dramatize the collective nature of the enterprise but to help with the actual fighting of a war that was getting more formidable every day. Limited support of the South Korean army such as Washington had originally envisaged was clearly not going to suffice. As early as June 30 the President announced that he was authorizing the Air Force "to conduct missions on specific military targets in Northern Korea wherever militarily necessary," had ordered a naval blockade of the entire Korean coast, and had authorized General MacArthur "to use certain supporting

[9] In the ensuing discussion the Egyptian delegate also drew attention to the Security Council's failure to take action on Egypt's quarrel with Great Britain over the position occupied by the latter under existing treaties.

ground units." [10] Meanwhile the Secretary-General had cabled
to each of the 59 United Nations governments to ask what assistance, if any, each was able to provide. The response was not
spectacular. All except the six Communist governments replied
positively enough to justify the claim that 53 nations were supporting the United Nations action in Korea. But some of the
Arab replies were highly perfunctory, and very few governments found themselves in a position to spare fighting men or
equipment.

In the first weeks of the crisis significant armed assistance,
apart from that of the United States, was provided only by
Great Britain and the older nations of the British Commonwealth. The United Kingdom immediately placed its naval
forces in Japanese waters at the disposal of the United States;
Australia provided two naval vessels and an air fighter squadron; New Zealand ordered two frigates to Korean waters;
Canada presently offered a long-range air transport squadron
to aid in the airlift of troops and supplies across the Pacific. It
was reserved for Nationalist China, least loved of all the
United Nations, to outbid all its fellow governments. Precluded
by the United States Seventh Fleet from attempting military
operations against the mainland, Chiang Kai-shek's regime
dramatically offered the United Nations three divisions, comprising 33,000 experienced ground troops, for use directly in
South Korea—an offer which, however, would have entailed
serious diplomatic complications and was eventually declined
on the ground that, as General MacArthur stated on August 1,
"such action at this time might so seriously jeopardize the defense of Formosa that it would be inadvisable."

As time passed and the gravity of the situation increased, the
same and other nations materially augmented their contributions.
Important units of British, Australian, Turkish, Philippine,
and other ground troops had fought alongside South Korean
and United States forces before the end of the year. Many

[10] For the legal basis of the President's action, which was challenged by Senator
Taft among others, see *Department of State Bulletin*, XXIII, July 31, 1950,
173-178.

other nations contributed specialized units, supplies, and medical aid in accordance with their special capabilities. By September 15, altogether 19 nations had offered or were contributing military aid in some form; 21 others, as well as many in the first group, were providing nonmilitary aid or civilian relief assistance or had signified their readiness to discuss an appropriate contribution.

This high over-all participation was gratifying to believers in the United Nations, but failed to disguise the fact that the Korean war was still being fought essentially by the United States and a very few close associates. This apportionment of burdens and responsibilities was duly noted in several quarters: by Communists who sought to interpret the Korean affair as a war of the United States against Asia; by non-Communist Asians and some Europeans who were predisposed to be critical and suspicious of this country; and by isolation-minded Americans who were congenitally disposed to find fault with this country's friends.

The appearance of a disproportionate American role in the Korean war was unavoidably heightened to some extent as a result of the designation of General MacArthur as United Nations Commander-in-Chief. Under the circumstances this was a logical and indeed inevitable step. There was an obvious need for establishing machinery to coordinate and direct the efforts of United Nations members who had responded to the Security Council's call. A unified command was essential, as Sir Gladwyn Jebb of the United Kingdom told the Council on July 7; and there was, "of course," no question that the United States should be requested to designate the commander. There was equally no question that the United States would designate General MacArthur. Inevitably, however, the appointment would make it more difficult to maintain the distinction between United States and United Nations activities in the Far Eastern theater.

The resolution setting up a unified command in Korea was introduced by Great Britain and France and adopted at the July 7 meeting by 7 votes to 0, with Egypt, India, and Yugoslavia abstaining. It recommended that all members providing military forces and other assistance under the resolutions of June 25 and June 27 should make them available to "a unified command under the United States"; requested the United States "to designate the commander of such forces"; authorized the unified command to display the United Nations flag in operations against the North Korean forces, "concurrently with the flags of the various nations participating"; requested the United States "to provide the Security Council with reports as appropriate on the course of action taken under the unified command"; but did not define further the nature of the unified command's responsibility to the United Nations. General MacArthur's appointment was made known the following day, and the flag of the United Nations was rushed to Tokyo for presentation to the new commander.

Militarily the arrangement proved remarkably effective. Administratively and politically it placed a heavy burden on the man in charge, whose efforts to carry out an almost impossible military assignment had to be combined with the exercise of three distinct kinds of national and international responsibility —as United Nations Commander-in-Chief in Korea, as Supreme Commander for the Allied Powers in Japan, and as Commander-in-Chief of United States Forces in the Far East. The position was one to tax the patience and discretion of angels, and was not made easier by the fact that General MacArthur held strong individual views on Far Eastern problems, was accustomed to wide latitude in the discharge of his responsibilities, and was an object of special veneration to American advocates of a "stronger" Far Eastern policy.

Contacts between General MacArthur's headquarters and the Security Council were maintained through the United States representative to the United Nations, another logical arrangement which, however, tended to limit the growth of mutual understanding between the United Nations and its Supreme Commander. Even within the American chain of command the Tokyo headquarters occupied a somewhat anomalous position, being unused to close direction by any Washington authority.

The arrangement dictated by circumstances was thus one that could produce all kinds of complications if the war were protracted or threatened to spread to other areas of the Far East. Under such circumstances, controversies about the personal role of General MacArthur would tend to exacerbate the impatience of some United Nations members with the United States and the impatience of some Americans with the United Nations.

Meanwhile it was becoming quite evident that a major military campaign would be required if there was to be any hope of carrying out the Security Council's directive to repel the armed attack and restore international peace and security in Korea. An insolent message to the Secretary-General showed that the North Korean "Democratic People's Republic" had no intention of heeding the Security Council's order or even recognizing its legality. While the diplomats were improvising at Lake Success, the well-trained, well-equipped, and well-indoctrinated North Korean forces had continued to exploit the advantages of surprise, superior preparation, and favorable terrain and weather. Seoul, the South Korean capital, had fallen on June 28, and Red tank columns and amphibious troops were already moving against the very heart of Republican territory. Apparently the North Koreans aimed at overrunning the entire peninsula before any substantial United Nations forces could be brought to the aid of the beaten, bewildered Republican army. They had an excellent chance of doing so unless the United Nations build-up was exceptionally rapid—or unless their masters in the Kremlin could somehow be persuaded to call off the campaign.

2. Mediation Fails

Why the Kremlin allowed the Korean aggression to occur in the midst of its own boycott at Lake Success is one of the more intriguing mysteries in the history of the Politburo's operations. It is an incontestable fact that the prompt and effective response of the Security Council was made possible only by the absence of Mr. Malik from the Council table. Had a Soviet representative gone to Lake Success on June 25 and June 27, it was inconceivable that he would have refrained from vetoing the historic resolutions adopted on those two afternoons. Failure to sabotage the Council's efforts seemed, at the very least, like a major tactical error on the part of the Soviet Union. It strengthened some observers in the belief that Premier Kim Il Sung's regime had ordered the invasion on its own responsibility and without prior approval from the Kremlin.

However that might be, events soon made it clear that Moscow, for the moment at least, was backing the aggressor to the hilt. The first Soviet press comments on the Korean situation repeated the North Korean fiction that Pyongyang was engaged in repelling a "surprise attack" by the South Korean "puppet government"—a seemingly untenable interpretation of the known facts, but one to which the Soviet Union and its allies were to adhere unwaveringly through the months to come.

A more detailed statement of the Soviet position was elicited by a direct diplomatic approach on the part of the United States. On June 27 Ambassador Alan S. Kirk, acting on instructions from Washington, presented a stiff note of inquiry at the Kremlin. Recalling the absence of the Soviet representative from the first meeting of the Security Council, the United States bluntly requested an assurance—"in view of the universally known fact of the close relations between the U.S.S.R. and the North Korean regime"—that the U.S.S.R. "disavows responsibility for this unprovoked and unwarranted attack, and . . . will use its influence with the North Korean authorities to withdraw their invading forces immediately." [11]

As was presumably expected, the Soviet reply was negative in all respects. Responsibility for the events in Korea, it said, rested not upon Pyongyang but "upon the South Korean authorities and . . . those who stand behind their back." Far from intervening in the manner of the United States, the U.S.S.R. remained firmly opposed to "interference by foreign powers in

[11] *United States Policy in the Korean Crisis,* 63-64. "Union of Soviet Socialist Republics" is spelled out in the original.

the internal affairs of Korea." For good measure the Kremlin restated its view that the situation regarding Chinese representation in the Security Council precluded Soviet attendance and deprived the Council's decisions of legal force.[12]

The full significance of these contentions was revealed five days later, on July 4, when Soviet Deputy Foreign Minister A. A. Gromyko issued a lengthy statement presenting the official Soviet view on all aspects of the Korean crisis.[13] This key declaration deserves rather full analysis because it was to provide the basis for all phases of Soviet-Communist political warfare in the Far East during the balance of the year. It illustrated once again the skill with which Soviet propagandists could build up a consistent and even convincing case by adapting truth, half-truth, and outright falsehood to the requirements of a preconceived political idea. And it revealed the nature of this idea beyond any possibility of doubt. For Moscow and for world Communism, the essential fact in the Far Eastern crisis was the armed intervention allegedly perpetrated by the United States against the interests of the people of Korea and of all Asia. "The United States Government," said Gromyko, "has committed a hostile act against peace, and . . . bears the responsibility for the consequences of the armed aggression it has undertaken."

This fundamental point was driven home from various angles. First, Gromyko asserted, the actual events in Korea had been touched off by a "provocative attack" by South Korean troops, in accordance with a "premeditated plan" which had been "blurted out from time to time by Syngman Rhee himself as well as by other representatives of the South Korean authorities." The signal for attack, he strongly hinted, had been given by John Foster Dulles when he visited South Korea following the Tokyo conferences with General MacArthur in June. After the initial South Korean defeats, Gromyko went on, the United States had resorted to open intervention with air, naval, and

[12] Soviet note, June 29, *ibid.*, 64.
[13] "Statement of Deputy Foreign Minister A. A. Gromyko on American Armed Intervention in Korea," *USSR Information Bulletin*, X, July 28, 1950, 420-423.

ground forces; thus it "passed over from a policy of preparing aggression to outright acts of aggression . . . demonstrating that, far from seeking to consolidate peace, it is on the contrary an enemy of peace."

Second, Gromyko demolished to his own satisfaction the claim that this American "armed intervention against Korea" was undertaken on the authorization of the Security Council. Not only was the American action begun *before* the resolution of June 27, he urged, but that resolution itself was adopted by a "gross violation" of the United Nations Charter. The absence of the U.S.S.R. and the "legitimate representative of China"—owing to "the United States Government's hostile attitude toward the Chinese people"—deprived the resolution of any legal force; all the more so because, as Gromyko somewhat inconsistently asserted, the Korean affair was "a matter of internal conflict between two groups of one State," and hence allegedly outside the jurisdiction of the United Nations in any case. "Gross pressure" by the United States, he said, had converted the United Nations into "a kind of branch of the State Department . . . a tool utilized by the ruling circles of the USA for unleashing war."

Having disposed of the Security Council resolution as "a hostile act against peace," Gromyko went on to vent Moscow's irritation against Trygve Lie, whose quest for peace had been so convenient to the Kremlin only a few weeks before. Far from fulfilling his duties as Secretary-General, said the former Soviet representative at the United Nations, Lie had "obsequiously helped the United States Government and other members of the Security Council grossly to violate the Charter." Thus he had shown that he was concerned "not so much with strengthening the United Nations organization and with promoting peace, as with helping the ruling circles of the USA to carry out their aggressive plans in respect to Korea." This comment was a fair sample of the implacable hatred that pursued any individual whose independence had destroyed his possible usefulness to the Kremlin.

Gromyko's third major point concerned "the real aims of

American armed intervention in Korea." These, he said, were (1) "to lay hands not only on South but also on North Korea," and (2) by "open war against the Korean people . . . forcibly to establish in Korea an anti-popular regime which would allow the ruling circles of the United States to transform that country into their colony and to use Korean territory as a military and strategic springboard in the Far East." This was in many ways the crucial part of the statement, since it compressed into a few sharp phrases everything that could be said about American action which would be most likely to arouse misgivings in Korea itself and still more in other Asian countries.

"The United States has . . . passed from a policy of preparing aggression to direct acts of aggression, simultaneously in a whole number of the countries of Asia," said Gromyko; and to prove it he offered his own interpretation of the actions announced by President Truman the week before. The order to prevent any attack on Formosa meant "the occupation by American military forces of this part of China's territory" and constituted "outright aggression against China"—a contention which was to be heard many times before the year was out. Reinforcement of American contingents in the Philippines was aimed at "intervening in the domestic affairs of the Philippine State and at kindling an internal struggle"; it showed that the United States "continues to consider the Philippines as its colony." Accelerated military aid to the Indochinese states reflected a policy of "kindling war against the people of Viet Nam for the sake of supporting the colonial regime in Indo-China—thereby proving that the United States Government is assuming the role of gendarme of the peoples of Asia."

To round off his indictment, Gromyko drew a historical parallel between the Korean fighting and the American and Russian civil wars, and then proceeded for the first time to hint at possible Soviet terms for ending the war. To anyone familiar with Soviet political terminology these seemed to be poles apart from the United Nations position. The Security Council had called on the members of the United Nations to help the

Korean Republic repel the armed attack and restore international peace and security in the area. Gromyko appeared to be suggesting just the opposite: cessation of United Nations assistance ("American military intervention," as he preferred to call it), and acceptance of the North Korean program for unification of the country.

It was characteristic of Soviet diplomatic methods that the aims of the Soviet Government were presented in the guise of "noninterference in the domestic affairs of other states" and, furthermore, were arbitrarily identified with the real interests and wishes of the people concerned. All Gromyko said was this: "The Soviet Government holds that the Koreans have the same right to organize their internal national affairs according to their wishes in the matter of the unification of the south and the north of Korea into a single national state as that which the North Americans had and exercised in the '60's of the past century, when they united [*sic*] the south and the north of America into a single national state." But, since the North Korean Communists controlled by Moscow were held to be the only qualified interpreters of the Korean national will, it was a legitimate deduction that the U.S.S.R. desired them to have their own way in creating a "united, democratic Korean state" on the approved Communist pattern.[14] This inference was strengthened by Gromyko's demand for removal of the one obstacle to the implementation of North Korean plans. "The United Nations organization," he wound up, "will accomplish its obligations concerning the maintenance of peace only if the Security Council demands the unconditional cessation of the American military intervention and the immediate withdrawal of the American armed forces from Korea." With American forces out, there would be no one to resist the Communization of the entire country.

The diplomatic technique that emerged from the Gromyko proposals was simple but effective. First, in June the North

14 The identification of the North with the interests of progress and national unity, both in Korea and in the United States of the 1860's, was clearly brought out in other sections of the Gromyko statement.

Koreans had offered a political settlement along lines favorable to their own and Soviet aims. When this was rejected, a stronger bargaining position had been seized by invading the Republic of Korea. Now Gromyko renewed the offer to negotiate on something like the original basis, with the overhanging threat of military disaster as an added inducement. Gromyko did not, indeed, describe his pronouncement as a full statement of Soviet demands. In the light of subsequent developments, it was noteworthy that he made no direct reference to the admission of Communist China to the United Nations, which was to become one of the major Russo-Chinese conditions for ending the Korean conflict. From his references to the "illegality" of actions taken by the Security Council in the absence of Communist China and the U.S.S.R., however, it could be inferred that a settlement of this issue would also be regarded as a precondition for liquidating the Korean affair. This was to be made a certainty by events of the next few days.

Neither the tone nor the substance of the Gromyko statement offered a very good basis for a negotiated settlement. Though issued at a time when the cause of the South Koreans and the few American units fighting with them looked all but hopeless, it is questionable whether the Soviet leaders really expected any major government to fall into the trap. Like all such Soviet manifestoes, it was adapted to a variety of purposes: to provide a broad, if spurious, moral and ideological platform for future action; to stake out an advantageous bargaining position against the day when negotiations might become possible; and meanwhile to encourage to the maximum all the weaknesses and divisions in the hostile camp. The relentless concentration on the United States, as the sole instigator of the Korean tragedy and the inveterate enemy of Asia, was of peculiar significance in this regard. Whether or not General MacArthur's command succeeded in retrieving the military situation, the Kremlin would plainly spare no effort to denude this country of foreign sympathy and support. Whatever the United States did, whether it won or lost, would be turned to account in Moscow's grand campaign to alienate us from our friends and extinguish the last sparks of pro-American feeling in the world at large.[15]

The Soviet effort to represent the United States as the real enemy of peace was unintentially abetted to some extent by the attempts of other powers to find a basis on which the U.S.S.R. might still call back the dogs of war and return to the United Nations. Even the shock of the aggression in Korea did not entirely dispel the belief that some accommodation might still be found among the interests of the great powers. The uncompromising stand of the U.S.S.R., by emphasizing the danger of war, made such an accommodation seem more imperative than ever. And, since there was little prospect of a diplomatic retreat by Moscow while its side was winning, attention inevitably focused on grievances the Kremlin was known to be nursing and which might go far to explain its present intransigence.

Everyone knew that the most prominent of these grievances was the refusal of the United Nations to oust the representatives of the "Kuomintang group" and admit Communist China to representation on the Security Council and other United Nations bodies. Since many non-Communists believed that Peking actually was entitled to speak for China at the United Nations, they felt little compunction in advocating a "compromise" on this basis even though they disapproved of the methods the U.S.S.R. had chosen to enforce its demand. Trygve Lie had proposed such an arrangement in the spring, before the Korean aggression; others were to go on proposing it as the only promising road to a peaceful settlement in Korea itself. It was recognized that this approach would involve substantial modifications in the existing policy of the United States; but to governments which disapproved of the American policy in any case it did not seem that this should be an insurmountable obstacle.

[15] One major phase of this campaign, as it was to develop through the summer, was barely hinted at in a critical reference to American "air power up to the 'Flying Fortresses' and jet aircraft attacking the civil population and the peaceful towns of Korea."

Shortly after the outbreak of hostilities in Korea an attempt had been made by the British Government to ascertain the conditions under which Moscow would be prepared to call off its belligerent satellite. No specific proposals were made, and despite a broad hint from Gromyko the British declined to discuss any "deal" involving other issues besides Korea. Although London differed sharply from Washington on the issue of Chinese Communist representation, it shared the view of the United States that the aggression in Korea was a separate issue and would have to be settled independently of what was done about other problems.[16]

A more spectacular attempt to end the conflict was initiated by Prime Minister Nehru of India, who now emerged for the first time as a principal actor on the international stage as well as the most authoritative spokesman of non-Communist opinion in many parts of Asia. Nehru, like Trygve Lie before June 25, was identified with neither of the two power blocs. Much as he deplored the use of violence in human affairs, he continued to believe in the fundamentally good intentions of the Communist rulers in Moscow and especially in Peking. Peace, he felt, was humanity's supreme need, nowhere more so than in his own impoverished India; and such was his confidence in the revolutionary government of China that he believed peace could best be safeguarded by satisfying that government's obvious political aspirations.

Nehru was not insensitive to the evils of aggression. He had "accepted" the Security Council resolution of June 27—though without offering any concrete assistance as yet.[17] But his doubts about Russia did not extend to Communist China, which was supporting the North Korean cause by propaganda but not, apparently, by any active measures. Moreover, they were balanced by strong misgivings about the tendency of Western policies in Asia. "We Asians," Nehru told the Indian parliament on August 3, "are in a better position to know what the people of

[16] Statement of Prime Minister Attlee to the House of Commons, July 20, 1950.
[17] On July 29 India offered to provide the United Nations with a field ambulance unit and, if needed, a small surgical unit from its regular defense forces.

other Asian countries, such as Korea, China and Indochina, really want."

On July 13 Nehru sent personal messages to Premier Stalin and Secretary Acheson, proposing in effect that the Korean problem be settled by admitting Communist China to the Security Council. "India's purpose," he said, "is to localize the conflict and to facilitate an early peaceful settlement by breaking the present deadlock in the Security Council so that representatives of the People's Government of China can take a seat in the Council, the U.S.S.R. can return to it, and, whether within or through informal contacts outside the Council, the U.S.A., the U.S.S.R., and China, with the help and cooperation of other peace-loving nations, can find a basis for terminating the conflict and for a permanent solution of the Korean problem." [18]

Stalin agreed with alacrity. "I welcome your peaceable initiative," he wrote. "I fully share your point of view as regards the expediency of peaceful regulation of the Korean question through the Security Council with the obligatory participation of representatives of the five great Powers, including the People's Government of China." The Soviet Premier added a suggestion of his own: "I believe that for speedy settlement of the Korean question it would be expedient to hear in the Security Council representatives of the Korean people." This innocent-sounding sentence had ominous implications. "Representatives of the Korean people" would certainly include North Korean Communists. North Korean Communists would certainly not travel to Lake Success without demanding new political arrangements in Korea, such as Gromyko had already hinted at. Stalin's answer indicated that he was delighted to use the Korean problem to force Communist China's admission to the Security Council, but it did not mean that he would tamely go back to the *status quo ante* in Korea as the Security Council

[18] The published documents on this episode are printed in *Department of State Bulletin*, XXIII, July 31, 1950, 170-171, and in *USSR Information Bulletin*, X, July 28, 1950, 419. "Union of Soviet Socialist Republics" and "United States of America" are spelled out in the originals.

had demanded. Nehru, nevertheless, found the reply "prompt and encouraging."

In Washington Nehru's message caused understandable annoyance. This was Trygve Lie's program all over again, with the added fault that the United States was now being asked to buy off a Communist aggression already under way. To accept Nehru's proposal, with or without Stalin's amendment, would simply encourage new acts of aggression whenever Moscow or Peking had new demands to make. It would also mean selling out Nationalist China on grounds of pure expediency, an undignified procedure which in any case would have been next to impossible in the existing temper of American opinion. Six or eight months earlier a case might have been made for complete disassociation from Chiang Kai-shek and accommodation with the Communists; but the United States was now "stuck" with Chiang and his island stronghold of Formosa, and there was no honorable or politically feasible way to get rid of them.

Yet to reject a proposal that Stalin and many others had pronounced reasonable would be to incur some of the moral onus for continuing the war—a burden that ought properly to belong only to the Soviet Union and its Korean satellite. Such projects as Nehru's not only put the United States in an uncomfortable position before world opinion but also distracted attention from the central issue of aggression. Thus they interfered with the task of maintaining the alignment of free nations which had condemned the aggression and undertaken to support the United Nations action in Korea.

The American reply, dispatched on July 18, tried to overcome these handicaps and put the Far Eastern problem into what the United States Government considered the correct perspective. "A breach of the peace or an act of aggression," Acheson wrote, embedding his answer in eight paragraphs of deferential platitudes, "is the most serious matter with which the United Nations can be confronted. We do not believe that the termination of the aggression from northern Korea can be contingent upon the determination of other questions which are currently before the United Nations. . . . In our opinion, the decision between competing claimant governments for China's seat in the United Nations is one which must be reached by the United Nations on its merits. It is a question on which there is at present a wide diversity of views. . . . I know you will agree that the decision should not be dictated by an unlawful aggression or by any other conduct which would subject the United Nations to coercion and duress." Nehru replied with some acerbity that his proposal had been made "on its merits" and that he did "not think that the admission of China now would be an encouragement of aggression."

There were further, unpublished exchanges, which betrayed some irritation on both sides but failed to alter anyone's position. The net effect of the Indian mediation effort was to confirm the basic divergence between American views and those of a government which, not altogether unwarrantably, claimed to speak for the whole of non-Communist Asia. Nehru continued to give nominal support to the principles of the two Security Council resolutions, but did not relinquish his hope of engineering a settlement on a larger pattern. Meanwhile the Indian delegation at Lake Success did what it could to limit the scope of United Nations action in Korea, minimize the risks of the conflict's spreading to other areas, and hold open the door to peaceful adjustment whenever a favorable opportunity might present itself.

This course of action made India a rallying point for other nations with roughly similar views on the Far Eastern crisis. American leadership of the free world, virtually unchallenged while the issue was simply one of resistance to aggression, was weakened to a potentially dangerous extent by the intrusion of these other issues on which the United States position had comparatively little international support. This was not because India or any other non-Communist country was consciously playing the Soviet game. They simply placed a different evaluation on the various factors in the world crisis. The position the United States had taken up in regard to China was one with which they could not sympathize, and which they feared might precipitate a major war. To them the prospect of such a war was infinitely more alarming than was the prospect of a diplomatic retreat by the United States.

The United States was undoubtedly right in contending that no real solution could be arrived at by "appeasing" Moscow and Peking, though there was room for argument about where diplomacy left off and "appeasement" began. In practice, every suggestion favorable to Communist China was to be turned down in Washington on the unchallengeable ground that acceptance of the Communist demands would be tantamount to the rewarding of aggression. Yet it was ironical, to say the least, that the United States was forced to invoke this principle in defense of policies which were deplored by many of its best friends. Whether or not the American ground in China was wisely chosen in the first place, it is undeniable that American diplomacy in the second half of 1950 was severely handicapped by the necessity of maintaining it. This country's unwillingness to consider any modification of its China policy halted all mediation efforts in their tracks, allowed world Communism to indulge in veritable orgies of anti-American propaganda, and inhibited the maintenance of a solid front of free nations against the real disturbers of the peace.

3. Mr. Malik Walks Back

The theory is widely held that the Soviet Government failed to anticipate the serious resistance offered to the North Korean aggressors by United States and other United Nations forces. If so, the error was natural enough. To judge by all previous indications, including the speech of January 12 by the Secretary of State, Korea was an area that lay beyond the effective range of American military power, one where the free nations could do little but wring their hands while one of their number was devoured.

Despite its tremendous moral effect throughout the free world, the prompt intervention of the United Nations under American encouragement did not immediately offset the overwhelming military advantage of the North Korean army.

Fighting with skill, savagery, and a total disregard for casualties, Communist troops repeatedly outflanked the light United States and South Korean holding forces, who fought stubborn delaying actions but were compelled to fall back steadily southward and eastward notwithstanding the complete United Nations control of the air. By late July the Korean Government and the United Nations had been pressed back into an area of roughly 10,000 square miles in the southeast corner of the peninsula, including the temporary South Korean capital of Taegu and the important port of Pusan. Complete expulsion seemed a strong possibility; at best, it appeared, the United Nations would have to face a protracted struggle through the fall and winter.

But meanwhile the balance was gradually shifting as new units became available to General MacArthur's command. Pusan was not only a potential evacuation port but also the main point of entry for the build-up of United Nations strength. American occupation troops were moved in from Japan, despite risk of possible disorder in that country; other Army and Marine contingents, together with much equipment, were shipped or flown directly from the United States. While the men already in the field traded space for time, a secure base was being established in southern Korea. As early as July 19, General MacArthur could report to the President that ultimate victory was assured. "With the deployment in Korea of major elements of the Eighth Army [from Japan] now accomplished, the first phase of the campaign has ended and with it the chance for victory by the North Korean forces. . . . Our strength will continually increase while that of the enemy will relatively decrease. . . . He has had his great chance but failed to exploit it. . . ."

No one can say definitely how this altered military outlook affected official thinking in Moscow and Peking. Even if the reaction was one of unmixed astonishment, however, it is unlikely that the Kremlin found itself at a loss even for a moment. North Koreans, after all, were expendable, and their misfortunes did not directly engage the position of the Soviet

Union. Soviet strategy always allowed a wide margin for possible miscalculations and tactical readjustments. Communist propaganda was well adapted to camouflage such shifts and squeeze advantages even from defeat. In the case of Korea there was still plenty of time to retrieve the situation; if needed, the whole manpower of continental China was available for that purpose, and there were already preliminary signs of the vast redeployment of the Chinese Communist armies that was to preface their open intervention late in October. In the meantime the protraction of military operations offered a continuing opportunity to further the moral isolation of the United States by pillorying this country as the ruthless enemy of Asia and of world peace.

This opportunity, rather than any sense of having incurred a major defeat, seems to have been primarily responsible for the Soviet Government's decision to call off its boycott of the United Nations, resuming the place in the Security Council which Mr. Malik had vacated on January 13. In the regular order of succession, Malik was slated to preside over the Council during the month of August; and on July 27 he laconically advised the Secretary-General that he would assume the presidency as scheduled and call a meeting for August 1. The two-point provisional agenda he submitted gave a foretaste of the line he would pursue. Instead of "Complaint of aggression upon the Republic of Korea," the realistic title under which the Security Council had been dealing with the one urgent issue before it, he proposed the speciously neutral language, "Peaceful settlement of the Korean question." And ahead of Korea he placed another item which had been the stock in trade of Soviet political warfare all through the year: "Recognition of the representative of the Central People's [Communist] Government of China as the representative of China."

One matter of urgent unfinished business was disposed of by the Security Council on July 31, the day before Malik's return, in order to obviate a likely Soviet veto. United Nations quarters were seriously concerned over the vast material damage and human suffering occasioned by even one month of hostilities in Korea. John M. Chang, Korean Ambassador to the United States, told the Council that over a million persons had been driven from their homes and were concentrated in an area where food, clothing, shelter, and medical care were gravely deficient. Hardship and want obviously would increase as the fighting continued and cold weather approached. Thus, on the proposal of France, Norway, and the United Kingdom, warmly supported by the United States, the Council adopted a resolution asking the Unified Command to determine requirements for civilian relief and support in Korea and to supervise their administration in the field. Other United Nations and related organs, including the Secretariat, the Economic and Social Council, the specialized agencies, and nongovernmental organizations, were requested to provide assistance as appropriate.

In effect this resolution provided authority to coordinate relief activities on the same basis as military contributions placed at the disposal of the Unified Command. Though it would make for efficiency in relief operations, it could not save the Korean people from the devastation of their country under the scourge of war. The growing destruction and mounting ferocity of the struggle, in which Koreans of both sides indulged in startling barbarities, were threatening to spoil the great page of history which the Security Council had started to write on June 25. Some of this disillusionment and distress was beginning to find an outlet in criticism of the United States and its leadership in the Korean campaign. Thanks to American air supremacy, and given the urgent necessity to bomb the North Koreans' communications and supply centers, General MacArthur's headquarters exercised a monopoly on destruction from the skies—a fact which the enemies and even the friendly critics of this country were not slow to publicize. As the war went on, people in all countries began to ask themselves whether the principle being upheld by the United States in Korea was worth the price that was being paid for it.

This illogical but very human reaction created precisely the kind of atmosphere in which Soviet representatives could most effectively explode their well-laid propaganda charges. Mr.

Malik, when he reentered the Council chamber at Lake Success on August 1, obviously was prepared to make the most of it. Never in the history of the United Nations had the Soviet Union commanded so large and expectant an audience. Over 20,000 persons had made application for the few available admission tickets; most of these, and many others, would follow the proceedings by radio and television. As always, however, Soviet tactics raised a question whether the Russians were not overacting their role and thus defeating their own ends. Mr. Malik's ferocious appearance on the television screen certainly made few new friends for the Soviet Union in this country. In other parts of the world, especially in Asia, his month-long diatribe against the United States and the "reactionary Kuomintang group" may have carried more weight. It is difficult to escape the conclusion that his performance accentuated the trend toward dissociation from the United States which had already begun to crystallize in the policy of the Indian Government and was to become more noticeable as the Communist shadow lengthened over the Far East.

Space is lacking for a detailed account of the 14 meetings of the Security Council which took place under Malik's presidency during the month of August, and of the further course of debate under Sir Gladwyn Jebb of the United Kingdom during the first half of September. Much of the drama, the tension, and the parliamentary learning and ingenuity displayed by the delegates is preserved in the Council's official records. But the chief significance of these sessions was not to be found in the procedural issues around which much of the debate technically revolved. The Soviet strategy was to turn the Security Council into an international court for the trial of the Far Eastern policy of the United States. Malik was prosecuting attorney; Ambassador Austin, ably seconded by Sir Gladwyn Jebb and by Jean Chauvel of France, was chief counsel for the defense. Judge and jury were the peoples of the world.

The articles of the indictment were contained in Gromyko's statement of July 4. The prosecutor had only to repeat them interminably, embroider and expand upon them, and docu-

ment them with his own interpretation of contemporary Far
Eastern events. The strategy of the defense likewise offered
few essential novelties. Finding itself enmeshed in a network
of falsehood and misrepresentation, the United States was reduced for the most part to refuting specific accusations, pointing out the rationale of its own actions and the irreproachabil-
ity of its motives, and trying to shift the burden of guilt back
where it belonged. Ambassador Austin performed this task
with energy but was handicapped by the necessity of defending
a line of policy that others besides the Communists found questionable. Logically and legally the American position on Korea
was impeccable. The difficulty was that the methods of the
prosecution had nothing to do with logic or legality and treated
Korea almost as a side issue.

Certain consistent tactical aims were visible through the
clouds of rhetoric. So far as possible the United States was
concerned to limit discussion to the vital matters already before the Security Council in connection with the Korean aggression. The U.S.S.R., on the contrary, sought by every means
to extend the scope of debate and subordinate the Korean situation to the broader picture of Far Eastern developments. Mr.
Malik's first move was an attempt to pick up the issue of Chinese Communist representation where it had been dropped in
January. With complete disregard for the Security Council's
rules of procedure, he opened the August 1 meeting by ruling
from the chair that the representative of Nationalist China was
disqualified from participating in further meetings of the
Council. After this highhanded act had been voided by a vote
of 3-8 [19] the better part of three meetings was devoted to beating down further attempts by the chairman to have the question of Chinese representation considered before the Council
resumed its work on Korea.[20]

[19] India, Yugoslavia, and the U.S.S.R. voted to uphold the chairman's ruling;
China, Cuba, Ecuador, Egypt, France, Norway, the U.K., and the U.S. voted
against it.
[20] The U.S. proposal to continue discussion of the Korean item in its original
formulation was eventually adopted on August 3 by 8-1 with 2 abstentions (India
and Yugoslavia).

Two draft resolutions on the Korean question were before the Council. The United States had introduced a proposal condemning the North Korean authorities for their continued defiance of the United Nations and calling upon all states (1) to use their influence with the North Koreans to cease their defiance, and (2) to refrain from assisting and encouraging them or from taking any action that might lead to the spread of the conflict. This proposal the U.S.S.R. now countered with a draft resolution calling for (1) a hearing of the Chinese Communists and "the representatives of the Korean people" on the Korean question, and (2) the ending of hostilities and the withdrawal of "foreign troops" from Korea.

At last the issue was fairly joined; but before it could be debated another procedural question had to be dealt with. Hitherto Dr. Chang, as representative of the Korean Republic, had sat at the Council table whenever Korean issues were under discussion. The Soviet chairman, however, refused to continue this practice unless the North Korean regime was also represented. Seven meetings were given over largely to debating this point. It was not settled until September 1, when Malik yielded the chair to his British equivalent and Dr. Chang was permitted to resume his place. Only then did debate on the two Korean resolutions formally get under way, to culminate on September 6 in a Soviet veto (the forty-fourth) of the American resolution and a decisive rejection of the Soviet counterproposal.[21]

In the meantime the U.S.S.R. had introduced (on August 8) a subsidary proposal concerned with what it called the "inhuman, barbarous bombing by the American Air Force of the peaceful population, towns, and populated areas in Korea," and asking the Council to call on the United States to desist from such practices. This resolution had also been held up in the procedural log jam and was not debated until September 7. Though concerned by the ever-growing destruction taking place

[21] The vote on the U.S. resolution was 9 in favor, 1 opposed (U.S.S.R.), and 1 abstention (Yugoslavia). Both Yugoslavia and Egypt abstained on the Soviet resolution, which was rejected by a vote of 1-8.

in Korea, most delegates were unimpressed by the mass of un-
verifiable anti-American "evidence" produced by Malik from
North Korean and other Communist sources, and refused to be
diverted from the central issue of responsibility for the aggression. Nine delegates voted against the resolution, and Yugoslavia abstained as it had consistently done since the beginning
of the crisis.

These were matters on which the majority of free governments could hardly fail to stand with the United States, whatever effect the Soviet delegate's philippics might be having on
the unsophisticated masses at which he directed them. Long
before the Korean resolutions reached a vote, however, the
emphasis of the Soviet attack had shifted to areas where the
solidarity of the free nations was less in evidence. Malik's
continuous harping on the issue of Chinese Communist representation was not designed merely to save Russia's face or
curry favor with the Peking regime. It was designed to extract
the last drop of poison from a matter on which American views
were still opposed by such influential governments as those of
Great Britain and India, to say nothing of Yugoslavia and of
various other United Nations members which were not represented on the Security Council. As summer advanced, additional
aspects of the China problem were brought into play in a manner that unmistakably revealed the Soviet view of China as the
rock that could split the free world.

The new American policy toward Formosa offered exceptional opportunities to forward this design. Militarily the protection of Formosa by the Seventh Fleet was a serious obstacle
to Communist plans for its conquest; by September the preparations for its invasion had been discontinued in favor of a
marked build-up of Chinese forces in Manchuria, the back door
to the Korean theater of war. Politically, however, American
intervention not only raised Chinese Communist fury to a new
pitch but was causing widening circles of dissatisfaction and
distrust in the free world. Although the President had gone
out of his way to assure the world that this country had no

selfish designs on Formosa,[22] each new American action in reference to that island deepened the feeling that the United States was pursuing aims far removed from those of the United Nations. The more prominently these actions could be played up by Soviet propaganda, the greater would be the strain on the concert of free nations resisting aggression in Korea.

For the United States, avoidance of the political pitfalls in this situation was made more difficult by the effects of the domestic conflict over Far Eastern policy, the anxiety of the State Department to avoid further charges of "softness" toward Communist China, and the tendency of military considerations to predominate in a war situation such as now prevailed in the far Pacific. General MacArthur, long-time advocate of a vigorous opposition to Asiatic Communism, had become for all practical purposes the arbiter of American action in the Far East. His immense personal prestige, his ill-defined sphere of responsibility, and his unique grasp of local military requirements were three powerful obstacles to effective control of Far Eastern policy from Washington. A succession of high-level emissaries—including, in October, the President of the United States himself—crossed the Pacific to confer with General MacArthur; yet even such drastic efforts failed to reconcile completely the differing views of the Supreme Commander, the United States Government, and the other non-Communist members of the United Nations.

The widespread concern generated by a visit of General MacArthur to Chiang Kai-shek on Formosa at the end of July provided a foretaste of the difficulties this country faced in

[22] The following statement was included in the President's message to Congress on July 19: "In order that there may be no doubt in any quarter about our intentions regarding Formosa, I wish to state that the United States has no territorial ambitions whatever concerning that island, nor do we seek for ourselves any special position or privilege on Formosa. The present military neutralization of Formosa is without prejudice to political questions affecting that island. Our desire is that Formosa not become embroiled in hostilities disturbing to the peace of the Pacific and that all questions affecting Formosa be settled by peaceful means as envisaged in the Charter of the United Nations. With peace reestablished, even the most complex political questions are susceptible of solution. In the presence of brutal and unprovoked aggression, however, some of these questions may have to be held in abeyance in the interest of the essential security of all."

attempting to pursue simultaneously a United Nations policy and a national policy in the Far East. The discussions, according to both participants, centered around the problem of coordinating American and Chinese forces for the defense of Formosa. This was obviously a United States rather than a United Nations matter, but one that did not lack embarrassing implications for the United Nations—especially when Chiang Kai-shek went on to speak of general "Sino-American military cooperation" and of final victory in "our struggle against Communist aggression." The display of mutual cordiality between the United Nations Commander and the Nationalist President caused a minor sensation and was followed by an urgent flight to Tokyo by Presidential assistant W. Averell Harriman, diplomatic inquiries in Washington, anxious official denials that the affair had political significance, and an explicit British disclaimer of responsibility for American actions relating to Formosa.[23]

More difficulties of this order were to come, but meanwhile the Peking government and the Soviet Union had taken the official step of bringing the Formosa problem before the Security Council. On August 24 Premier and Foreign Minister Chou En-lai cabled to Malik, as president of the Security Council, a highly tendentious protest against the American actions as "a direct armed aggression on the territory of China, and a total violation of the United Nations Charter." The Security Council, he declared, was obligated "to condemn the United States Government for its criminal act" and "take immediate measures to bring about the complete withdrawal of all the United States armed invading forces from Taiwan [Formosa] and from other territories belonging to China."

For the United States to oppose consideration of this complaint would have run counter to a well-established American policy of favoring the full airing of international controversies in the United Nations. The legal and factual distortions in Chou En-lai's complaint would not be difficult to refute. Moreover, United Nations participation in dealing with Formosa

23 *New York Times*, August 16, 1950.

would relieve the United States of some of the embarrassment it was now carrying alone. "The United States would welcome United Nations consideration of the Formosa problem," was the State Department's immediate rejoinder. "We would approve full United Nations investigation here or on the spot," Ambassador Austin wrote to the Secretary-General. "We believe that United Nations consideration would contribute to a peaceful, rather than a forcible solution of that problem." In the same communication he offered a preliminary rebuttal of the Chinese Communist contentions and reiterated that United States action was "without prejudice to the future political settlement of the status of the island."

Referral of Formosa to the Security Council—which four days later placed the Chinese Communist complaint on its agenda, over the protest of Nationalist China and Cuba—was calculated to reassure those who feared the United States was pursuing egoistic aims in the Pacific. But the soothing effects of this gesture were immediately canceled by an incident which raised doubts in some quarters about the ability of the United States Government to control its own agents. While official Washington was preparing to hand the issue to the United Nations, General MacArthur had been composing a lengthy public statement setting forth the consequences—utterly catastrophic, in his view—of allowing the island to fall into the hands of a "hostile military power." [24] Addressed to the national encampment of the Veterans of Foreign Wars, the document was also made available to newspapers, press associations, and magazines but was not submitted to the author's military or civilian superiors in Washington.

Whatever the merit of the General's strategic opinions—which went far beyond those attributed to the Joint Chiefs of Staff—the tone, manner, and timing of his statement contrasted sharply with the efforts the administration was making to calm suspicions and hold together the common front. On August 26, two days before its scheduled release, President Truman directed the Secretary of Defense to order the message with-

[24] Text *ibid.*, August 29, 1950.

drawn. General MacArthur complied; but it was already too
late to prevent publication. A new national and international
scandal ensued, too sensational to be allayed by the President's
explicit reaffirmation of the American position as presented at
Lake Success.[25] Those who agreed with General MacArthur,
especially in the United States, were merely confirmed in their
dissatisfaction with the official foreign policy and its representatives; those who disagreed with him, especially abroad, became a prey to growing uneasiness. To the first group General
MacArthur became more than ever a demigod incapable of
error; to the second, he was to symbolize the element of rash-
ness that seemed to them to be taking possession of American
foreign policy.

Serious debate on Formosa in the Security Council did not
begin until late September, after the commencement of the
regular session of the General Assembly. In the meantime
Peking and Moscow continued their joint anti-American crusade on a new issue, also growing out of the American leadership in Korea. On August 28 Peking complained to the United
Nations that American aircraft had attacked various nonmilitary objectives on the Manchurian side of the Yalu River, the
international boundary between Korea and China. Next day it
alleged that the violation of Chinese air space had been "consciously and deliberately" repeated, "with malicious intent of
widening the scope of the war and destroying peace." From
the United States, Peking asked compensation and punishment
of the alleged offenders; to the Security Council it suggested
condemnation of this country's "provocative and atrocious action," plus "immediate measures to bring about the complete
withdrawal of all the United States aggression forces from
Korea."

Since the days of the Greek civil war, such unverified accusations had been a standard Communist weapon. It was, however,
impossible to be sure that the Chinese allegations were ficti-
tious. Although United Nations forces had strict orders to keep

[25] Letter from the President to Ambassador Austin (also sent to General Mac-
Arthur) made public August 28, 1950.

away from Chinese and Soviet territory bordering Northern Korea—notwithstanding the fact that they were thereby debarred from interfering with the supply of North Korean forces in the field—there was always the possibility of isolated mistakes. Ambassador Austin later told the Security Council that from evidence in his possession it was possible that one such incident might have occurred. But the American record was clean, and the United States had nothing to lose by submitting it to impartial scrutiny. Austin immediately suggested an on-the-spot investigation by a commission appointed by the Security Council.

This realistic approach had little to recommend it to Chinese or Soviet Communists. Their interest was not in ascertaining the truth but in vilifying the United States, splitting the anti-aggression front, and forcing a way for Communist China to Lake Success. Once again Mr. Malik proposed that a Chinese Communist representative be heard by the Security Council. This proposal seemed hardly necessary for purposes of establishing the facts, but served the more important purpose of putting the United States for once in the minority. Some delegates who were alarmed by the growing bellicosity of the Chinese Communists felt that the presence of a Communist representative would provide opportunities for mollifying the Peking government and perhaps weaning it away from its present dependence on Moscow. When a vote was taken on September 11, only two delegations (Nationalist China and Cuba) joined the United States in opposing the invitation. France, India, Norway, the United Kingdom, and Yugoslavia voted with the U.S.S.R., providing one less than the required seven affirmative votes. Next day the Council voted on the substance of the American proposal for an investigation. France, Norway, and the United Kingdom returned to vote with the United States, but Malik cast the U.S.S.R.'s forty-fifth veto to kill the project. A Soviet draft resolution condemning the United States out of hand was rejected by a vote of 1-8.

One more incident involving aircraft came before the Security Council during this period and lit up for a moment the explosive potentialities of the Far Eastern situation. On September 4 a Soviet twin-engined bomber was shot down by United States fighter planes over the Yellow Sea, somewhere between the west coast of Korea and the Soviet base at Port Arthur. The United Nations command, in a report transmitted to the Security Council by the United States, claimed that the bomber had approached United Nations naval forces "in a hostile manner" and opened fire on the fighter patrol; the U.S.S.R., in a note to the United States, claimed that the plane had been attacked and destroyed "without any justification or excuse" while entering the limits of the Port Arthur naval base.

As with the American plane that was downed in the Baltic in April, the two versions were impossible to reconcile. The chief significance of the incident, once it became clear that Moscow did not intend to treat it as a *casus belli,* lay in the two governments' opposite approaches to a solution. United States representatives in Moscow and Washington steadfastly refused to accept the Soviet protest, contending that the fighter planes in question had been operating under United Nations, not American command, and that any correspondence in the matter should be addressed to the United Nations. The U.S.S.R. just as stubbornly refused to recognize this distinction. For Mr. Malik this was just one more instance in which the United States was using the United Nations to cover what he called its "aggression against the Korean people."

Through the name-calling at Lake Success could occasionally be heard undertones of the war still raging in the Korean peninsula as United Nations forces fell back toward their last defense lines around Pusan. To all appearances the war was not going well for the United Nations. North Korean troops, many of them experienced veterans of the Chinese civil war, still hurled themselves against United Nations positions, infiltrated United Nations lines, and made effective use of the abundant modern equipment, much of it demonstrably Soviet-manufactured, that flowed to them across the Manchurian border. The sea and air superiority of the defending forces was insufficient to turn the scale against an enemy whose preponderance in manpower was still very great. Each of General MacArthur's semimonthly reports to the Security Council wound up with an urgent plea for more United Nations assistance, especially for more ground forces.

These appeals were not unheeded. As early as July 26 Australia, New Zealand, and the United Kingdom offered to provide special combat formations to the United Nations command. Canada followed suit in August. Better still, Thailand and Turkey decided late in July to furnish combat forces of 4,000 and 4,500 respectively. Their action, shortly followed by the Philippines, had particular importance as a demonstration of Asian interest in repelling aggression against another Asian state. Early in September Greece, France, the Netherlands, and Belgium decided to contribute small ground forces to the international army.

These increments, combined with the steady build-up of United States fighting power, would help to turn the tide when the time came to carry out the daring plan that had taken shape in the mind of the United Nations Commander. As August drew into September, the fate of this great international action still hung in suspense. If the military balance could be decisively righted, the United Nations would be immeasurably strengthened and much of the verbal poison spattered upon the United States would lose its potency. Failure in the military sphere would destroy confidence in the United Nations, undermine United States prestige, and leave to the Soviet Union the grateful task of exploiting the free world's disillusionments.

CHAPTER SIX

REMOBILIZATION: THE NORTH ATLANTIC AREA

THE REPERCUSSIONS of the aggression in Korea were immediate and world-wide. No previous event had demonstrated so clearly the incompatibility of Soviet ambitions with the maintenance of a peaceful international order. After June 25 it was more difficult than ever to believe that Soviet expansionism could be held in check unless and until the existing disparity in the strength of the Communist and non-Communist worlds was remedied. The vital question was whether time still remained to create the armed strength which alone might deter the Kremlin from undertaking further and even more dangerous adventures.

The one great fact brought home by the Korean aggression was that, militarily speaking, the free nations of Europe and Asia were living practically on the sufferance of the Soviet Union. The latter, it now appeared, possessed not only a decisive military superiority over its neighbors but also a much greater readiness to exploit this advantage than had been generally assumed. The Atlantic powers, and to a certain extent all the free nations, had counted on their relationship with the United States and its power of retaliation with atomic bombs to discourage the Soviet leaders from taking advantage of their immediate weakness. The Korean attack, and its support by the Soviet Government even after the United States had decided to intervene, suggested that the deterrent effect of our atomic bomb stockpile was less absolute than had been hoped. Not only was the atomic bomb of little use under field conditions such as obtained in Korea, but its availability for retaliation against the U.S.S.R. itself evidently would not prevent that country from proceeding in its own way against nations that lay within reach.

To judge by the Korean experience, the atomic bomb would not be wholly effective as either a political or a military weapon unless it was more adequately correlated with other forms of military strength as part of a global strategic conception. Such a conception, based on the intimate collaboration of ground, sea, and air forces, was in existence only for the North Atlantic area, where its translation into reality was still in the initial stages. Elsewhere nothing comparable existed. Nearly all the countries of the Middle and Far East, whether or not they had been recipients of American or other foreign military aid, bore a family resemblance to Korea in their intrinsic weakness, their strategic isolation, and their exposure to attack by superior forces under Soviet control.

One of the potential lines of action that seemed open to the U.S.S.R., assuming that it was prepared to press its advantages, was to precipitate a whole series of Koreas or "little hot wars" in widely separated areas and under varied conditions of climate and terrain. Such a strategy might drain off the strength of the free world as rapidly as it could be built up, forcing the free nations to fight under adverse conditions of the Kremlin's choosing while leaving the U.S.S.R.'s own strength unimpaired. It was true that this method would so increase the general international tension as to involve a constantly greater danger of general war, and there was no positive evidence as yet that the Kremlin desired such an outcome. But the danger of war was considerable in any case, and the prospect was one that no nation exposed to possible Soviet invasion could view with equanimity. Past policies aimed at preventing further Soviet expansion had proved insufficient. New measures were clearly required if the free nations were to succeed in their basic purpose of discouraging Soviet aggression, and safeguarding their independence if aggression should come.

The attempt to devise remedies for this situation occupied the free nations throughout the latter half of 1950, while the initial United Nations reverses in Korea were converted first

into overwhelming victory, then into threatened disaster as
Communist China threw its weight into the scale. As always,
the leading role devolved upon the United States, whose official policy continued to avoid extremes but sought the rapid
creation of maximum strength at home and abroad within the
framework of established policies. The keynote was sounded in
President Truman's message to Congress on July 19: "The attack on the Republic of Korea gives added urgency to the efforts
of the free nations to increase and unite their common strength
in order to deter a potential aggressor. To be able to accomplish this objective, the free nations must retain a sufficient defensive military strength in being, and, even more important, a
solid basis of economic strength, capable of rapid mobilization
in the event of emergency."

Few could quarrel with this general reasoning, provided rearmament was carried out along lines which were militarily
and politically sound and was properly subordinated to the
abiding aims of the free nations. The concept enunciated by
the President was to become the basis of official action both in
the United States and throughout the North Atlantic community, with considerable indirect effects on the rest of the world
and the United Nations organization. The scope and tempo of
the actions undertaken, however, varied considerably. The
United States began immediately a process of large-scale military and economic remobilization that was meant to serve as an
example to its North Atlantic allies. But the sense of urgency
that inspired this effort was still only partially shared by the
governments of Western Europe. Remobilization in the North
Atlantic area had to start from a position of absolute physical
inferiority which the psychological state of Western Europe
made it doubly difficult to overcome.

The reluctance of Western Europeans to face the full implications of Korea was understandable, if sometimes discouraging. From their point of view the situation could be made to
look almost unbelievably bad. Given the "new" determination
of Soviet policy, the position of Western Europe as a whole
was scarcely more favorable than that of Finland, whose po-

sition within the lion's jaws had forced it to relinquish even
the pretence of an independent foreign policy. Even if present
weaknesses could eventually be overcome, no one could promise that the Soviet Union would refrain from marching into
Western Europe before this happened. While the United
States pressed unremittingly for measures to strengthen Europe's military position, a good many Europeans, especially in
France, began to feel that it was more essential to avoid taking
any action that could provoke the Kremlin. This profound uneasiness, in combination with Western Europe's still incomplete physical and moral recovery from World War II, produced an attitude of hesitancy under American prodding, often
accompanied by a tendency to criticize American policy for allegedly bringing war closer.

The American government continued its steadfast adherence
to the doctrine that the creation of strength was not a step to
war, but the only possible way to safeguard peace. The British,
French, and other European governments officially accepted
this view, though with some reluctance because they had more
to fear from the possible consequences of an armaments race
and were correspondingly anxious to keep the door open for
negotiations with the U.S.S.R. Within this broad frame of
agreement, moreover, the North Atlantic governments both
collectively and individually had to face a host of subsidiary
questions about the proper direction of their activities. For the
United States the central problem was, How much of our effort
should go to the upbuilding of our own national strength, and
how much to that of our friends in Europe and elsewhere in
the free world? All kinds of imponderables would influence
the decisions to be made on this point. Among them would be
differing judgments about the ability and will of individual
free nations to defend themselves, about the real worth of
their friendship to the United States, about the significance of
the moral and contractual obligations the United States had already assumed toward them, and about the deeper affinities,
independent of formal commitment, which bound the free nations in a common destiny.

Remobilization would bring other problems to challenge the wisdom and ingenuity of statesmen. Rearmament might accentuate the danger of Soviet intervention while the West was still relatively defenseless, and yet it would also have to be geared especially to the necessity for parrying sudden thrusts by the U.S.S.R. or its satellites at the most vital points on the Soviet periphery. Emphasis on military requirements would accentuate the tendency to neglect the political, economic, social, and psychological fronts where East-West hostilities were already in full swing. Soviet strategy was aimed at dividing the United States from its friends, and the dangers ahead would put an extra premium on maintaining confidence and good understanding between this and other like-minded countries. They would also put a premium on the exercise in the United States of the same realism and maturity with which this country had risen to the lesser emergencies of 1946, 1947, 1948, and 1949.

The efforts of the North Atlantic countries to grapple with these problems fell into two distinct chronological phases, only the first of which will be fully considered in this chapter. For approximately four months after June 25 the progress of the remobilization effort was governed by conclusions flowing from the North Korean attack and the experience of the United Nations forces confronting the well-trained North Korean army. The first steps toward an accelerated rearmament program coincided with the turn of the tide in Korea and the rapid destruction of the North Korean forces after the United Nations landing at Inchon in September. A totally new phase, requiring a further reassessment of the global politico-military outlook, began with the commitment of large Chinese Communist forces in Korea in November. The North Atlantic reaction to this "new war" was one element in the general year-end crisis which will be considered in the final chapter of this volume.

1. America Sets the Pace

Four characteristics were uppermost in the American response to the new state of affairs created by the Korean attack. One was a general determination to meet the situation with strong and resolute action. The second was the lack of any general consensus about what kinds of action were most appropriate—coupled, perhaps, with some reluctance to examine the situation in its totality before reaching decisions. Third was the continuance, with undiminished bitterness, of the internal political battle that had raged through the first part of the year. The interaction of these three factors helped to produce a fourth which could legitimately be described as a tendency toward extremism or, at any rate, toward impatience with the moderation, balance, and circumspection that had hitherto characterized American postwar foreign policy. This tendency revealed itself in too many ways to be fully described here, but formed a definite element in the world situation and a distinct handicap to efforts to solve emerging problems by the ordinary processes of diplomacy.

A revealing indication of the new trend was the virtual disappearance of belief in the possibility of "normal" relations with the Soviet Union. Although Dr. Harold Stassen was to ventilate at least one more proposal for American-Soviet conversations based on the apparent assumption of Soviet good faith,[1] even Henry A. Wallace no longer professed belief in the pacific intentions of the Kremlin. At the other extreme, advocates of all-out action against the Soviet bloc seemed to gain confidence in their favorite remedies even as the summer setbacks in Korea were revealing the deficiencies of American military preparedness. Exasperation over the immediate difficulties of General MacArthur's command not only gave rise to demands for use of the atomic bomb against the North Ko-

---

[1] See Stassen's letter to Stalin of October 2, urging "that you change the policy of the Soviet Union and move toward world peace and freedom for mankind," which was strongly denounced by *Pravda* on October 20, 1950.

reans but also gave some currency to the idea of a preventive war against Russia itself.

Even certain governmental quarters appeared infected with this notion, which largely ignored the military arguments against one-sided reliance on atomic bombing, the seriously unbalanced condition of the national military establishment, and the profound antiwar feeling which still existed in the United States as well as elsewhere. In August the administration was compelled to disavow a speech by Navy Secretary Francis P. Matthews suggesting "a war to compel cooperation for peace"; and partiality for the same type of thinking was generally understood to have been a factor in the abrupt dismissal of Defense Secretary Johnson in mid-September.[2]

A kindred state of mind was discernible in various other developments of the summer and fall. A stringent Communist-control bill, the Internal Security Act of 1950, which Congress passed over the President's veto on September 22-23, illustrated the growing tendency toward strong but precipitate action in matters affecting foreign relations. Strict enforcement of the provisions barring alien adherents or former adherents of "totalitarian" organizations from the United States caused unnecessary hardship to hundreds of well-disposed foreign visitors during the autumn, and entailed considerable diplomatic complications with the United Nations as well as with governments as anti-Communist as those of republican Italy and fascist Spain.

The somewhat indiscriminate character of this anti-Communist feeling was conducive to an intensification of the special type of political campaign that was being waged against the administration and its foreign policy record. Earlier international crises had usually brought with them some subsidence of domestic quarreling in the interests of a united stand against the external danger. In this, the gravest crisis that had yet arisen since World War II, evidences of such a spirit were

[2] The Matthews speech is printed in *Vital Speeches of the Day*, XVI, September 15, 1950, 730-732. Johnson's resignation, submitted September 12, was ostensibly motivated by the fact that, as he wrote the President, he had made "more enemies than friends" as Secretary of Defense.

hard to find. A good many politicians seemed to see the Korean situation primarily in terms of its effect on the November elections, and to regard the United Nations military reverses chiefly as a source of fresh ammunition to be used against the administration, the State Department, and the Secretary of State. "The blood of our boys in Korea is on his [Acheson's] shoulders, and no one else," Senator Wherry told his colleagues on August 16. Graver insults were in store for General of the Army George C. Marshall, an American uniquely respected the world over, on his appointment to the vacant post of Secretary of Defense.[3]

This belligerent temper inevitably left its imprint both on the new legislation specifically related to the Korean crisis and on the general character of American world policy. The overall effect was a further strengthening of every policy trend that was identifiable with straightforward anti-Communism, and a further weakening of such trends as lacked an obvious anti-Communist character. American policy thus tended to become more "tough" and "realistic," less concerned with psychological and diplomatic subtleties, and less tolerant of hesitation at home or abroad. The nations of the Soviet bloc became the objects of intensified hostility. New and more exacting standards were set for the performance of nations already established in American friendship. Scruples about the rehabilitation of "anti-Communist" nations like Western Germany, Spain, and Japan were thrown to the winds. With them went the last chances of speedy action on such "internationalist" measures as the Genocide Convention and the I.T.O. Charter, which reflected the preoccupations of a more peaceful era.

This general simplification and "toughening up" of American foreign policy certainly could not be ascribed solely to public or political pressure in the United States. Changes of emphasis and concentration on essentials were obvious require-

<hr>

[3] Cf. especially the record of the Senate debate of September 15 on the bill to waive the legal requirement that the post of Secretary of Defense he held by a civilian. A more temperate summation of Republican views on the administration's general foreign policy record was issued by the minority members of the Senate Foreign Relations Committee and reprinted in *New York Times*, August 14, 1950.

ments of the new world situation. It was noticeable, however, that the administration abandoned old objectives and adopted new ones a good deal more slowly than congressional spokesmen seemed to desire. Responsible officials of the executive branch, trained to appreciate the complexities of world affairs and the problems and viewpoints of other nations, knew there were limits this country could not exceed without endangering its own interests and risking the support of its friends. Internationally, the task of the State Department was to urge reluctant foreign government to intensify their mobilization efforts, support American foreign policy, and forget all lesser preoccupations. Domestically it faced an equally difficult assignment in trying to hold American foreign policy on a steady course amid the increasingly violent winds of opinion.

Acceleration of this country's defense preparations was one clear necessity which, for the moment, was subject to little political or technical controversy. The scale of the effort projected in this field was impressive, and it was characteristic of the new temper that administration targets were criticized for being too low rather than too high. In August Congress completed action on the regular $15.5 billion national defense appropriation for 1950–1951; less than a month later it enacted a supplemental appropriation bill carrying an additional $12.6 billion for the defense establishment. Selective Service and other mobilization procedures were tightened with the object of doubling the size of the armed forces, from 1.5 million to roughly 3 million by mid-1951. Concurrently, preliminary steps toward economic mobilization were taken; certain export controls were reimposed, and a National Defense Production Act gave the President new powers over a wide sector of the national economic life. Orders were placed for huge quantities of strategic materials for military production and stockpiling. Only one phase of preparedness was conspicuously neglected: no attempt was being made as yet to prepare the nation for civil defense against atomic attack, except through publicity aimed at forestalling panic and assuring anxious citizens that atomic bombs need not be fatal.

Parallel with the beginnings of the national rearmament effort, the foreign military assistance program was stepped up even more sharply. Even before Congress passed the $1,222.5 million Mutual Defense Assistance appropriation for 1950–1951, the President had requested an additional allocation of $4 billion for the same period—$3,504 million for the North Atlantic area, $193 million for Greece, Turkey, and Iran, and $303 million for Southeast Asia and the Philippines. This allocation reflected the administration's increased concern with the Far East as well as Europe; hitherto the only funds available for that area (except for Korea and the Philippines) had come from two annual appropriations of $75 million each for the general area of China. This request, too, was granted with a minimum of resistance. There were few as yet who questioned the President's assertion that "The security of the United States is inseparably bound up with the survival of the free nations associated with us in the common defense." [4]

Amid the prevailing emphasis on military preparedness, economic assistance legislation tended to suffer, despite the President's reminder that "military power rests on economic strength" and his insistence that "we must continue to give full support to the European Recovery Program." The suggestion that the U.S.S.R. might aim at wrecking Western Europe by throwing its economy out of gear and depressing its living standards aroused comparatively little interest. Considerable attention was, however, devoted to the problem of combating Communism on the political and ideological levels. The Internal Security Act aimed at protecting the United States against Communist subversion and sabotage; other measures were directed at defeating the Communist psychological offensive in foreign countries by letting them know the "truth" about America.

The impulse behind the proposed "campaign of truth," which received a powerful stimulus from the Korean crisis, was

[4] Letter of the President to House Speaker Sam Rayburn, August 1, in *New York Times*, August 2, 1950. The full $4 billion was included in the supplemental appropriation bill (Public Law 843, approved September 27, 1950) which also carried increased funds for the Department of Defense.

a somewhat tardy awakening to the importance of international propaganda in the modern world. The Voice of America and related activities had survived the hostility of the early postwar years, and were now criticized not so much for existing at all as for being too weak and ineffective to gain the world's ear. From underestimating their importance, opinion had swung round to overestimating their potentialities in a world already deafened by propaganda from so many sources.

In July, on the heels of the Korean aggression, the President requested a supplemental appropriation of $89 million for an "expanded campaign of truth"; in September, after a series of congressional cuts and restorations, a total of $79 million (including $15 million in Marshall Plan counterpart funds) was set aside for this purpose. Meanwhile the State Department had set up a "national psychological strategy board," on which the defense agencies were to be represented, "to assess and prepare for the psychological aspects of the cold war." [5] These measures went only a small part of the way toward meeting the views of public opinion specialists, but would enable the Voice of America to expand its coverage and increase its technical efficiency.

What was the message that the expanded Voice would carry to the world? Amid much discussion of administrative and technical problems, this matter had received comparatively little attention, and the answers that were conventionally given seemed to underestimate the difficulty of establishing a common understanding between Americans and other peoples. One eminent group of 28 Senators had written the President, "Let us tell the Russian people that we want to live in peace with them and hope their rulers will not compel us to fight them"; [6] but they could not specify how the Russians were to be convinced. Others, impressed by the difficulty of penetrating the Kremlin's curtain of secrecy, laid more stress on the need to counteract Soviet misrepresentations of America in the outside world. Since Communist untruths were detrimental to the

[5] *Department of State Bulletin*, XXIII, August 28, 1950, 335.
[6] *Ibid.*, September 11, 1950, 424.

United States, they reasoned, knowledge of the truth would necessarily operate in our favor.[7]

A few saw that the problem was deeper—that what was needed was not merely improved mechanical facilities but a vital creed, a dynamic idea capable of galvanizing the world's masses as American democracy had done in earlier decades and as Soviet Marxism was doing now. Soviet publicists laughed at the "truth campaign" idea and held that "imperialists" were simply incapable of generating productive ideas.[8] That the United States was at a real disadvantage in this respect had been conceded by John Foster Dulles in a book that went to the heart of various issues touched upon in this narrative. "There is no use having more and louder Voices of America," he had written early in 1950, "unless we have something to say that is more persuasive than anything yet said. To find that message is, above all, a task for the spiritual leaders of our nation. . . ." [9]

Unquestionably, belief in its professed ideals was one of the qualities with which the free world as a whole seemed insufficiently equipped as it endeavored to gird itself in face of the Korean challenge. No amount of informational activity, moreover, could have much effect unless national policies were kept reasonably in accord with national principles. Aspects of this problem were to exert an inconspicuous but omnipresent influence on the success of American efforts to rally the free nations against the manifest threat of advancing Stalinism.

2. New Look at North Atlantic Defense

European and North Atlantic affairs lost none of their complexity after June 25. A bewildering interplay of aims, opinions, projects, and interests continued to operate at every level

[7] See especially the President's address of April 20, 1950, to the American Society of Newspaper Editors.
[8] B. L. Leontyev, "The Struggle for Peace—Mighty Movement of Modern Times," *Voprosy filosofii*, No. 1, 1950 (*Current Digest of the Soviet Press*, II, No. 38, November 4, 1950, 8).
[9] John Foster Dulles, *War or Peace* (New York, The Macmillan Company, 1950), 271.

of discussion, influencing the policies of nations in ways that were sometimes plain but often obscurely intangible. Few of the problems under debate were strictly new, but some that had seemed acute before now took on the gravity of life and death, while others acquired a fresh wrapping of uncertainty and would remain in a state of suspense until the over-all trend of North Atlantic affairs was clarified.

Still preeminent among the problems of the area was the future relationship of the United States to Europe—a relationship clouded by growing doubts in the weeks following June 25. The revelation of Soviet boldness in the Far East reemphasized Western Europe's own undefended condition and its utter dependence on continuing American support by whatever means were available. Yet the very fact that aggression had come in the Far East made it likely that American attention and resources would be directed increasingly to that theater and away from Europe. Spokesmen for the American administration were at pains to assure Western Europe that its requirements would not be forgotten, provided Western Europe itself contributed its share to the joint effort; but Europeans could not shut their eyes to the indications of a powerful contrary current in American opinion.

To this uneasiness were added the effects of reciprocal irritations on both sides of the Atlantic. If Europeans questioned the reliability of the United States, there were plenty of Americans who doubted the reliability of Europe. Not only were certain countries like France and Italy known to be "riddled" with Communism; even some non-Communists in Western Europe were anything but pro-American. Whatever excuses might be found for the slow pace of European "unification" and military revival, accomplishments to date were certainly unimpressive compared to the targets that had been set. Some Americans openly questioned whether it was wise to go on trying to build up Europe unless Europe showed more determination to defend itself. Not altogether consistently, they also complained at the small number of Europeans who had been sent to fight in Korea. But such expressions, instead of spurring the Europeans to greater effort, seemed only to stimulate the growth of anti-American and "neutralist" tendencies in Europe. This vicious circle held the threat of a serious deterioration in American-European relationships which might offset the constructive achievements of the North Atlantic Treaty Organization.

Officials of the North Atlantic governments were immune to these sentiments in their extreme and irrational forms, but had nevertheless to take them into account in their endeavor to put strength into the empty framework of the North Atlantic alliance. Each government had also to reckon with various hard facts that still limited the effectiveness of their joint endeavors. One such fact was that the United States really had been forced to take on world-wide commitments of tremendous scope, and could not possibly save Europe without maximum effort by the Europeans themselves. Equally plain was the fact that Europe, still painfully struggling back from the catastrophe of World War II, had few idle resources and little physical or psychological energy to spare for a greatly increased defense program. As a result, the dignified meetings of the North Atlantic Treaty Organization were faintly suggestive of encounters between an irresistible force and a set of immovable objects. The United States continually adjured, prodded, and appealed to the European governments to intensify their efforts; the latter, not quite unmoved, still resisted, clung to established policies, and asked for solid proofs that the United States would not leave them in the lurch.

This diplomatic contest revolved mainly about two specific issues. The first concerned the rebuilding of European military establishments and military production, hitherto explicitly subordinated to the needs of the economic recovery program. Everyone recognized that these tasks must now be pushed with greater vigor, but there was a wide gap between American and European ideas of what was necessary and possible. The United States insisted on a maximum effort in Europe itself, to be primed with equipment, machine tools, and other aids under the expanded Mutual Defense Assistance Program. European governments were more interested in preserving their recent economic gains and keeping domestic tax rates and living standards within politically tolerable limits; thus they tended to expect more from the United States and proportionately less from their own peoples.

The second issue was that of the rearmament of Western Germany, which now entered for the first time into the very foreground of official discussions. From a military standpoint, the insufficiency of the prospective North Atlantic Treaty ground forces pointed strongly to a need for letting Western Germany bear a share in the common defense, all the more so if any attempt was to be made to hold the area in case of war and thus deny its communications network and industrial potential to the enemy. In common with the United States, most of the North Atlantic governments recognized the force of these considerations and repressed their misgivings about the ultimate implications of German rearmament—a course which conceivably might provoke drastic retaliation by the U.S.S.R., and in any case threatened to encourage a revival of German militarism and possibly a German attempt to regain the lost territories in the East. Only France held firm in its resistance to rearming the traditional enemy, devising one expedient after another to sidetrack and delay the project.

In its simplest terms the struggle over German rearmament at this stage could be viewed as a duel between the United States and France, with most of Western Europe lukewarmly supporting American views. In reality, however, the issue was enmeshed in a dense tangle of political and technical interests that prevented its being considered in isolation or solely on its own merits. Among the factors involved in any decision on Germany were the form of the "integrated" European or North Atlantic defense organization which would be necessary to quarantine a rearmed Germany, if for no other reason; the methods of reconciling German demands for "equality" and for security against Russia with Western European insistence on security against Germany as well as Russia; and, not least, the readiness of the United States to commit enough forces to Europe to counterbalance the added threat of Russian intervention if Germany were rearmed. Intertwined with these broad issues were others involving German internal politics, the still unsolved relationship between East and West Germany, and the problems of Western Germany's general position in Europe —questions of occupation costs, of a provisional peace settlement, and of German integration into Western Europe through such projects as the Schuman Plan. That Western Germany itself would be willing to participate in the joint defense was generally taken for granted, despite evidences of considerable opposition to rearmament on the part of the West German youth, the Social Democratic opposition, and various other quarters in the Federal Republic.

Closely interrelated as these problems were, there was no single forum available for their discussion and solution. German problems, the special concern of the United States, Great Britain, and France as occupying powers, had thus far been largely outside the purview of the North Atlantic Treaty Organization, while American aid under the Mutual Defense Assistance Program had been handled by direct negotiation between the United States and individual North Atlantic governments. The North Atlantic Treaty Organization itself suffered from a superabundance of committees and planning groups, all built on the principle of the sovereign equality of the treaty partners, which impeded the rapid discharge of business. The council of Foreign Ministers' deputies, set up by the North Atlantic Council in May and chairmaned by Charles M. Spofford of the United States, was to become a useful instrument of intergovernmental contact and coordination, but its authority was limited even within its own field. Thus it served less as a policy-making body than as an indicator of the trend of thought in North Atlantic circles.

The initial meetings of the North Atlantic deputies in late July and August afforded the first clear intimation of the changes in North Atlantic thinking that were taking place as a result of Korean developments.[10] Two points especially stood out in their occasional communiqués. First, the interdependence of rearmament and economic progress was still recognized, but the latter was now definitely relegated to second place. Economic requirements, particularly in the view of the United States, would henceforth be subordinated to the overriding needs of the military program. Second, the concept of "balanced collective forces" which had been approved in May was already being superseded by the pressure of events. Increasing stress was laid on the second adjective, "collective," which was shortly to be replaced by the more far-reaching term "integrated" as the 12 governments edged closer to genuine pooling of their military resources.

The first and all-important task was to accelerate the build-up of allied military strength on the European continent. The problem had been adequately stated by Winston Churchill in the House of Commons on July 27 when he contrasted the 10 unarmored and 2 armored Western European divisions available in Europe with an opposing force of over 80 Soviet divisions, 25 to 30 of which were armored. Existing plans called for increasing the Western divisions in Europe to around 20 in 1951 and 35 in 1954; but it was now clear that the sights would have to be raised.

To start the ball rolling, the United States addressed a formal inquiry to its European partners asking what supplementary contributions to the common defense each was able to make, both through its own efforts and with increased assistance under the American military aid program. Without substantially greater European efforts, American spokesmen implied, Congress would be unlikely to approve increased expenditure for European aid. The replies were indicative of

[10] The fullest documented study of the work of the North Atlantic Treaty Organization and cognate bodies during the second half of 1950 is a series of articles by Wilhelm Cornides and Hermann Volle in *Europa-Archiv*, V, 1950, 3464-3474, 3504-3514, 3576-3593, and VI, 1951, 3655-3676. Further information and documentation is presented in *Chronique de politique étrangère*, III, November 1950, 605-631, and IV, January 1951, 5-41, and in Vera Micheles Dean and Howard C. Gary, "Military and Economic Strength of Western Europe," *Foreign Policy Reports*, XXVI, October 15, 1950, 118-128.

the differing approach of the American and European governments. A considerable augmentation of the various national
forces was proposed, but the main emphasis was laid on the
difficult economic situation of the countries concerned and
their need for very substantial American assistance if they were
to finance any important increase in their defense establishments and military production.

Of the ten European signatories of the North Atlantic
Treaty, it had been evident that only Great Britain and France
could make really substantial contributions to European rearmament in terms of either military forces or economic potential. For both of them, moreover, the task of rearmament
presented problems much more serious than was apparent from
hasty examination of the statistics on their economic recovery.
It was unlikely that any amount of determination and efficiency
would enable either of them to expand their military production significantly without a corresponding reduction in living
standards that were already low, and without encountering
major difficulties of reconversion and readjustment and disturbances of their balance-of-payments situations. Britain's industrial production was far above the 1938 level, but its economy
was fully stretched and there was little margin for further
curtailing personal consumption or slackening production for
export. France, with a less productive economy, faced equally
difficult problems, with the additional handicap of an inadequate tax system that tended to accentuate the burden thrown
on the politically disaffected poorer classes. Its special sensitivity to social disturbances exemplified the dangers that would
be involved in any attempt to build military strength at the expense of popular welfare.

Both the British and French governments nevertheless announced rather far-reaching plans, based on the assumption
that American aid on a large scale would be available in carrying them out. Their adequacy, in terms of the actual military
situation and the state of the two economies, was a matter for
technical debate. Politically, however, they appeared to represent what the British explicitly called an "upper limit." If

American aid was not forthcoming in the expected volume, the targets might not be met; it seemed unlikely that they would be exceeded in any case, barring a complete change in the international climate such as in fact was to occur in November and December.

Great Britain, which was about to demonstrate its seriousness of purpose by raising its conscription period to two years and announcing plans to form three new divisions, offered a program which would increase defense expenditures from 8 percent to 10 percent of the national income. From the previous annual average of £780 million ($2,184 million), the outlay over the next three years would rise to a total of £3,400 million ($9,520 million, later increased to £3,600 million or $10,080 million). This, said the British note, was "the largest program practicable within the period envisaged . . . without restoring the direction of labor, the requisitioning of factories, or embarking on the slow progress [process?] of building and equipping new industrial capacity. . . ." A larger program would be inconsistent with the attainment of economic goals whose importance was still recognized by the United States. Furthermore, "how far it will be possible to progress toward the new and upper limit will depend on the amount of United States assistance forthcoming." [11]

French objectives were stated more concretely. During the next three years, Paris reported, it was planned to modernize and reequip the five divisions of the existing French army and add to them 15 completely new divisions, at an estimated cost of 2 trillion francs ($5.7 billion). Like the British, the French detailed at some length the sacrifices this program would impose on the French people and its heavy dependence on outside financial aid. The French note also reflected the chronic French fear of being left alone on the Continent. The proposed efforts, it said, "would be useless if ground and air forces sufficient to assure the maintenance of peace should not be stationed in Continental Europe. . . . It is necessary that the United States and Great Britain, notably, should participate in the defense

[11] *New York Times*, August 4, 1950.

with a sufficient number of divisions stationed in Continental Europe." [12]

In line with its well-established view that the defense of the North Atlantic area must be regarded as a genuinely collective enterprise, the French Government also seized the opportunity to press once again for the creation of central political and economic organs, a unified military command, and more effective machinery for centralized financing within the North Atlantic Treaty Organization. To the French, close association of the Atlantic powers seemed desirable not only on general grounds but also because it would offer France a larger measure of protection in relation to both the U.S.S.R. and Germany. It would also tend to promote a more efficient use of resources and a more equitable distribution of burdens as between countries with low living standards and national incomes like France and Italy and those with high ones like Canada and the United States.

The other European members of the Atlantic Pact, with the exception of Iceland and Portugal, announced parallel plans for increasing their military expenditures and defense forces within the limits of their smaller capabilities. Belgium and Luxembourg doubled their periods of military service; the Netherlands promised three reserve divisions; Italy proposed to build its army up to the peace treaty limit of 250,000 men (including national police); Norway prepared to embark on a three-year armament program. The economic impact of rearmament on these countries would vary. Italy, in particular, had idle capacity and idle manpower which could be put to good use in a coordinated rearmament effort if raw materials and technical and financial aid were available.

These programs, if tackled with energy and determination, would undoubtedly mean more exertion and rather less comfort for the peoples affected. Yet one had only to add them together to see how far they fell short of providing a counterpoise to the Russian power in Europe. One computation placed at 30 divisions the total ground force that might be available

[12] *Ibid.*, August 8, 1950.

in Western Europe at the end of three years if all the programs were fully carried out. Even if Soviet preparations stood still in the interval, as they certainly would not, it was doubtful that 30 divisions would represent an adequate deterrent force in 1953.

The United States was unwilling to accept these estimates as the last word. At the same time it recognized that its own actions would have great influence on the scale and tempo of European efforts. European governments would not act without a clearer assurance that this country, too, intended to assume a major role in the defense of the Continent. Though the United States had already announced plans to strengthen its Air Force in Great Britain and to augment its Mediterranean Fleet, it had yet to reveal its position on the vital matter of European ground defense. Commitment of additional American ground forces to supplement the two divisions already in Germany and the scattered units in Austria, Trieste, and elsewhere would be the best way of showing that the United States would not be swayed from its determination to keep Western Europe out of enemy hands.

An important assurance in this sense was given by President Truman on September 9, on the eve of a new meeting of the North Atlantic Council. His statement was obviously designed both to allay European doubts and to stimulate greater European efforts. "On the basis of recommendations of the Joint Chiefs of Staff, concurred in by the Secretaries of State and Defense," said the President, "I have today approved substantial increases in the strength of the United States forces to be stationed in Western Europe in the interest of the defense of that area. The extent of these increases and the timing thereof will be worked out in close coordination with our North Atlantic Treaty partners. A basic element in the implementation of this decision is the degree to which our friends match our actions in this regard. Firm programs for the development of their forces will be expected to keep full step with the dispatch of additional United States forces to Europe. Our plans are based on the sincere expectations that our efforts will be met with similar action on their part. . . ."

This statement went far to dispel European misgivings about the intentions of the United States, and made clear that future developments would be based on the principle of mutuality. The difficulty was that for the present the United States, with the best will in the world, had very few troops available to supplement the two divisions already in Europe. It would take time to mobilize and train the men provided for in the new defense legislation, and Europe's needs would have to be very carefully balanced against those of the de facto war in the Far East. At best the presidential statement was more a declaration of intent than an immediate solution. It removed an important psychological barrier, but the concrete difficulties remained.

These difficulties came out clearly in the bilateral discussions the United States was undertaking with individual treaty partners concerning the expansion of their defense programs and the utilization of roughly $4.5 billion provided by the two congressional appropriations for military assistance to North Atlantic Treaty countries in the fiscal year 1950–1951. The amended Mutual Defense Assistance Act authorized the shipment of various kinds of production equipment as well as military items and machine tools, and questions of military production in Europe played a much larger role than the year before. The American objective was to allocate the funds in a way that would yield maximum results in the form of armed strength and military potential, geared to the requirements of the North Atlantic Treaty Organization; the objective of the European participants was to do this in a way that would impair their hard-won economic gains as little as possible. The discussions were complicated by the fact that the rearmament drive was already bringing about a revolutionary transformation in the world economic picture, with as yet unforeseeable effects on prices, costs, balance-of-payments trends, and dollar requirements of the individual European countries.

Only with France was a formal and fairly detailed understanding worked out during the autumn, an obvious priority in view of the fact that France was expected to supply the bulk of the ground forces for European defense and was by far the largest single claimant to American military aid. Early agreement was indispensable if the French were to carry out their plan to raise 20 divisions by 1953. In mid-October the French Defense and Finance ministers came to Washington for conferences with top American officials and secured a promise of up to $2.4 billion in military aid during the fiscal year. A part of this sum was to go to Indochina, which had been given highest priority in distribution of the approximately $500 million in military aid funds available for the Far East. Also included was a preliminary allocation of $200 million to support France's increased military production program.[13]

Arrangements with Great Britain proved more complicated, partly because Britain's gold and dollar position was rapidly improving under the impact of increased raw material purchases in the sterling area. British officials did not feel that this development lessened the need for American support of their military expansion program, which could still be carried out only by withdrawing people, facilities, and materials from productive enterprise. The British estimated that their $10 billion three-year program would require about $1.5 billion in American aid, and they attached importance to having a good part of this amount in "free dollars" which could be spent anywhere in the world. This arrangement, however, was wholly unacceptable to American officials. Put on ice pending a decision on German rearmament, the disagreement helped to explain the coolness toward the United States which was to become evident in some British quarters during the troubled days of November and December.[14]

[13] Communiqué, October 17, in *Department of State Bulletin*, XXIII, October 30, 1950, 704; and *New York Times*, October 18, 1950.
[14] Negotiations between the U.S. and Italy did not commence until early 1951, on the basis of an Italian memorandum of December 19 proposing to raise 12 infantry divisions and two armored brigades and manufacture $400 million worth of military equipment, on the assumption that U.S. aid in both cash and raw materials would be available.

3. The German Stumbling Block

Limitations on the scale of Western European rearmament plans helped to explain a growing concern in North Atlantic circles with the status of Western Germany, which represented an important increment of unused industrial capacity and, perhaps even more important, a potential source of military manpower to help fill the gap between Soviet and Western ground strength. In the United States, Korea had convinced official quarters that the question of West German rearmament must be faced and solved without further delay. To judge by Chancellor Adenauer's frequent allusions to Germany's present insecurity, the Bonn government had reached an identical conclusion. No one professed to desire the reestablishment of a separate German army, a course that would be strongly repugnant to Western European and probably to American and German opinion. But in any case the whole trend of official thinking was away from the idea of separate national forces and in the direction of "integrated" defense. In this framework, American officials reasoned, it should not be impossible to find a way for Germany to take its share of responsibility for the common defense, under conditions that would be militarily sound and politically acceptable both in Germany and in the allied states.

One possible method was suggested in the Council of Europe, whose Consultative Assembly commenced its second regular session at Strasbourg early in August. The presence of an 18-member delegation from the German Federal Republic, signalizing the formal reentry of Western Germany into European political life, underlined the importance of the occasion and of the influence that Germany was destined to exert on the future evolution of Europe. "I am very glad the Germans . . . have come here to share our perils and augment our strength," Winston Churchill told the Assembly on August 11. "They should have been here a year ago. A year has been wasted, but still it is not too late. There is no revival of Europe, no safety or freedom for any of us except to stand together, united and unflinching. I ask this assembly to assure our German friends that we shall hold their safety as sacred as our own."

Although the Statute of the Council of Europe debarred that organization from concerning itself with "national defense" matters, one of the most significant actions taken at this gathering directly involved the defense of Europe, its relation to the defense of the North Atlantic area, and, by implication, the role of Germany. Georges Bidault of France, speaking for many who wished to see Europe endowed with stronger political institutions, proposed the designation of a (Western) European minister of defense; Mr. Churchill, obsessed as always with the insufficiency of current preparations to meet the Russian military threat, called for the immediate creation of a unified European army. The two proposals were amalgamated and on August 11 the Assembly adopted a resolution calling for "the immediate creation of a united European army, under the authority of a European Minister for Defense, subject to proper democratic European control, and acting in full cooperation with the United States and Canada." [15]

The resolutions of the Consultative Assembly had no official force, and this particular recommendation did not look like one that the North Atlantic governments as a group would view with sympathy, though they were to come back to it after some of the difficulties of alternative courses of action had become apparent. For the moment the official trend was toward dealing with the German problem in a North Atlantic rather than a European framework. Definite decisions on Germany were high on the agenda of the American, British, and French Foreign Ministers, who had arranged to meet together and with their colleagues of the North Atlantic Council in New York in mid-September, shortly before the opening of the United Nations General Assembly. The occasion would provide opportunity for a general review of North Atlantic Treaty affairs

[15] The vote was 89 in favor, 5 against (4 Irish representatives and 1 British Laborite), and 27 abstentions (mostly Swedes, British Laborites, and German Social Democrats).

and was expected to result in the establishment of an "integrated" North Atlantic defense force with an American, possibly General of the Army Dwight D. Eisenhower, as its commander. An integrated North Atlantic force, as distinguished from the purely European force envisaged at Strasbourg, would be the logical culmination of previous North Atlantic planning efforts, and the naming of an American commander would further emphasize the solidarity of the United States and Europe in the defense of the entire area.

It is unnecessary to trace in detail the intricate history of the New York negotiations, which passed back and forth between the three Foreign Ministers and the North Atlantic Council and required an urgent summons to the British and French Defense Ministers to come and advise their Foreign Office colleagues. As in past meetings, the decisive factor was the gap between American and French views on the role of Germany. This gap proved to be so wide that the completion of other business had to be deferred. Agreement was reached on the organizational structure of the integrated defense force, but it was doomed to remain largely a blueprint until the differences on Germany were narrowed.

The American proposal, as put forward by Acheson, was to decide then and there on the formation of German military contingents; ten divisions, according to generally accepted report, was the figure suggested. These units would not constitute a German army or require the reestablishment of a German general staff, but would form part of the new "integrated" North Atlantic defense force; and their equipment needs would not be allowed to interfere with the prior requirements of the North Atlantic Treaty countries. But this proposal, though carefully qualified to take account of probable French objections, went far beyond what the French were willing to accept. Mr. Bevin and, more hesitantly, most of the other foreign ministers aligned themselves with the American view; M. Schuman was adamant. Since the United States had already made known its intention of stationing additional ground forces in Europe and its willingness to accept the supreme command of the integrated defense force, it had few inducements left with which to secure acceptance of its proposals.

Thus the "Big Three" got no further than a negative statement that "the re-creation of a German national army would not serve the best interests of Germany or Europe." As to German participation in "an integrated force for the defense of European freedom," they confined themselves to taking note of "sentiments recently expressed in Germany and elsewhere" in favor of such a course, and stated that the problems involved were under study. With its three leading members in disagreement, the North Atlantic Council could do nothing more positive. Its only action in the matter was a request to the North Atlantic Defense Ministers to examine, as a matter of urgency, "the methods by which Germany could most usefully make its contribution" to European defense.[16]

Though unable to agree on a formula for German rearmament, the Big Three did recognize more explicitly than ever before that the security of Germany was related to the security of Europe as a whole, and that some concrete steps were needed to allay the existing sense of insecurity in the Federal Republic—which Chancellor Adenauer lost no opportunity of bringing to their attention. Not only would the three governments "increase and reinforce their forces in Germany," including Western Berlin, said the Foreign Ministers; they would also "treat any attack against the Federal Republic or Berlin from any quarter as an attack upon themselves." This was practically tantamount to admitting Germany to the benefits of the North Atlantic Treaty, without as yet imposing any corresponding obligation on the government of the Federal Republic.

In addition to this guarantee of support in a crisis, the three governments took various steps to bolster the status of the Bonn government in relation to both East and West. As a partial offset to the "outright military units" which had been created in the Soviet zone of Germany, they agreed to authorize

---

[16] Tripartite communiqué, September 19, in *Department of State Bulletin*, XXIII, October 2, 1950, 530-531; North Atlantic Council communiqué, September 27, *ibid.*, October 9, 1950, 588.

the formation in Western Germany of "mobile police formations," organized on a *Land* (state) basis but subject to call by
the federal government in an emergency. In the political and
economic fields they promised a series of readjustments which
would not affect their own position in Germany but would relieve the Bonn government of many of the remaining disabilities connected with the occupation regime. Steps would be
taken to terminate the nominal state of war with Germany; the
Occupation Statute would be amended; the federal government would be enabled to conduct its own foreign relations;
internal controls would be reduced; security restrictions on
German industry would be relaxed—including both those on
shipbuilding and the ceiling on steel production "where this
will facilitate the defense effort of the west." [17]

All of this, as the ministers pointed out, represented "a
major advance toward the progressive return of Germany to
partnership in Western Europe." Its fundamental significance
could be gauged from the reaction of the Soviet Union and its
satellites, which loudly asserted that the tripartite New York
decisions "are another gross violation of obligations which
these Governments assumed under the Potsdam Agreement,
that they contain a threat to peace in Europe and are contrary
to the interests of all peace-loving peoples, including the national interests of the German people." [18]

The other major result of the New York meetings was the
agreement of the North Atlantic Council upon "the establishment, at the earliest possible date, of an integrated force under
centralized command, which shall be adequate to deter aggression and to ensure the defense of Western Europe." Pending
the settlement of technical details, important principles were
laid down to govern the organization and direction of the integrated force. It was to be organized under the North Atlantic
Treaty Organization (not under any "European" authority, as
proposed at Strasbourg), which would be responsible for its

[17] Tripartite communiqué, September 19, cited.
[18] Statement of the Prague conference of Eastern Foreign Ministers, October 21,
in *USSR Information Bulletin*, X, November 7, 1950, 666; cf. below, pp.
408-409.

"political and strategic guidance." For its "higher strategic direction" it would look to the Anglo-French-American Standing Group in Washington. Its Supreme Commander, supported by an international staff, would have "sufficient delegated authority to ensure that national units allocated to his command are organized and trained into an effective integrated force in time of peace as well as in the event of war." Not all the national forces of the treaty powers would be placed under the Supreme Commander, but decisions regarding "the precise character and composition of the forces to be allocated to the integrated force" would be sought from governments at an early date.[19]

In many ways this decision marked the coming of age of the North Atlantic Treaty Organization, founded at Washington just a year earlier. The period of preliminary planning was over; from now on it was a question of putting the plans into effect as rapidly as possible. Much still remained to be done in the way of simplifying the unwielding structure of the organization, strengthening the machinery for coordinating defense production in the 12 treaty countries, and arranging for the absorption or supersession of the Western Union military headquarters already functioning at Fontainebleau. The main task henceforward, however, would be to convert charts and plans into actual military formations equipped with the guns, tanks, planes, and ships they would need to defend the soil of Western Europe.

American officials felt that not much could be accomplished along this line until a decision was reached on the German problem. The North Atlantic Deputies could go to work on some of the production and financial problems of rearmament, but any decisions they might reach would be highly provisional as long as the question of German participation remained in suspense. The New York discussions had made it clear that only France among all the North Atlantic powers still strongly opposed the inclusion of German contingents in an integrated defense force. Even the French, moreover, had seen the writing

[19] North Atlantic Council communiqué, September 27, cited.

on the wall and were now concerned less with blocking German rearmament as such than with devising alternative methods less sharply violative of French instincts. The Germans, of course, had not been present in New York. Chancellor Adenauer had sent a message emphasizing that they would have to be given equal status in any defense program in which they might participate; but they were presumably still expected to fall in with any arrangements the Western powers were able to agree upon.

Seeing the inevitability of accepting some kind of German military units, French officials hoped to minimize the damage in two principal ways. First, they sought to put off the evil day as long as possible—preferably until a strong and well-armed Western force was actually in being, and until French security was further assured by the integration of French and German war-making potential under the Schuman Plan. Second, they were determined that the future German units should be so small, so entirely without operational autonomy, and so completely "integrated" into the larger international force that they could not possible act as a military arm of the German government. The less they resembled the German army of 1870, 1914, or 1940 the less difficult it would be for French opinion to accept them.

Acheson had suggested the formation of ten German divisions, to be placed under the operational control of the North Atlantic commander-in-chief. Back in Paris, French statesmen went to work on an alternative concept which was to become known as the Pleven plan in honor of France's Prime Minister. Its basis was the concept of a European army as formulated at Strasbourg. Development of a European army, in the French view, could proceed simultaneously with that of the integrated North Atlantic defense force envisaged in New York. Germany, unlike the North Atlantic Treaty countries, would have no national army and would not participate directly in the North Atlantic force, but might, under suitable safeguards, contribute units to the European army.

Such a European army, acccording to the French plan, would also form part of the eventual North Atlantic force, but would be responsible in the first instance to a European defense minister and an appropriate European political authority. It would be a true international army, including units from all the participating nations. These units would be incorporated at the lowest possible organizational level, thus ensuring that units of any one nation would be powerless to act in common. German units, too, might be admitted to such a force, M. Pleven told the National Assembly, provided the Schuman Plan was first accepted and the European defense minister and political authority had been duly chosen. On the night of October 25-26 the Assembly endorsed the government plan, 349 to 235; at the same time it reaffirmed its opposition to German "rearmament" as such by the much larger majority of 402 to 168.

Although the French plan envisaged full cooperation of the European army within the framework of the North Atlantic Organization, it offered no solution of the immediate problem before the latter. Aside from the doubtful military worth of such a polyglot force, the preliminary arrangements would delay indefinitely the utilization of German manpower for the common defense. Thus a very chilly atmosphere awaited Defense Minister Jules Moch when he came to Washington at the end of October to present the program to the North Atlantic Defense Committee, presided over by General Marshall. It had been hoped that this meeting could reach definite agreement on the national contingents to be contributed to the integrated defense force, thus clearing the way for the appointment of a supreme commander. The Defense Ministers did reach a number of decisions affecting the integrated force, and arrived at a definite recommendation—subject, however, to further review by the governments—as to the military contingents to be provided by each country. But Moch's insistence on the French plan destroyed the hope of an understanding on the central issue of Germany. Unable to agree, the Defense Ministers passed the problem to other authorities for further study.

In the meantime German agitation over the whole question of rearmament had been growing steadily, though without producing anything like a clear-cut German stand. The exposed position of the Germans was far from enviable, but their attitude was not one to arouse enthusiasm. Prevailing German opinion seemed compounded of the most varied and largely irrational elements—national sensitivity, fear of Russia, and impatience with the West, shot through with internal animosities and resting on an unstable foundation of injured innocence, apathy, and cynicism. Rearmament had become the chief subject of the perennial Adenauer-Schumacher debate, but it would be too simple to assert merely that the Chancellor was in favor of rearmament and the Social Democratic leader against it. Both men seemed curiously incapable of taking a definite, unequivocal position. The most that could be said with assurance was that Adenauer showed more consciousness of Western Germany's present insecurity and the need to do something about it; Schumacher seemed more intent on the demands which would have to be met by the Allies before Germany considered taking up arms again. Not only did he appear to insist on equal status for Germany; he seemed also to be stipulating that before Germany rearmed, the Allies must first be strong enough to prevent that country from becoming a battlefield.

Traces of the same incertitude and lack of realism were discernible all through the West German population. Basically the German state of mind seemed almost wholly negative. The Western Germans, with the possible exception of some of the expellees from the East, clearly did not want war; except for some former *Wehrmacht* officers and other scattered elements, they evidently did not want a national army; still less did they want to take up arms merely to rescue the Western powers from their difficulties, and least of all under what they considered the humiliating conditions proposed by M. Pleven. If they consented to participate in an integrated defense force, it must be on terms of absolute equality; but there would not be much enthusiasm in any case.

Although the Germans did not want to be overrun from the East, they feared that rearmament would be as likely to bring on this calamity as to prevent it. Some Germans found in this situation a powerful argument for the neutrality of Germany between East and West; others, convinced that neutrality was a delusion, still saw no reason to set a low price on German cooperation with the West. Sheer lack of military spirit gave Germany a bargaining power such as it had not enjoyed since Hitler's heyday. It was beginning to look as though German as well as French objections might become a serious obstacle to erecting an adequate collective defense along the lines hitherto envisaged.

4. Integration or Disintegration?

Uncertainties over Europe's defense prospects were matched by others which involved unfinished business in the economic and political fields. With the decision of the United States to rearm and encourage its partners to do likewise, the North Atlantic world had entered a period in which military requirements would take definite precedence over economic and political goals. Previous objectives were having to be reappraised in terms of their relationship to novel requirements. Such well-established targets as the completion of the European Recovery Program in 1952 lost much of their significance when it was realized that the United States and Europe were in for a prolonged period of joint exertion which was sure to make unprecedented demands on their combined resources.

In this atmosphere the status of programs concerned with European economic integration and political unification became somewhat problematical. In one sense, the concept of Western European unity was already beginning to look a trifle obsolete now that the official emphasis in defense planning had shifted decisively to a North Atlantic basis. The latent opposition of the two concepts was clearly apparent in the controversy over a European versus a North Atlantic defense force. The United States now seemed rather less interested in promoting European unity as such than in building up over-all defense capabilities and strengthening its own ties with Canada,[20] Great Britain, and other strategically situated nations in or outside of the North Atlantic Pact.

Yet there undoubtedly were fields in which closer cooperation within Western Europe would be serviceable to North Atlantic aims, notably in relation to states like Sweden and Switzerland that did not belong to the North Atlantic Treaty Organization. On the economic side, increased productivity gained through rationalization and the cooperative use of resources and facilities would tend to lessen the added burdens of rearmament and the sharpness of the "guns-or-butter" dilemma. Politically, the European idea still had value as an emotional symbol which would help to give meaning to the sacrifices that Europeans would have to make. And many in Europe were still conscious of a need to stand together as closely as might be feasible in a world that was so largely dominated by huge, somewhat unpredictable superpowers.

The second half of 1950 brought no full clarification of these issues, but disclosed a number of novel trends and witnessed a full-scale crisis in the Council of Europe, the principal meeting ground of divergent tendencies affecting the organization of the Old World. The session of the Consultative Assembly which began by producing the resolution on a European army later brought to a head the long-standing conflict between "federalists" and "functionalists," or, more properly, between the French-led group which urged the development of European political institutions and the British Laborite-Scandinavian bloc which insisted on doing nothing that would impair the sovereignty of individual governments.

A series of stormy meetings at Strasbourg, from August 7 to 28 and again from November 18 to 24, resulted in a severe setback for the "federalists." The British, with their veto in the Committee of Ministers, their strong representation in the Consultative Assembly, and their influence on Continental Social-

---

[20] On October 26 the U.S. and Canada exchanged notes in Washington embodying a "Statement of Principles for Economic Cooperation" in defense along the lines of the Hyde Park agreement in 1941 (texts in *Department of State Bulletin*, XXIII, November 6, 1950, 742-743).

ists, successfully beat off each of the multiple efforts of Paul Reynaud, André Philip, and others to liberalize the Statute and procedure of the Council and make a start in the direction of European federation. Plainly, the British were not going to change their minds on this issue; but few were willing to go ahead without them. Nothing remained but to adjust the pace of progress to the slow steps of His Majesty's Government. On November 23 the Assembly virtually shelved the "federalist" program by adopting a resolution that called for the creation of specialized, "functional" European authorities in the economic, social, cultural, and defense fields, starting with the Schuman coal-steel pool.[21] How far Britain would go along even on this limited program remained to be seen.

The implications of this disagreement for the future of the free world as a whole were difficult to gauge. They were probably less serious than would have been the case if there had been no North Atlantic Community to serve as a balance wheel for divergent trends within Western Europe. "Federalists" and "functionalists" alike subscribed to most of the general aims of the North Atlantic grouping, with which all but a few Western European states were by now directly or indirectly associated. Their differences concerned rather the methods of reaching these same aims than any definite idea of setting up a substitute for them. It was noteworthy that United States pressure for a more dynamic approach was much less in evidence than formerly. Fully preoccupied with the development of the North Atlantic alliance, Washington evidently viewed these intra-European differences with a certain equanimity so long as they did not interfere with urgent practical programs.

Before suspending its labors for the year, the Strasbourg Assembly once again endorsed the two outstanding current examples of the functionalist approach, the Schuman Plan and the proposed European army. This time the inclusion of German contingents on a basis of equality was specifically

21 The door to federation was left open in a proposal (referred to an expert committee for further study) to convert the Assembly into a limited parliament which might ultimately take over the authority of such functional organizations as the O.E.E.C. and the Brussels Treaty organization.

mentioned; the vote was 83 to 7, with British Laborites and German Christian Democrats abstaining and the German Social Democrats voting in the negative. Since this question was now in the hands of the North Atlantic Treaty Organization, the vote was largely academic, though it might serve to strengthen the French hand in the event that the majority approach to the German problem failed to yield results.

As for the Schuman Plan, negotiations for a treaty establishing a European coal-steel authority were still going forward among the six governments that had sent representatives to the Quai d'Orsay in June. Some momentum had been lost, partly because more critical matters had supervened and partly because the delegates had run into complex technical problems such as disparate productivity, costs, and wages, vested interests of national producers and the old coal and steel cartels, and the unresolved ownership status of the Ruhr industries. Nevertheless progress was made. The delegates derived encouragement from an election-eve commendation by President Truman, and Hugh Dalton pleasantly surprised his auditors at Strasbourg by confirming on behalf of the British Government that once the High Authority was set up the United Kingdom would consider how it could associate itself with the sponsoring governments. French statesmen were somewhat concerned lest American pressure for the rearmament of Germany should lessen German enthusiasm for the plan, and also feared the influence of Great Britain in the Allied High Commission; but prospects for a treaty early in 1951 seemed good enough to warrant their continuing to emphasize the Schuman Plan as a necessary preliminary to any form of German rearmament.

On the broader economic front, progress toward the goal of a unified European market was conditioned by the radical changes that were taking place in the world economy as a whole with the commencement of serious rearmament. On the one hand, developments following the Korean crisis actually accelerated the trend toward successful completion of the Marshall Plan in terms of the original target, i.e., European independence of extraordinary dollar aid by mid-1952. By the end of the year new peaks had been attained in Western Europe's industrial production, export volume, and intra-European trade. European hard-currency balances continued to grow, and the dollar gap to contract. From a monthly average of $360 million in October-November 1949, Western Europe's trade deficit with the Western Hemisphere fell to a monthly figure of $242 million in October-November 1950.[22] Great Britain's gold and dollar position improved to such a point that it was found possible to suspend further Marshall Plan assistance effective at the end of the year.

But the advent of a new armament program, superimposed on the existing industrial structure, suggested that Europe's balance of payments would henceforth be a matter of secondary concern. More vital would be its ability to produce, with American help, sufficient goods to equip its armies and still maintain civilian consumption at reasonable levels. Already there were signs of a renewed inflationary trend, and shortages of coal and other vital materials were beginning to loom where surpluses had threatened a few months before. American stockpiling of scarce materials from overseas, though greatly relieving the immediate world shortage of dollars, raised serious questions about how Europe was to obtain and pay for the materials to run its own industrial plants. Some method of allocating strategic materials within the free world, whether through the North Atlantic Treaty Organization, the O.E.E.C., or some other agency, would clearly be necessary. Equally essential would be some plan for shielding the European economies (and the American economy as well) against rapid increases in the prices of imported raw materials, which were rising much faster than the prices of manufactured goods for export.

In these circumstances, the objective of a closer integration of the Western European economies had certainly lost none of its importance, although there were some signs of a reverse trend as European nations individually joined the competitive

[22] Economic Cooperation Administration, *Recovery Guides: Participating Countries,* No. 18, February 1951, ii-ix.

scramble for raw materials and took measures to protect their economies against the vagaries of the world market. The drive to eliminate quantitative restrictions on intra-European trade lost some momentum as successive reductions began to bite into protected industries, and there were frequent complaints of a growing resort to autarkic practices in Europe and a lack of guidance from the Economic Cooperation Administration. A change of emphasis had appeared in E.C.A. operations as rearmament entered the picture, coinciding roughly with the retirement of Administrator Paul G. Hoffman and his replacement on October 1 by his former deputy, William C. Foster. But the lapse of interest in integration, if any, was only temporary. "Closer integration of the economies of the countries of Western Europe was never more vital," said E.C.A.'s report to Congress for the third quarter of 1950. ". . . Trade liberalization measures, as steps in this direction, can be expected to contribute to the more efficient utilization of economic resources and the expanding economy required to assure a combination of reasonable living standards and an adequate military establishment." [23]

Above and beyond these intra-European problems there remained the question of what policies the United States was going to adopt regarding the whole question of future aid to Europe, which would have to be viewed henceforth from a military even more than from an economic angle. Its form and extent would be determined, in the last analysis, by the value that Congress attached to having a strong Europe as a partner in an increasingly perilous world situation. Full clarification on that point would have to await the assembly of the new Congress in 1951; meanwhile the trend of administration thinking was indicated by the *Report to the President on Foreign Economic Policies* which Gordon Gray and the experts associated with him submitted in November after a seven-month intensive survey. Their conclusion, so far as Western Europe was concerned, was that rearmament had forced "a postponement of

[23] *Tenth Report to Congress of the Economic Cooperation Administration* (Washington, 1951), 22.

the time when the United States, consistent with its own interest, can end economic assistance."

Western European nations, said Mr. Gray, had "not yet felt the unfavorable impact of their own accelerated rearmament. It seems clear that a sufficiently large and rapid growth in military strength is beyond the capacity of Western European countries solely through their own efforts or with aid only in the form of military equipment." While continuing to insist on maximum European efforts, therefore, "the United States should be prepared to continue supplying aid, apart from military equipment, for another 3 or 4 years beyond the present time." The amount of aid required would depend on the actual rearmament effort of individual countries and its total impact on their economies.[24]

At the basis of this recommendation was the assumption that "Western Europe is the most critical area from the standpoint of our own security and the security of the free world." But this principle, axiomatic though it had been in postwar American foreign policy, was no longer unchallenged. Beneath the surface, as the United States became more fully engaged in the Far East, interest in Europe had waned and dissatisfaction with Europe's record of accomplishment had grown. Herbert Hoover brought some of this feeling to a head in a speech on October 19. If Western Europe wanted defense against the Communist tide, he said, "they must do most of it themselves—and do it fast." No more American aid, in money or men, should be provided "until a definitely unified and sufficient European army [sic] is in sight," said the former President, leaving Europeans to ask themselves how fully the United States really had grasped the complexities of the situation and how far it recognized the solid community of interest that was supposed to underlie the Atlantic community.

[24] *Report to the President on Foreign Economic Policies* (Washington, November 10, 1950), 10-11.

5. Mediterranean Readjustments

While working to build up the North Atlantic community as the main bulwark of the free world in Europe, the United States did not lose sight of other European countries which stood outside that grouping but occupied vital points of the North Atlantic security structure. The actual membership of the North Atlantic Treaty group had been determined by a variety of factors of which strategic significance was only one. Now that military and strategic considerations had officially moved into first place in American and North Atlantic calculations, attention was bound to focus more sharply on the position of these "outside" powers and their possible contribution to the common defense.

Two of these states, Sweden and Switzerland, were qualified to play a significant role in the defense of the West but were excluded from closer association with the North Atlantic group by their firm adherence to a policy of neutrality. Ireland, another of the World War II neutrals, flatly refused its cooperation as long as its territorial claim on the United Kingdom remained unsatisfied. Somewhat less immutable prospects obtained in the Mediterranean, where the North Atlantic powers had assumed considerable responsibilities through the inclusion of Italy and the Algerian departments of France among the areas they were pledged to defend.

From the point of view of global strategy the Mediterranean was, as always, a crucial area. Some authorities held that it might provide facilities for offensive and defensive warfare even if the West European plain were overrun. The geographic and political complexity of the region was, however, an obstacle to the development of coherent national or international policies. The inherent instability of the young countries along its southern and eastern shores, a source of standing concern to the American government, had to be viewed primarily in relation to the problems of an awakening Asia. More directly involved in the immediate fate of Europe were the nations

of the Northern Mediterranean, from the Iberian peninsula
to Turkey. Four of these—Spain, Yugoslavia, Greece, and Turkey—were nonmembers of the North Atlantic alliance whose
status underwent significant alterations in the wake of the
Korean attack.

Greece and Turkey already possessed an indirect relationship to the North Atlantic community through their participation in the Organization for European Economic Cooperation,
the Council of Europe, and especially the American military
aid program, of which they had been the earliest beneficiaries.
Their position on the borders of the Soviet bloc had made
them vital elements in the original policy of "containing"
Soviet expansionism, and their importance as outposts of the
free world had in no way diminished as the containment policy
broadened into a general plan of European reconstruction.
Their proximity to Yugoslavia would have great significance
in case of a Soviet or satellite attack on that country.

Although too remote for inclusion in the original North
Atlantic coalition, Greece and Turkey remained objects of special American and British solicitude, and their gradual recovery
offered one of the most striking vindications of the American
policy of substituting strength for weakness in the free world.
Greece had turned the corner with the successful liquidation
of Communist-led guerrilla resistance in 1949. Although its
economic situation remained perilously weak and its politics
were too turbulent to dispense altogether with American guidance,[25] its eventual stabilization seemed probable if only it was
spared further interference by the Communist states to the
north.

Turkey's progress was even more gratifying. Not only had

[25] The United States intervened strongly in Greek affairs when Ambassador Henry
F. Grady addressed an emphatic letter to the Greek Prime Minister on March 31
intimating that American aid would cease unless a "stable and efficient" government was formed and far-reaching economic and financial reforms were undertaken without delay (*Department of State Bulletin*, XXII, April 17, 1950, 600-
601). On September 16 the State Department announced that Greece's allotment
of E.C.A. funds was being reduced since "the rate of progress in the Greek
program has not been sufficient to allow complete and effective utilization of the
amount originally contemplated" (*New York Times*, September 17, 1950).

it stood unshaken against Soviet pressure in all its forms, but its people gave evidence of remarkable discipline and adaptability to democratic ways. National elections held in May 1950 led to the retirement, absolutely without incident, of the old-established People's party founded by Kemal Atatürk and the replacement of President Ismet Inönü's regime by a new government under Celal Bayar, former leader of the opposition. The change brought no deviation from Turkey's steadfastly pro-Western policy, and the prompt arrival and courageous performance of the 4,500 Turkish troops dispatched to the Korean front established a standard which few other United Nations members could meet.

Turkey's ready compliance with the recommendations of the Security Council may have helped incline the United States in favor of its government's frequently expressed desire for closer association with the North Atlantic Treaty Organization. In any case there were good reasons for tying in this sector of the Mediterranean more closely with the defense planning for the North Atlantic area. Cordiality already prevailed between Greece, Turkey, and Italy. There had been intermittent talk of linking the three nations in an Eastern Mediterranean pact associated with the North Atlantic alliance. Greece and Turkey were due to continue receiving American military aid on a considerable scale—$120 million under the regular allocation for 1950–1951, and $193 million (with Iran) under the post-Korean appropriation. But, though based on the apparent assumption that Greece and Turkey would be with the North Atlantic powers in any general conflagration, such assistance had so far been administered on a purely bilateral basis, without reference to the work of the "Southern European-Western Mediterranean Regional Planning Group" (France, Italy, United Kingdom, and United States) under the North Atlantic Treaty.

At its New York meeting in September the North Atlantic Council took steps to correct this anomaly by offering to "associate" the Greek and Turkish governments with "such appropriate phases of the military planning work of the North

Atlantic Treaty Organization as are concerned with the defense of the Mediterranean." Acheson, as chairman of the Council, informed the Turkish and Greek ambassadors of the Council's view that such a relationship "would contribute significantly to the defense of that area." Both governments accepted,[26] and prepared to coordinate their staff planning with that of the North Atlantic powers. Although this was not the same thing as membership in the North Atlantic Treaty, it was a further recognition of the principle that military defense of the free world was an indivisible whole, not a series of isolated fronts.

This principle was less easy to apply in the case of Spain and Yugoslavia, both of which served as a reminder that other factors beside the military were relevant to the free world's defense. Both countries represented totalitarian political trends that were incompatible with the professed principles of the North Atlantic community; both had long been on bad terms with most of the North Atlantic governments; both were at the center of complex, highly explosive political situations on which sentiment within the North Atlantic countries themselves was far from uniform. Under such circumstances neither Spain nor Yugoslavia could be readily associated with the North Atlantic system in the fashion of Greece and Turkey, though individually they might be treated in such a way that any potential value they might possess for the North Atlantic powers would not be entirely wasted. To the United States, at least, it seemed that these potentialities outweighed the political difficulties which counted more heavily with some of its European allies.

Any contribution Franco Spain might make to the strength of the North Atlantic community would probably be limited entirely to the military realm. The importance of its strategic position between Atlantic and Mediterranean was well known, and the mountain barrier of the Pyrenees might take on great significance in war if it should unhappily prove impossible to hold the Russians at the Elbe, the Rhine, or the Seine. Spain was reputed to have 22 divisions of troops, badly equipped

[26] *Department of State Bulletin,* XXIII, October 16, 1950, 632-633.

but supposedly good fighters, and perhaps half a million trained reserves; their sheer number was impressive when compared with the forces available to the North Atlantic powers. True, the real worth of this Spanish army was debatable on military grounds; there was a question whether Generalissimo Franco would be willing to face the political risks of mobilizing it, or, if mobilized, to let it serve outside of Spanish territory; and it was even more doubtful whether Spain's worn-out economy was capable of supporting a major military effort. The fundamental obstacles to association with Spain, however, were the unrepentantly antidemocratic character of the Franco dictatorship and the profound aversion it had aroused in liberal and left-wing circles, both Communist and anti-Communist, throughout the world. Anti-Franco sentiment was especially prevalent in the democratic labor movement of Western Europe, which had strong influence on official policy in France, Britain, and the Scandinavian countries.

The symbol of this moral indignation was the resolution adopted by the United Nations General Assembly in 1946, recommending that member states recall their ambassadors and ministers from Madrid and barring Spain from membership in the specialized agencies as well as the United Nations. The United States had never been enthusiastic for this resolution, preferring to regard diplomatic relations as a technical matter that had nothing to do with approval or disapproval of another government. Compliance with the resolution by other governments had been spotty; if anything, moreover, it seemed to have strengthened Franco's position in Spain instead of paving the way for his removal. Furthermore, not everyone in the United States or elsewhere shared the anti-Franco sentiment which had been predominant in 1946. Various members of the Senate were particularly distressed by the policy of ostracizing a government which, whatever might be thought of its political practices, was at any rate strongly anti-Communist. Pressure to send an ambassador to Madrid and to include Spain among the beneficiaries of American economic and military aid programs was a recurrent feature of each session of Congress.

As the world situation darkened and American policy veered toward straight anti-Communism, the force of these considerations seemed to grow. As early as January 18, 1950, Secretary Acheson wrote to Senator Connally that the United States would like to see the Spanish anomaly resolved, and was "prepared to vote for a resolution in the General Assembly which will leave members free to send an Ambassador or Minister to Spain if they choose." In the same letter he expressed the opinion that Spain's association with the rest of Western Europe, though ultimately desirable, was "a matter in which the Western European nations must have a leading voice"; participation of the present Spanish Government in Western European cooperative programs, he said, would be a source of weakness rather than strength, "unless and until there has been some indication of evolution toward more democratic government in Spain." As to the development of mutually beneficial economic relations between the United States and Spain, he strongly intimated that it was up to the Spanish Government to adopt a more positive and cooperative attitude in its official dealings with this country.[27]

That this qualified stand did not by any means go far enough to satisfy the congressional friends of Franco was demonstrated by the passage of the McCarran rider to the General Appropriation Act, calling for the extension of $62.5 million in loans to Spain.[28] Concurrently, agitation grew for a new policy that would enable Spain to play a part in the military defense of Europe. Franco himself showed no intention to modify his regime in a way that would make it more palatable to the Western democracies, but appeared willing to cooperate with the United States, at least, provided the cooperation was on his own terms.

By the time the General Assembly convened in New York on September 19, events in Korea had further tilted the bal-

[27] *Department of State Bulletin,* XXII, January 30, 1950, 156-159.
[28] Cf. above, p. 95.

ance in Franco's favor both in the United States and abroad. Eight Spanish-speaking nations brought in a proposal to revoke the two key sections of the 1946 resolution, thus authorizing member governments to reaccredit ambassadors or ministers to Madrid and paving the way for Spain's admission to the United Nations specialized agencies at the discretion of the latter. After perfunctory debate the new resolution was adopted by the safe majority of 38-10.[29] Although the vote was sufficiently large to vindicate Franco's policy of immobility in the eyes of the Spanish public, it was far from an endorsement of his regime by the free world. No member of the North Atlantic community opposed the resolution, but only the Benelux countries, Canada, Iceland, and the United States supported it. Denmark, France, Norway, and the United Kingdom were among the 12 nations that abstained from voting.

President Truman had told reporters two days before the vote that it would still be "a long, long time" before the United States decided to reaccredit an ambassador to Spain. But old-established attitudes were crumbling fast before the pressure to get ahead with building up the anti-Communist front. On December 27 the President announced that he was appointing Stanton Griffis, previously Ambassador to Egypt and Argentina, to fill the post that had been vacant for the last five years. Great Britain also decided to accredit an ambassador to Madrid, though a similar move by France was temporarily blocked by opposition of the Socialists in the cabinet. On other fronts, too, Spain's reacceptance seemed to be gaining momentum. The United Nations Food and Agriculture Organization decided to admit Spain as well as Western Germany to membership; and on November 15 the Economic Cooperation Administration announced, contrary to previous indications, that a program of American loan aid to Spain would get under way immediately under the authority of the General Appropriation Act.[30]

[29] U.N. Document A/1487, adopted November 4, 1950. Still in effect was an earlier United Nations decision barring Spain from membership in the United Nations itself as long as the Franco regime remained.
[30] *Department of State Bulletin*, XXIII, November 27, 1950, 857.

Franco, it appeared, was winning his battle. By sitting tight and refusing to modify his repressive policies in the slightest, he was bringing the free world to his doorstep. This he owed less to any peculiar sagacity of his own than to the anti-Communist tide which Moscow's actions had encouraged in the world outside. Whether his government, which had thus far assumed no obligations toward the Western nations, would ever become a source of positive help to them remained to be ascertained. While awaiting the next gestures from the West, Franco chose to raise his bargaining price or simply display his contempt for Western sensibilities by letting the controlled press revive Spain's old claim to Gibraltar, still the western anchor of Britain's position in the Mediterranean. Plainly, he would not be an easy or acquiescent partner if ever the West was forced to depend on his good will.

Yugoslavia, like Spain, lived under a dictatorial regime, but one that played a much more direct and obvious role in the East-West conflict. Whatever the Western nations might think of Tito's Communist government, its two-year-old revolt still represented the most serious political and strategic breach in the world-wide Stalinist front. Unlike Franco, Tito was doing the free world a service by his mere existence, which deflected a goodly share of the Kremlin's animosity and kept the idea alive in leftist circles that it was possible to be "progressive" without being Stalinist. Thus far the Yugoslav leadership had evinced no interest in rapprochement with the "bourgeois" states of the West. In the United Nations, Yugoslavia had continued to plead the cause of Communist China, and had carefully avoided taking sides in the Korean conflict. As yet the United States and its Atlantic associates hardly thought of Tito as a potential ally, but Washington and London had considered it a worth-while enterprise merely to help the Yugoslav regime stay afloat and perpetuate the damage it was doing in the Stalinist community. Tito's 32 divisions might not be exactly comrades in arms, but it was useful to have them there to engage the attention of Russia's rearmed Balkan satellites. In case of a general war it would be good to have them fighting on the same side.

During the latter part of 1950 this relationship tended to grow considerably closer. Contrary to the Spanish experience, moreover, there were manifestations of a friendlier feeling on both sides. Tito was discovering that strict neutrality between East and West was suicidal for a country in Yugoslavia's position. The conviction was driven home by a calamitous drought during the summer of 1950 which gravely impaired Yugoslavia's food supplies and might easily entail the destruction of the regime unless outside help could be secured. The United States was quick to recognize the implications of this situation. No "bargain" was struck. The Yugoslav Government continued to insist on its complete independence of action, a claim which the United States Government had no reason to dispute. But there could be no question that as American relief shipments began to materialize, Yugoslavia's general attitude began to undergo a distinct change for the better.

The change of outlook on the part of the Yugoslav leaders seems to have been motivated in part by genuine disillusionment with the course followed by the Kremlin, not only in relation to Yugoslavia but throughout the world. A fresh study of Marx and Lenin confirmed their impression that Moscow, having forsaken the true path of "socialism," had actually become the leading threat to world peace. In line with this discovery, Yugoslavia's attitude on the Korean and other questions progressed from one of complete neutrality to one much closer to that of states like India and Israel—still independent, still highly critical at times of the "Western bloc," but less dogmatic and more realistically aware of the true nature of the world crisis.

Concurrently the Yugoslav Government moved to eliminate some frictions nearer home. Amid bitter denunciations from the Soviet bloc, relations with Greece were "normalized" for the first time since before the Greek civil war. Tension with Italy slackened and a reparations and financial settlement was reached, although their conflicting claims to Trieste still prevented the growth of anything like cordiality between the two Adriatic nations. Some of the stringency of Yugoslavia's internal policies was also relaxed, at a time when the repressive character of Communist rule in the neighboring satellite states was being more and more accentuated. The lessened severity of the police and the mildly liberal reforms introduced into the state administrative machinery did not affect the regime's totalitarian essence, but at least indicated a healthy trend away from the rigid Stalinist pattern.

The counterpart, if not the inspiration, of these developments was a succession of American moves to assist in meeting the internal food crisis. Congress being in recess during the early autumn, the administration used a variety of methods to start relief on its way.[31] Cash was made available through the Export-Import Bank; large quantities of wheat flour were supplied by the Economic Cooperation Administration; somewhat paradoxically, $16 million for army rations was provided under the Mutual Defense Assistance Act, which authorized limited aid to any threatened European nation whose strategic location made it important to the defense of the North Atlantic area. Stopgap assistance of this nature totaled some $31.4 million. Authorization of a further $38 million in Yugoslav aid was the principal foreign policy business before Congress when it reconvened late in November. Spurred by the administration's emphatic assurances that the matter was really urgent,[32] Congress enacted the necessary legislation with a minimum of quibbling or ideological objection and sent it to the White House in time for signature on December 29.

These actions, accompanied by the usual detailed stipulations designed to assure equitable distribution and safeguard

---

[31] *Ibid.*, XXIII, December 4, 1950, 879-880. For background cf. *Aid to Yugoslavia: A Fact Sheet* (Department of State Publication 4030, Washington, 1950). [32] *Ibid.*, XXIII, December 11, 1950, 937-940. In its final form the Yugoslav Emergency Relief Assistance Act of 1950 (Public Law 897, 81st Congress), authorized the expenditure of a total of $50 million (including $12 million already disbursed by E.C.A.) out of funds previously appropriated for the European Recovery Program.

American interests,[33] relieved the Tito regime of any immediate danger of internal collapse. So far as the United States was concerned, they were frankly based on considerations of expediency, not on any early expectation of gaining Tito as an ally or turning his Communist regime into a liberal democracy. Somewhat similar reasoning appeared to inspire the British Government, which provided financial assistance on a smaller scale. The future course of the Yugoslav Government would be a fascinating laboratory study in the behavior of "emancipated" Communists under completely unpredictable conditions. But whether Tito ultimately aligned himself with the West or tried to build some kind of neutral "third force," American interests would be well served if he would simply hold on and keep the Soviet power away from the head of the Adriatic.

How long Tito could survive if the Kremlin actually gave orders for a march into Yugoslavia was anybody's guess. His army was still the second largest in Europe and presumably the best in the Balkans, but it might soon be surpassed by the armies of the surrounding satellite states, which were being built up well beyond peace treaty limits and equipped with modern Soviet material. But in this respect Yugoslavia's problem was no different from that of the rest of non-Soviet Europe. It was distinctly possible that the Soviet and satellite armies could sweep forward across Europe at any time. Neither in Yugoslavia nor farther northward, however, was the United States willing to encourage a Soviet advance by neglecting opportunities to strengthen the potentialities of resistance. There might still be considerable merit in the idea of "deterring" the Soviets from aggression by showing that aggression would be met with strength. Such strength was now definitely in the making in Europe. The outlook was far from hopeless provided the rearmament effort was carried forward with resolution, mutual trust, and due recognition of the human factors which might spell the difference between success and failure.

[33] Among other things Yugoslavia undertook to supply the United States with reciprocal assistance in the form of raw and semiprocessed materials (*Department of State Bulletin*, XXIII, December 18, 1950, 985-986; XXIV, January 22, 1951, 150-151).

CHAPTER SEVEN

REMOBILIZATION: ASIA AND THE
WESTERN HEMISPHERE

A FAVORITE occupation of world affairs analysts in the latter part of 1950 was the preparation of balance sheets designed to compare the military and economic strength of the free nations with that of the Soviet world. Such tabulations were useful adjuncts to the study of current developments, but too tentative and too restricted in scope to offer more than a rough indication of some of the free world's problems. The picture they presented was basically a simple one. The major part of the world's population and known resources was still beyond the Kremlin's reach; much of it was at least nominally in the custody of the United States and its Western European associates. The Communist world, however, had far outstripped the free nations in effective mobilization of the resources it controlled, and its unquestionable military superiority over the whole Eurasian land mass enabled it to threaten many areas of vital significance to the West. Finally, the latent strength of the free world was widely scattered and uncoordinated; its effective utilization required not only improved military protection in certain areas but also a closer articulation between the industrial complex of North America and Western Europe and the largely underdeveloped, primarily raw material-producing regions of Asia, Africa, the Pacific, and Latin America.

These latter countries, which overshadowed the North Atlantic community itself in terms of area, population, and natural resources, played a dual role in the world power balance. On the one hand they represented an indispensable source of oil, rubber, tin, wool, uranium, and other vital materials and also an important segment of the free world's moral and military strength, as attested by the participation of Australia and New Zealand, among others, in the United Nations action in Korea. On the other hand, many of these same countries lay on the fringe of the Stalinist empire and were directly menaced by Soviet expansionism. Thus for the free world it was essential not only to find ways of utilizing their potential contribution to the defense of freedom but also to keep them from falling into the hands of world Communism and thus swelling the power of the opposing camp.

Although it would be an oversimplification to describe American actions outside Europe in the second half of 1950 as expressions of an integrated over-all policy, the interaction of these two sets of requirements—one primarily economic, the other primarily military—was plainly evident. In non-Communist parts of Asia, where the danger was great and immediate, primary emphasis was laid on the attempt to remedy acute weaknesses, eliminate outstanding sources of friction, and lay foundations for stable growth. In Indochina and certain other countries it took the form of expanded economic and military assistance; in Japan, it led to intensified efforts to clear the ground for a peace settlement which would bind Japan to the free nations. Not without some relation to these efforts was an American initiative in the United Nations General Assembly, directed toward strengthening the world organization as an instrument of collective security against aggression, which will be considered in the next chapter.

In areas unaffected by the Communist threat, American action was dictated primarily by the needs of the evolving rearmament program. During the early stages of remobilization, United States interest in the "rear" areas (and in some "forward" areas like Malaya) was manifested principally by a hasty buying up of available raw materials to feed the American industrial machine and augment the stockpile of scarce materials. This action had the beneficent effect of loosing a flood of dollars on the free world at large, but by the end of the year it had caused serious complications pointing to an imperative need for international machinery to assure the orderly procurement and allocation of raw material stocks.

Although the tempo of American activity throughout the world was quickened as a result of Korea, its underlying objectives and its operating methods underwent no essential change. Established agencies and programs like the Economic Cooperation Administration and the Mutual Defense Assistance Program were still considered the logical tools of American policy and were adapted to the new requirements without great difficulty, although improved coordination of the various foreign economic and assistance programs would certainly be necessary as remobilization progressed. A significant newcomer among the instrumentalities of American world policy was the Point Four program, formally authorized by Congress in June. Despite its many limitations, technical assistance under Point Four had an important role to play in resource development for the free world's arsenals as well as in its original function of pointing the way to a more tolerable life for millions of human beings more or less open to Stalinist seduction.

In the threatened areas of the Far East, American military and economic aid programs supplemented to some extent the efforts of the French in Indochina and the British Commonwealth nations in Southern and Southeast Asia. This was the point of maximum concentration of Western assistance, but it was also, next to Korea, the area in greatest danger from Sino-Soviet aggression. Aid to Southeast Asia took the form of a desperate race against internal disintegration and outside pressure. No one could foresee the outcome, but the necessity for strenuous efforts to hold the area was clear. Any major breach in the existing ring of non-Soviet lands around the periphery of Eurasia might threaten the entire security structure of the free world.

But the difficulty of building a wall of resistance around a power which possessed the advantages of interior lines, overwhelming material superiority, and freedom from observation was aggravated by the almost insouciant attitude of many of the governments and peoples in question. Most Asian leaders, from Nehru downward, showed reluctance to visualize the problem in Western terms or to recognize the peril that Stalinist imperialism represented for their own countries. Realization of the need for basic reform in Asia and obsession with asserting their new-found independence vis-à-vis the West had the effect of blinding them to the much graver threat to that independence which was looming in the East. The tendency of Asian opinion to belittle the danger from Peking and Moscow and to dissociate itself from the interests of the Western nations, particularly the United States, was a source of weakness almost as grave as the more obvious weaknesses in the military sphere. The apparent indifference of the United States to Asian ways of thinking helped to explain this prevalent attitude but in no way curbed its negative effects.

To some extent the awareness of danger seemed to increase as one drew farther away from the immediate danger zone. The extreme anti-Communism of the Chinese Nationalists on Formosa was a matter of course. The Japanese public, with its long experience of Far Eastern power politics, showed a livelier appreciation of the Soviet threat than did the less sophisticated peoples of the Asiatic mainland. Australia and New Zealand, the Pacific members of the British Commonwealth, showed considerable realism in their appreciation of Oriental problems; Australia, in particular, sought the closest possible accord with the United States, and tirelessly urged a Pacific security pact to harness the strength of the free nations not only against Communist aggression but also against the menace of a reviving Japan. Latin America had become something of a backwater of world politics in the years of the East-West struggle, but the average Latin-American government evinced a lively preoccupation with supposed Communist dangers at home and tended to take an outspokenly anti-Soviet position in the United Nations.

No single standard was available by which to measure the success of American policy as it set out to galvanize these far-flung but vital sectors of the free world. The nature and intensity of American effort, and its relationship to the efforts of other powers, varied radically from one country to another. The only adequate test of particular actions was how effectively they contributed to the over-all aim of preserving the free world against piecemeal destruction. Confronted by an agency whose material power, revolutionary skill, and aggressive intentions were no longer doubtful, the free nations found themselves at a considerable world-wide disadvantage in which their lack of a common purpose loomed even larger than their material unpreparedness. A universal meeting of minds was hardly to be expected in the particular generation that had to face the Stalinist revolution. But it was in terms of movement toward or away from such a common understanding that the significance of particular gains and losses would have to be gauged.

1. The Economic Aspect

In the economic field the advent of rearmament solved some old problems, raised some new ones, and left still others to be dealt with along lines laid out before the Korean crisis but subject to modification in the light of the new situation. The most immediate effect was a dramatic rise in the world market prices of strategic raw materials, which climbed to sensational levels in anticipation of increased demands for armaments production and strategic stockpiling, particularly by the United States, and, to a minor extent, as a result of speculative hoarding. The increases were particularly spectacular for such commodities as wool, rubber, and tin, which more than doubled in the last half of 1950, with copper and zinc running close seconds.[1]

The cumulative impact of these price increases was accentuated by the fact that they were superimposed on an already high price level, especially in terms of European currencies, which resulted from the devaluations of 1949 and the increased level of prosperity in the United States in the first half of 1950. In Europe, as we have seen, the effects were inflationary and on the whole adverse; the raw material-producing countries, on the other hand, particularly in Southeast Asia and Latin

[1] *The Economist,* CLIX, December 30, 1950, 1223-1224.

America, experienced a boom in production and exports as well as an improvement in their terms of trade (i.e., the relation between import and export prices). Countries like Malaya with its rubber, Indonesia with its tin, Australia with its wool, and the Latin American republics with their nonferrous metals faced the agreeable probability of continued high levels of production and exports.

A prolonged uncontrolled boom in raw material prices would not, of course, be an unmixed blessing for the producing countries. The gap between prices of raw materials and manufactured goods was sure to be narrowed in the long run, and the twin specters of inflation and overexpansion hovered just around the corner. But the initial impact over large sections of the free world, including the British Commonwealth and the sterling area, was highly gratifying. In the year that followed the devaluation in September 1949, the sterling area's gold and dollar reserves rose by over $1.4 billion to a level of $2.8 billion.[2] The trend could be expected to continue in the wake of rising raw material prices and expanding trade in sterling area products. Thus one major effect of rearmament, and particularly of the massive American purchases for strategic stockpiling, had been to reduce further the world's dollar gap problem. Even in the 12 months prior to October 1950 the world's dollar deficit had shrunk from $3.3 billion to $1.1 billion.[3]

The ultimate significance of this development would depend on how it affected the over-all economic and political situation of the free world in a period of total crisis. It was noteworthy that the direct advantages were chiefly felt in Canada, Latin America, and the sterling area, whereas continental Europe, though benefiting somewhat from the increased availability of dollars outside North America, faced serious difficulties in obtaining and paying for the materials it was going to need for its increased rearmament effort. In economic

[2] *Report to the President on Foreign Economic Policies* (Washington, November 10, 1950), 43.
[3] "Next Step for O.E.E.C.," *The Economist*, CLIX, October 14, 1950, 595.

terms a three-way division was already appearing in the free world, between raw material producing and consuming countries and, within the latter group, between economically powerful consumers like the United States (which was also an important raw material producer) and less favorably situated nations which were adversely affected by American (and British) forays into the raw materials market. Aspects of this division were continually coming to the surface throughout the autumn in the deliberations of the Organization for European Economic Cooperation, in the Torquay meeting of signatories to the General Agreement on Tariffs and Trade, and in international commodity conferences on wool, tin, and other materials. Not until after the December meeting of President Truman and Prime Minister Attlee were decisive steps taken to reestablish a degree of order in world raw material markets.[4]

So far as the producing countries themselves were concerned, two basic questions had to be asked about the way in which their potentialities were being exploited. First, how effectively was it promoting maximum growth in the economic strength of the free world as a whole? And, second, how effectively was it promoting the long-range economic and social growth of the producing countries themselves, most of which fell into the category of "underdeveloped territories"? To a considerable extent the two questions were interrelated and complementary, since the same set of factors largely governed both effective exploitation and sound development. Increased productivity was the basic need of the underdeveloped areas— more efficient operation of mines, plantations, and processing plants, aided by better transportation and communications facilities, improved public health and education, and more adequate nutrition and housing. Some progress along these lines would be needed merely to expand the flow of materials to the arsenals of the West. Ideally, it would also contribute to building foreign exchange and purchasing power in the underdevel-

[4] White House communiqué, December 8, 1950, and statement by France, U.K., and U.S., January 12, 1951, in *Department of State Bulletin*, XXIII, December 18, 1950, 959-961 and XXIV, January 22, 1951, 149-150.

oped countries and raising barriers of material and moral well-being against the Communist tide.

Yet the net effect of rearmament on the various programs for assistance to underdeveloped countries was problematical to say the least. Rearmament would, without doubt, bring into many of these countries a flow of investment capital and technological skills for which sufficient inducements had thus far been lacking. Development would take place at an accelerated rate; but its incidence would be very uneven, and its nature would be governed more by economic and military considerations than by the long-range interests of the inhabitants. Some countries would derive little or no net benefit from the new trend; in others, comprehensive development plans were likely to be shelved in favor of short-range programs to increase the output of scarce materials. As a result, existing inequities in the distribution of income among different social groups might be accentuated; the widespread need for agricultural reforms and diversification of production might remain largely unfulfilled, and hoped-for increases in general living standards might be indefinitely deferred, at the very time when the worsened international situation increased the threat of external conquest and/or internal disintegration in underdeveloped countries all round the Sino-Soviet periphery.

It was thus against a highly uncertain background that the United States, the United Nations, and the British Commonwealth prepared to begin the implementation of their respective programs designed to benefit the vast neglected portions of the modern world. These programs, though representing somewhat differing conceptions as to technique and area of application, were all directed toward the same general goal. All of them, moreover, depended ultimately on support from the United States as the principal source of funds available for development purposes.

In this country the "bold new program" of January 1949 had at last become law with the passage of the Act for International Development in June 1950 and the subsequent allocation of $34.5 million to support the program during its first fiscal year.[5] Once Congress had acted, the United States moved rapidly to create the necessary administrative apparatus. A Technical Cooperation Administration was established in the State Department under Dr. Henry G. Bennett, a specialist brought in from the educational world. Existing interdepartmental committees were superseded by an Interdepartmental Advisory Council on Technical Cooperation, of which Dr. Bennett would be chairman. Nelson A. Rockefeller, a former Assistant Secretary of State, was appointed to head the 12-man International Development Advisory Board which would advise and consult with the Secretary on policy matters.[6] A preliminary allocation of funds had already been worked out— $12.75 million for the United Nations technical assistance program, $10.5 million for direct assistance in Latin America, $5 million for the Near East and Africa, and $2 million for the Far East, which would also benefit from the United Nations program and from the activities of the Economic Cooperation Administration under special legislation pertaining to that area. Before the year was out, nine countries[7] had concluded bilateral agreements with the United States covering various phases of their future technical cooperation with this country.

Action by the United States enabled the United Nations to begin work on the expanded technical assistance program authorized by the General Assembly in 1949, which had been held up by uncertainty about United States participation. The Technical Assistance Conference originally scheduled for 1949 was held at Lake Success on June 12-14, 1950. Fifty-four countries attended, the Soviet bloc being unrepresented because of its stock objections to the presence of Nationalist China. Total contributions of $20,012,500 were pledged for the period July 1, 1950–December 31, 1951, the bulk of the funds to be distributed between the United Nations and the various special-

[5] Above, pp. 95-98.
[6] Department of State Bulletin, XXIII, September 25, 1950, 499-500; November 13, 1950, 793-795; December 4, 1950, 880-881; December 18, 1950, 971-974. Capus M. Waynick served as acting Technical Cooperation Administrator until the end of November.
[7] Brazil, Burma, Ceylon, India, Indonesia, Iran, Liberia, Paraguay, and Thailand.

ized agencies in proportions already determined by the General Assembly. The United States, with a pledge of $12,007,500 or 60 percent of the total, emerged as the largest single contributor, followed by the United Kingdom with £760,000 ($2,128,-000) and 48 other countries which pledged smaller amounts, partly in dollars but largely in their own currencies. While waiting for the contributions to materialize—always a hazardous period in United Nations affairs—three policy and administrative boards established for the purpose went to work processing and reviewing the multiple requests for technical assistance which had already been submitted by 18 countries.[8]

Both the United States and the United Nations programs were limited to relatively low-cost technical aid and made no provision for the expanded capital investment in underdeveloped countries which, in the opinion of most authorities, would be necessary if such aid was to be fully effective. As already indicated, this omission was due not to oversight but primarily to the fact that there was no source from which investment funds could be readily made available in sufficient volume. The lending capacity of the two major institutions in this field, the International Bank for Reconstruction and Development and the Export-Import Bank, could not be materially increased except through a diversion of United States public funds, which would be difficult to bring about in view of the other demands on American resources and the adverse sentiments of the American financial community. The same objections would apply to any new international investment authority. Private foreign investment was not particularly welcomed by most underdeveloped countries, and in any case had hitherto remained far below economically desirable levels despite American emphasis on the need to create a more favorable investment "climate" abroad. The concentration on technical assistance, therefore, reflected the realities of international finance

[8] Cf. *United Nations Technical Assistance Conference: Resolutions and Final Act*, U.N. Document E/CONF. 10/11, June 15, 1950, as corrected; *First* and *Second Reports of the Technical Assistance Board to the Technical Assistance Committee*, U.N. Documents E/1742, July 4, 1950 and E/1911, January 24, 1951.

in mid-1950 much more than it did the actual needs of under-developed areas.

This arbitrary division of the problem was avoided in the greatly expanded "Colombo Plan for Cooperative Economic Development in South and Southeast Asia" which the British Commonwealth governments made public in November. A six-year development program covering India and Pakistan, Malaya and Singapore, North Borneo, Brunei, Sarawak, and any other Southeast Asian countries that desired to participate, it envisaged a combination of capital investment and technical aid with an estimated over-all cost of £1,868 million ($5.2 billion). The largest share of new investment funds was to be channeled into transport and communications, with agriculture second; mining and industry came very low on the list. Only 15 percent of the proposed expenditures was allocated to Southeast Asia proper; India alone would absorb 70 percent, and Pakistan 15 percent.[9]

The Colombo Plan was by far the most comprehensive attempt yet made to come to grips with the problems of economic underdevelopment in an entire area which was also a uniquely unstable portion of the earth's surface. It was not far removed from the concept of an "Asian Marshall Plan" which had sometimes been mooted as the only adequate way of putting non-Communist Asia on its feet. From the standpoint of the British Commonwealth, it was a realistic attempt at identification with progressive, constructive tendencies in a region of major Commonwealth interest. If it contained an element of unreality, it lay in the supposition that such far-reaching plans could be carried through in the midst of a world rearmament drive. British financial participation was to be largely in the form of released sterling balances held on behalf of other participants; but these would cover only a fraction of the total costs, and the possibility of any additional British contribution would depend largely on how successfully the

[9] *Colombo Plan for the Co-operative Economic Development in South and South-East Asia: Report by the Commonwealth Consultative Committee* (Cmd. 8080, London, September-October 1950).

United Kingdom could manage the new burdens of rearmament. Ultimately the prospects for the Colombo Plan depended on how far the United States conceived it to be in this country's interest to participate. Even if the United States chose not to participate directly—as it would have to do, to the extent of perhaps $2 billion, if the announced targets were to be reached —its actions would still have a decisive indirect effect because of its influence on the economic situation of the major countries involved.

Experience with the Point Four legislation had shown that it would take time to convince American opinion that this country really had a stake in the welfare of underdeveloped areas, and one that was closely related to its interest in frustrating the ambitions of the Kremlin. How long it would take for this truth to win general acceptance was problematical, but the process of national education was certain to be furthered by the analysis presented late in 1950 in Gordon Gray's *Report to the President on Foreign Economic Policies.* Social and economic progress in underdeveloped areas, this report declared, was "more important than ever to the security and well-being of free countries"; furthermore, it roundly asserted that activities to date "have not been pressed with the vigor that the situation requires and . . . have not yet been fused into a sufficiently effective program." [10]

The boldest recommendations of the Gray report were concerned with means of overcoming this handicap. Private investment, public loans, technical assistance, and grants all had a significant role to play, the report argued. Private investments should still be considered the most desirable means of providing capital, but "under present conditions a heavy reliance on public lending must be recognized as essential for an aggressive development program." The International Bank and the Export-Import Bank should aim at "a net outflow of capital to underdeveloped areas in the range of 600 to 800 million dollars a year, of which half or more should be supplied by the International Bank from sources other than the United States

[10] *Report to the President on Foreign Economic Policies,* cited, 5, 9.

Treasury." This compared with a net outflow of $144 million during the fiscal year 1950, of which $70 million had come from the International Bank and $74 million from the Export-Import Bank. Direct grants for development and technical assistance, currently being provided by the United States at a rate of $150 million a year, would also be required in certain cases: "It seems probable that a needed, feasible, and effective [grant] program would require funds of up to about 500 million dollars a year for several years, apart from emergency requirements arising from military action." Finally, the report insisted, the administration of all such programs "should be much more closely coordinated than is now the case." [11]

These recommendations were commended by the President to the special study of the Advisory Board on International Development, which was expected to submit its views in time for action by the new Congress early in 1951. But it was easy to foresee that the case for an expanded Point Four, like Mr. Gray's parallel recommendations dealing with the promotion of a multilateral and nondiscriminatory system of world trade, would be difficult to put across at a time when the direct costs of rearmament would be monopolizing national attention. Even if the needs of the underdeveloped countries were not entirely overlooked, they would almost certainly be further subordinated to immediate military requirements. This type of emphasis, however, would considerably impair the political effect of the program—especially in Asia, where there was already a prevalent feeling that any economic assistance provided by the West was motivated by the selfish aim of gaining new allies against the Soviet Union. Local sensitivities and American preoccupation with other matters made it certain that the rebuilding of Asia's crumbling bastions would proceed under severe difficulties.

[11] *Ibid.*, 12-14, 64. It was further recommended that the lending authority of the Export-Import Bank be increased from $3.5 to $5 billion "in order to make advance planning effective," and that borrowers be permitted to spend the loans outside the U.S.

2. Middle East No Man's Land

In few segments of the ring of free countries around the Soviet bloc did conditions in 1950 give as little cause for satisfaction as in the area loosely called the Middle East, from Egypt and the Levant States to Iran and the Indian Ocean. In global strategy this area might well outrank the Far Eastern theater which had occasioned such lively concern since the fall of Nationalist China. A traditional objective of Russian expansionism, the region seemed almost to invite a Soviet push that would split the free world along its North-South axis, deny it the abundant oil resources of Iran, Iraq, and the Arabian peninsula, and open a path for the extension of Soviet influence westward across Africa and eastward into Pakistan and India. This was a region that seemed to call preeminently for creating a "situation of strength"; yet the actual situation was one of notorious and dangerous weakness. Great Britain held only shreds of its former prestige and influence in the area; the United States had not come in to fill the vacuum effectively; and the capacity of the local governments to fend for themselves in such troubled times was doubtful to say the least.

Failure by the West to maintain a sounder footing in these countries resulted not so much from willful neglect as from the difficulty of keeping in step with the social and psychological transformations that were taking place in the Middle East as a feudal society gave place to modern national states. The whole movement of recent Middle Eastern history had been directed toward shaking off Western control, at a time when the societies of the region were not ripe to appreciate the political values of Western democracy or even to make effective use of such Western technological aid as was available for the modernization and strengthening of their economies. Though there were outstanding exceptions, the Middle Eastern mind was still largely frozen in an obsolete political and social outlook that impeded genuine reform at home and substituted violent xenophobia and anti-Westernism for the discriminating appraisal of world trends which the position of the region made desirable. These traits, common in some measure to the entire Middle East, seemed especially prominent in the nations of the Arab world, which had lost their fight to block the creation of Israel in 1948 but still allowed their chagrin over this reverse to blind them to larger issues in the world outside.

The Jewish state of Israel, with its predominantly Westernized population, advanced technology, and progressive outlook, was an exception to the general rule of backwardness and political myopia. There were friends of Israel in the United States who urged that that country be made the anchor of an American position in the Middle East, through inclusion in the European Recovery Program and even the North Atlantic Treaty. It was a fact that the Israeli outlook was in many respects closely akin to that of the West; yet it was very doubtful how far the country was qualified to uphold Western interests in the area. Barren, overcrowded Israel would have all it could do to survive in its hostile environment; its government was almost as sensitive as India's about taking sides in the East-West struggle. Furthermore, Western partiality to Israel implied continued bad relations with the surrounding Arab states, which the West had thoroughly antagonized but could ill afford to write off in view of their vital petroleum resources and commanding position in world strategy and communications.

Revolutionary economic and social changes would be needed before the Middle East as a whole was ready to take its legitimate place in the councils of the free world—changes which the slow and cautious methods associated with the Point Four concept might or might not suffice to bring about while time was available. Meanwhile, a settlement of the Palestine quarrel was obviously of first importance if the region was ever to break loose from its local fixations and begin adjusting itself to present-day reality. Yet even this seemed impossible without profound changes in the Israeli and Arab outlook.

Appropriate organs of the United Nations labored through 1950 to bring peace to Palestine, as they had done through 1949, but with no greater success. The armistice agreements concluded early in 1949 remained in effect—save for occasional armed clashes and reciprocal accusations, some of which came before the Security Council during the autumn, that bore witness to the continued state of tension. But except for Jordan's annexation of the Arab area in eastern Palestine (to the disgust of its fellow members of the Arab League) there was virtually no progress toward a definitive settlement. The questions of Israel's permanent frontiers, of the status of Jerusalem, and of the 800,000-odd Arab refugees congregated outside the provisional Israeli boundary still remained as seemingly irreducible obstacles to pacification.

The United Nations Conciliation Commission for Palestine reported in a communication dated October 23 that its efforts to bring the parties together had failed and that it was now up to the General Assembly to urge them to engage in direct discussions under United Nations auspices.[12] But the 60-nation General Assembly, now in session in New York, was even less able to promote agreed solutions than the three-member Commission. It could and did urge negotiations, as requested;[13] but only on the problem of the Arab refugees, whose tragic plight the Commission had signalized as the most urgent motive for a quick peace, did it take any formal action. It failed either to retract or confirm its unenforceable demand of the year before for the internationalization of Jerusalem, and the Holy City remained split between Israel and Jordan.[14]

The problem of the Arab refugees was more acute than any territorial issue, not only because of the human misery involved but also because Arab and Israeli tempers would never cool as long as these people's status remained unsettled. Neutral authorities, if not the Arab governments, had virtually given up

[12] *Supplementary Report of the U.N. Conciliation Commission for Palestine,* October 23, U.N. Document A/1367/Add. 1, October 24, 1950; cf. also the Commission's *General Progress Report,* September 2, U.N. Document A/1367, September 22, 1950, and the maps in *The United States in World Affairs, 1948–1949,* 380.

[13] U.N. Document A/1754, adopted December 14, 1950.

[14] The only proposal on Jerusalem which came to a formal vote in the Assembly was a Belgian draft resolution calling for further study of the problem, and this failed to gain the necessary two-thirds majority when a vote was taken on December 15.

hope of returning the refugees to Israel as originally intended, and were concentrating on the idea of getting them integrated into the local Arab economies. But the outlook for progress in this direction was dim. The "relief and works" program authorized by the Assembly in 1949 had received inadequate financial support and produced only insignificant results; if anything, the material and moral state of the refugees was worse than the year before.[15] The Assembly had no real solution to offer, but authorized the Relief and Works Agency to go on administering direct relief for another 18 months while continuing to seek the permanent reintegration of the refugees through agreement with the Arab governments. The necessary funds, estimated at $50 million, were to be sought through later negotiations.[16]

These issues were the outstanding sore spot of the Arab world, but even without them there would still have been plenty of the unrest and instability that sooner or later invited Stalinist penetration. The Arab governments, insecurely rooted in the shallow soil of Arab society, were suspicious of each other and of their own peoples. Their own insecurity was partly accountable for their habit of catering to nationalist Arab opinion, while their mutual jealousies were a bar to the effective pursuit of common interests. In so far as they did manage to act together, it was usually in opposition to Western interests rather than in harmony with them. To the Western governments—which themselves often pursued conflicting aims in the Middle East—it seemed that the primary interest of the area was to consolidate itself against the growing menace of Soviet imperialism. The Arab governments, though not wholly blind to this necessity, subordinated it to the aim of consolidation against Israel and against the remaining traces of the older, Western imperialism. Until satisfied that their independence had been secured against the West, they were un-

[15] *Assistance to Palestine Refugees: Interim Report of the U.N. Relief and Works Agency for Palestine Refugees in the Near East,* U.N. Document A/1451, October 19, 1950.
[16] U.N. Document A/1603, adopted December 2, 1950.

willing to think seriously in terms of securing it against the East.

This divergence of aims was the fundamental obstacle to the kind of Arab-Western partnership that would otherwise have been indicated. The Arab League, which Great Britain had originally encouraged in the hope of establishing a bulwark of its Middle Eastern position, had instead functioned—rather ineffectively, it is true—as an instrument for common military action against Zionism and, implicitly, as a common political front against the West. Great Britain continued its attempts to cultivate Arab good will, and continued to supply some military equipment to Egypt, Jordan, and Iraq, with which it had special treaty relations; but whether this activity would redound to Britain's ultimate advantage was more than questionable. In May 1950 the three Western Foreign Ministers affirmed that both the Arab states and Israel were entitled to maintain "a certain level" of armed forces in the interest of their own security and that of the Middle East.[17] Anything like large-scale extension of the Mutual Defense Assistance Program to this area would, however, have been unthinkable while Israeli-Arab relations remained so tense and the political allegiance of the Arab governments was so uncertain.

In November, a renewal of the chronic anti-British agitation in Egypt and Iraq pointed up the precariousness of the Western position at a time when the Chinese Communist intervention in Korea had confronted the free world with a supreme crisis. The Egyptian Government, spurred by an unusual degree of internal unrest, chose this moment to open a new offensive against Britain's treaty position in the Suez Canal Zone and the Anglo-Egyptian Sudan. King Farouk's speech from the throne, read on November 16, declared that the Anglo-Egyptian treaty of 1936 and the 1899 agreements on the Sudan had lost their validity as a basis for Anglo-Egyptian relations and would be "abrogated." Iraq took up the cry; on November 17 Premier Nuri al-Sa'id affirmed his country's solidarity with Egypt,

[17] Tripartite declaration, released May 25, in *Department of State Bulletin*, XXII, June 5, 1950, 886.

adding that the 20-year-old Iraq-British treaty was "outdated and incompatible with current world developments" and that "no foreign nation should have the right to military bases on our territory in peacetime." Mr. Bevin replied in the House of Commons that the United Kingdom stood on its treaty rights and had no intention of leaving the Middle East "defenseless."

These declarations, which provoked a wide echo in the Arab world, reflected well-known Arab national aims which had occasioned repeated crises in earlier years. It was not certain that the Arab governments, especially Egypt's, were really as anxious for the British trops to leave as they sounded. Britain's presence still had some value to them as a stabilizing influence, and there were at least a few Arabs who felt genuine concern over the aggressive policies of the U.S.S.R. and deemed the moment ill chosen for pushing matters to a break with London. The Arab League had sponsored an Arab collective security pact which had been accepted by all the governments except Iraq and Jordan, and a section of Arab opinion was for going ahead with this project and possibly linking it in some way with the North Atlantic-Mediterranean security system. But the general preference was for making a clean sweep of Western influences before turning to other problems. The vehemence of anti-Western feeling, the sensitive Arab concern for "independence" and "sovereignty," and the distractions of the Palestine issue were grave psychological obstacles that would have to be overcome before this part of Asia could begin to pull its weight in the reconstruction of the free world.

Iran in some ways reduplicated the situation in the Arab world, though with the difference that it had no interest in Palestine, was directly exposed to Soviet pressure, had a considerable pro-Soviet movement within its own borders, and consequently was somewhat more circumspect in its dealings with foreign powers of both sides. Without British and especially American support, Iran would have no chance of permanently resisting Russian encroachments as it had managed to do since World War II. This point had been strongly brought out by Shah Mohammed Reza Pahlevi himself on his visit to the

United States late in 1949. On the other hand, acceptance of Western support had the effect of antagonizing the Russians and thus aggravating the very dangers that made it desirable. Furthermore, Iran's effort to strengthen the foundations of its independence was hampered by local factors similar to those prevailing in the Arab world: an antiquated social system which ensured great wealth for a few and bitter poverty for the majority; intense unrest among various groups of the population, which not infrequently sought relief in harassing such foreign interests as the British-owned Anglo-Iranian Oil Company; and the lack of a sound tradition of public administration which frustrated impulses toward reform.

As in various other countries, American action in relation to Iran had sufficed to underline this country's interest in the independence and integrity of free nations, but not to offset in any decisive way the negative factors in the situation. The year 1950 failed to bring any significant advance beyond the general affirmation of American-Iranian solidarity which had marked the high point of the Shah's visit; [18] if anything, it was a period of growing Iranian disillusionment because the concrete results of the visit had been so inconsequential. Iran's share in the global American military assistance appropriations was not significantly augmented, nor was American economic assistance forthcoming on the hoped-for scale.

A $25 million developmental credit for Iran was announced by the Export-Import Bank on October 10, and $500,000 in technical assistance funds was set aside to support the work of an Iranian-United States Joint Commission for Rural Improvement. But release of the credit was delayed by technical obstacles, and the technical cooperation project would make slow headway at best against the massive poverty of Iranian village life. Meanwhile the hopes initially aroused by Iran's own seven-year development plan were being dissipated, as funds and personnel were drained off for current operations and quarreling broke out between Iranian bureaucrats and American engineers retained to direct the project. New tensions were

[18] *The United States in World Affairs, 1949*, 395.

building up over the status of the Anglo-Iranian Oil Company, and the precarious tenure of Premier Ali Razmara symbolized the uphill character of the Shah's fight for reform against the regime of privilege and vested interest with which his parliament was identified.

Iranian coolness toward the West was further evidenced in November by the revocation of rebroadcasting privileges previously accorded to the Voice of America. Meanwhile signs of a warmer relationship with Russia had been climaxed at the beginning of November by the conclusion of a one-year trade pact and an agreement to discuss other outstanding issues. It was wholly unlikely that Iran would voluntarily enter the orbit of the Soviet Union. Soviet intrigues in Iran's northern province of Azerbaijan had not ceased, and the Iranian reaction to the Chinese Communist intervention in Korea showed a realistic awareness of the direction from which danger would come. But it was equally evident that Iran had its own demands to be presented to the West and meanwhile was determined to shun close political association with the Western bloc.

More appealing to Iranian diplomats was the idea, frequently discussed in Middle Eastern circles, of some kind of neutral Middle Eastern or Moslem bloc stretching from Iraq in the west to Pakistan in the east. Theoretically such an arrangement might not have been entirely amiss from the Western point of view if Soviet actions were to precipitate war. It would deprive the West of bases of action close to southern Russia, but, if successfully maintained, would also contain the Soviet pressure toward the Persian Gulf.

In practice, however, it was difficult to see how such an association of inherently weak Middle Eastern states could successfully maintain neutrality against their powerful Soviet neighbor. Unsatisfactory as was the Western position throughout the area, the only solution seemed to lie in adjusting relations with the individual states in a manner that took account of their national aspirations and would enable them to begin developing their potential strength in cooperation with the West.

3. The India-Pakistan Enigma

Conditions bearing upon the future of the free world failed to improve significantly as one proceeded eastward from Iran to Afghanistan, Pakistan, and India, the countries that separated the Sino-Soviet realm of Stalin and Mao Tse-tung from the Indian Ocean. Here there was less immediate motive or threat of Soviet aggression, but an even more striking prevalence of the sort of conditions that favored the slow advance of the Communist tide. The 430 million people of India and Pakistan, in particular, could be said to represent the keystone of non-Communist Asia. Their advance toward harmonious co-existence and social and political health would radiate a spirit of firmness and confidence throughout the Moslem world and Southeast Asia; their collapse into economic chaos or a war of mutual extermination would destroy a major prop of Asian independence.

In the context of world politics in 1950 this area figured chiefly as the seat of tendencies which had proved highly embarrassing to the United States in its effort to maintain the alignment of free nations against the Soviet-sponsored aggression in Korea. The refusal of the Indian Government to accept this country's interpretation of the Far Eastern crisis and to endorse our various protective actions against Communist China had caused lively annoyance in Washington and for the time being destroyed the possibility of coordinated action with Asia's leading non-Communist government. India's policy mirrored with painful clarity the distrust of the West, the insistence on the rights of Asia's reborn peoples, which animated the governments of all the Asian and Arab states from Indonesia to Syria, Lebanon, and Egypt. The fact that India itself was engaged in a bitter feud with Pakistan, its sister nation of the British Commonwealth, in no way lessened the significance of Prime Minister Nehru's opinions as spokesman for governments that represented at least a quarter of modern humanity.

It was not always realized that the non-Communist powers

were fortunate in having a statesman of Nehru's caliber at this vital crossroads of the free world. The validity of some of his views about the dynamics of Soviet and Chinese Communism might be disputed, but he also saw clearly into some aspects of the world situation that the West would disregard at its peril. He realized that Asian nationalism had become a force that could no longer be trifled with; that the indescribable poverty and backwardness of his continent clamored for alleviation; and that its political allegiance could not be bought. He perceived that Asia as a whole would never permit its interests to be subordinated to the exigencies of an ideological and power struggle in which its own sympathies were not deeply engaged.

In a lesser man these perceptions would have resulted in mere anti-Western demagogy of a type that was not unknown among Asian politicians. But Nehru combined with them a breadth of mind and an ethical outlook that prevented their being turned to petty uses. Neither in foreign nor in domestic policy was Nehru's conduct of affairs immune from serious criticism, but even his critics were forced to admit that his acts were guided by deeply felt moral principle and rarely betrayed any compromise with expediency. In this respect he offered the sharpest possible contrast to a man like Stalin, his principal competitor for the moral leadership of Asia. Where Stalin aimed at Asia's "liberation" as a major phase in the drama of totalitarian world conquest, Nehru sought to realize the same goal within an ethical and spiritual framework informed largely by Western ideals. In his own stricken country his leadership represented the principal bulwark against several types of virulent extremism; on a larger plane it was an important barrier to Asia's submergence by the materialistic and amoral tendencies associated with Stalinism.

Under the circumstances Nehru's leadership in Asia was probably less disadvantageous to the West than any alternative that turbulent continent was likely to produce. Any change would most probably be for the worse. Yet changes were obviously on the way, for the situation of the impoverished, overpopulated, and internally divided Indian subcontinent was inherently unstable. As India and Pakistan entered their third year of independence from the British crown they faced readjustments which would demand statesmanship of the highest order. The partition of the subcontinent between these two mutually antagonistic nations had disrupted its economic and politico-strategic unity and aggravated beyond measure the task of governing its discrete fragments. Meanwhile the southward pressure of Stalinism lessened both nations' security against military attack and added the threat of possible invasion to that of an explosive internal situation.

In both India and Pakistan the fundamental task of government was to establish a more decent livelihood for the variegated, continually increasing mass of human beings who crowded their exhausted soil. If Pakistan's needs in this respect appeared secondary, it was only because those of India were so glaringly apparent and so tremendous in scale. The abject, almost universal poverty of Indians and Pakistanis alike was sufficient explanation of their governments' distaste for the East-West struggle, and also, perhaps, for the tensions and blind hatreds that permeated both nations. These emotional forces had been the primary cause of India's partition in 1947, and remained the most intractable obstacle to a beginning of sound reconstruction. Though most conspicuously operative in the many-sided quarrel between India and Pakistan, they also expressed themselves in internal life, especially in India, with such force that the situation perpetually threatened to get out of control. Professed Communists, against whom the Indian Government frequently took strong action, were still a numerically insignificant element in the sea of India's population, but there were few countries where hunger, agrarian discontent, and industrial strife created a more favorable situation for quick Communist gains.

The strife between India and Pakistan handicapped efforts to improve the situation by accentuating the economic problems of both countries, absorbing the attention of their leaders, and keeping nationalist and communal passions at fever pitch. A fresh outbreak of Hindu-Moslem rioting in East and West

Bengal early in 1950 claimed an estimated 3,000 lives, caused the flight of well over a million refugees of the two faiths in opposite directions, and brought relations between the two countries very close to war. For the moment the situation was saved by the joint action of Nehru and Pakistan's Prime Minister, Liaquat Ali Khan. In April they managed to conclude a pact for the reciprocal protection of minorities and took various other steps to alleviate the most acute tensions. Such efforts, however, were strenuously condemned by extremists on both sides and provided only the frailest of barriers against a resurgence of religious and social violence.

No lasting understanding between the two nations was to be hoped for while they remained at odds over the disposition of the former princely state of Kashmir, claimed by India but partially occupied since 1947 by Pakistani and pro-Pakistani as well as Indian armed forces. Three years of effort by the United Nations had failed to eliminate this problem as a threat of war or to disentangle its intricate legal, political, and military aspects in a manner satisfactory to the two governments. Through 1948 a special United Nations commission had labored to secure a formal cessation of hostilities; through 1949 it strove to bring the two parties to agreement on conditions for a truce and a plebiscite. In 1950 this effort was transferred to other hands, with no greater success. An Australian mediator, Sir Owen Dixon, was appointed to the task in April but reported in September that he had completely failed to secure agreement on either a plebiscite or a partition of the disputed state.[19] Meanwhile the danger to peace persisted, and mobilization continued to drain the scanty resources of both countries. The military manpower which in British times had twice helped to save the free world was now tied down in an exhausting and dangerous confrontation within the subcontinent itself.

Superficial analysis of the Kashmir controversy often pro-

[19] *Report of Sir Owen Dixon, United Nations Representative for India and Pakistan, to the Security Council,* U.N. Document S/1791, September 15, 1950. Cf. maps in *The United States in World Affairs, 1947–1948,* 205, and above, p. 176.

duced the impression that India was at fault for rejecting various equitable-sounding proposals that were acceptable to Pakistan. The Indian position, however, was that all Kashmir was legally and rightfully India's and that any concessions to the Pakistani viewpoint were concessions to an aggressor—an interpretation that the Pakistanis for their part strenuously repudiated. No just or satisfactory solution would be found while both parties insisted on pursuing their narrowly exclusive state interests and disregarding the larger interests they had in common. Like the Saar dispute between France and Germany, this was an issue that could only be settled on some higher political plane, just as the Schuman Plan aimed at resolving the Franco-German antagonism by creating a solidarity of interest in place of an historical rivalry. But India and Pakistan showed few signs of readiness to transcend their mutual antagonisms. The two premiers were not insensible to their countries' broader needs, but in the face of such primal animosities their scope of action was tragically limited.

The situation was one that the pooled statesmanship of the British Commonwealth had thus far been powerless to mend, and about which the United States could do comparatively little despite its preoccupation with eliminating sources of irritation in the free world. An Anglo-American attempt to press for a settlement in Kashmir in 1949 had miscarried; Nehru's visit to the United States in the autumn of that year had confirmed the impression that India and this country were thinking along radically different lines; a visit by Liaquat Ali Khan in May 1950 was equally devoid of tangible results.

Economic assistance was, of course, a prime need of both countries, particularly India, which had become a grain-deficit area as a result of partition and, in addition to its other troubles, faced a catastrophic famine as the result of widespread crop failures during 1950. But the normal impediments to effective economic assistance were accentuated here by extraordinary political and psychological difficulties, notably American dissatisfaction with India's position in the East-West conflict and an equally sharp feeling in India that this country was interested only in "buying" allies for the cold war. To some extent the United States was handicapped by a prevalent notion that it had supplanted Great Britain as the leading exponent of Western "imperialism" in the area. In any case the limited sums of money available for economic assistance programs in Asia were in no way proportionate to the magnitude of the needs in this part of the world.

Both India and Pakistan would derive benefit from the Colombo Plan, whose relatively modest goals, however, presupposed a much higher rate of investment than either had been able to obtain thus far from either domestic or foreign sources. The Point Four agreement which the United States and India concluded late in 1950, providing for technical assistance to a value of $1.2 million in the fields of agriculture, river valley development, and transportation,[20] was a constructive step which might produce valuable results if unlimited time were available; but time was short, and meanwhile the population of the subcontinent was growing at the rate of 5 million a year.

That these matters had more than academic or humanitarian interest was emphasized by developments elsewhere in Asia which pointed up their relationship to the transcendent problems of the free world's survival. In the past, India and Pakistan had been shielded from direct contiguity with Stalinist Asia not only by their own mountain defenses but also by a belt of intervening territories comprising Afghanistan on the northwest and the nominally Chinese or Chinese-protected lands of Sinkiang and Tibet on the northeast. Through 1950 the Afghan barrier stood firm—a small, primitive nation whose position on the Soviet periphery resembled Iran's except that it had been the object of somewhat less solicitude on the part of either Russia or the United States. Afghanistan's territorial

[20] *Department of State Bulletin,* XXIV, January 8, 1951, 67. During 1950 the U.S. also allocated $4.5 million in "China area" aid funds to enable India to alleviate its food shortage by purchasing 500,000 tons of grains below the U.S. domestic support price (*Tenth Report to Congress of the Economic Cooperation Administration,* Washington, 1951, 92-93).

demands against Pakistan [21] made it anything but a comfortable neighbor, but its imperialistic aims were at least its own and not Moscow's or Peking's.

Very different was the outlook to the northeast, where the conquest of China was destined to bring Communist power right down to the India-Pakistan borders, a process that was virtually completed by the Chinese Communist invasion of Tibet toward the end of 1950. The prospect of having Communist China as a next-door neighbor undoubtedly had something to do with Nehru's reluctance to antagonize the Peking government, and its accomplishment had ominous potentialities for the future course of events. The campaign in Tibet failed to shake Nehru's insistence on what he considered a fair deal for the Chinese Communists, but did lead him to take certain precautionary steps to strengthen India's position in Nepal and other buffer-like states along the line of the Himalayas. Despite these expedients there could be no doubt that geographical contiguity, in conjunction with long-standing Indian-Chinese frontier disputes, would provide the Moscow-oriented Peking government with new opportunities for pressure and intrigue in a region that was already one of the major weak spots of the free world.

4. Southeast Asia and the Pacific

Throughout most of non-Communist Asia the second half of the twentieth century posed an identical problem. Was emancipation from European political dominance to become an opportunity for growth and development within the liberal-humanistic tradition still nominally upheld by the West, or was it to be merely the prelude to political and social chaos and probably the imposition of a new, more systematic, and more tyrannous imperialism rationalized by the dogmas of Marx and Lenin? In the Middle East, India, and Pakistan, this was still a question for the future; in Southeast Asia and the

[21] *The United States in World Affairs, 1949*, 418-419. In connection with this and the following paragraph, cf. the map on p. 176, above, and the discussion of the Tibetan invasion on pp. 404-405, below.

Pacific the gage had been already thrown down and Stalinism was on the march. Communism had won in China. Local Communist movements in Burma, Malaya, and Indochina, to say nothing of the Philippines, had been at open war with constituted authority for two years or more. Conditions appeared ripe for a vast revolutionary push from China outward which might sweep away the last vestiges of Western influence from that portion of the Asiatic mainland.

It is a truism to state that American policy in this area had thus far rested on no single, generally accepted set of principles and reflected no general consensus about the nature of the Far Eastern problem or the kind of action it demanded from this country. Opposition to Communism was a sentiment on which most Americans agreed, but one which gave rise to the most varied recommendations when applied to the complexities of the Far Eastern situation. The political debate over China policy, in which these differences came out most sharply, tended increasingly to take on the character of historical recriminations as the administration itself became more firmly fixed in a policy of maximum resistance to Peking. Even after the Korean aggression and the neutralization of Formosa, however, American action in the Far East continued to show traces of two distinct conceptions, not necessarily incompatible but difficult to reconcile in a consistent whole.

One of these was the global conception of the Truman Doctrine and the "containment" policy, which conceived the defense of the free world as an indivisible unity and called for resistance to Communist expansion at any threatened point along the Soviet (or, by logical extension, the Sino-Soviet) periphery. This had been the basis of American efforts to strengthen the non-Communist forces throughout Asia, and its principles had been specifically applied to Southeast Asia by the Secretary of State himself.[22] The other conception looked at the Far East from the more conventional, unilateral standpoint of national rather than global defense, and gave special emphasis to those territories whose protection was deemed

[22] Speech before the Commonwealth Club of California, March 15, 1950.

essential to the defense of the continental United States. Thus originated the doctrine of the so-called "defensive perimeter" embracing the Aleutians, Japan, the Ryukyus, and the Philippines—and now, apparently, Formosa, which had been placed under the protection of the Seventh Fleet until hostilities in Korea should be terminated.

Through the latter part of 1950 the United States continued to pursue this dualistic national policy, in addition to prosecuting its mission in Korea on behalf of the United Nations. Economic and military aid to the countries of Southeast Asia was intensified, along lines which represented the best attainable compromise between local requirements, American availabilities, and the political interests of the various Asian and European authorities involved. But relatively increasing emphasis was laid upon the countries of the "defensive perimeter," which it was clearly intended to safeguard even if Southeast Asia should prove indefensible. Japan, in particular, emerged more clearly than ever as the central concern of United States policy in the Pacific.

This emphasis was not altogether welcome to the other free governments of the Pacific, some of which still hoped to escape involvement in the East-West conflict while others resented the implied indifference to their own defense needs. It was widely remarked that strategic considerations were inducing the United States to display special solicitude for those countries and governments which were least in harmony with the present mood of Asia. No one was happy about the revival of Japan, which for many still loomed as a potential menace to the security of the Far East. The other recipients of American favors—Chiang Kai-shek on Formosa, French-supported Bao Dai in Vietnam, the Quirino regime in the Philippines—were generally unpopular in Asia and could contribute little to the popularity of the United States itself. Spokesmen for the Pacific members of the British Commonwealth (especially Australian External Affairs Minister P. C. Spender, leading advocate of a Pacific defense pact modeled on the North Atlantic Treaty) bemoaned Washington's apparent unconcern for advance planning of a coordinated area defense which would include its friends outside the defensive perimeter.

No policy would satisfy everyone in this complicated area; but at least the United States was able to move with some rapidity thanks to the imminence of the Communist threat. Increased military aid to the Philippines and Indochina had been announced by the President within two days of the Korean outbreak, and the tempo of both military and economic assistance measures was steadily increased through the summer and autumn. The supplemental Mutual Defense Assistance appropriation enacted in September carried $303 million for Southeast Asia and the Philippines, in addition to the $75 million for the general area of China and $27.5 million for the Philippines, Korea, and Iran which had been included in the original appropriation for 1950–1951. Economic assistance on a more limited scale was possible under the Point Four legislation and a provision of the Foreign Economic Assistance Act which allotted up to $40 million of unexpended China aid funds for use in the general area outside China proper and Formosa.[23]

The decision to accord both military and economic aid to the associated states of Indochina had been reached months before the Korean aggression. Indochina was in the front line of the struggle with Communism, and there were indications that the Vietminh insurgents, having established contact with the Chinese across the border, were embarking on bolder tactics. By October a guerrilla offensive, evidently Chinese-backed, in the northern border region of Tonking had compelled the French to abandon a number of frontier posts and placed the cities of Hanoi and Haiphong in some danger. In Washington the French Defense and Finance Ministers were informed that the bulk of the military assistance funds available for the Far East was being allocated to Indochina, and that the operations in progress were deemed sufficiently important to justify

[23] See above, p. 93, note 33.

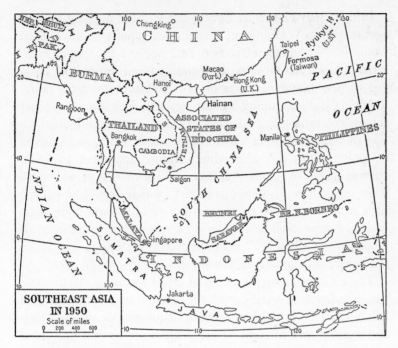

SOUTHEAST ASIA
IN 1950
Scale of miles
0 200 400 600

"a particularly high priority" in the shipment of American
military equipment, including light bombers.[24]

Such assistance might be helpful in stabilizing the situation,
provided Communist China did not intervene directly and provided French and Vietnamese could find a way out of the
political stalemate symbolized by the rule of the Emperor Bao
Dai. Thus far, however, Bao Dai had signally failed to capture
the public imagination in Vietnam, and the French had fallen
equally short of satisfying the political ambitions of even those
tame nationalists who formed Bao Dai's cabinet. While French
administrators and Vietnamese politicians haggled over details,
the entire country threatened to burst into flames. Among the
disillusioned in France, sentiment was growing for dumping
the whole problem into the lap of the United Nations, as
though Korea were not a sufficient strain on the solidarity and
resources of that organization.

[24] Communiqué, October 17, in *Department of State Bulletin*, XXIII, October 30,
1950, 704.

In this crisis French statesmen, not without insistent encouragement from Washington, moved more rapidly than was their wont. In November, after two field surveys by special emissaries, the French Government promised and secured the backing of the National Assembly for a more energetic policy involving the regrouping and strengthening of French military forces, centralization of French political responsibility, formation of national armies by the Indochinese states, and transfer of practically the entire administrative apparatus to Indochinese hands by January 1. The State Department welcomed these evidences of determination,[25] which would, however, have been even more reassuring if they had come some years earlier, before their effect could be offset by the presence of 80,000 or so Chinese Communist troops encamped just across the border in Yunnan and Kwangsi.

The military assistance needs of other Southeast Asian countries had been surveyed during the summer by a special United States mission, but the emergency requirements of Indochina and the coolness of some of the Asian governments prevented any other distribution of American equipment on a large scale. Thailand, which had been spared Communist attack thus far, concluded a military assistance agreement with the United States in October, with the expectation that most of the assistance provided would go to strengthen the security of its troubled frontier with Indochina.[26] In November, ten river patrol craft were assigned to Burma,[27] which, however, was still looked upon primarily as a British responsibility and whose government had shown extreme reluctance to identify its local civil war against Communist-led insurgents with the general East-West conflict. Military assistance to the British forces in Malaya was limited to whatever equipment might become

---

[25] Statement by Assistant Secretary of State Dean Rusk, November 27, *ibid.*, December 11, 1950, 940. In December General Jean de Lattre de Tassigny was vested with full civil and military powers to direct the French effort in Indochina.
[26] *Thailand: Its People and Economy* (Department of State Publication 3958, Washington, 1950), 8; *Department of State Bulletin*, XXIII, October 30, 1950, 701-702; *New York Times*, November 30, 1950.
[27] *Department of State Bulletin*, XXIII, November 27, 1950, 856.

available indirectly as a result of American military aid to the United Kingdom.

The complementarity of British and American responsibilities in Southeast Asia was even more evident in the economic field. Burma had received a British Commonwealth loan of £6 million ($16.8 million) after the Colombo conference in January. The Colombo Plan, although open to all Southeast Asian countries that wished to participate, signalized the special interest of the Commonwealth in the British territories of Malaya, Singapore, and the East Indies. American representatives, while making no commitments, had several times expressed their sympathy with the Commonwealth effort; and United States plans were directed primarily to areas not immediately covered by the Colombo project. Economic cooperation agreements providing a framework for technical and economic assistance through the Economic Cooperation Administration were concluded with Burma and Thailand in September, and with Indonesia in October;[28] in the two latter countries, development would be facilitated by loans from the International Bank and the Export-Import Bank respectively.[29] Shortly thereafter it became known that the E.C.A. was putting the finishing touches on an economic aid program for the fiscal year 1950–1951 which would provide about $21.4 million for the Indochinese states, $13 million for Indonesia, $8 to $10 million for Burma, and $8 million for Thailand.[30]

The island republics of Indonesia and the Philippines offered two different variants on the general problem of Southeast Asia. On trial in Indonesia was the ability of a people just freed from colonial rule and still beyond range of the East-West struggle to put its house in order and set its relations with the West on a basis of mutual advantage and respect.

---

[28] *Ibid.,* September 25, 1950, 500; October 30, 1950, 702. Preliminary agreements were also negotiated with the three Indochinese states.

[29] Thailand was granted $25.4 million in International Bank loans on October 30 (*New York Times,* October 31 and December 11, 1950) ; Indonesia had received a $100 million line of credit from the Export-Import Bank in February.

[30] *Tenth Report to Congress of the Economic Cooperation Administration* (Washington, 1951), 78-93; cf. above, p. 178.

The United States was anxious for the experiment to succeed, and welcomed Indonesia's unanimous acceptance by the General Assembly on September 28 as the sixtieth member of the United Nations. It was too early to judge as yet whether the Indonesian Government would serve as a stabilizing force in Southeast Asia. Its foreign policy as unfolded in the General Assembly showed what seemed an exaggerated distrust of the West, while its internal policy was still concentrated on undoing the work of the Dutch and substituting a strongly centralized regime for the federal system established under United Nations auspices in 1949. The breakdown in December of a Dutch-Indonesian conference to settle the future allegiance of Dutch New Guinea called forth an expression of American concern [31] and demonstrated once again how difficult it was for the West to reach any satisfactory accommodation with the impetuous temper of Asian nationalism.

The Philippines, in whose fate the United States was far more directly concerned, had been independent for four years but had still to demonstrate the capacity to manage its own affairs acceptably. Thanks to the relatively altruistic record of American policy in the islands, relations with the United States were much easier than those of Indonesians with Dutch or Indochinese with French. Internal conditions, however, left much to be desired. Inefficient production, an inequitable system of land tenure, low income levels, and governmental corruption were notoriously prevalent, and on the island of Luzon a fullfledged guerrilla insurrection flourished in the Communist-led Hukbalahap movement. With the tapering off of United States subsidies in the form of reconstruction payments and veterans' benefits, the Republic's financial and balance-of-payments position had deteriorated to a point where bankruptcy and political chaos seemed a reasonable expectation unless strong remedial action was taken.

In July President Truman, acting on the request of Philippine President Elpidio Quirino, appointed a special survey

[31] *New York Times,* January 8, 1951.

mission to examine the Republic's economic and financial problems and recommend measures that would enable it to become and remain self-supporting. Headed by Daniel W. Bell, a Washington banker and former Treasury official, the mission spent two months in the Philippines and in October submitted a comprehensive report confirming both the seriousness of the situation and the need for prompt, drastic measures. Joint action by the Philippine and American governments, it found, would be essential to provide an environment in which the people of the Philippines could work out a "reasonable" solution of their problems. Its recommendation—a five-year program of economic development and technical assistance, involving a thorough overhaul of the economy, the bureaucracy, and the fiscal and tax system—amounted to an application of the Point Four principle on the grand scale. The estimated need for American loans and grants was set at $250 million, the expenditure to be supervised and controlled by an American technical mission.[32]

President Truman approved the report and commended it to his Philippine colleague, who could hardly fail to concur in its conclusions despite the sharp criticism of his administration. But Philippine problems had been diagnosed before; the essential question was whether the doctor's prescription would be followed. Under an agreement concluded in Manila by William C. Foster, the new E.C.A. Administrator, the Philippine Government undertook to propose immediate enactment of an "equitable" tax increase, agricultural minimum wage legislation, and an appropriate declaration of policy, on the understanding that the American administration would recommend congressional action to implement the Bell recommendations.[33] If vigorously prosecuted, the program would go far to reconvert the Philippines into a "showcase" of progressive democ-

[32] *Report to the President of the United States by the Economic Survey Mission to the Philippines* (Department of State Publication 4010, Washington, October 9, 1950).
[33] Shirley Jenkins, "Philippine White Paper," *Far Eastern Survey*, XX, January 1, 1951, 6.

racy. How rapidly it got under way would depend in the first instance on the actions of the Philippine and American congresses.

In the defense field the principles of American-Philippine cooperation were so firmly established that the expansion of the Mutual Defense Assistance Program after Korea raised few questions of more than technical interest. Considerably graver problems faced the United States in assuring the protection of more northerly segments of the recently expanded "defensive perimeter": the Ryukyus, Japan, and Formosa. For the moment the Ryukyus and Japan were under American occupation, and it remained only to ensure that American interests were adequately safeguarded in settling their permanent status. This was a delicate political problem which would have to be handled on the diplomatic level. In contrast, the even more delicate issue of Formosa was dealt with on a strictly military basis under the aegis of the Far East Command.

Military necessity had been the basis for proclaiming Formosa's protection by the Seventh Fleet in June; and the same type of reasoning plainly underlay the decision late in the year, after a lapse of many months, to resume shipments of arms and ammunition to Chiang Kai-shek's forces. Recommendations along this line had been submitted by General Mac-Arthur's headquarters after the Supreme Commander's visit to Formosa in July, and Washington decided to act upon them as soon as it became convinced that the Chinese Communists were bent on aggressive aims in Korea.[34] This change of policy, revealed early in 1951, in no way substantiated the charges of American "aggression" against Formosa with which the Communists were filling the air at the United Nations, nor did it necessarily mean that the United States was going to support a Nationalist invasion of the China mainland such as some American political quarters were advocating. It did, however, strengthen this country's commitment to a particular position on the Formosa problem, thus narrowing the area available for diplomatic negotiations on the Far East as a whole.

[34] New York Times, January 7 and April 26, 1951.

In Japanese affairs the principal impact of Korea was to fortify the United States determination to effect an early and liberal peace settlement, thus crowning the work of reconstruction and regeneration carried out in the five years of occupation. Japan was far and away the most important strategic position in the farther Pacific; concern for its security against external attack could be discerned in various acts of American policy, including the attempt that was shortly to be made to eliminate Communist power from the whole of the neighboring Korean peninsula. The Korean affair further reduced the likelihood of agreement on a Japanese treaty between the democratic and Communist states, but provided additional incentives to put relations between Japan and the non-Communist world on a sound, permanent, and friendly basis. In September the President anounced that informal discussions to this end would be undertaken with the other governments represented on the Far Eastern Commission.[35] Shortly thereafter John Foster Dulles began a round of conversations with representatives of these governments in New York and Washington.

Although a basic decision had already been reached to proceed, if necessary, without Soviet participation, the Soviet Government was not excluded from these exchanges. Indeed, the Russians appeared unusually receptive, thus reinforcing the conciliatory tone that distinguished their political warfare during the early autumn weeks when the United Nations seemed to be winning in Korea. Mr. Malik went so far as to intimate that his government might drop its traditional insistence on negotiation through the veto-ridden Council of Foreign Ministers and accept an 11-power peace conference as suggested by the United States. But this tentative procedural concession served only to accentuate the substantive Soviet-American differences which emerged in the course of later conversations.

Strategic considerations were clearly predominant in the

[35] White House release, September 14, in *Department of State Bulletin*, XXIII, September 25, 1950, 513.

draft proposals which Mr. Dulles submitted as a basis for discussion with the representatives of the other Far Eastern Commission governments.[36] They differentiated sharply between
Japan proper, whose territory was to be limited to the four
main islands in accordance with the terms of surrender, and
the various components of Japan's former island empire, which
were to be dealt with in a fashion that would assure the United
States of a strategic position at least as favorable as it enjoyed
at present. The Ryukyus, including Okinawa, and the Bonin
Islands were to be placed under United Nations trusteeship
with the United States as administering authority, thus ensuring this country's continued control in an area of major strategic importance. Further, the United States proposed to reopen
the question of Formosa and the Pescadores, which had been
provisionally allotted to China, and of South Sakhalin and the
Kuriles, which had already been annexed by the U.S.S.R. The
permanent status of all these territories, provisionally regulated
at the Cairo and Potsdam conferences, was now to be determined in concert by Great Britain, the U.S.S.R., China, and
the United States; if (as seemed probable) they failed to decide the matter within a year, it would be passed to the United
Nations General Assembly, where the Western powers presumably could expect majority support.

In regard to Japan proper, years of deliberation had brought
the United States to the concept of a simplified peace treaty
whose main purpose would be to relieve Japan of the various
burdens and disabilities usually imposed on a defeated aggressor. Aside from the limitation of Japanese sovereignty to
the four main islands, there would be no punitive provisions—
no reparations, no economic restrictions, and, even more important, no limitations on rearmament or the recreation of
armed forces. This concept was the result of two types of considerations. First, it was felt, a magnanimous settlement would
be more likely to bind Japan to the democracies than one

[36] Memorandum to Governments on the Far Eastern Commission, *ibid.*, December
4, 1950, 881.

burdened with petty restrictions. Second, it left ample room for arrangements to deal with the problem of Japanese security, and its relation to the security of the Pacific area as a whole, in the light of conditions actually existing.

Japan itself was debarred by its postwar constitution from maintaining armed forces even for its own defense; yet it could not, in the view of the United States and of many Japanese, be left undefended in the present state of international tension. Eventually it might be necessary to contemplate a constitutional amendment and some measure of Japanese rearmament; but the immediate problem, realistically stated, was to find a basis on which some United States troops might remain after the occupation ended. The solution proposed in the American memorandum was ingenious. As a prospective member of the United Nations, it said, Japan would be expected to contribute in some way to the "collective security" arrangements that were being developed within the world organization. Provisionally, and even before Japan's admission to the United Nations, this contribution might take the form of "facilities" (i.e., military bases and installations) which would be made available cooperatively to United States and perhaps other forces "for the maintenance of international peace and security in the Japan area." Thus foreign troops who were in Japan as a result of military victory would remain for Japan's defense, with the concurrence of the Japanese Government and the other treaty signatories.

These suggestions had evidently been drawn up without much expectation that they would be acceptable to the U.S.S.R. or to Communist China, which was not represented on the Far Eastern Commission in any case and would certainly resent the proposal to reexamine its claim to Formosa. How far the State Department's ideas would prove acceptable to other interested governments, and to the Japanese, also remained to be ascertained. They seemed to offer a basis on which divergent viewpoints might ultimately be compromised, but the divergences were still wide and many more conversations would be needed before the non-Communist governments could enter a peace conference with any prospect of final agreement. Chinese intervention in Korea further complicated the problem by emphasizing the threat to Japanese security and strengthening the tendency in American circles to advocate the outright rearmament of Japan, a course that did not seem to be greatly favored by the Japanese themselves or any of the other peoples concerned with Pacific affairs.

Up to the end of 1950 the principal result of the deliberations had been to confirm the opposition of the Communist world to the line of action favored by the United States. In November Moscow raised a whole series of objections, cast in the form of requests for clarification, which bore most heavily on the proposals affecting the former Japanese possessions and the security arrangements for the Japanese homeland. A few days later *Pravda* reprinted a lengthy statement by Chou En-lai, the Chinese Communist Premier and Foreign Minister, reiterating Communist China's claim to participate in the negotiations and condemning the American proposals with typical violence. In December the United States furnished a detailed answer to the Soviet questionnaire, the gist of which, however, was contained in one sentence: "The United States does not . . . concede that any one nation has a perpetual power to veto the conclusion by others of peace with Japan." [37] If the Soviet Government refused to play, that need not prevent other Pacific governments from acting, collectively or even individually, to end the Japanese war in 1951.

The mere conclusion of one or more peace treaties would not by itself restore Japan to a place of dignity, trust, and economic health among the free nations. The perennial problem of Japan's position in world trade would have to be solved outside the treaty framework, as would questions affecting the permanent political orientation of the Japanese people. Economic recovery had progressed faster than expected in recent months, and Korean rehabilitation, Southeast Asian develop-

[37] Soviet aide-mémoire, November 20, *ibid.*, 881-882; U.S. aide-mémoire, December 28, *ibid.*, XXIV, January 8, 1951, 65-66; statement by Chou En-lai (December 4), in *Pravda*, December 6, 1950.

ment, and Western rearmament all might create important new outlets for Japanese manufactures. One of the most optimistic notes in the Gray report was the intimation that American economic aid to Japan might be unnecessary after the fiscal year 1950–1951.[38] Japanese self-support, however, was a secondary concern in relation to the great objective of reintegrating Japan into the life of the free world. This process would require wisdom and forbearance on all sides, allied no less than Japanese. To many it seemed a risky venture at best; if it succeeded, the free nations would be entitled to congratulate themselves in later years on a signal work of statesmanship.

5. Inter-American Relations in the World Crisis

On December 16, 1950, while President Truman was proclaiming a state of national emergency in view of the "grave threat to the peace of the world" resulting from events in Korea, Secretary Acheson announced that the American representative in the Council of the Organization of American States was being instructed to request a meeting of the American Ministers of Foreign Affairs "to consider problems of an urgent nature and of common interest to the American States." "The aggressive policy of international communism," Acheson explained, ". . . has brought about a situation in which the entire free world is threatened. . . . What is at stake in the present situation, with respect to this inter-American community of ours, is the survival of all that it stands for in the world. The United States, having embarked on urgent mobilization for the common defense, wishes to consult its fellow-members in the inter-American community with respect to the situation which we all face and on the coordination of the common effort required to meet it." [39]

This announcement was virtually the first official sign of exceptional United States interest in Latin American problems

[38] *Report to the President on Foreign Economic Policies*, cited, 12.
[39] *Department of State Bulletin*, XXIV, January 1, 1951, 8.

since the outbreak of the Korean crisis nearly six months earlier. The extraordinary procedure proposed by this country and its speedy acceptance by the other 20 republics reflected both the seriousness of the world situation and the eagerness of Latin American governments to capitalize on the fact that the United States was once again becoming aware of their existence.

Only three meetings of American Foreign Ministers had occurred since the establishment of the inter-American system in 1890—at Panama in 1939, at Havana in 1940, and at Rio de Janeiro in 1942. Each of them had been held in the midst of world war, and each had resulted in important measures to coordinate the action of the Americas in face of the situation created by Axis aggression. The kindred nature of the fourth meeting, eventually scheduled for March 1951, was evident from the agenda proposed by the United States. It included (1) political and military cooperation for the defense of the Americas; (2) cooperation to strengthen the internal security of the American republics; and (3) emergency economic cooperation, embracing both (a) production and distribution for defense purposes, and (b) the basic requirements of the civilian economies for products in short supply.[40]

That a formal inter-American consultation could have been delayed to such a relatively advanced stage of the world crisis was due primarily to two factors: the absence of any direct, immediate Stalinist threat to the Western Hemisphere, which had enabled the United States to concentrate its main attention on more critical theaters; and the existence of a common tradition, symbolized and reinforced by the existence of the Organization of American States, which encouraged a roughly similar approach to the problems of world policy on the part of nearly all the American republics.

The strife-torn world of 1950 had abundantly attested the value of this institutional expression of inter-American solidarity. "In a world shaken by conflict," as Edward G. Miller, Jr., Assistant Secretary of State for Inter-American Affairs, re-

[40] *Ibid.*, January 8, 1951, 66.

marked with no more than normal diplomatic overstatement, "there is, in the Americas, peace among nations. . . . In all sincerity, I believe that our 21 Republics afford an example that should inspire and hearten other regions of the earth. The Americas have proved that countries can discuss their common problems at a common council table and find pacific solutions on a basis of perfect equality and complete respect." [41]

Two occasions earlier in the year had demonstrated the utility of the inter-American machinery, perfected at the Bogotá conference of 1948.[42] In the preceding winter a mounting wave of revolutionary disturbances and international tension in the Caribbean area had prompted the Council to sponsor an exhaustive investigation of the conspirational activities which had kept the region in a state of turmoil for a number of years. Its report, submitted in March 1950, drew attention to the grave implications of this situation for inter-American peace and progress and resulted in the adoption of a series of resolutions admonishing the responsible governments and calling for a study of preventive and remedial measures. This action served to clear an atmosphere which had become exceedingly murky and helped to account for the fact that no further foreign-supported uprisings occurred in the Caribbean during the balance of the year.[43]

As an expression of inter-American solidarity in world affairs the Organization of American States rose with equal propriety to the challenge of Communist aggression in Korea. On June 28, three days after the violation of the 38th parallel and one day after the crucial June 27 meeting of the Security Coun-

[41] Ibid., 62.
[42] The Charter of the Organization of American States, drawn up at Bogotá, was ratified by the U.S. Senate on August 28, 1950. A reservation on the Charter provisions relating to cooperative effort with respect to social, economic, and cultural standards made it clear that the Federal-State relationship under the U.S. Constitution remained unaffected.
[43] Background in The United States in World Affairs, 1949, 477-479; text of report (March 13) in Annals of the Organization of American States, II, No. 3, 1950, 231-252; text of resolutions (April 8), in Department of State Bulletin, XXII, May 15, 1950, 771-774. A summary account by Edward A. Jamison appears ibid., XXIII, July 3, 1950, 18-25.

cil, the Council of the inter-American body unanimously adopted a resolution recalling that all of its members were also members of the United Nations and bound to comply with United Nations decisions; declaring its "firm adherence" to the actions of the Security Council; and reaffirming "the pledges of continental solidarity which unite the American States." [44] All 20 of the Latin American republics backed up this declaration by officially endorsing the Security Council resolution, and, by the beginning of August, 17 of them had promised at least token assistance to the United Nations action. Bolivia placed 30 army officers at the disposal of the Unified Command, and in December Colombia's offer to provide an infantry battalion of 1,080 troops was gratefully accepted.[45]

Yet these positive manifestations of inter-American solidarity had to be evaluated in terms of an over-all situation which was unhappily by no means without negative features. Latin America, for all its attachment to the high-sounding principles of democracy and international harmony, was not an area that could be viewed with much complacency by its inhabitants or by anyone who was genuinely concerned for the health of the free world. Its salvation in the postwar years had been its remoteness from the disintegrating and aggrandizing force of Stalinist imperialism, rather than any peculiar advantages deriving from proximity to the United States. Critically examined, conditions below the Rio Grande were uncomfortably reminiscent of the poverty, instability, and social disorganization that invited subversion and conquest in less fortunately situated lands.

Even the Americas were certainly not free from Communist penetration, the actual extent of which was a subject of lively controversy throughout much of the hemisphere but eluded precise measurement. It seemed clear that the Communists, working primarily through the labor movements, had gained

[44] *Annals of the Organization of American States,* II, No. 3, 1950, 222.
[45] *Korea and the United Nations* (United Nations Publication 1950.I.3, Lake Success, 1950), 89-93; *Department of State Bulletin,* XXIII, November 27, 1950, 870, and XXIV, January 1, 1951, 12.

considerable influence in Guatemala, Cuba, Chile, Argentina, and perhaps other countries, and had even managed on occasion to sway personalities of governmental rank. Not less clear, however, was the unlikelihood that the Communists by themselves could seriously damage the fabric of Latin American society as long as they lacked the close support of any outside power. The real weakness of Latin America was not Communism but the retrograde economic, social, and political situation of which Communism was only one expression. Latin America could be described with only slight exaggeration as a seventeenth-century survival among the free nations of the twentieth century. It was this fundamental backwardness, relieved here and there by a deceptive glitter of modernity, that decisively limited its potentialities as a source of strength to the free world.

Secretary Acheson, in an important speech delivered in the more tranquil atmosphere of September 1949, had defined three distinct aspects of the United States interest in Latin America: national and hemisphere security, encouragement of "democratic representative institutions," and economic cooperation as an aid to both.[46] This formula provided an adequate basis for appraising Latin American trends in the ensuing year, but seemed to reverse the emphasis of actual United States policy during that period. Matters of military security claimed relatively little direct attention, and encouragement of democratic representative institutions received scarcely more. The weight of American interest and activity fell in the economic field—mainly for practical reasons such as the need for strategic materials, but also because it was generally realized that a massive overhauling of Latin American economic life along the lines of the Point Four program was the precondition for progress in other directions.

Washington's comparative indifference to military cooperation in the Americas was readily understandable in terms of the global strategic problem imposed by the Soviet menace.

[46] For an extended analysis of Acheson's speech of September 19, 1949, cf. *The United States in World Affairs, 1949*, 478-485.

The idea of "hemisphere defense," which had attained its greatest popularity in the isolationist days of 1940 and 1941, had never commanded universal assent and had little relevance to a situation in which the United States was committed to a policy of containing Soviet expansionism on the Eurasian continent itself. The Inter-American Treaty of Reciprocal Assistance (Rio Pact) of 1947, unlike the North Atlantic Treaty, was not buttressed by any positive arrangements for collective defense in face of aggression, since the eventuality of aggression against the Western Hemisphere seemed remote. Not until the very close of 1950, when the unavoidable difficulties and dangers of American world policy had become fully manifest, was there a revival by Herbert Hoover and others of the demand for concentrating of our defenses upon "this Western Hemisphere Gibraltar of Western civilization." [47]

In the meantime the United States had continued its intimate military collaboration with Canada, both bilaterally and within the framework of the North Atlantic pact, but had confined its military relations with the Latin American republics to the maintenance of various advisory and training missions and the provision of some surplus military equipment. As signatories of the Rio treaty, the Latin-American nations were entitled under the Mutual Defense Assistance Act to purchase United States military equipment for cash, though not to receive it as gifts. Negotiations with Argentina, Brazil, and Chile for the purchase by each of two light cruisers which had been declared in excess of United States mobilization reserve requirements were completed at the beginning of 1951.[48] The collective aspects of inter-American military cooperation were the province of the Inter-American Defense Board, which, however, could accomplish little until its mission under mid-century conditions was more clearly defined. The summoning of a consultation of Foreign Ministers made it likely that hemispheric military problems would receive closer attention in the year ahead.

[47] Cf. below, pp. 439-440.
[48] Department of State Bulletin, XXIV, January 15, 1951, 104.

In the political field, too, various considerations prevented the United States from exercising strong leadership in Latin America.[49] Chief among them was a considerable doubt as to whether a policy based on ideological preferences was actually suited to Latin American conditions or would serve the best interest of the United States and the hemisphere. Democratic practices did not readily take root in the Latin American soil, and perhaps would not do so until the soil itself had been more thoroughly prepared by education and economic and social improvement. Instability and revolutionary violence might hold back this process even more than did the rule of military dictators allied with clerical-agrarian reaction. Hence the United States generally leaned over backward—too far, as some felt—to avoid interposing in the long, slow process of Latin American democratization.

From the standpoint of political stability, Latin American conditions in 1950 reflected considerable improvement over the turmoil of the three preceding years. There was only one coup d'état, in Haiti, and one assassination of a chief of state, in Venezuela. Orderly changes of government through free elections were initiated in Brazil, El Salvador, Guatemala, Nicaragua, and Uruguay, and comparable developments were in prospect for Bolivia and Venezuela—whose military junta claimed, at least, to be getting ready to return power to elected representatives. Other elections in Haiti, Paraguay, and Peru took place without incident, but reflected at best a partial application of democratic processes since there were no opposition candidates. Of more than ordinary interest was the election of Getulio Vargas to the Brazilian Presidency in November, which conferred a democratic mandate on a former long-time dictator who had distinguished himself for loyal collaboration with the United States during World War II.

[49] That Latin Americans were highly sensitive about even the suggestion of United States interposition in their concerns was evidenced afresh in the furor that arose in March 1950 when Guatemala produced vague charges of such interference (categorically rejected by the United States) as grounds for requesting the withdrawal of the U.S. Ambassador, who was subsequently transferred to another post.

That these developments did not signify a general democratic trend was further evidenced by the undiminished repression practiced in certain Latin American countries. A conspicuous example was the continued outlawry of the APRA, Peru's largest political party, and the continuing confinement of the fugitive APRA leader, Víctor Raúl Haya de la Torre, in the sanctuary of the Colombian Embassy at Lima.[50] Even more revealing was the absence of any perceptible liberalizing tendency in Argentina, wealthiest and most influential of the South American republics, where the demagogic dictatorship of President Juan D. Perón continued to flout civil liberties, freedom of the press, and the canons of just and orderly government while pursuing a foreign policy in which unenlightened self-interest seemed to be the principal component. Although Perón's supporters were not accused of fomenting any new revolutionary disturbances in neighboring countries in 1950, Perónismo as an inherently antidemocratic political and social movement still showed unmistakably expansionist tendencies, and there were definite indications of an attempt to build up Argentine influence in the labor movements and other sectors of Latin American society.

United States relations with Argentina, however, afforded a clear-cut demonstration of the triumph of "practical" over ideological considerations in American foreign policy. The year 1950 completed the reversal of the anti-Perón trend which had been predominant in the early postwar years and saw the United States extending economic benefits to Perón's government on a scale that compared favorably with those accorded to the most democratic of friendly nations. This tendency toward a closer rapprochement had been implicit in certain United States-Argentine financial negotiations undertaken during 1949, and was sealed in February 1950 when Assistant Secretary Miller visited Buenos Aires and conferred with Perón in

[50] Cf. *The United States in World Affairs, 1949,* 475. On November 20, 1950, the International Court delivered an ambiguous ruling which generally favored the Peruvian standpoint but failed to specify whether the fugitive should be surrendered. He therefore remained under Colombian protection pending clarification of the Court's judgment.

the course of a tour of South American capitals. The most conspicuous results, apart from declarations of mutual interest in placing commercial and financial relations on a sound basis, were Argentina's belated ratification of the Rio treaty and the extension by the United States of an Export-Import Bank credit of $125 million to permit the settlement of outstanding Argentine commercial debts.[51]

This step, whose first beneficiaries would be the United States creditors of delinquent Argentine commercial firms, was characterized by the State Department as "an indivisible part of the foundation of a new era of economic collaboration between the two countries." "Healthy economic relations between the United States and Argentina and an increasingly prosperous Argentine economy," said the Department, "can redound only to the benefit of all of the other countries in this hemisphere." In addition, it was hoped that the arrangement would contribute to the furtherance of multilateral world trade and, by increasing trade between Argentina and Europe, assist toward closing of the dollar gap.[52] Naturally, the credit would not be a cure-all. It could not, for instance, avert such situations as developed late in the year when an impasse in Anglo-Argentine trade negotiations had the effect of reducing the meat ration of this country's British allies to the lowest point in history.

The difficulties which had prompted this extraordinary rescue operation resulted in part from the Argentine Government's unsound economic policies in previous years, and in part from conditions which were common to postwar Latin America as a whole—heavy imports from the United States, insufficient exports to Europe, inconvertibility of currencies, depletion of foreign exchange reserves, and inflationary pressure at

[51] Announced on May 17, the Export-Import Bank credit was made available to a consortium of Argentine banks following conclusion of a detailed agreement on November 13 (*New York Times,* November 14, 1950). An explanation of the economic background appeared in *Department of State Bulletin,* XXII, May 22, 1950, 801-803.
[52] *Ibid.,* May 29, 1950, 860-861.

home. Some though not all of these difficulties would be alleviated as a result of the rearmament drive, which greatly increased world demand for Latin American agricultural and mineral products and helped to convert the dollar deficit of earlier postwar years into a 1950 surplus.[53]

Latin American countries would find themselves better able to pay for their imports of capital and consumers' goods from the United States than for some time past; but it was questionable whether the United States, on its side, would be in as good a position to supply Latin American requirements, especially at prices Latin Americans would be willing to pay. The new orientation of the world economy would confront the Western Hemisphere with its own difficult problems in the allocation of scarce materials and manufactured goods and in the control of inflationary forces let loose by rearmament. The Gray report noted a danger that additional higher export earnings by Latin America would "raise the cost of living and promote inflationary profits, on the one hand altering the distribution of real income to a degree that will create social unrest and political instability, and on the other dissipating the additional foreign exchange earnings in wasteful imports of luxury consumers goods." [54]

The rearmament program would also bring changes in the pattern of economic development in Latin America, through private investment, Export-Import and International Bank loans, and technical cooperation under United States and United Nations auspices. Purposeful participation in economic development was a well-established phase of United States policy in Latin America, an area in which, moreover, more than

[53] The following figures for the 20 American republics (in millions of dollars) illustrate this development:

	1947	1949	1950
Imports from U.S.	3,858	2,721	2,668
Exports to U.S.	2,168	2,301	2,907
Excess of imports (—)			
or exports (+)	—1,690	—420	+239

Source: *Foreign Commerce Weekly*, XLIII, April 16, 1951, 30.
[54] *Report to the President on Foreign Economic Policies*, cited, 52.

one-third of all United States private foreign investment was concentrated; thus the advent of Point Four had signified not a new departure as elsewhere but an invigoration and systematization of existing activities which were now endowed with a formal philosophy. The opening in 1950 of an important steel plant in Chile, largely financed by the Export-Import Bank, and the shipment of a small quantity of Chilean pig iron to the United States [55] exemplified the slow transformation of Latin American economies which the United States was helping to bring about.

Development activities continued on various levels through 1950, in forms adjusted to local circumstances. One significant novelty was the new Treaty of Friendship, Commerce, and Economic Development with Uruguay, ratified by the Senate on August 9, whose provisions on the reciprocal treatment of foreign economic enterprises were meant to serve as a standard for bilateral arrangements of the type envisaged under the Point Four program. [56] Two of the new series of Point Four agreements were concluded late in the year. The United States and Paraguay established a permanent four-man joint commission to make studies and recommendations on the expansion of existing programs in the fields of food and agriculture, health and sanitation, and education. With Brazil a similar joint commission was set up to carry forward the work of the Brazil-United States Technical Commission which had surveyed the country in 1948–1949. [57] Colombia, meanwhile, prepared to embark on a comprehensive development plan growing out of a survey by the International Bank, [58] for which it looked primarily to assistance from United Nations sources.

It was noteworthy that the focus of most of this activity was

[55] *Department of State Bulletin*, XXIII, November 27, 1950, 857.
[56] Text *ibid.*, September 25, 1950, 502-509.
[57] *Ibid.*, December 18, 1950, 974-975, and XXIV, January 1, 1951, 25-26. Brazil and the United States also concluded an important cultural agreement, signed October 17 (text *ibid.*, XXIII, October 30, 1950, 697-698).
[58] *The Basis of a Development Program for Colombia: Report of a mission headed by Laughlin Currie and sponsored by the International Bank for Reconstruction and Development in collaboration with the Government of Colombia* (Washington, International Bank, 1950).

national rather than regional or continental, and that it emphasized technical cooperation more than large-scale development projects. Schemes for coordinated development of Latin American countries as a group were a favorite theme of hemisphere economic conferences, and a blueprint for an inter-American program of technical cooperation, approved at an extraordinary session of the Inter-American Economic and Social Council in March and April,[59] represented a modest step in this direction. Most Latin American governments, moreover, would have been only too happy to embark on more grandiose industrialization and development programs. The basic obstacle was the same that was encountered in Point Four operations the world around—namely, the sheer unavailability of the requisite investment capital on terms that would satisfy both foreign borrowers and United States lenders. There was still a wide, perhaps impassable gulf between the Latin American desire for large public loans and grants and the insistence of the United States that the job must be done mainly by private capital. Specific arrangements for developmental aid, whether under governmental or private auspices, were in the nature of slender bridges flung across this chasm.

The rearmament program was likely to mitigate the difficulty in some respects, though certainly not in all, by enabling the Latin American governments to finance a larger proportion of their own development needs and by stimulating a larger volume of United States private investment, particularly in minerals development. The United States Government, for its part, had no intention of shelving its program for cooperative economic development, as Mr. Miller pointed out in an important discussion of the problem on December 6.[60] Continuing attention, he promised, would be directed to assisting the realization of sound development programs and also to "fair and considered treatment of Latin American requirements of goods and services subject to allocation controls." In return, he

[59] *Annals of the Organization of American States,* II, No. 3, 1950, 259-267.
[60] *Department of State Bulletin,* XXIII, December 25, 1950, 1011-1016.

expressed the hope that Latin American governments would take care to avoid the economic and political pitfalls of the road ahead, and that mutual understanding and forbearance would minimize the "frictions and misunderstandings" that were inevitable as the free nations entered a situation just short of all-out mobilization.

Frictions and misunderstandings were certain to occur as the Latin-American nations moved to exploit the new state of affairs. Their cooperation would not come cheap. But such stresses and strains in the inter-American family, though undesirable from any non-Soviet viewpoint, were in a different category from those obtaining in United States relations with most of the Asian nations considered earlier in this chapter. Latin Americans, whatever their feeling about the "colossus of the North," could hardly avoid recognizing that their interests were ultimately bound up with those of this country; and there was no Russian or Chinese colossus waiting to seize upon and exploit every sign of weakness.

Neither of these conditions obtained in the countries of the Middle East and Asia. Those countries were already open to Stalinist attack; yet their other preoccupations were so compelling that they recognized only fitfully, if at all, the fundamental coincidence of their interests with those of the Western world. Much as they needed Western help, they suspected that it would be given not for the sake of improving their condition but only for the purpose of entangling them in an anti-Communist front in which they had no desire to participate. Even in Latin America—even in Europe, for that matter— there were traces of the feeling that the United States was really interested only in strengthening its own military position vis-à-vis the Soviet Union, not in helping other free peoples to solve their problems.

This feeling would have to be taken into account if the remobilization of the free world was to be fully effective. The United States would have to exert itself more effectively to convince other free nations that they, too, had a primary interest in disarming the Stalinist drive toward world power. And at the same time it would have to convince them that military exigencies had not caused this country to forget its interest in the promotion of better living standards and wider opportunities for mankind at large.

CHAPTER EIGHT

THE FIFTH GENERAL ASSEMBLY

THE Charter of the United Nations provides that the General Assembly of all members of that organization shall meet in regular annual sessions and in such special sessions as occasion may require, may discuss any matters within the scope of the Charter, and in general may make recommendations on all such matters as are not under active consideration by the Security Council. By 1950 the Assembly had held four regular and two special sessions, meeting, as John Foster Dulles pointed out on October 9, "in an atmosphere of steadily mounting tension." The Fifth Regular Session was scheduled to convene at the temporary United Nations headquarters on Long Island on September 19.

That the session would be a momentous one was made certain by the hectic condition of international affairs resulting from the Korean aggression; that it would witness another sharply contested round in the political and propaganda battle between East and West was ensured by the arrival of Foreign Minister Vyshinsky at the head of a powerful Soviet delegation. Having called off their boycott of the United Nations, the Soviets clearly intended to use the propaganda facilities of Flushing Meadow and Lake Success to the utmost. Mr. Vyshinsky, unlike his Western colleagues, did not limit himself to a few *pro forma* appearances in the early days of the session. He settled in for weeks of hard slugging in committee and plenary meetings, assuming personal direction of the anti-American crusade which Malik had been conducting in the Security Council through the hot days of late summer.

As usual, the Assembly faced a crowded agenda, comprising over 73 items in the fields of political, economic, social, legal, and administrative affairs, non-self-governing territories, and trusteeship. But much of the detailed work of the session was noticed only on the inside pages of the largest newspapers. Inevitably the serious, many-sided effort to put some reality into the Charter's promises of human betterment was drowned out by the clash of an ideological and power conflict which had by now become global and universal. Every council chamber of the United Nations re-echoed as seldom before with the themes of war and cold war, now given over to the full orchestra of 60 nations.

For the United States, as leader of the free world's resistance to Stalinist imperialism, this transposition and amplification of the world's debate had both advantages and disadvantages. Experience of the past three years had amply confirmed the soundness of this country's practice, inaugurated under Secretary of State Marshall in 1947, of supporting measures to strengthen the role of the General Assembly as the body in which majority sentiment could be brought to bear without the crippling limitation of the Soviet veto. Since majority sentiment on the key issues of the postwar world had invariably been aligned with the United States, the increasing utilization of the Assembly had proved well worth while despite the fact that its recommendations lacked the binding force which the directives of the Security Council were supposed to possess. Through its sponsorship of the Interim Committee and other devices, the United States had helped raise the Assembly to a position of moral ascendancy in which it had had no competitor—none, at any rate, until the Security Council, thanks to the absence of the Soviet delegate, responded in such an exemplary fashion to the events of June 25, 1950.

Through the critical month of July the Security Council had proved itself an admirably effective guardian of interests which were common to the United States and to the free world as a whole. But the total impasse which followed Mr. Malik's return to Lake Success on August 1 had demonstrated afresh that the Security Council was powerless to deal effectively with East-West questions when functioning in the manner foreseen by the Charter. It was reasonable to assume that the Soviets would not make the same mistake twice: the next aggression would probably find a Soviet representative on hand to sabotage the Council's operation from the start. The only reasonable preventive—apart from the highly risky expedient of trying to have the Soviet Union read out of the United Nations—seemed to be a further tapping of the powers of the General Assembly, which the Soviets would certainly denounce as illegal but would be unable to prevent. Thus the major innovation sponsored by the United States at the Fifth Session was the creation of machinery which would enable the Assembly to act, even in cases of aggression, if "lack of unanimity of the permanent members" prevented the Security Council from exercising its responsibilities.

This broad reliance on the General Assembly was based on the assumption that at least two-thirds of the United Nations would continue, as in the past, to see eye to eye with the United States on vital matters. The assumption seemed amply justified in the light of world response to the Korean situation; and, by announcing early in the session that it would also lay the problem of Formosa before the General Assembly, the United States demonstrated its confidence in that body's ability to reach equitable decisions that would not be in conflict with American policy. Later developments, however, made it necessary to ask whether this confidence was entirely warranted. From the standpoint of other United Nations members there was a world of difference between supporting American action against aggression in Korea and supporting American policy in Formosa and in the Far East generally. This wider American policy had already called forth emphatic opposition within the free world, an opposition which tended at times to dampen enthusiasm for American leadership in Korea itself.

The convocation of the General Assembly, while broadening the basis of international support for the United States in many matters, magnified also these currents of objection, criticism, and resistance. On the Security Council, India had represented practically the only serious non-Communist opposition to the American-sponsored course in the Far East. In the General Assembly this function was taken over by an Arab-Asian bloc of 12 or 13 nations, constituting one-fifth of the world organization's membership. Moreover, the prevalent tendency toward political dissociation from the United States continued to spread as this country's opposition to the Chinese Communists continued to harden. Not only would-be neutrals but also some of the staunchest friends of the United States were affected by this movement, which reached a climax in November and December with the confirmation of Chinese Communist intervention in Korea. By that time most of the routine business of the Assembly had been disposed of, leaving the United States battling virtually unassisted to hold together its disintegrating majority in the face of a possible Far Eastern war.

The net effect of the Assembly session, therefore, was to carry a step further the gradual isolation of the United States which seemed to be one of the fundamental objectives of Communist strategy. The Assembly settled to its work in an atmosphere of confidence, engendered by the prospect of total victory in Korea following the successful amphibious landing of United Nations forces at Inchon on September 15. Despite ominous mutterings from Peking, it interposed no serious objection to the pursuit of the broken North Korean armies, first across the 38th parallel and then right up to the Manchurian frontier at the Yalu River. Discounting the peaceful protestations of Mr. Vyshinsky, it gave the usual broad support to American proposals aimed at countering the aggressive tendencies of the Soviet Government. It reached at least partial decisions on a number of important matters not directly involved in the East-West struggle.

Throughout the session, however, from the opening day until December 15, when the Assembly recessed except for one committee left to grapple with the problems of the Far East, the rift over Far Eastern policy had been continuously present as a source of embarrassment and irritation between the United

States and other delegations. Many governments that shared the American conviction concerning the aggressive intent of the U.S.S.R. simply were not prepared to follow this country in applying the same standards to Communist China. Their belief in the reasonableness of Peking's demands was, in some cases, so intense as to blind them to the impropriety of the methods Peking was using to enforce them. Peking's dispatch of an army of "volunteers" into Korea, confronting the United Nations with attempted blackmail on a gigantic scale, disclosed the full extent of this cleavage and brought to a head the opposition to American policy that had been gathering within the free world for some time past. These developments, to be considered more fully in the final chapter, may usefully be kept in mind in judging the positive accomplishments recorded in the following pages.

1. Crossing the Parallel

Through the months that preceded the opening of the Assembly, the international debate on the Far East had centered around two distinct though interrelated problems. One was the status of Communist China, with its demand for representation in the United Nations and, since the American "neutralization" order of June 27, for a free hand against the Nationalists on Formosa; the other was the aggressive war being conducted by Soviet-supported North Korean Communists against the Republic of Korea and the United Nations. The two situations were interrelated because the Chinese Communist demands were supported by the U.S.S.R. and their acceptance was one of the conditions on which the Eastern bloc would clearly insist in any negotiated settlement of the Korean affair. In a negative sense, too, they were interrelated because an important segment of United Nations opinion regarded the Chinese demands as justified and was less than enthusiastic about the insistence of the United States on keeping the two issues separated.

In the course of the Assembly session this interrelationship was to be brought out even more sharply by Communist China's

open intervention in the Korean war, an action that Peking
seemed to regard primarily as a method of enforcing respect
for its wishes. The United States had always taken the view
that Peking was at least a tacit partner in the Korean venture,
and American sources were later to claim that open Chinese
participation had been contemplated "from the beginning." [1]
Thus far, however, there was no indication of Chinese Communist involvement in the Korean hostilities, except through
propaganda supporting the North Korean cause. General Mac-
Arthur had stated in a report to the Security Council that
40,000 to 60,000 Korean troops who had received training and
combat action with the Chinese "People's Liberation Army"
had been released and integrated into the North Korean forces
before the conflict began, but cited no evidence of "direct or
overt" Chinese participation.[2] The new equipment in the hands
of the North Koreans was of Soviet, not Chinese origin; and
United Nations operations were proceeding on the assumption
that the only enemies to be faced were the North Koreans
themselves.

Even before the fact of Chinese intervention came to light at
the beginning of November, however, it was a foregone conclusion that the Chinese as well as the Korean phase of the
Far Eastern problem would get a thorough airing in the General Assembly. The Korean question and some aspects of the
China situation were already on the agenda; the question of
Chinese representation in the United Nations was sure to be
raised again by both Soviet and non-Soviet spokesmen; and the
United States itself took the initiative in asking the Assembly
to consider the problem of Formosa.[3] However much other

[1] Statements of General MacArthur and Assistant Secretary Dean Rusk in *New
York Times*, December 3 and 30, 1950.
[2] U.N. Document S/1796, September 18, 1950.
[3] In view of this action the Security Council, which had at length turned to the
Chinese Communist complaint of American "aggression" (above, p. 238), decided on September 29 to postpone further debate until after November 15 and,
furthermore, to invite a representative of the Peking government to attend its
meetings on the matter. This decision (opposed only by the U.S., Nationalist
China, and Cuba) represented a first important victory for those governments
which for different reasons had been urging that the Chinese Communists be
given a hearing. Nationalist China endeavored to veto the resolution as a matter

governments might disagree with American actions affecting that island, no one could accuse the United States of trying to exclude the question from international consideration as the U.S.S.R. was accustomed to do in similar circumstances.

Of the three questions, that of Chinese representation in the United Nations was clearly of central importance, not only because it was the one on which Soviet and Chinese Communist spokesmen laid chief emphasis but also because the manner in which it was settled might decisively affect the outlook in Korea and Formosa as well. Consciousness of this fact was evidenced at the very first meeting of the Assembly on September 19, an occasion usually confined to ceremonial and routine observances.

The session had hardly been called to order when Sir Benegal N. Rau of India, anticipating a probable move by the Soviet delegation, was on his feet to propose that the matter be settled there and then in Communist China's favor. India, he said, was introducing a draft resolution under which the Peking regime would be identified as the representative of China in the Assembly, and other organs of the United Nations would be invited to follow the Assembly's example. The obligations of United Nations membership, said Sir Benegal, could be carried out only by a government "which, with a reasonable expectancy of permanence, actually exercises control over the territory of that Member and commands the obedience of its people"; and, he added, the Peking regime was "the only such Government functioning in the Republic of China as now constituted."

The passage of such a resolution was clearly within the competence of the Assembly, which, like every other major United Nations organ, had full power to judge the qualifications of any government claiming to represent a member state in its councils. A good many delegations undoubtedly would have been glad to vote for the Indian resolution and dispose of the

of substance, but was overriden by a vote of 1-9; Ernest A. Gross explained that the U.S., though strongly opposing the resolution, considered that it dealt with a procedural matter and therefore was not subject to the veto.

issue once for all. But, if the legal claims of the two Chinese governments were controversial, their political status was more so, as the Assembly was immediately reminded when Vyshinsky burst into a continuation of the tirade against the "reactionary Kuomintang group" which he had carried on throughout the Assembly's 1949 session. Dr. T. F. Tsiang of Nationalist China, in turn, made an effective reply to the Indian and Soviet arguments and declared that the Assembly must choose between what he called a legitimate democratic regime (that of Chiang Kai-shek) and a regime which he described as un-Chinese in origin and character and in no way representative of the Chinese people.

The United States, though officially opposed to the seating of Communist China, was in no hurry to launch into a general debate on the merits of the issue. There would be ample time for that later in the session, said Mr. Acheson, reminding the Assembly that the governments of 43 United Nations members recognized Nationalist China while only 16 recognized the Communists. The "orderly and sensible thing to do," he suggested, "is to vote down this resolution and do it quickly, to organize this Assembly and get on with its work."

A compromise proposal was offered by Canada—a special committee of seven to examine the question and report back with recommendations, pending which the Chinese Nationalist delegation would be seated with the same rights as other delegations. This resolution was presently adopted by a vote of 42-9; [4] but meanwhile the vote on the Indian resolution showed how profoundly the question had divided the free world. Sixteen delegates voted for immediate acceptance of Communist China; among them were not only the five Soviet bloc representatives but also those of Great Britain, the Netherlands, Denmark, Norway, Sweden, Yugoslavia, India, Pakistan, Israel, Afghanistan, and Burma, all of which had previously moved to

[4] A seven-nation committee (Canada, Ecuador, India, Iraq, Mexico, Philippines, Poland) was set up on December 12 to implement this resolution but had not reported before the end of the year. Formation of the committee was intentionally deferred until after the Assembly had considered a Cuban proposal dealing with the general problem of U.N. representation (cf. below, pp. 380-381).

recognize the Peking regime. Only 33 nations—barely more than half the Assembly—cast negative votes. Ten delegations abstained; in this group were France, Canada, Argentina, Ecuador, Guatemala, and five Arab governments.

The lack of general support for the United States on one of the most important issues before the Assembly could hardly have been brought out more clearly, but the full significance of the situation was not to become apparent until later. Meanwhile the Assembly turned down two provocatively phrased Soviet resolutions on the same question and proceeded to elect Nasrollah Entezam of Iran to preside over the session. After a few days of formal speeches—the traditional "general debate" —concrete work on the Korean and other pressing problems began in the Assembly's committee rooms at Lake Success.

On both general and technical grounds the Assembly had an interest in all phases of the Korean situation, including the progress of military operations. With the spectacular amphibious assault on the Inchon area in mid-September, these had taken a startling turn for the better. Almost from one day to the next, victory appeared to have come within the grasp of the United Nations. A much-battered Seoul was liberated in the last week of September, while the main body of United Nations forces in the southeast, breaking out of their encirclement around Pusan, fought their way rapidly across and up the peninsula, inflicting heavy losses on the enemy in personnel and equipment. A junction with the advance force in the Seoul area on September 26 led to the entrapment of more than half the North Koreans in the southwestern part of the peninsula. Other thousands were lost in headlong flight toward the 38th parallel.

By October 1 General MacArthur could claim unqualified success. "The early and total defeat and complete destruction of your armed forces and war-making potential is now inevitable," he declared in a broadcast message to the North Korean commander-in-chief. "I . . . call upon you and the forces under your command, in whatever part of Korea situated, forthwith to lay down your arms and cease hostilities . . . and

. . . at once to liberate all United Nations prisoners of war and civilian internees under your control. . . ." On the same day small units of Republic of Korea troops crossed the 38th parallel in an advance up the east coast.

The speed of these operations took the United Nations by surprise and left little time for deliberation on the grave decisions which they made necessary. The collapse of North Korean resistance offered an opportunity which could not have been foreseen three months earlier, when the Security Council had called for aid to the Republic of Korea "to repel the armed attack and to restore international peace and security in the area." At that time it would have been foolhardy to think of anything more far-reaching than a restoration of the status quo along the 38th parallel. Secretary Acheson had explicitly stated in a speech on June 29 that United Nations action was "solely for the purpose of restoring the Republic of Korea to its status prior to the invasion from the north and of reestablishing the peace broken by that aggression."

Now, however, the military position had been reversed. With its present military preponderance there seemed nothing to prevent the United Nations from going further, eliminating the source of the aggression once for all, and bringing about the unification of Korea which it had been vainly urging since 1947. The legal basis for such a course might be somewhat novel, since it would derive from past resolutions of the Assembly rather than from the Security Council recommendations which had actually brought United Nations armed forces into Korea. This, however, would not be the first time the United Nations had been forced to adapt itself to unforeseen situations growing out of violations of the Charter committed or condoned by the U.S.S.R.

The tone of the discussion in the Assembly's Political Committee indicated that the governments supporting the United Nations action were in general not subject to exaggerated legalistic qualms. A more important question, however, was the political wisdom of conducting major operations north of the 38th parallel. This, after all, would constitute an armed action within Communist-controlled territory; and there were no precedents to indicate how Moscow, which was certainly not overscrupulous about military incursions into the free world, would react to a violation of its own domain. Also to be considered was the attitude of Communist China, which had a long frontier with North Korea and whose Manchurian industry was dependent on certain hydroelectric installations situated on the south bank of the Yalu River.

Some students of the Far East who had noted the northward movement of Chinese troops during the summer believed Peking was genuinely concerned over the proximity of United Nations military forces to its own territory, and was preparing to take major precautions in view of what it considered the hostile disposition of the United States and its Far Eastern commander-in-chief. This opinion was fortified to some extent when Chou En-lai, Premier and Foreign Minister of the year-old Communist government, made a major speech on September 30 in which he bitterly denounced the "frenzied and violent acts of imperialist aggression" of the United States and described this country as "the most dangerous foe of the People's Republic of China." A spreading of American "aggression" under General MacArthur's auspices was possible at any moment, Chou En-lai warned; but the Chinese people, notwithstanding their wholehearted love of peace, would neither tolerate "foreign aggression" against themselves nor would they "supinely tolerate seeing their neighbors being savagely invaded by imperialists." The Korean people, he predicted, would overcome their present difficulties and win final victory.[5]

This warning did not receive the attention it perhaps deserved in view of later developments. Official Washington was inclined to accept the judgment of General MacArthur, who did not expect any untoward consequences to result from advancing into North Korea. Quite possibly the risks of an advance would be less than the risk of standing still and leaving a Communist North Korea in existence, a standing threat to the Republic and to Japan as well. Other governments, though

[5] Peking broadcast in English, October 1, 1950.

not necessarily sharing General MacArthur's confidence in "the pattern of the Oriental psychology to respect and follow aggressive, resolute and dynamic leadership," [6] offered no convinced resistance to leaving matters in the discretion of the Unified Command.

Thus the decision to carry the war across the 38th parallel, which seems momentous in retrospect because it was shortly followed by the open intervention of Communist China, was arrived at with remarkably little preliminary soul-searching. The Security Council did not even discuss the issue. The General Assembly, however, by reiterating its aim of "a unified, independent and democratic Korea," implicitly endorsed the attempt to unify the country by United Nations arms.

The comprehensive resolution which provided this mandate was presented by Great Britain and sponsored by eight governments from four continents. Its crucial provisions, deliberately drafted in vague terms to avoid unduly tying the hands of the United Nations Commander, recommended (a) "all appropriate steps . . . to ensure conditions of stability throughout Korea"; (b) all "constituent acts," including United Nations-sponsored elections, to establish "a unified, independent and democratic Government in the sovereign State of Korea"; (c) cooperation of both South and North Koreans in this process; and (d) that "United Nations forces should not remain in any part of Korea otherwise than so far as necessary for achieving the objectives specified in sub-paragraphs (a) and (b) above." [7] This language was generally viewed as an authorization to General MacArthur to proceed as he saw fit. American and other Western spokesmen gave the fullest assurances that it meant exactly what it said, and concealed no plans for permanent occupation of Korea or the establishment of military bases there.

The utterances of Mr. Vyshinsky gave no particular reason to expect an adverse Soviet reaction. His main concern seemed

[6] Message to the Veterans of Foreign Wars, in *New York Times*, August 29, 1950.
[7] U.N. Document A/1435, sponsored by Australia, Brazil, Cuba, Netherlands, Norway, Pakistan, Philippines, and U.K., and adopted October 7, 1950.

to be with demonstrating the essential reasonableness of the
U.S.S.R., to which end he had introduced a specious proposal
for solving the Korean problem on the basis of a cessation of
hostilities, withdrawal of foreign troops, and the holding of
all-Korean elections under supervision of a United Nations
committee—which, however, would include both the U.S.S.R.
and Communist China.[8] Such delusive offers were no longer
taken seriously. The worst that Vyshinsky could say of the
eight-power resolution, however, was that it could not be implemented—not because any foreign power planned to intervene, but because, according to him, it clashed with the will
of the "Korean people."

The Indian Government, which had managed to accredit an
ambassador to Peking and claimed inside knowledge of Communist China's intentions, later took considerable credit for
warning the United Nations against the contemplated action.
The actual words of Sir B. N. Rau, however, were not so very
categorical. India, he told the Assembly on October 7, just
before the vote, "fears that the result may be to prolong North
Korean resistance, and even to extend the area of conflict. Our
fears may turn out to be wrong, but each government has to
judge the situation upon the best information at its disposal
and to act accordingly. Thus we view with the greatest misgivings the particular recommendation that I have mentioned"
—i.e., the language that was held to sanction the crossing of
the parallel.

With this mild warning echoing in its ears, the Assembly
proceeded to adopt the eight-power resolution by 47 votes to 5,
with India, Yugoslavia, and five Arab states abstaining and
Indonesia not voting. Two days later United Nations forces
crossed the 38th parallel in strength in the western sector and
drove northward toward Pyongyang, the Communist capital.
At the same time General MacArthur broadcast a new surrender message, this one addressed "to the Premier and Govern-

[8] This "phony" resolution, as the New Zealand delegate called it, was rejected in
the Political Committee by a vote of 5-46-8 (5 in favor, 46 opposed, 8 abstentions), and by a paragraph-by-paragraph vote in the Assembly.

ment of North Korea," calling upon them "for the last time" to lay down their arms and cease hostilities or face "such military action as may be necessary to enforce the decrees of the United Nations."

The response was unexpectedly defiant. A message disseminated in the name of North Korean Premier Kim Il Sung instructed the Communist troops to fight to the end, and promised them final victory. Stalin, extending greetings on the second anniversary of Soviet-North Korean diplomatic relations, wished the Korean people "successful completion of their long years of struggle for the establishment of a united, independent, and democratic Korea." [9] A spokesman of the Chinese Communist Foreign Ministry, quoted by the Peking radio, denounced the decision to cross the 38th parallel as "illegal" and declared that the Chinese people could not "stand by idly" while Korea was "invaded" by the United States and its accomplices.[10]

It was later established that the first organized units of Chinese Communist troops crossed the Yalu River into Korea on October 16, just one week after the full-scale crossing of the parallel.[11] For the moment, however, this intervention in no way alleviated the plight of the beaten North Koreans, whose total destruction was now the announced aim of the ground, air, and naval forces operating under the Unified Command. Through the second half of October United Nations forces, fighting their way through rugged, mountainous terrain, advanced on an average of better than 10 miles a day.

[9] Almost simultaneously, on October 9, the Soviet Government protested against another alleged impropriety by American aircraft, claiming that two U.S. planes from Korea had fired on an airfield 100 kilometers inside Soviet territory (USSR Information Bulletin, X, October 27, 1950, 610). Again the U.S. refused to accept the protest on the ground that it should be addressed to the U.N. In a communication to the U.N. Secretary-General on October 19 the U.S. acknowledged that an attack had occurred as a result of "navigation error and poor judgment," expressed regret, and offered to pay any damages determined by a U.N. commission or other appropriate procedure (U.N. Document S/1856, October 19, 1950).

[10] Peking broadcast in English, October 11, 1950.

[11] Special report of General MacArthur to the Security Council, November 5, U.N. Document S/1884, November 6, 1950.

Pyongyang was occupied on the 21st, as parachute drops north of the capital barred the main escape routes. "The wholesale retreat before unrelenting U.N. pressure," General Mac-Arthur reported, "has been extremely expensive to the enemy both in men and in matériel. Enemy prisoners of war have reached an approximate figure of 135,000." [12] Not until late October did the enemy achieve a partial stabilization along a line roughly 50 miles south of the frontier, suggesting to some observers that the task of mopping up in the northern mountains might be prolonged through the winter.

Military victory, in any case, would be only the beginning of the United Nations task in Korea. Behind the battle lines was appalling destruction, destitution on a mass scale, hatred and political confusion. The opportunity to construct a "unified, independent and democratic Korea" had been purchased at a high price and under conditions that would make its realization difficult even if hostile outside influences were excluded. Two paramount questions demanded immediate answers: how was the political reconstruction of the country to be undertaken, and what was to be done about the enormous task of relief and rehabilitation? The eight-power resolution of October 7 had set up a framework for dealing with these problems, but detailed policies had still to be established.

The problem of political reconstruction was essentially the problem of what to do with the existing Republic of Korea government, headed by President Syngman Rhee and previously recognized by the Assembly as the only legitimate government in Korea. Rhee's own view, reputedly shared by General MacArthur, was simple: his government's jurisdiction should be extended to North as well as South Korea, and should serve as the basis for any elections and constitutional changes needed to unify the country. But the Rhee government was not much esteemed in United Nations circles, and the vengeful behavior of some of its representatives in liberated territory did nothing to add to its popularity. The Assem-

[12] U.N. Document S/1885, November 6, 1950.

bly, without excluding the existing regime from playing a role in reconstruction, had stipulated that "all sections and representative bodies of the population of Korea, South and North," should be invited to cooperate with the United Nations. To carry out this intention it set up a new seven-nation United Nations Commission for the Unification and Rehabilitation of Korea, and an interim group with the same membership which should "consult with and advise" the Unified Command beginning immediately.[13]

This decision left open the question whether new elections should be held in South as well as North Korea, and also whether Rhee's government should be given temporary authority over civil administration in liberated parts of North Korea. This was what seemed actually to be happening, and there was some reason to fear that South Korean representatives would not be overscrupulous in trying to eliminate anti-Rhee sentiment among their liberated brethren. The United States, which was anxious to give no basis for charges that it was pursuing a reactionary or imperialistic policy in Korea, made no attempt to influence the seven-nation committee in Rhee's favor. On October 12, largely at the instance of Australia, the interim group took the position that the Republic of Korea had jurisdiction only in South Korea and asked General MacArthur to assume provisional responsibility for all government and civil administration north of the 38th parallel. Syngman Rhee, however, loudly denounced this decision and evinced every intention of contesting its application in the field. Thus the future of his government was still in suspense when the appearance of Chinese units at the end of the month threw a new veil of uncertainty over Korea's destiny.

Chinese intervention also overtook United Nations deliberations on the problem of Korean relief and rehabilitation. Extensive civilian relief work had already been carried out by United States and United Nations agencies under the auspices

---

[13] Australia, Chile, Netherlands, Pakistan, Philippines, Thailand, and Turkey were named to the Commission. The United States, which did not seek membership, attached importance to the heavy Asian representation.

of the Unified Command,[14] but existing plans had to be revised in light of events since the Inchon landing. In its resolution of October 7 the Assembly had asked the Economic and Social Council to develop quick plans for post-hostilities relief and rehabilitation, as well as a long-term program to promote Korean economic development and social progress. There was some delay in obtaining firm estimates of relief requirements for the whole country, and the figures submitted by the Unified Command, the Republic of Korea Government, and the United Nations Secretariat varied considerably among themselves. Eventually, on November 7, the Economic and Social Council adopted plans for a new relief agency, the United Nations Korean Reconstruction Agency, and sent them to the General Assembly with an intimation that relief operations in 1951 and early 1952 would cost something like $250 million. The Assembly approved the proposed administrative arrangements on December 1, and a negotiating committee was appointed to solicit contributions from both members and nonmembers of the United Nations.[15]

In all these actions relating to Korea the United States avoided any attempt to impose its own views in opposition to the wishes of other non-Communist nations in the Assembly. Even the decision to carry the war across the 38th parallel, though clearly in consonance with official preferences in Washington and Tokyo, was a spontaneous act of the Assembly which could not be said to have been made under American pressure. In this respect American policy struck the observer as much more conciliatory than it did in the matter of Chinese Communist representation and some other questions before the Assembly.

Yet it would be incorrect to suggest that this display of moderation inspired universal confidence. The temporary victory in Korea went far to restore respect for American military leadership, but failed to dispel the old misgivings about the

[14] These activities are summarized in U.N. Document E/1851/Rev. 1, October 11, 1950.
[15] U.N. Document A/1595, adopted December 1, 1950.

general drift of American policy. To some extent these were heightened by American discussions of the idea of "preventive war" and the bellicose tone of political campaign speeches on the Far East in anticipation of the November 7 election. From gatherings as unlike as the Institute of Pacific Relations conference in Lucknow and the British Labor party conference at Margate came evidence that the aims of the United States were frequently misunderstood and its intentions widely distrusted.

In mid-October, speculation about American intentions was greatly stimulated by the sensational decision of President Truman to fly to Wake Island for a face-to-face talk with General MacArthur. Neither the motivations nor the results of this meeting were fully disclosed at the time, nor can they be adequately set forth in a history written so soon after the event. Although the President took with him an imposing array of diplomatic and military talent, no witnesses were present at the crucial conversation—"primarily . . . about the problems in Korea"—which took place in a quonset hut on Wake Island on Sunday morning, October 15. Subsequent disclosures—confirming, among other things, the supposition that the United Nations Commander had greatly underestimated the likelihood and eventual consequences of Chinese Communist intervention in Korea—were to figure largely in the national controversy that followed the removal of General MacArthur in April 1951. The immediate significance of the conference, however, lay principally in its confusing effect on world opinion.

The President's own views on Far Eastern policy were abundantly set forth at all stages of the journey. There could be no doubt that he and his advisers were deeply impressed by foreign misgivings about the role of the United States, and anxious to dispel them as far as possible. Repeatedly the President emphasized that the United States, though resolute and rapidly gaining in strength, was unwaveringly devoted to peace, had no thought of pursuing selfish advantages in Korea or elsewhere, and was determined to act in harmony with the peace-loving majority of the United Nations. Yet these assurances were not fully effective. A joint communiqué, drafted by the President and initialed by General MacArthur, stressed the conferees' "very complete unanimity of view" but somehow failed to allay suspicions that the two men still differed on some of the crucial problems with which both were concerned in their different capacities.

On his return journey the President delivered a major address in San Francisco (October 17) which seemed specifically aimed at soothing Asian doubts and assuring the Asian peoples that the United States was their friend. "Let this be crystal clear to all," he said, "we have no aggressive designs in Korea or in any other place in the Far East or elsewhere. No country in the world which really wants peace has any reason to fear the United States." Nor did we, in our necessary preoccupation with preventing aggression, overlook the positive needs and aspirations of the Far Eastern peoples—their sense of freedom and independence, their problems of social injustice, land distribution, productivity, standards of living. We were not "trying to push blueprints upon them as ready-made answers for all their complicated problems," but we did stand ready to help those who desired it. "We seek full partnership with the peoples of Asia, as with all other peoples, in the defense and support of the ideals which we and they have written into the Charter of the United Nations. This is the partnership of peace."

2. Uniting for Peace

A week after his San Francisco speech the President delivered another important address before the General Assembly itself on the occasion of United Nations Day, October 24. Once again he solemnly reaffirmed the dedication of the United States to peace and to the purposes of the United Nations. Three fundamental ideas formed the groundwork of his remarks: (1) The United States refused to believe war was inevitable, and always stood ready to negotiate with other countries on a basis of mutual good faith; (2) under present conditions, however, the United States and the other peace-loving nations had no choice but to create the armaments needed to make the world secure against aggression; (3) nevertheless the search for a settlement of differences and for the reduction and control of world armaments must never be relaxed. Effective disarmament, said the President, "would release immense resources for the good of mankind. It would free the nations to devote more of their energies to wiping out poverty, hunger, and injustice. . . . As the cost of maintaining armaments decreased, every nation could greatly increase its contributions to advancing human welfare. All of us could then pool even greater resources to support the United Nations in its war against want."

This emphasis was well suited to the atmosphere that had settled over the General Assembly in the course of five weeks' work. As usual, the Assembly's main concern in nearly all phases of its agenda had been with the problems created by Soviet imperialism in a world which, for the most part, was still free and wanted to remain so. As usual, the United States had led the effort to mobilize the moral and material power of the United Nations in ways that would effectively counter Soviet ambitions. The Soviet Union and its bloc of satellites had, as usual, denounced this effort as the work of megalomaniacs and warmongers, and gone to great lengths to contrast the "saber-rattling" of the "American warlords" with the allegedly pacific aims of the Soviet-ruled "camp of peace and democracy." And, as usual, the great majority of the free nations had followed the American lead—not, however, without the usual fears that the United States was going too far and too fast and inadvertently dragging the world farther along the road to war.

These typical attitudes emerged most clearly in the discussion of the various "peace" plans which occupied much of the Assembly's attention during its first two months. Differing widely in source, nature, and purpose, these proposals had in common the fact that they professedly aimed at peace and thus paid deference to the prevailing sentiment of the mid-century. Actually they fell into three major categories: (1) American-sponsored proposals for strengthening the United Nations in its primary task of maintaining international peace and security through collective action; (2) Soviet proposals, and Western counterproposals, designed essentially to place moral responsibility for the international tension on the other side; and (3) "neutral" proposals aimed at encouraging the settlement of great-power differences and a return to the original constructive purposes of the United Nations.

The most significant single action of the 1950 Assembly, with the possible exception of its decisions on Korea and on the former Italian colonies, was its adoption of the resolution on "Uniting for Peace" which the United States had put forward as an answer to the permanent deadlock in the Security Council. This plan, first unfolded by Secretary Acheson in his formal opening address to the Assembly on September 20, was a logical development in the American policy of equipping the General Assembly to take over responsibilities which the Security Council had proved incapable of exercising. It owed something to earlier American discussions of United Nations reform as well as to the experience of Korea, which had shown what the United Nations could accomplish when it was temporarily not inhibited by the Soviet veto.

Like the North Atlantic Treaty, the "Acheson plan" was designed to remedy a practical shortcoming of the United Nations by methods that were implicitly authorized in the Charter itself, thus avoiding the hazards of overt Charter revision. Unlike the Atlantic Treaty, which was primarily designed to deter or meet a possible large-scale attack in a key area, the new plan would have no geographical limitations and would probably not be backed by force on any comparable scale. Its greatest utility might come not in a major war but in a recurrence of comparatively small-scale aggressions on the Korean pattern. Among other advantages, it would provide a framework for "collective security" measures such as were then under consideration in connection with the proposed Japanese peace settlement.[16]

As adopted by the Assembly on November 3, the "Uniting for Peace" resolution had five major provisions: (a) It authorized the General Assembly to meet on short notice in an emergency in which the Security Council was prevented from acting, and to recommend appropriate collective measures, including the use of armed force when necessary.[17] (b) It established a 14-nation Peace Observation Commission to observe and report on dangerous situations in any part of the world. (c) It asked all member states to maintain in their armed forces special elements which could be made available for United Nations service on call of the Security Council or the General Assembly. (d) It established a 14-nation Collective Measures Committee to study and report on these and other methods for maintaining and strengthening international peace and security. In addition, (e) the resolution urged all United Nations members to renew their fidelity to the United Nations, honor its decisions, and promote respect for human rights and achievement of economic stability and social progress.

Six members joined the United States in sponsoring this resolution,[18] which was adopted by the overwhelming majority of 52 to 5, with only the Soviet bloc opposed and only Argentina and India abstaining. Even the Soviet bloc supported sections (b) and (e), and Czechoslovakia and the U.S.S.R. accepted places on the Peace Observation Commission. This result, however, was not achieved without long and arduous debate and a number of concessions to the views of the smaller non-Soviet powers. Included in the same package, under the general heading of "United Action for Peace," were two further resolutions which did not conflict with the "Uniting for Peace" program

16 Cf. above, p. 333.
17 If not in session, the Assembly could be convoked on 24 hours' notice at the request of either (a) any seven members of the Security Council, or (b) a majority of the members of the U.N. Recommendation by the Assembly of the use of armed force was limited to cases of a breach of the peace or act of aggression.
18 U.N. Document A/1481 (A), originally sponsored by Canada, France, Philippines, Turkey, U.K., U.S., and Uruguay, and adopted November 3, 1950. Resolutions B and C, discussed below, are included in the same document.

but were designed to encourage pursuit of United Nations aims by more orthodox methods. One (Resolution B), developed from a Soviet draft but so thoroughly amended that the Soviet bloc ultimately refused to vote for it, urged the Security Council itself to perform the jobs assigned it by the Charter and to implement the Charter's unfulfilled provisions on United Nations armed forces. The second (Resolution C), proposed by Iraq and Syria and adopted unanimously, was a new appeal to the Big Five to get together and resolve their differences.[19]

The failure of the Soviet bloc to offer more determined opposition to the "United Action for Peace" resolutions was the result of a complicated tactical situation in the Assembly rather than any fundamental change of heart in Moscow. Concerning the key provisions of the Acheson plan, the ones that would enable the Assembly actually to circumvent a Security Council veto, Eastern spokesmen made it clear that they considered them just as illegal and inadmissable as earlier actions to develop the powers of the Assembly. But the debate came at a moment when the U.S.S.R. was exerting itself to appear in a conciliatory light and undo some of the unfavorable effects of the Korean adventure by a display of peaceful intentions. Despite some contemporaneous manifestations of truculence in the Far East, in Europe, and in the United Nations itself, Soviet "peace" talk was intensified in these early autumn weeks to a point where some observers believed that the Politburo, having suffered an initial defeat in Korea, was planning a radical shift in its political strategy.

In the forefront of these pacific manifestations was Mr. Vyshinsky, a veteran of several "peace" campaigns waged at

[19] Somewhat related to the purposes of the "Uniting for Peace" resolution was a resolution introduced by Yugoslavia on "The Duties of States in the Event of the Outbreak of Hostilities," which called on any state which became involved in armed conflict to declare immediately its readiness to cease military operations and withdraw its military forces from any territory they had occupied. (U.N. Document A/1529, adopted November 17, 1950 by 49-5-1.) Another Yugoslav idea, the establishment of a Permanent Commission of Good Offices to promote pacific settlement of disputes, was referred for examination to the Assembly's Interim Committee. (U.N. Document A/1530, adopted November 17, 1950 by 45-5-3.)

earlier sessions of the Assembly. Instead of flatly rejecting the Acheson plan, Vyshinsky professed to accept large parts of it and merely offered a series of emasculating amendments, accompanied by broad hints that the United States should renounce its policies of "aggression" and live at peace with its neighbors. On October 13, while Chinese Communist "volunteers" massed behind the Yalu River frontier, he openly appealed to the United States to give up its "new tough policy" and return to its wartime practice of great-power cooperation. "Why do you not get back to that situation?" he asked. "If you do, things might change. I am profoundly convinced that things would change. Why do you not give up the attempt of trying to dictate your will to states which are on an equal footing with you and which have equal rights with you? Perhaps then you would clean up that sorry mess which you have created and these obstacles which you have erected on the path to cooperation." [20]

That the U.S.S.R. itself often tried to "dictate its will" to the United Nations was known to everybody, and had been demonstrated anew in the Security Council only the day before when Mr. Malik cast the forty-sixth Soviet veto in order to prevent the nomination of Trygve Lie for a new five-year term as Secretary-General. It was performances like these that made normal cooperation with the Soviet Government impossible. The later history of the Lie case, however, showed that the United States was also willing to insist on its own view if it believed a sufficiently important principle was at stake. While the U.S.S.R. professed its readiness to accept almost anyone except Lie, the United States insisted that the Norwegian was the only acceptable candidate and that to disqualify him would be tantamount to punishing him for his support of the United Nations action in Korea.

Most delegations, though feeling that it would be unfair to penalize Lie for his stand in the Korea case, would have been willing to settle for some other candidate acceptable to both

[20] Statement in the First (Political and Security) Committee: unofficial verbatim translation as reported in *New York Times*, October 14, 1950.

East and West, such as Charles Malik of Lebanon, Lúis Padilla Nervo of Mexico, or General Carlos P. Romulo of the Philippines. Not so the United States, which insisted that Lie must be vindicated in order to establish the independence of his office and its immunity from reprisals. If the Security Council would not recommend him for a new term, the United States argued, the Assembly should extend his present term. On October 25 Ambassador Austin announced that the United States itself would, if necessary, use its first veto to defeat any alternative candidate. Some grumbling ensued, but eventually 14 delegations were persuaded to join the United States in sponsoring a three-year extension of Lie's term by the General Assembly— long enough to constitute a vote of confidence, but not long enough to constitute an overt usurpation of the powers of the Security Council.[21]

While this interlude was being played out, the Assembly's Political and Security Committee had turned to other "peace" resolutions, and in the first instance to a major propaganda item proposed by the U.S.S.R. in Vyshinsky's opening speech. The Soviet delegation was accustomed to submit a tendentious "peace" resolution to each session of the Assembly, and the 1950 model incorporated features from several previous drafts as well as novelties borrowed from the Stockholm "peace" appeal. In language heavily loaded with unacceptable political inferences, it called on the Assembly to condemn "propaganda in favor of a new war," demand unconditional prohibition of atomic weapons and "strict" international control to enforce the ban, declare that the first government using atomic or other means of mass destruction would be a war criminal, and invite the Big Five to conclude a "peace" pact and reduce their armed forces by one-third during 1950.

Experience had taught the non-Communist members of the Assembly not to waste time unraveling sophistries of this nature, but to repudiate them and devote their ingenuity to a

[21] U.N. Document A/1475, adopted November 1, 1950 by 46-5-8. Vyshinsky, however, announced that the U.S.S.R. would refuse to recognize Mr. Lie after his present term expired in February 1951.

positive restatement of those pristine United Nations ideals which the Soviet Union itself perpetually violated. Accordingly, the Soviet resolution was decisively voted down, first in committee and then in plenary session. In its place the Assembly adopted on November 17 two resolutions under the general rubric of "Peace Through Deeds," both inspired by the idea that United Nations goals could be attained "if all the Members of the United Nations demonstrate by deeds their will to achieve peace."

The first resolution, an eight-nation draft which started by recognizing "the profound desire of all mankind to live in enduring peace and security, and in freedom from fear and want," effectively turned the tables on the U.S.S.R. by pointing out that "any aggression, whether committed openly, or by fomenting civil strife in the interest of a foreign power, or otherwise, is the gravest of all crimes against peace and security throughout the world." As indispensable means toward the realization of lasting peace and security it listed (1) "prompt united action . . . to meet aggression wherever it arises," and (2) universal agreement to accept "effective" control of atomic and other armaments under the United Nations, and to promote the application of the resources thus made available "for the general welfare, with due regard to the needs of the underdeveloped areas of the world." [22] The second resolution, submitted by Chile, was a reaffirmation of earlier Assembly resolutions condemning propaganda against peace and measures "hindering mutual comprehension and understanding between peoples." [23]

Before turning its attention to the intricate details of atomic energy and armaments control, the Assembly had also to take a position on the "Twenty-year Program for Achieving Peace through the United Nations" which the Secretary-General had elaborated before the Korean aggression. In distributing his

[22] U.N. Document A/1531, sponsored by Bolivia, France, India, Lebanon, Mexico, Netherlands, U.K., and U.S., and adopted November 17, 1950 by 50-5-1. The defeated Soviet resolution is U.N. Document A/1376, submitted September 20, 1950.
[23] U.N. Document A/1532, adopted November 17, 1950 by 43-0-8.

memorandum on June 6, [24] Mr. Lie had reserved the right to place it on the Assembly's agenda, a step which he had since proceeded to take despite the mixed reception originally accorded his program and the subsequent darkening of the international skies.

As already noted, the principal American objections to the Lie program arose not from its detailed recommendations but from its linkage with the issue of Chinese representation, which Mr. Lie felt must be settled before progress in other directions would be possible. The substance of the memorandum, with its plea for a new effort at agreement on atomic energy, disarmament, and other questions, was unexceptionable if it could be shown that the U.S.S.R. was really disposed to arrive at fair agreements—which seemed more unlikely than ever in the light of the Soviet record since June. It seemed even less probable after Mr. Vyshinsky, while again professing sympathy with some of the ideas under discussion, had denounced the memorandum and its author in such terms as "loudspeaker of the United States of America, of the Anglo-American bloc" and had substituted his own draft 20-year program embodying the standard Soviet views on China, the Security Council, atomic energy, and other subjects covered by the Lie memorandum.

The Soviet counterdraft was voted down, and Mr. Lie energetically denied that his program had been, as Vyshinsky said, "sanctioned by the State Department . . . visaed by the Foreign Office . . . and . . . countersigned by Schuman in Paris." But nothing much could be done with the program in a positive way except to endorse its principles and give the Secretary-General another personal vindication. Acting on a proposal submitted jointly by nine of the smaller powers, the Assembly on November 20 noted that progress had already been made on some of the ten points, commended the Secretary-General for his initiative, and asked the appropriate organs of the United Nations to give consideration to those portions of the memo-

[24] Cf. above, pp. 192-195.

randum with which they were particularly concerned.[25] Actual agreement on the points at issue depended on the outlook of the respective great powers, not on the desires of Mr. Lie or the Assembly.

The fate of the Lie memorandum illustrated the besetting difficulty of all "peace" efforts in 1950, in or outside of the General Assembly. In the political vernacular of the mid-century the word "peace" stood for at least three different kinds of ideas, reflecting as many different interpretations of the world crisis. To the Stalinist mind it was a device for tying the hands of the "imperialists" and promoting the extension of Soviet influence and control—a sugar-coating for the expression of more fundamental political aims. For the majority of the free governments, on the other hand, "peace" meant the right to maintain their own national integrity against the clear threat of Stalinist aggression. Their quest for peace thus expressed itself primarily in a search for more effective forms of collective security, typified by the heavy vote in favor of the "Uniting for Peace" resolution.

Both of these conceptions rested on the idea of a fundamental antagonism between the two worlds, Soviet and free. Somewhere between them lingered the hope that this idea was mistaken, that the opposition of the two worlds was not irreconcilable, and that a real "peace" might yet be brought to birth by restoring contact and confidence between the two sides. This third view, which constantly waxed and waned in intensity, was the inspiration of proposals like Trygve Lie's for the resumption of negotiations on outstanding issues. It had a natural appeal to everyone who was not satisfied with the one-sided "peace" of Stalinism or the equally partial though more constructive "peace" sought by the West. Unlike the latter, however, it was doomed to remain sterile until the great powers began to trust each other—in other words, until the Western governments became convinced that Moscow had ceased to plot their extinction. The second half of 1950 brought

[25] U.N. Document A/1539, adopted November 20, 1950 by 51-5-1.

no development that would have justified the Western governments in coming to any such conclusion.

3. East-West Scrap Heap

Though the majority in the Assembly was at liberty to express opinions on the international situation and could make some progress toward promoting collective security within the free world, it could do virtually nothing toward relieving the basic conditions that made this effort necessary. Its allusion to progress already made on some points of Mr. Lie's memorandum had reference mainly to accomplishments in the economic and social fields and in promoting the advancement of dependent peoples—matters which were peripheral to the East-West struggle and which will be briefly considered later in this chapter. But no real progress had been or would be made toward breaking the East-West deadlock in those matters enumerated by Mr. Lie where an impasse had already been reached, such as the control of atomic energy and conventional armaments, the provision of armed forces to be made available to the Security Council, and the admission of long-standing applicants for United Nations membership.

Equally without decisive effect were the Assembly's actions during this session on a variety of old East-West issues such as the deprivations of human rights and fundamental freedoms in Bulgaria, Hungary, and Rumania. It is true that on one ancient United Nations problem, relations with Franco Spain, the majority of the Assembly registered a change of heart and revoked a part of the anti-Franco measures it had recommended, in concert with the Soviet bloc, in 1946.[26] But on strictly East-West controversies it could only cast about vainly for new solutions and reaffirm opinions already on record. In most instances these opinions were clearly in harmony with those of the United States and condemnatory of the Soviet position; a few of them, notably those on United Nations membership, reflected a feeling that one or more of the Western powers also

[26] Cf. above, pp. 288-289.

had needlessly obstructed progress toward United Nations goals. The essential feature of all these resolutions, however, was the fact that they left the central deadlock untouched. The Assembly might bewail the results of the East-West antagonism, but was powerless to alter the Soviet stand or the consequent positions of Washington, London, and Paris.

The net effect of these miscellaneous Assembly actions was scarcely proportionate to the lengthy debates and the liberal interchanges of East-West invective that preceded them. In most instances a bare record of the eventual decision will suffice. On the matter of human rights and freedoms in Bulgaria, Hungary, and Rumania, for example, the Assembly adopted on November 3 a resolution reiterating the concern it had expressed the year before over the flagrantly totalitarian practices of those countries' Communist regimes. Noting that all three governments had flouted their peace treaty obligations and the opinions of the International Court of Justice and conducted themselves in a manner that showed them to be "callously indifferent to the sentiments of the world community," it sharply reminded them of their duty and—being quite powerless to correct the situation—provided for the collection and circulation of relevant information by the Secretary-General's office.[27]

A second Balkan issue, that of threats to the political independence and territorial integrity of Greece, was still on the Assembly's agenda despite the collapse of guerrilla resistance to the Greek Government in the fall of 1949. The United Nations Special Committee on the Balkans (UNSCOB) had continued to observe conditions along the northern Greek frontier, and reported during the autumn that an external threat to Greece still existed and that Albania, in particular, was continuing to give aid to Greek guerrillas reentering Greece for subversive purposes. The Committee also drew attention to the large number of fugitive guerrillas in the satellite countries, whose disarmament had never been verified, and particularly

[27] U.N. Document A/1486, adopted November 3, 1950 by 40-5-12. For background cf. *The United States in World Affairs, 1949,* 249 and 271-272, and the opinions of the International Court delivered on March 30 and July 18, 1950.

to the thousands of deported Greek children who were still held captive in Eastern Europe. After the usual acrimonious debate the Assembly adopted on December 1 a three-part resolution (a) recommending the voluntary repatriation of Greek military personnel who had been captured and abducted by the guerrillas; (b) continuing UNSCOB for another year; and (c) urging a renewed effort to secure the early return of the Greek children to their parents.[28]

On the same day the Assembly dealt with a parallel piece of unfinished business from the other side of the globe, the item on "threats to the political independence and territorial integrity of China" which had been brought up by the Chinese Nationalist delegation at the 1949 session and referred to the Interim Committee for study and report. Unlike the current Chinese issues which were continually cropping up in the most varied guises, this one dealt with the historical question of whether the Soviet Union, as alleged by Nationalist China, had intervened in Chinese affairs in violation of international treaties and the United Nations Charter. No action was taken, because the Interim Committee reported that it had refrained from considering the matter in view of the many related issues before the Assembly and the existing political situation. The Assembly, never enthusiastic about rushing into this controversy and by now shuddering under the impact of Chinese intervention in Korea, limited itself to (a) instructing the Interim Committee to continue its studies, and (b) asking all states to observe international propriety in their Far Eastern policies.[29]

Still to be reviewed were two old issues of a more general nature, United Nations membership and disarmament. The

---

[28] *Report of the United Nations Special Committee on the Balkans*, U.N. Document A/1307 (General Assembly *Official Records, Fifth Session*, Supplement 11); U.N. Document A/1423, October 9, 1950; U.N. Document A/1584, adopted December 1, 1950 by 53-5-1 (part a), 53-6 (part b), and 50-0-5 (part c).

[29] U.N. Document A/1586, adopted December 1, 1950 by 35-17-7 (part a) and 39-6-14 (part b). For background see *The United States in World Affairs, 1949*, 308-312. The United States originally supported Nationalist China's demand for a U.N. fact-finding commission, which, however, was withdrawn for lack of other support.

"saddest chapter" in United Nations history, as a Brazilian delegate remarked, concerned the 14 nations which had unsuccessfully applied for admission to the world organization between 1946 and 1950—particularly the nine non-Communist states (Austria, Ceylon, Finland, Ireland, Italy, Jordan, Republic of Korea, Nepal, and Portugal) whose claims had been endorsed by the Assembly but lacked the indispensable approval of the Security Council. Security Council approval was unobtainable because the U.S.S.R. refused to clear any of these countries unless the Western powers would drop their opposition to the admission of five Communist states (Albania, Bulgaria, Hungary, Rumania, and the Mongolian People's Republic) concerning whose admissibility they entertained strong doubts.[30]

At the 1950 session the new state of Indonesia, backed by a certification from the Security Council, was admitted to membership as the sixtieth of the United Nations; but there was little that the Assembly could do about the waiting list except to renew its request to the Security Council for favorable consideration of the nine non-Communist applicants.[31] Although it took no specific action on the five Communist states, the tone of debate betrayed some impatience with the position of the Western powers on their applications. The smaller countries generally favored the idea of "universality" of the United Nations, if only because it would increase their voting strength in relation to the great powers. There was a growing feeling that the Western stand was costing more than it was worth and that universality was the only way around great-power disagreements on the merits of this or that particular applicant.

This same disposition to accept political facts which could not easily be altered was evident in the Assembly's handling of a somewhat similar issue which concerned the representation of countries that were already members of the United Nations but had undergone a revolutionary change of government

[30] For background see The United States in World Affairs, 1949, 288-289. The inability of the Assembly to accept new members without recommendation by the Security Council was confirmed by the International Court on March 3, 1950.
[31] U.N. Document A/1624, adopted December 4, 1950 by 46-5-2.

such as had occurred in China. Disagreement on the specific case of China was largely responsible for the Assembly's failure to work out a set of criteria to govern future action in matters of this kind. The debate, initiated at the behest of Cuba, revealed a fundamental disagreement between (1) those governments, including both Great Britain and the U.S.S.R., which supported Communist China's claim to representation and accepted Trygve Lie's view that effective control of a country was the essential criterion; and (2) those governments, headed by the United States, which opposed Communist China and insisted that political factors such as attachment to United Nations principles must also be considered. In the end the Assembly could only agree that such controversies should be promptly considered by the Assembly or the Interim Committee, and decided "in the light of the purposes and principles of the Charter and the circumstances of each case"—leaving the essence of the problem untouched.[32]

In contrast to the division that appeared whenever Chinese matters were under discussion, the Assembly's decision on atomic energy and disarmament found the Western nations as solidly aligned as ever. Though it involved no break in the long-standing deadlock between the majority and the Soviet-controlled minority, this decision offered a theoretical possibility of adjustment through the transference of the dispute to a new forum. This was the direct result of an American concession— not, indeed, a very dangerous one—which had been announced by the President in his address on October 24.

Hitherto the impasse in this field had been threefold. Agreement on international control of atomic energy had been ruled out by Soviet rejection of the only plan for international inspection and control which the majority of the United Nations considered realistic and effective. Progress toward reduction and control of other (conventional) armaments had been barred by the U.S.S.R.'s unwillingness to accept international scrutiny of its military arrangements. And a concerted attack upon the problem of *all* world armaments, atomic and nonatomic, had

[32] U.N. Document A/1753, adopted December 14, 1950 by 36-6-9.

been prevented by American insistence that the two problems be kept separate and dealt with by separate United Nations commissions.

Since the disclosure of the Soviet atomic explosion in 1949 there had been a widespread feeling that the United States ought to make some attempt to meet Soviet views on atomic energy control while there was still hope of agreements which might avert an atomic war. The United States had continued to insist that the "majority plan" already approved by the Assembly must be upheld until someone produced another that was as good or better. It continued to insist that an atmosphere of confidence, coupled with effective inspection, was a prerequisite to disarmament in conventional weapons. But it did at length recede from its position on the separation of the two problems. On October 24, while the chairman of the Atomic Energy Commission in Washington was telling the press that the United States had made great gains in the atomic field during the preceding year, the President suggested that the work of the two United Nations disarmament commissions might profitably be brought closer together. "One possibility to be considered," he said, "is whether their work might be revitalized if carried forward in the future through a new and consolidated disarmament commission."

Although the U.S.S.R. had long chafed at the existing set-up, the explosive response of Mr. Vyshinsky to this suggestion showed how far it fell short of satisfying Soviet requirements. What the Russians had wanted, and still wanted, was an international agreement that would tie the hands of the United States in atomic matters while leaving them free to continue their own atomic development work behind a curtain of secrecy.[33] Knowing that no other great power (except, presumably, Communist China) would concur in such an arrangement, the U.S.S.R. preferred to use the armaments problem as a basis for further propaganda along the lines of the Stockholm

[33] In an address to the Political Committee on October 23 Vyshinsky offered a reinterpretation of the Soviet proposals on atomic energy control which was widely understood as a concession but actually represented no departure from the established Soviet position.

appeal. Thus, as an alternative to the President's proposal—a typical expression of the "atomic bombolatry" of United States ruling circles, according to Vyshinsky—it brought forward once again its frequently rejected demand for simultaneous conventions on (1) unconditional prohibition of the atomic weapon, and (2) international control of atomic energy in accordance with the generally unacceptable Soviet plan.

This move the Assembly decisively rejected on December 13. Instead it adopted an eight-power resolution inspired by the Truman speech. A committee of 12, consisting of the 11 members of the Security Council plus Canada, was set up to consider and report to the 1951 Assembly on "ways and means whereby the work of the Atomic Energy Commission and the Commission for Conventional Armaments may be coordinated and on the advisability of their functions being merged and placed under a new and consolidated disarmament commission." The preamble of the resolution emphasized principles that most nations outside the Soviet bloc agreed were essential to effective disarmament: universality of application, and safeguards to ensure compliance. Not without irony at such a moment, it also drew attention to the fact that effective regulation and reduction of armaments would "substantially diminish the present danger of war, relieve the heavy economic burden placed upon the peoples of the world in the absence of a system of armaments control, and permit the greater use of man's resources to projects devoted to his betterment." [34]

One novel East-West issue still faced the Assembly as the result of a Western decision to hale the U.S.S.R. before the United Nations as a violator of its obligations to repatriate German and Japanese prisoners of war captured in 1945 and earlier. As already noted, the Soviet Government claimed that substantially all prisoners in its hands had been repatriated by the spring of 1950, but had failed to account for up to 1.5 million Germans and between 350,000 and 400,000 Japanese and had resisted all attempts to ascertain their fate. Having exhausted every other recourse, the United States together with

[34] U.N. Document A/1722, adopted December 13, 1950 by 47-5-3.

Great Britain and Australia laid the matter before the General
Assembly, requesting it to consider how information on the
remaining individuals might be obtained and repatriation
brought about for those still living.[35]

As was to be expected, the Soviet Union claimed that this action had no justification in fact, was contrary to the Charter, and
was inspired by propagandistic rather than humanitarian aims.
Equally to be expected was the action of the Assembly in a
matter which, as the American delegate reminded it, was also
of vital interest to Austria, Italy, and various other countries
that had been at war with the U.S.S.R. Though with little hope
of practical results, the Assembly on December 14 expressed
its concern over the evidence presented to it, called upon "all
Governments" to honor their obligations in this regard and
submit full information on all nonrepatriated individuals, and
provided for establishment of an *ad hoc* commission to offer
its good offices "with a view to settling the question . . . in a
purely humanitarian spirit and on terms acceptable to all the
Governments concerned." [36]

4. Progress on the Sidelines

From this record of well-intentioned impotence it is a relief
to turn briefly to other fields in which United Nations action
was less inhibited by the effects of the East-West conflict. That
conflict made itself felt in all phases of United Nations activity,
but with an intensity that varied according to the extent to
which Soviet purposes or interests were directly involved. The
United Nations still could act, after a fashion, in countries like
Palestine and Indonesia; and expressions of the Soviet viewpoint did not prevent it from steering its own course in regard
to what the Charter had designated as "international problems
of an economic, social, cultural, or humanitarian character."
As long as 55 of the United Nations remained outside the
Soviet fold, they were at liberty to organize affairs in their part
of the world according to their own preferences and abilities.

[35] U.N. Document A/1339, August 28, 1950; cf. above, pp. 170, 172, 182.
[36] U.N. Document A/1749, adopted December 14, 1950 by 43-5-6.

It would be misleading to suggest that the record of the United Nations in these more tranquil fields was wholly positive, in 1950 any more than in earlier years. Disagreements and antagonisms within and among the free nations, combined with the universal preoccupations of the "cold war," limited their collective impact on the stupendous problems of twentieth-century international life. Their failure to strengthen the shaky peace in Palestine has already been noted,[37] and other evidences of irresolution and ineffectiveness would be easy to produce. Nevertheless the future of organized humanity was being shaped in this work, perhaps no less decisively than on the bomb-scarred terrain of Korea. By democratic process, decisions were being reached that would profoundly influence the development of all nations, both those that had achieved statehood already and those that still awaited the dawn of independence.

Among the most significant achievements of the General Assembly's five-year history were its decisions of 1949 and 1950 which set Italy's former colonies of Libya and Somaliland on the road to nationhood and prescribed an autonomous existence for Eritrea. In three toilsome sessions of negotiation and debate, from April 1949 to December 1950, the Assembly succeeded in hammering out simple, clear-cut, and not unhopeful solutions for a three-headed diplomatic problem of baffling complexity. In so doing it demonstrated not only the capacity of the United Nations for serious executive action but also the strength of the movement toward independence for the world's remaining colonial and semicolonial peoples. That this movement was one of the dominant forces of the time, one that no government could safely disregard, was demonstrated again and again in reference to the Italian colonies, as it was habitually demonstrated in reference to United Nations responsibility for the administration of trust territories and non-self-governing areas generally.[38]

Four years of United Nations debate prior to 1950 had

[37] Above, pp. 308-310.
[38] For background discussion cf. *The United States in World Affairs, 1949,* 350-382. An eddy of the same movement reached the United States itself on Novem-

clarified both the major problems and the basic international alignments involved in colonial issues—on the one hand, a group of recently emancipated "anticolonial" nations generally supported by the Soviet bloc; on the other, Britain, France, and a handful of lesser countries with direct responsibility for administering colonial and trust territories; in the middle, the United States, whose general political interests identified it with the second group but which endeavored to promote compromise and pay due heed to the aspirations of colonial peoples. In the case of the former Italian colonies, this alignment was complicated both by the strategic interests of the various great powers and by the susceptibilities of Italy itself, which exacted considerable deference because of Italy's membership in the North Atlantic alliance and because its claims were supported by a large number of Latin American governments.

At its 1949 session the Assembly had cut its way through this tangle far enough to settle in broad outline the future of Libya and Italian Somaliland, leaving Eritrea for future consideration. Libya was to become an independent, sovereign state by January 1, 1952, the interval to be occupied in constitution-making and other preparatory activities under United Nations guidance. By the fall of 1950 this process had advanced so far that the Assembly had only to lay down a timetable for the remaining stages and indicate its desire that the new state should receive the benefits of United Nations membership and participation in the United Nations technical assistance program.[39]

Before the end of the year a Libyan national assembly representing the three territories of Tripolitania, Cyrenaica, and Fezzan had met and invited the Emir Sayid Idris al-Sanusi to become King. It was still possible to doubt that Libya had either the political experience or the economic resources to

---

ber 1, 1950 in an attempt on the President's life by persons associated with a small nationalist group in Puerto Rico.
[39] U.N. Documents A/1528, adopted November 17, 1950 by 50-0-6, and (on technical assistance) A/1533, adopted unanimously on the same date.

make its way in the world unassisted, but strategic interests ensured that the United Kingdom, which had been thrown on the defensive in more developed parts of the Moslem world, would do what it could to help the new nation get off to a proper start. The United States, too, had an interest in the success of the experiment, and as a preliminary gesture of friendship announced on November 24 that Libya would be included in the Point Four program.

Somaliland's rise to independent status was scheduled to proceed more slowly. On December 2 the Assembly, completing its action of the year before, approved a trusteeship agreement under which Italy would administer its former colony on behalf of the United Nations for a period of ten years, meanwhile promoting, under the eye of a United Nations Advisory Council, its political, economic, and social preparation for independence.[40]

Eritrea would also have become independent, if the Soviet bloc and some of the anticolonial nations had had their way. But the ethnic, geographic, and political factors in this last remnant of Italian East Africa were so extraordinarily involved that a special United Nations commission had found itself totally unable to agree on a recommendation, and even the usual bloc of anticolonial governments lost its cohesion when the issue was discussed in the Interim Committee and then in the Assembly itself.[41] The solution eventually adopted—largely through the efforts of the United States—was federation of Eritrea with Ethiopia, in a complicated relationship designed to assure the Eritreans control of their domestic affairs while foreign affairs, defense, and finance would be regulated from Addis Ababa. The arrangement was really satisfactory to nobody but seemed to be the only solution capable of winning

[40] U.N. Document A/1617, adopted December 2, 1950 by 44-6-0; see also *Draft Trusteeship Agreement for the Territory of Somaliland Under Italian Administration*, U.N. Document A/1294 (General Assembly, *Official Records, Fifth Session*, Supplement 10).

[41] Cf. *Report of the United Nations Commission for Eritrea*, U.N. Document A/1285 (General Assembly, *Official Records, Fifth Session*, Supplement 8); *Report of the Interim Committee of the General Assembly*, U.N. Document A/1388 (General Assembly, *Official Records, Fifth Session*, Supplement 14), 2.

enough votes to get the matter off the agenda. A United Nations Commissioner was designated to help the Eritreans prepare for their part in a collaboration which, Ethiopia's Foreign Minister assured the Assembly, would write a new chapter demonstrating the verity and justice of United Nations work.[42]

No other executive decisions of comparable scope faced the Assembly in the colonial field, but it adopted a number of recommendations designed to implement and in some cases extend its responsibility for the welfare and progress of dependent peoples. Eleven resolutions dealing with the trusteeship system were adopted on December 2, mostly in the form of directives to the Trusteeship Council. Aside from various procedural recommendations, the Assembly expressed special interest in promoting educational advancement, improved land use, broader technical assistance, and abolition of corporal punishment in trust territories. With respect to the much more numerous non-self-governing territories which were outside the trusteeship system, the Assembly adopted five resolutions on December 12 which likewise emphasized the importance of technical assistance, educational progress, and protection of the inhabitants' rights and freedoms.

Most of these resolutions were adopted without adverse vote. Although the debate produced abundant evidence of the differing philosophies of administering (colonial) and non-administering (anticolonial) governments, the agenda was not of a nature to provoke many of the acrimonious exchanges that had disfigured some previous sessions. The administering powers, however, continued to distinguish sharply between general declarations of principle and specific procedural innovations that signified a further United Nations encroachment on their freedom of action in administering territories for which they were responsible. Particularly noteworthy was the opposition generated by two proposals tending to impose additional obligations on the administering countries. One re-

42 U.N. Document A/1605, adopted December 2, 1950 by 46-10-4. Eduardo Anze Matienzo of Bolivia was elected United Nations Commissioner in Eritrea for the transition period ending September 15, 1952.

quested the Secretary-General to report on compliance or non-compliance by trust administering powers with the recommendations of the Trusteeship Council and the Assembly; the second invited countries administering non-self-governing territories to submit information concerning the implementation of the Universal Declaration of Human Rights in their possessions.[43]

Once again the Assembly faced a special problem in the refusal of the Union of South Africa to place its mandated territory of South West Africa under the trusteeship system, despite four previous Assembly resolutions inviting it to do so and an International Court opinion which clearly implied that, although not obligatory, it would be a good idea. This, however, was another case in which the Assembly lacked means to implement its opinions in the face of noncompliance by the country principally affected. A move to censure South Africa severely was headed off, partly through the efforts of the United States, which disapproved the Union's position but did not wish to see it driven into a corner. Eventually the Assembly confined itself to (a) setting up a committee to work with South Africa, if possible, in attempting to carry out the Court's intricate judgment, and (b) reiterating its own previous opinions in the matter.[44] On another explosive South African issue, meanwhile, the Assembly offered fresh but somewhat unhopeful suggestions for settling India's and Pakistan's perennial quarrel with South Africa over that country's treatment of people of Indian origin.[45]

As in previous sessions, questions of an economic and social nature occupied much of the Assembly's time and gave rise to a number of significant though hardly spectacular decisions. Aside from the concrete effect of its actions in certain specialized fields, the most interesting feature of the Assembly's work

[43] U.N. Documents A/1611, adopted December 2, 1950 by 33-11-12, and A/1694, adopted December 12, 1950 by 37-10-9. The U.S. voted against the first and in favor of the second resolution.
[44] U.N. Document A/1721, adopted December 13, 1950 by 45-6-5 (part a) and 30-10-16 (part b).
[45] U.N. Document A/1604, adopted December 2, 1950 by 33-6-21.

in this area was, perhaps, the frequency with which the United States found itself in the minority. That the Communist countries, with their specialized viewpoint on economic and social questions, should seldom agree wholeheartedly with their fellow United Nations members was a matter of course. Somewhat more startling were the divergences between American and majority opinion on both principles and operational questions. Although these differences did not always come out in formal votes and in general were neither so dramatic nor so serious as those that were coming to light in the political field, they illustrated once again the atypical character of the American position on many international issues.

Several such differences were directly reducible to questions of economics—specifically, how far this country had an obligation or an interest in utilizing its superior economic resources for the benefit of less happily situated peoples. Since the overall scope of United Nations activity for world economic advancement and for the relief of emergencies depended directly upon the scale of the American contribution, which usually amounted to well over half the total, this country often found itself obliged to dampen the enthusiasm of other governments with less onerous responsibilities.

A typical case was that of the United Nations International Children's Emergency Fund (UNICEF), whose widely appreciated welfare activities depended heavily on American grants of funds for which Congress had shown decreasing enthusiasm. For the second successive year the United States endeavored, without success, to have UNICEF replaced by a permanent child welfare program which would emphasize long-range assistance to governments rather than direct relief. Instead the Assembly unanimously extended UNICEF for another three years; [46] the United States abstained from voting, after warning that the willingness of Congress to appropriate additional funds would be greatly influenced by the extent of contributions from other quarters.

[46] U.N. Document A/1597, adopted December 1, 1950 unanimously with 1 abstention (U.S.). On congressional action during 1950 cf. above, pp. 91 and 98.

A similar, though less clear-cut, difficulty was discernible in the debates on world economic problems and policies, especially those on technical assistance and economic development. Among the various pertinent topics which were designated for study by the Economic and Social Council and the Secretariat— questions of national income, land tenure, agricultural unemployment, and commercial policy—none possessed greater general interest than that of methods for financing the economic development of underdeveloped countries. The resolution which the Assembly unanimously adopted on this point [47] repeated truths on which virtually all authorities agreed: sound development required not only technical assistance but also an accelerated rate of capital investment; not only more effective mobilization of domestic savings but also a larger, steadier flow of foreign capital, both private and public. Once again the Economic and Social Council was invited to consider practical methods of bringing these things about; and once again the question in everyone's mind was what, if anything, the world's wealthiest nation was going to do to help make them possible.

In one important respect the United States had aided significantly in reducing the scope of an international humanitarian and social problem through its acceptance of European refugees and displaced persons under the amended Displaced Persons Act of 1950.[48] Although the number of refugees still awaiting resettlement (some 293,000 as of early December) had necessitated postponement of the International Refugee Organization's liquidation date from January 1 to September 30, 1951, the end was in sight for this segment of the world's homeless population, and the principal problem remaining concerned the legal protection of refugees in their new countries. Thanks largely to the negotiating efforts of Mrs. Eleanor Roosevelt of the United States delegation, the Assembly was able to approve final arrangements for a High Commissioner's

[47] U.N. Document A/1541, adopted November 20, 1950.
[48] Above, p. 83.

Office for Refugees, under G. J. van Heuven Goedhart of the
Netherlands, which would assume responsibility in this field at
the beginning of 1951.[49]

Finally, the United States sustained definite defeats on two
important questions whose implications were both practical
and philosophical. One of the major phases of United Nations activity, in which American representatives had played a
conspicuous part, lay in the systematization and development
of international law and its extension into the field of human
rights and fundamental freedoms. That the American form of
government, with its emphasis on the autonomy of the 48
States, posed certain obstacles to full United States participation in these endeavors has already been noted in connection
with American nonratification of the Convention on Genocide,
which was to go into effect on January 12, 1951.[50] The minority
position of the United States was even more strikingly illustrated in discussions of the draft United Nations conventions
on Human Rights and Freedom of Information.

The debate on the 18 completed articles of the draft Covenant on Human Rights clearly reflected the variety of national
backgrounds, philosophies, legal systems, and social practices
that made up the United Nations, and which produced official
attitudes so diverse that some delegates frankly questioned
whether it was profitable to seek a common denominator in
the form of a binding international convention. Eventually the
Assembly returned the document to the Commission on Human
Rights with instructions to rewrite it along prescribed lines
for submission to the 1951 session.[51] Although this directive
was not formally opposed by the United States, it embodied
features that the American and some other delegations had

[49] U.N. Document A/1750, adopted December 14, 1950. Not yet foreseen were
the complications resulting from new restrictions on immigration into the U.S.
under the Internal Security Act of 1950 (above, p. 250).
[50] Cf. above, pp. 82-83.
[51] U.N. Document A/1620, adopted December 4, 1950 by 38-7-12; for background cf. *The United States in World Affairs, 1949,* 320. By another resolution
(Document A/1622, same date, adopted by 36-11-8) the Assembly decided that
the future covenant should apply to all dependent territories administered by
the signatory states. The U.S. voted for the first but against the second resolution.

fought throughout the session. Most notable of these was an instruction to include in the Covenant a "clear expression of economic, social and cultural rights" together with the civil freedoms already spelled out. The rights belonging to this second category—such as the right to work, to social security, to leisure, and to education—were constitutionally guaranteed in many countries, and their inclusion in the covenant had been vigorously advocated not only by the Soviet bloc but also by the Arab and certain Latin American states. Further difficulties were promised by United States insistence that the covenant include a federal-state clause, which the American delegation deemed essential to safeguard States' rights but which not a few delegations seemed to regard as a potential loophole for American evasion of obligations imposed by the covenant.

The human rights debate, though it found the United States in the minority, witnessed no important division among the North Atlantic governments such as occurred in discussion of the draft Convention on Freedom of Information. This document, originally inspired largely by the United States, had become unacceptable in its worked-out form because of its many restrictions on freedom of the press and other information media; but it was favored for that very reason by various smaller countries which were not too sympathetic to the American concept of informational freedom and were particularly loath to give free rein to foreign-controlled newsgathering organizations. At the Assembly's 1949 session the United States, Britain, and the Netherlands had secured a year's postponement of this controversial item; at the 1950 session France revived the issue and placed itself at the head of the small-power, "restrictionist" group, which succeeded this time in swinging the Assembly around to its point of view. The key issue was the composition of a 15-nation special committee which was to redraft the convention for eventual submission to a special international conference. The inclusion, in addition to the Big Four, of ten small countries that were known to favor the restrictionist approach made it certain that the proponents of freedom of information in the American sense would be heavily outnumbered.[52]

Many of these actions received comparatively little attention at the time because the eyes of the world were focused on the Assembly's efforts to cope with the new situation created by the all-out offensive of the Chinese Communists in Korea. These efforts, it was clear, would indefinitely delay the Assembly's formal adjournment. Meanwhile, by mid-December the agenda had been completed except for Far Eastern questions, which were momentarily in the hands of the Political Committee, and there was no further reason to maintain large delegations on the scene. Vyshinsky and other key figures were on the point of leaving. On December 14 the Assembly decided to hold its next regular session in Europe; this would be the last session before the scheduled completion of the permanent United Nations headquarters in New York City. Next day the Assembly recessed, to be reconvened whenever developments in the Far Eastern crisis might require it.

[52] U.N. Document A/1748, adopted December 14, 1950 by 44-0-12 with the United States abstaining; for background cf. *The United States in World Affairs, 1949*, 323-325. In other actions on the same date the Assembly condemned the practice of radio jamming as carried on by the U.S.S.R. (Document A/1746) and recommended minimum limitation of freedom of information and the press by governments declaring a state of emergency (Document A/1747).

CHAPTER NINE

A WORLD IN CRISIS

IN THE last two months of 1950 the nations of the world
suddenly found themselves engaged in an ordeal as darkly
perilous as any in human history, one whose outcome is still
hidden in the future and whose final evaluation may lie generations or even centuries hence. In its bearing upon the des-
tinies of mankind it could be compared without presumption
to the era of the Persian wars, the fall of Rome, or the pagan
incursions into medieval Europe; in scale and universality of
impact, if not in violence, it exceeded even the two global con-
tests already recorded in the annals of the twentieth century.
Much more was involved than the future of the Far East, the
United Nations, the North Atlantic community, or the United
States. Events accompanying and flowing from the Chinese
Communist intervention in Korea were capable of inflicting
irreparable damage not only on the structure of immaterial
values known as Western civilization but even on the physical
and technological apparatus by which that civilization had been
perpetuated and diffused.

This crisis differed from earlier postwar tensions both in its
greater seriousness and in its geographic scope. For the first
time the free world, already habituated to the expansionist
menace centered in Moscow, faced the full implications of
Communism's rise to power in China and its voluntary or involuntary association with Soviet Communism. Peking and
Moscow, for the time being at least, were partners acting
together on a global scale. While China poured men into
Korea and reiterated its Far Eastern demands in louder tones,

the U.S.S.R. continued to build its military strength and renewed its political offensive against the heart of the North
Atlantic position in Europe. Between them they thus exploited
their geographic advantage to the utmost, confronting the free
nations with a challenge of world-wide dimensions and thereby
accentuating the inherent weaknesses of the free world's position. By demonstrating their opponents' incapacity to meet the
challenge simultaneously at all points, they precipitated a reaction very close to panic and brought to the surface all the sub-
terranean tensions and antagonisms that had been gathering in
the United States, the Atlantic community, and the free world
for many months.

As usual the strategists of world Communism dropped a
minimum of clues as to their over-all view of the world situation, the precise advantage they hoped to gain, or the risks they
were prepared to take in pursuing them. It was possible to
construe their activities either as a coordinated drive with limited, tangible objectives, as a concerted assault upon the unity
of the free nations, as preparation for all-out war, or as all
three together. Some risk of war was certainly inseparable from
their activities, even though either power could—unlike the
West—always beat an orderly retreat at the very last moment.
But with or without war, their underlying purpose clearly was
to "call the bluff" of the Western world by confronting the
latter with a situation too big for it to handle.

Divided counsels in the West added to the inherent discom-
forts of the situation. In demanding simultaneous showdowns
on German rearmament and on the position of Communist
China in the Far East, the Communist leaders selected the very
issues on which Western sentiment was already least united.
In both instances the United States was identified with aims
that had no more than half-hearted concurrence from some of
its allies. Lukewarm toward the policy of rearming Germany,
several of these were positively frigid toward the policy of opposing Communist China's demands for Formosa and admission to the United Nations. Behind their specific reservations
was a more general apprehension over what seemed to them a

lack of restraint in American policy. Thus Peking and Moscow could count on a good deal of sympathy for their concrete demands even among people who had no sympathy with their methods and ultimate aims. This lack of firm conviction and mutual confidence was to be a definite hindrance to the free nations in taking the steps which their common peril made indispensable.

As the crisis progressed, the alienation of the United States from its friends became more marked. American reaction to the new turn in Korea was of a nature to aggravate all the differences on which Moscow and Peking had evidently reckoned. The tone of public and political utterances in this country became more bellicose, and increasingly drastic courses of action were advocated on many sides. American diplomacy, always at a disadvantage when emotions gained the upper hand, was further handicapped by an intensification of the attacks on the State Department and Secretary Acheson. Republican gains in the November 7 election encouraged a formal attempt to destroy the Secretary of State which reached its climax in mid-December, at a time when he could well have used maximum national support in maintaining the shaken allegiance of our North Atlantic allies.

Elsewhere in the free world a contrary spirit was predominant. Where the United States wanted quick and decisive action, especially in the Far East, others were for proceeding with the utmost circumspection. Some Americans ascribed this "foot-dragging" tendency to the fact that this country was doing most of the fighting in Korea, a factor which undoubtedly had some influence in the sense that others were less subject to that particular form of emotional stress. But it must be admitted that this country's friends had more substantial reasons for caution, both in the behavior of the Communist powers and in the uncertain intentions of the United States. Moscow and Peking had brought about a situation that could easily lead straight to war. To judge by available indications, American tempers had risen to a point where the challenge might be accepted, and on Stalinist terms. Under such circumstances it was not surprising that nations within reach of the Communist military machine should be loath to provoke it unnecessarily and anxious to restrain the United States as far as possible.

In the United Nations these misgivings inspired a series of frantic efforts to find a conciliatory solution of the Far Eastern problem. To judge by the behavior of the Chinese Communist delegation which appeared at Lake Success in November, Peking did not want these efforts to succeed; but they were bound to fail in any case because Peking demanded a price that the United States, for one, was unwilling to pay. Settlement of the Korean issue on Communist terms, admission of Communist China to the United Nations, and a free hand in Formosa were the three conditions stipulated; and the United States, which had been opposed to them before, was even less willing to see them accepted at the point of a gun. Other countries were less firmly set against them, but their efforts to find common ground and avoid antagonizing Peking resulted in antagonizing American opinion to a degree that held definite dangers for the future of the United Nations.

No open break occurred between the United States and its partners in the North Atlantic Treaty Organization, although the possibility of such a break seemed serious enough at one point to justify an emergency flight of the British Prime Minister to Washington. On the contrary, some new advances were made under the spur of expanded Communist aggression. The interallied dispute about German rearmament was resolved, General Eisenhower was appointed to head the integrated North Atlantic defense force, and Canada and the European treaty partners prepared to follow the United States lead in carrying through a greatly accelerated production and mobilization effort.

Yet the success of the Brussels meeting in December, at which the key decisions were formalized, was subject to important qualifications. Notable differences persisted among the Big Three concerning the way to handle the U.S.S.R's sharp protests against the proposed rearmament of Western Germany. The Germans themselves were showing unexpected reluctance to cooperate. Meanwhile, reciprocal disillusionment between the United States and Europe was growing by leaps and bounds. Before the end of the year various leaders of American opinion were openly repudiating the whole basis of postwar American policy in Europe and advocating a return to quasi-isolation. Adoption of such extreme remedies seemed unlikely, but 1950 was to close in an atmosphere of recrimination and irresolution as dangerous in its own way as was Moscow's and Peking's continued, remorseless pressure against the free world's vulnerable spots.

1. Peking-Moscow Axis

In seeking to understand the partnership that was now taking control of international events, it is not unprofitable to recall a similar alignment that flourished briefly in the Europe of the 1930's and early 1940's. The Rome-Berlin Axis, which linked the two leading fascist powers of the Hitler era, resulted from a somewhat comparable set of ideological and material factors and functioned for a time with similar devastating effects on the international community. In both cases a state that was originally free to choose its own friends gravitated, or was forced, into the orbit of a stronger, highly dynamic power with which it had definite ideological affinities but also definite long-term conflicts of interest.

For Communist China, as for Fascist Italy, ideological attraction was reinforced by the prospect of specific advantages that could be achieved only by joining hands against the democratic powers. The logical path of expansion for Mussolini's Italy lay in the Mediterranean regions dominated by England and France. Ten years later Mao Tse-tung's China, as the leading revolutionary force in the Far East, found its aspirations blocked by a coalition of "imperialist" nations of which the United States was now the leader. Thus objective conditions as well as innate preference dictated the alliance with Soviet Russia which had been implicit in the outlook of the Chinese

Communist leaders and was formalized during Mao's visit to Moscow early in 1950.

Both the ideological attractions and the latent centrifugal factors were probably stronger in the Sino-Soviet partnership than in its fascist prototype. The common Marxist-Leninist foundation of the two regimes was an incomparably firmer basis for common action than the loose, unsystematic doctrinal affiliation of Fascism and Nazism, and the outlook of a serious revolutionary figure like Mao Tse-tung was hardly to be compared with the opportunism of the adventurer Mussolini. But, though there could be little doubt of the collusion of Moscow and Peking in late 1950, not everyone was convinced that the subservience of China was final and irrevocable. Italy had been materially incapable of maintaining its independence against Germany, once the latter had regained power beyond a certain point. China's situation was inherently less unfavorable, and some observers continued to look for its eventual resurgence as an independent factor in world affairs.

Through 1950 there were certainly few evidences of any conscious antagonism between Peking and Moscow. Mao's government was no "satellite" regime, to be manipulated in the manner of Rumania or Bulgaria; the relationship appeared much more nearly one of equals. But Mao and his associates seemed to have remained completely loyal to the Kremlin, and their confidence in the U.S.S.R. appeared no less genuine than their loudly expressed hatred of the United States. Meanwhile, uncertainty in the free world concerning the exact nature of Soviet-Chinese relations was actually of service to the two powers in the pursuit of their respective aims because it prevented the free nations from adopting anything like a common policy.

How far Chinese Communist actions in late 1950 were inspired by genuine misapprehensions about the aims of the United States will long be a matter of dispute—as will, for that matter, the true opinions of Moscow itself concerning American intentions. At times it seemed inconceivable that Chinese spokesmen could really believe their own lurid fabrications about what Chou En-lai described as this country's "frenzied and violent acts of imperialist aggression." Nevertheless it was useful to remember that American intentions had been widely misunderstood even in quarters sympathetic to this country; that the Chinese Communists relied largely on their Soviet brethren for their picture of political trends in the outside world; that the United States actually had figured for some years as the principal obstacle to Chinese Communist ambitions; that prominent Americans often had advocated out-and-out warlike actions against Communist China; that the United States actually had intervened in China's civil war through the neutralization of Formosa, and was giving aid and comfort to a rival government; and that General MacArthur, who commanded the predominantly American force that was approaching the Yalu River frontier in late October, had not been precisely well-disposed toward the Peking regime. Chou En-lai may have exaggerated the significance of particular facts, but there was at least a grain of truth in his general characterization of the United States as "the most dangerous foe of the People's Republic [i.e., the Communist regime] of China." [1]

This conception, whether well or ill founded, had occupied a central place in the developing pattern of Sino-Soviet political warfare. The grand strategy of this political warfare, as it was perfected in the last months of 1950, flowed naturally from the two powers' positions spanning the Eurasian continent from the Sea of Japan to the Elbe River. While one party riveted the attention of their joint adversaries in Asia, the other had only to distract and throw them off balance by stepping up the pressure in Europe. This kind of warfare did not necessarily require close tactical coordination. Each party could pursue its own aims more or less independently of the other. For maximum effect it was necessary only that the timing of their actions on both sides of the globe should roughly coincide, thus strain-

[1] Report by Chou En-lai to the National Committee of the People's Political Consultative Conference, September 30 (Peking broadcast in English, October 1, 1950).

ing the nerves and the resources of the free nations to the utmost and minimizing the possibilities of successful all-round resistance. In 1950 the pressure was confined mainly to the psychological level and military force was brought to bear only in the restricted Korean theater. But what made the strategy so peculiarly disturbing to the West was the realization that it could also be employed in full-scale war.

Not the least significant feature of this combined action was the division of labor whereby each party contributed what would best serve their joint purposes. To some observers, it is true, China's belated entry and lavish expenditure of manpower in Korea suggested that Peking either was being victimized by the U.S.S.R. or had insisted on elbowing its way in to finish a job the Soviet-supported North Koreans had failed to complete. Even such well-placed observers as the Yugoslavs were inclined to interpret the whole Korean affair in terms of a basic Sino-Soviet rivalry. Moscow, according to this somewhat wishful view, had originally planned the Korean campaign as an attempt to "impose its tutelage" on Peking by asserting itself as a "big Asiatic power"; its failure had enabled Peking to put itself forward in a former Soviet sphere of influence.[2]

But such interpretations seemed to overlook both the evidence of coordinated staff work by Russians, Chinese, and North Koreans in the Far East [3] and the fact that from the standpoint of international Communism the arrangement actually represented the most economical and politically effective use of joint resources. China's manpower reserves were more or less inexhaustible; its allocation of over a million men to the Manchurian-Korean theater enabled Russia to keep its own forces intact but did not prevent China from simultaneously invading Tibet and maintaining heavy pressure against Indochina and other peripheral areas. Politically, moreover, the appearance of Chinese troops in Korea provoked a very different world

[2] Observator, "China 1950," *Review of International Affairs* (Belgrade), I, No. 15, December 20, 1950, 4.
[3] The existence of a Soviet-Chinese-North Korean "joint staff headquarters" at Changchun, Manchuria, was reported in *New York Times*, December 14, 1950.

reaction from what would have followed the commitment of the Soviet army. Soviet intervention would in all likelihood have consolidated the anti-Soviet front of free nations; Chinese intervention tended to dissolve it by confusing the Korean struggle with ideas of defending Asia against American "imperialism."

Furthermore, there was good evidence to show that the Chinese Communists themselves were looking at the conflict in global terms and saw their own activities as part of an overall plan. Chinese commentaries repeatedly stressed the interdependence of the European and Asiatic fronts and made no exaggerated claims for the importance of their own theater. Thus a prominent provincial governor predicted in October that the spreading flame of "American imperialist aggression" would involve the three continents of Europe, Asia, and Africa. "The major and decisive battlefield will be Europe," he said; Korea was "the major battlefield of secondary importance in East Asia." [4] And in November a Chinese analysis of this country's immediate superiority in material resources pointed out that it was actually Europe that held the balance of industrial potential between the two camps. "As soon as the United States starts the world war," it said, "Western Europe will soon be liberated [sic]. Then . . . the apparent United States superiority will vanish." [5]

2. Setting the Stage

It is impossible to determine just when or how Moscow and Peking arrived at the crucial decisions that precipitated the year-end crisis. The exact relationship between Vyshinsky's and Malik's peaceful protestations of mid-October and the warlike actions which were evidently in preparation at the same time cannot be established, nor do we know to what extent, if at all, Communist intentions were influenced by the United Nations

[4] Speech of Gen. Yeh Chien-ying, Governor of Kwangtung Province, October 6, reported *ibid.*, December 24, 1950.
[5] *Shih-Shih Shou-Tse (Current Affairs Journal)*, November 5, quoted *ibid.*, December 10, 1950.

crossing of the 38th parallel on the heels of the resolution of October 7. All that can be definitely stated is that during the second half of October things began to happen in the Far East and in Europe which looked like elements of a coordinated action, some parts of which must presumably have been planned well in advance. On November 3-5 these manifestations culminated in the disclosure of Chinese intervention in Korea and in a Soviet note to the Big Three demanding a meeting of the Council of Foreign Ministers on the German question.

On the Chinese side the signal for action seems to have been the lengthy speech which Chou En-lai delivered on September 30, the first anniversary of the Communist "People's Republic," which has already been mentioned in connection with the General Assembly's deliberations on Korea. In addition to warning that further American "aggression" might occur at any time, the Communist Premier and Foreign Minister made three significant announcements. The people of China, he said, were determined to "march westward to liberate the Tibetan people and defend the frontiers of China"; they were determined to "liberate Taiwan [Formosa] and other Chinese territory from the clutches of the U.S. aggressors"; and they "absolutely [would] not supinely tolerate seeing their neighbors being savagely invaded by imperialists." This declaration might have been, but was not, the prelude to an assault on Formosa. Such a venture would have been even more hazardous than the course of action actually adopted, which involved action of different kinds on widely separated fronts in Tibet, Indochina, and Korea.

The Tibetan affair, which began first—Tibetan sources later claimed that Chinese troops crossed their boundary on October 7 [6]—was of least international concern because of Tibet's

[6] Tibetan complaint to the United Nations, dated November 7, received November 13, and printed *ibid.*, November 14, 1950. The boundary in question (indicated by a dotted line in the map on p. 176) had been fixed in general terms by the treaty of Simla in 1914 but was not recognized by China, which held that the true boundary lay some hundreds of miles farther west. For a balanced account of the Tibetan affair see Fred W. Riggs, "Tibet in Extremis," *Far Eastern Survey*, XIX, December 6, 1950, 224-230.

isolated position and because most governments recognized China's suzerainty over the country despite the failure of an earlier Chinese government to ratify the relevant international treaty. For over a year there had been recurrent indications that Peking was preparing to assert its authority, and a Tibetan delegation had for some time been waiting in India for the opportunity to negotiate a modus vivendi with China's new rulers. Peking, however, having carefully prepared the ground by political and psychological methods, preferred military action to diplomacy. By October 24, when the Chinese radio formally disclosed that People's Army units had been ordered "to free 3 million Tibetans from imperialist oppression and to consolidate national defenses of the western borders of China," the campaign was already in an advanced stage. The curt dismissal of India's protests [7] indicated that Peking was not disposed to tolerate outside interference in settling what it chose to regard as a strictly internal affair.

In Indochina there were still no signs of open Chinese intervention, but multiple indications that the character of the local civil war was changing in a way that could only indicate a tie-up between the Vietminh insurgents and the Chinese Communists in the South China hinterland. This was the period of the Vietminh offensive in northern Tonkin which forced the French to abandon a chain of frontier posts with heavy losses and gave the Vietminh unrestricted access to their Chinese friends. On October 11 Jean Letourneau, French Minister for the Associated States in the Far East, declared in Paris that France was now facing not guerrilla bands but a regular, fully equipped army. On October 19 Premier Pleven, outlining the recent French reverses in a statement to the National Assembly, catalogued large quantities of modern armaments furnished the Vietminh rebels by Communist China and revealed that 20,000 Vietminh troops had been sent back to Indochina with full equipment after training in Chinese territory.

But neither of these undertakings involved the same risks as the direct intervention against the United Nations in Korea,

[7] *New York Times*, November 3, 1950.

which, as already noted, began within a few days of the crossing of the 38th parallel by United Nations forces. By the end of October, units of Chinese troops had been encountered as far as 50 miles south of the Korean-Manchurian frontier. Though cold weather had set in and the campaign had seemed virtually finished, Chinese propaganda organs suddenly stepped up their attacks on "American imperialists" and began to call for "volunteers" to aid the "heroic Korean brethren" and eliminate the "threat to China's frontiers." Intervention, to be effective at this late stage, would have to be on a grand scale. That it lay well within Chinese capabilities was made clear by the special communiqué which General MacArthur issued on November 6.

"In the face of this victory of United Nations arms," declared the United Nations Commander, "the Communists committed one of the most offensive acts of international lawlessness of historic record by moving without any notice of belligerency elements of alien Communist forces across the Yalu River into North Korea and massing a great concentration of possible reinforcing divisions with adequate supply behind the privileged sanctuary of the adjacent Manchurian border. . . . A new and fresh army now faces us, backed by a possibility of large alien reserves, and adequate supply within easy reach to the enemy but beyond the limits of our present sphere of military action. Whether and to what extent these reserves will be moved forward to reinforce units now committed remains to be seen and is a matter of the gravest international significance. . . ."

To the United Nations General MacArthur reported officially that his forces were "presently in hostile contact with Chinese Communist military units deployed for action against the forces of the Unified Command." "The continued employment of Communist forces in Korea," he said, "and the hostile attitude assumed by such forces, either inside or outside Korea, are matters which it is incumbent upon me to bring at once to the attention of the United Nations."

While considering what to do about this new and monumental challenge to United Nations authority, the leading non-Communist powers had also to consider the different but equally serious challenge the Soviet Union had thrown down in Europe. There, no less than in the Far East, they were suddenly confronted with what looked like a complete refusal to accept their actions and policies of the preceding months. Unlike Communist China, the Soviet Union did not back up its demands by moving troops into any new areas of vital significance. On the contrary, as an integral part of its challenge to the West, it intensified its "peace" propaganda, obtained further millions of signatures for the Stockholm appeal, staged an all-U.S.S.R. peace conference on the theme that "Peace will triumph over war, because the leader of this struggle is Stalin," and in general continued to dramatize its determination to frustrate by peaceful means "the American-British imperialists" who, it was claimed, had now "passed over from the cold war to direct aggression." [8] But the appearance of Chinese "volunteers" in Korea only emphasized how quickly force could be brought to bear if the leaders of international Communism so chose. Their presence was an additional inducement to careful consideration of Soviet views on the German question.

Before renewing its campaign against Western policies in Germany the U.S.S.R. had proceeded to strengthen its grip on the Soviet-occupied section of that country by carrying out the parliamentary elections which had been postponed when the puppet "German Democratic Republic" was set up a year earlier. In the last elections held in Eastern Germany, in May 1949, over a third of the electorate had dared to vote in opposition to Soviet wishes. Pro-Soviet sentiment had hardly increased in the interval, but this time the Russians and their German Communist agents took no chances. The election of October 15, conducted on approved totalitarian lines, produced a 99.71 percent favorable vote for the Communist-approved

---

[8] "Letter to J. V. Stalin from the Second All-USSR Conference for Peace" (October 16-19), *USSR Information Bulletin*, X, November 7, 1950, 683. This agitation was continued at the "Second World Peace Congress" (November 16-22) originally scheduled to meet in Sheffield, England, but transferred to Warsaw after the British had denied entry permits to a large number of foreign delegates.

slate of candidates. While Secretary Acheson voiced American sympathy for "the East German people who have been treated in such a contemptuous and humiliating fashion by their oppressors," [9] the latter set about exploiting their electoral success by further moves toward the conversion of the puppet republic into a fully bolshevized "workers' state."

But, while accentuating the totalitarian features of the "Democratic Republic" and the ruling Socialist Unity party, the Russians did not by any means relinquish their long-run objectives—first, the prevention of West German rearmament under allied auspices, and, second, the reunification of the entire country under Soviet-Communist control. A reinvigoration of the agitation for German "unity" was the positive side of the campaign they now opened against allied purposes in Western Germany. While doing their best to frighten the Allies and the West Germans out of their plans to include German contingents in a North Atlantic or Western European defense force, they held out to the latter the attractive alternative of a peacefully reunited nation—though reunited, of course, only up to the Oder-Neisse line and on the basis of Soviet "popular" democracy, without benefit of the democratic safeguards the Bonn government and the Western Allies had offered at intervals throughout the year.[10]

To emphasize the seriousness with which it regarded the Western governments' recent decisions on the German problem, the Kremlin chose a method that recalled its protest in 1948 against the original plan to set up a separate West German government. First, a note was addressed to the Western "Big Three" in which the U.S.S.R. (1) rejected their four-month-old contention that the People's Police in the Eastern zone included military formations; (2) accused them of maintaining regular Germany military units in the guise of police forces in their own zones of occupation; and (3) warned them against carrying out the plans for German participation in the

[9] *Department of State Bulletin,* XXIII, October 30, 1950, 695.
[10] Above, pp. 169, 172. The proposal was renewed in a letter of October 9 from the three High Commissioners to the head of the Soviet Control Commission.

collective defense force which the three Foreign Ministers had discussed in New York in September. "The Soviet Government," it said, ". . . will not tolerate such measures . . . aimed at reviving the German regular army in Western Germany." [11]

Next, a conference of Eastern European Foreign Ministers met under Molotov's chairmanship at Prague on October 20-21, apparently for the sole purpose of denouncing the Big Three program and restating the Communist position. As always, this position was based on the rather artificial hypothesis that German questions were still capable of being regulated by the four occupying powers in accordance with the Potsdam agreement of 1945. Four specific demands were put forward in the name of the U.S.S.R., Albania, Bulgaria, Czechoslovakia, Poland, Rumania, Hungary, and the "German Democratic Republic": (1) a statement by the four occupying powers, barring German remilitarization and reaffirming the principles of the Potsdam agreement; (2) removal of restrictions on the German peace economy, and prevention of the reestablishment of a German war potential; (3) prompt conclusion of a German peace treaty, and withdrawal of occupation troops within a year; and (4) a novel but obviously unacceptable proposal for the political reunification of Germany, through the formation of an "All-German Constituent Council" on which the Eastern zone would have equal representation with the three Western zones.[12]

The advancement of this specious program, which contained the usual number of traps for the politically unwary, would not simplify the Allies' psychological task in Western Germany; but it had no official standing so far as they were concerned, and required scarcely more notice than the strongly worded commentaries in which the Soviet press had been belaboring the proposals for West German rearmament—always, of course, without reference to the remilitarization already

[11] Soviet note, October 20, as released by TASS and printed in *New York Times,* October 20, 1950. Nominally this was a reply to the Western note of May 23 (above, pp. 172-173).
[12] *USSR Information Bulletin,* X, November 7, 1950, 666-668.

well under way in Eastern Germany. Secretary Acheson declared that the time was long past when the world could be "stirred to hope by general phrases from the Soviet Union about disarmament and peace and German unity." The Prague declaration, he added, should have been addressed to the U.S.S.R., not to the Western powers.[13]

Quite different in its implications, however, was a second diplomatic note which the Kremlin formally addressed to the American, British, and French governments on November 3. In this communication the Soviet Government explicitly endorsed the Prague declaration and, in addition, demanded a four-power conference "to discuss these questions without delay." Requesting an answer "at a very early date," it officially proposed a meeting of the Council of Foreign Ministers to consider "the question of fulfillment of the Potsdam Agreement regarding the demilitarization of Germany." [14]

The Council of Foreign Ministers had not met since the spring of 1949, at which time it had failed completely to agree on means of implementing other provisions of the Potsdam agreement. But by calling for another meeting and a showdown on the rearmament question, the Russians showed that they meant business; and initial reactions in Paris and London, which coincided with the bad news from Korea, suggested that the Western powers might have some difficulty in establishing a solid front against them. Those who remembered that a somewhat similar political maneuver on the part of the North Koreans had prefaced the Korean aggression a few months earlier might well wonder whether Moscow would confine itself to writing notes.

That the Kremlin would spare no effort to frighten its antagonists out of their intentions was made doubly clear in the speech which Deputy Premier N. A. Bulganin delivered in Moscow on November 6, the anniversary of the "Great" October Revolution. In accordance with standard procedure, Bul-

[13] Statement of October 25 in *Department of State Bulletin*, XXIII, November 6, 1950, 727-728.
[14] *Ibid.*, XXIV, January 1, 1951, 12.

ganin predicted that the aggressive plans of the "warmongers" would be thwarted. In doing so, however, he castigated their policies in terms that were unusually forceful even by Soviet standards. The loudest applause of the occasion was reserved for a passage with definitely menacing undertones: "It is time these gentlemen realize that the Soviet people are not of the weak nerved sort (*Applause*) and are not to be intimated by threats. (*Prolonged applause*) History shows that our peaceful policy is not a sign of weakness. It is time these gentlemen realize that our people are capable of standing up for themselves, (*Prolonged applause*) of standing up for the interests of their country if need be, with arms in hand. (*Stormy prolonged applause*)." [15]

It is somewhat paradoxical that an American congressional election should demand inclusion in this review of major elements in a world diplomatic crisis. Yet students of international affairs can hardly escape the conclusion that in its own way the election of November 7 influenced the subsequent course of events to a degree that justifies comparison with the quite different influences emanating from Peking and Moscow. The working of the democratic process always entails some disturbance of the orderly course of foreign relations, just as foreign relations have increasingly encroached on the internal politics of all democratic countries; and in the case of the United States the world-wide impact of every election is magnified by this country's central position in the international community. In 1950 the impact was redoubled because the electoral campaign revolved mainly around foreign policy issues and the election itself occurred at a time of unprecedented world tension.

At such a moment an endorsement of the main principles of the national foreign policy would have considerably strengthened this country's position in relation to both allies and opponents, giving the former renewed confidence in the stability of American leadership and proving to the latter that the voice of the administration was in fact the voice of the American people.

[15] *USSR Information Bulletin,* X, November 24, 1950, 697.

But the balloting on November 7 produced no such endorsement; if anything, it reflected a rather widespread dissatisfaction with the administration's foreign policy achievements and an unexpected readiness to accept the type of criticism associated with the name of Senator McCarthy. Technically, the administration retained a slender majority in both houses—in the Senate, a majority of two. Actually, in domestic affairs it would be at the mercy of a Republican-Southern Democratic coalition, while its range of action in foreign affairs would be further restricted by the defeat of several staunch supporters such as Senators Lucas and Tydings, the triumphant return of such strenuous critics as Senators Taft, Millikin, Hickenlooper, and McCarran, and the advent of a number of new Senators who were known to be strongly imbued with McCarthyist views.

More significant than the outcome of any particular contest was the general frame of mind which apparently had gained prevalence in the country as a whole. That the administration's policies in Europe and Asia and the management of the State Department were exposed to strong criticism had been sufficiently evident before November 7, but that the criticism was really representative of national opinion had been less clear. After November 7 there could no longer be any doubt that large numbers of Americans were out of sympathy with the administration's methods and dubious about its objectives. In earlier times it would probably have been said quite plainly that the mood of the country had turned isolationist. That term, however, like the ill-omened word "appeasement," had acquired unsavory overtones and was rejected by those who claimed to represent the current outlook. "Only an idiot would be an isolationist today," said Senator Taft; and it was a fact that he and his associates seemed to favor a more active policy, in the Far East at any rate, than the isolationists of a decade earlier. But the difficulty of finding an alternative name showed how close were the resemblances to an earlier and supposedly obsolete frame of mind.

For some time past the critics of the official foreign policy had been roughly agreed on four desiderata: more energetic opposition to Communism, especially to Communist China; less deference to Europe; less emphasis on internationalist economic and social programs, and less deference to foreign opinion generally; and a thorough "housecleaning" of the State Department—beginning with Secretary Acheson, whose critics had continued their agitation against him despite their complete failure to produce grounds for his removal. All these demands were now renewed with a vigor that was stimulated by the feverish atmosphere of international affairs. To none of them did the administration openly yield, but it would be rash to assert that they had no influence in shaping the rigid line American diplomacy was to adopt, without benefit of bipartisan consultation, in the developing international emergency. It would be even more rash to overlook the dismay they produced among Europeans who felt they had everything to lose from a victory of the new tendencies.

It was Senator Taft, now a leading candidate for the Republican presidential nomination in 1952, who first indicated the trend of opposition sentiment by proposing a revision or "reexamination" of the whole program of American military aid to Europe, as it had developed in the framework of the Vandenberg Resolution, the North Atlantic Treaty, and the Military Assistance Program. "Is Europe our first line of defense?" the Senator asked on November 10. "Is it defensible at all?" He did not suggest that existing policies be abandoned, yet he evinced strong doubt that they were justified. Secretary Acheson, a week later, ridiculed this "reexaminist" approach as that of "a farmer that goes out every morning and pulls up all his crops to see how they have done during the night." [16] It was true that what Senator Taft proposed to reexamine was not the incidental details but the very foundation of American military and foreign policy. That its soundness should be questioned at this late stage was a measure of the uncertainties that the United States was experiencing and com-

[16] Remarks of November 17 in *Department of State Bulletin*, XXIII, November 27, 1950, 839.

municating to its allies as it endeavored to cope with one of the most difficult international crises in its history.

3. Crisis in the United Nations

Two distinct phases are discernible in the history of the Chinese Communist intervention in Korea and in the efforts of the United Nations to deal with a situation more precarious than any the world organization had yet faced. Until late in November the Chinese "volunteers" from General Lin Piao's Fourth Field Army confined themselves to fighting limited actions against United Nations forces, without engaging them in strength or stalling the United Nations advance toward Korea's northern boundary. During this period the problem created by their intervention was under continuous consideration by the Security Council, which was immediately convoked at the request of the United States but failed to take decisive action primarily because of a Soviet veto on November 30. Meanwhile the second phase had begun on November 24 when the United Nations command launched a "general assault" which was followed almost immediately by a massive Chinese offensive and the rapid reconquest of North Korea by the Communists. Through the month of December the General Assembly's Political Committee, to which the issue was formally transferred on its relinquishment by the Security Council, labored hopefully but vainly to halt the fighting on the basis of some adjustment between the diametrically opposed political stands of Peking and Washington.

One highly significant characteristic distinguished United Nations action in this crisis from the actions taken in earlier phases of the Korean conflict. Where previously the majority of the United Nations had unhesitatingly recognized that an aggression had been committed and the aggressor must be curbed, with the appearance of the Chinese the emphasis shifted from the repelling of aggression to the idea of mediation and conciliation as between equals. This trend was strongly but unsuccessfully resisted by the United States, which was unable to communicate to other nations its indignation over the Chinese action. Most of the non-Communist world seemed less troubled by Peking's bullying of the United Nations and generally lawless behavior than by the chance that the quarrel between the United States and Communist China would precipitate general war. As has been frequently pointed out, Peking's specific demands commanded widespread sympathy in the United Nations. In continuing to resist them even at the risk of war, the United States maintained its record for consistency but forfeited much of the good will it had previously enjoyed in United Nations quarters. A good many delegations now seemed to consider restraint of Communist China less important than restraint of the United States.

Of the three fronts on which Chinese pressure was being felt, only Korea directly concerned the United Nations. The defense of Indochina, which was to escape actual invasion at least through the winter, was left to France. Tibet had appealed for aid, but its legal status was so obscure that the United Nations was delighted to sidestep the problem.[17] Even in the case of Korea, there was evident from the first a widespread reluctance to meet the issue head-on. A quite disproportionate emphasis was laid on the necessity of "reassuring" Peking and allaying any doubts it might entertain concerning United Nations aims. All through November the Chinese Communists were receiving direct and indirect assurances from United Nations bodies, British diplomatic representatives, and even the President of the United States himself [18] that the United Nations action in Korea involved no idea of encroaching on Chinese territory or interests.

Although it is possible that the Chinese had been entitled to feel some uncertainty on this point, their subsequent actions made it obvious that they were seeking much more than the

[17] Tibet's appeal for help was eventually brought before the General Assembly by El Salvador, but its consideration was postponed at the suggestion of India and other governments.
[18] See especially President Truman's press conference statement of November 16 (read in the Security Council the same day), which, however, seemed directed primarily toward reassuring non-Communist opinion.

protection of Chinese interests in the Manchurian frontier zone. Specifically, as they themselves were to make clear beyond any possible doubt, they were seeking (1) withdrawal of United Nations forces from Korea, (2) withdrawal of American protection from Formosa, and (3) admission to represent China in the United Nations. More generally, they appeared to be doing their best to provoke the United States into retaliatory action against them, discredit this country in the eyes of Asia and the world, and strain the frayed bonds among the free nations to the breaking point.

At least a volume would be required to trace in detail the impact of these efforts in the various United Nations bodies and to describe the tensely dramatic scenes enacted at Lake Success in the presence of the Chinese Communist delegation which was at last permitted to make its appearance at United Nations headquarters. That a representative from Peking should be present while the new turn in Korea was being discussed had been decided by the Security Council as early as November 8, this time with the concurrence of the United States; [19] but serious complications developed because Communist China was not interested in discussing its own actions and wanted only to talk about American "aggression" against Korea and Formosa.

Thus it was not until November 24 that General Wu Hsiuchuan and his associates appeared in New York, and not until November 28 that Ambassador Austin was able to put to him the 20 questions which had been drawn up by the United States delegation with a view to elucidating Chinese intentions in Korea and Formosa. And Mr. Wu's only reply was a lengthy, bitter rehearsal of Chinese Communist grievances against this country, coupled with sharp reproaches to the United Nations over the alleged "illegality" of its proceedings and a demand that the Security Council apply "severe sanctions" against the

[19] The vote on this proposal, introduced by the U.K., was 8-2, with Nationalist China and Cuba opposed and Egypt abstaining; the U.S. voted in favor although it objected to the fact that Peking was being "invited" and not "summoned." Technically Communist China rejected this invitation while accepting the Council's earlier invitation (above, p. 354n) to participate in the debate on Formosa.

United States "for its criminal acts of armed aggression against the territory of China, Taiwan [Formosa], and armed intervention in Korea."

The acrimony of this confrontation could be attributed at least in part to intervening developments in Korea, where General MacArthur had chosen the day of Mr. Wu's arrival in New York to launch a full-scale offensive which, if successful, his headquarters said, should "for all practical purposes end the war." The wisdom of this initiative, for which the United Nations Commander did not attempt to evade responsibility, has been strenuously attacked and defended on both political and military grounds. There seems to be no serious question that General MacArthur was acting within the limits of the broad authority delegated to him on behalf of the United Nations. But there is equally no question that United Nations circles found the moment singularly ill chosen in view of the effort that was being made to keep the door open for a diplomatic settlement through Mr. Wu. These circles had already been perturbed by General MacArthur's restiveness about his inability to take action against the "privileged sanctuary" of the Communists beyond the Yalu River. His decision to attack at this moment was immediately bracketed with his utterances on Formosa and—somewhat unfairly—with the crossing of the 38th parallel as another proof of unadaptability to United Nations views.

From a military standpoint, General MacArthur was to claim that the "fortunate" and "timely" operation undertaken by his command resulted in partially frustrating a Communist plan which, he said, had involved "massing . . . such a powerful force as to enable the complete destruction of the United Nations command and conquest of all Korea . . . in one invincible movement." [20] At all events, as the United Nations attack bogged down, it was learned for the first time that there were over 200,000 Chinese soldiers in Korea, with perhaps another 300,000 just beyond the frontier. "We face an entirely new war," reported General MacArthur in a special com-

[20] Statements reprinted in *New York Times*, December 2 and 26, 1950.

muniqué on November 28, adding that "this situation . . .
poses issues beyond the authority of the United Nations military command—issues which must find their solution within
the councils of the United Nations and the chancelleries of the
world."

This statement, which many interpreted as an appeal for
authority to take military action against China itself, was an
indication that the world was rapidly approaching one of those
fateful moments when war and peace hang in the balance.
While General MacArthur talked of "a state of undeclared
war between the Chinese Communists and the United Nations
forces," Chinese Communist sources in Peking were demanding that the American "imperialists" be thrown into the sea.
Chinese Nationalists on Formosa, and some American congressmen in Washington, were calling for full-scale hostilities
against continental China. In Moscow, the Soviet press was
accusing the United States of sponsoring participation by Japanese in the Korean War, thereby hinting that the Soviet Union
might intervene under its alliance treaty with Communist
China.[21]

"This new act of aggression has created a new crisis, a situation of unparalleled danger," declared Secretary Acheson on
November 29. ". . . No one can guarantee that war will not
come." "We are fighting in Korea for our own national security and survival," said President Truman on November 30. In
response to questions from the press, he added some im-
promptu remarks which could be taken to mean that, if
military action against China was authorized by the United
Nations, the United States might authorize General MacArthur
to use the atomic bomb at his own discretion.

Although immediate efforts were made to assure the world
that there had been no change in American policy with respect
to the atomic bomb, the reaction to this statement was tremendous and, outside the United States, uniformly unfavorable.
Prime Minister Attlee decided at an hour's notice to fly to

[21] For U.S. denials see *Department of State Bulletin*, XXIII, November 27, 1950,
870; December 11, 1950, 936.

Washington for conferences with the President. Not only the millions who had signed the Stockholm appeal, but statesmen as far apart politically as Nehru and Tito deprecated the idea of atomic bombardment in the strongest terms. The resultant slump in United States prestige cannot be precisely measured, but there can be no question that for the time being the incident seriously undermined world confidence in American leadership. During the remainder of 1950 foreign criticism of the United States showed little of the restraint that had been normal at times when this country was proceeding in rough consonance with world opinion.

It was in this superheated atmosphere, while United Nations forces in Korea were beginning their costly, hard-fighting withdrawal before the Communist steam roller, that the issue reached its negative climax in the Security Council. After hearing from Mr. Wu, that body required only two more meetings to reach the end of its tether. Three draft resolutions were voted down on November 30—two irrelevant proposals of Communist origin, and one moderate but highly relevant one directed to the actual situation. Defeated by 1 vote to 9 were (1) a Soviet-sponsored resolution submitted by Mr. Wu, calling on the United States to get out of Formosa and Korea, and (2) a Soviet resolution (originally submitted September 2) calling on the United States to get out of Formosa. Then Mr. Malik used one, two, or three vetoes, depending on the method of counting, to defeat a six-power resolution on Korea which had been introduced almost three weeks earlier and which in effect combined an assurance to China concerning its "legitimate interests" with an urgent appeal to desist from its intervention in Korea.[22]

Thanks to its recent adoption of the "Uniting for Peace" resolution, the General Assembly was well equipped to deal with such issues when the Security Council fumbled. Before taking the matter to the Assembly, however, the United States was

[22] U.N. Document S/1894, November 10, 1950, sponsored by Cuba, Ecuador, France, Norway, U.K., and U.S. and rejected by 9-1 (U.S.S.R.) with India not voting. The Chinese Communist and Soviet resolutions are U.N. Documents S/1921, November 30, and S/1757, September 2, 1950, respectively.

hopeful of coming to an understanding with the British, who had co-sponsored the defeated resolution but, as Mr. Attlee's sudden visit showed, were unenthusiastic about the trend of American policy and had not abandoned hope of persuading the Chinese to adopt a more reasonable attitude. While Sir B. N. Rau, Trygve Lie, and other advocates of conciliation endeavored to penetrate the mask of Mr. Wu in New York, the President and the Prime Minister sat down in Washington on December 4 before a mountain of accumulated Anglo-American differences which the "military disaster" in Korea had made critical.

Some conflicts were resolved and various misunderstandings were removed, but in Far Eastern matters the two leaders could agree only on abstract principles like support of the United Nations and avoidance of "appeasement." When the conference broke up on December 8, they were still at one as to the desirability of a peaceful but effective settlement in Korea, and still in essential disagreement on the problems of Formosa and Chinese representation in the United Nations.[23] Still less were they agreed on what to do if Chinese Communist intransigence continued and the United Nations forces were obliged to evacuate Korea. The United States was openly toying with the idea of a "limited war" against continental China, to be carried on principally by naval blockade and air action. The British were wholly unsympathetic to such a venture, which, they suggested, would be militarily ineffective, internationally unpopular, and unlikely to remain localized. Any war with China would be all too likely to bring in China's ally, the U.S.S.R.; in the best of cases, it would entail the diversion of men and weapons that were badly needed for the defense of Europe.

Thus neither the British nor any other major government was prepared to support the United States in requesting strong action from the General Assembly, which formally added the question of Chinese intervention in Korea to its agenda on December 6 at the request of the six co-sponsors of the vetoed Se-

[23] White House communiqué, December 8, 1950.

curity Council resolution. Instead, a similar resolution was introduced by the same six governments in the Assembly's Political Committee. It contained no suggestion that Communist China be branded an aggressor, or that the Assembly have recourse to the machinery of collective security established earlier in the session. The General Assembly was not interested in collective resistance, least of all at this stage. The last thing it desired was to antagonize Peking at a time when many still hoped the conflict could be settled without more fighting. Americans who watched the swelling casualty lists from Korea [24] were understandably impatient; not less understandably, the majority of the United Nations insisted on making every effort, reasonable and unreasonable, to extinguish the conflict in preference to extending it.

These mediatory efforts held the center of the stage throughout December, while the multinational United Nations army in Korea was forced back across the 38th parallel and the United States Tenth Corps accomplished its epic withdrawal via the Hungnam beachhead in the northeast. A bewildering variety of peace plans was introduced in the First Committee or mooted in the corridors and in delegates' apartments. In addition to the six-power resolution calling for Chinese evacuation, Vyshinsky resubmitted the stock Russian proposal demanding the withdrawal of all "foreign" troops—leaving it somewhat unclear whether or not Chinese "volunteers" were included [25]—and settlement of Korea's future by "the Korean people." Thirteen Asian and Arab nations, later joined by Britain and Yugoslavia, published an appeal to the North Koreans and Chinese Communists to declare that they would refrain from crossing the 38th parallel and thus allow time for deliberations on the larger problem of the Far East. The Arab League suggested a military and propaganda truce, to be followed by United Nations-sponsored talks between President Truman and Premier Stalin. India's delegate spent many hours conferring with

[24] U.S. casualties in the Korean war as announced through January 5, 1951, totaled 40,176, including 6,761 dead (*New York Times,* January 6, 1951).
[25] Malik intimated to the Committee on December 13 that acceptance of the Soviet proposal would also settle the problem of the "Chinese volunteer corps."

his Asian colleagues on a cease-fire plan and a related program for a Far Eastern conference.

All of these Asian-inspired proposals were based more or less explicitly on the idea that a cessation of the fighting would be only the prelude to some kind of general conference on the Far East, in which Peking's various demands would be stated and, presumably, satisfied. India understood from its ambassador in Peking that Mao's government would not negotiate on Korea alone but insisted that all Far Eastern problems be considered together, with the "People's Republic" participating as an equal. Just as at earlier stages of the Korean crisis, therefore, acceptance of China's demands outside of Korea was being put forward as the price of a local settlement in Korea. And, as before, the principal obstacle to a "package" settlement in the Far East was the formally correct but diplomatically unpopular stand of the United States. "If those who are challenging the United Nations believe that we will give up our principles because they threaten us with mighty force," Senator Austin told the Political Committee on December 7, "let them know that they are tragically mistaken. . . . Only when [the Korean] question has been disposed of can the other pressing questions concerning the peace and security of Asia be settled."

This diametrical opposition failed to discourage the mediatory zeal of the Indian and other Arab-Asian delegates, some of whom had been in conference with Mr. Wu and convinced themselves that China was genuinely interested in a peaceful settlement. On December 12, therefore, Sir B. N. Rau introduced on behalf of the Arab-Asian bloc a double-barrelled proposal for (1) a cease-fire in Korea, and (2) a conference on the Far East. As a concession to the American view, the two elements of the plan were presented in separate resolutions, with priority given to the cease-fire project.[26] This resolution was adopted by the committee on December 13 by 51-5 and next day passed the full Assembly by 52-5, with Nationalist

[26] The cease-fire plan was supported by all 13 Asian-Arab states; the conference proposal was supported by all except the Philippines.

China abstaining. A three-man group, consisting of Assembly President Entezam, Sir B. N. Rau, and Canadian External Affairs Minister Lester B. Pearson, was charged with consulting the two high commands or their representatives and reporting to the Assembly on the most suitable basis for a cease-fire. All other business was suspended pending the group's report.[27]

This procedure, though acceptable to the United States because it involved no political commitment, was unacceptable to Peking for that very reason. Mr. Wu refused to meet with the cease-fire group, but called a special press conference at which he denounced the plan as a "trap," reiterated his insistence that the United States withdraw from both Korea and Formosa, complained that he had been given no opportunity to discuss the American "aggression" against that island, and announced that he was returning to China. Before boarding the plane on December 19 he sardonically wished the American people a Merry Christmas and a Happy New Year, adding that he was sure they did not wish to "start a world war by the aggression against Taiwan and the intervention in Korea." Since the United States had in the meantime frozen Chinese Communist assets in this country, forbidden American ships to call at Communist ports, and resumed military aid shipments to Chiang Kai-shek, prospects for a peaceful outcome were not bright.

The cease-fire group labored long and diligently to carry out its mission, sparing itself and the United Nations virtually no humiliation in the interest of dispelling the Chinese Communists' suspicions and enlisting their cooperation. It offered to go to China; it appealed to Peking to defer Mr. Wu's departure; it all but promised that general negotiations would begin as soon as a cease-fire was arranged. All, however, was to no avail. Representatives of the Unified Command had agreed with the group that a satisfactory cease-fire could be put into effect by establishing a demilitarized zone 20 miles wide just north of the 38th parallel. The "People's Republic" refused even to discuss such details, preferring to regard the whole

[27] U.N. Document A/1742, adopted December 14, 1950.

procedure as an illegal device engineered without Chinese participation and designed solely to give "American invading troops" a breathing space.

On December 23 Peking cabled the official reply which was to give the quietus to the efforts of the cease-fire group. A lengthy, violently anti-American diatribe by Chou En-lai, it concluded with an unequivocal restatement of the Chinese terms: "We firmly insist that, as a basis for negotiating a peaceful settlement of the Korean problem, all foreign troops must be withdrawn from Korea, and Korea's domestic affairs must be settled by the Korean people themselves. The American aggression forces must be withdrawn from Taiwan. And the Representatives of the People's Republic of China must obtain a legitimate status in the United Nations. These points are not only the justified demands of the Chinese people and the Korean people; they are also the urgent desire of all progressive public opinion throughout the world. To put aside these points would make it impossible to settle peacefully the Korean problem and the important problems of Asia." [28]

While the United Nations was recovering from this rebuff, attention shifted to the military front, where the Unified Command had succeeded in redeploying its forces in the general neighborhood of the 38th parallel. A temporary lull had followed the evacuation of the Tenth Corps from Hungnam, but on December 24 General MacArthur's headquarters reported new concentrations of enemy forces which made an offensive appear imminent. The North Koreans were back in the fight, with a new army as big as the one they had originally sacrificed; and beside and behind them, in Korea and Manchuria, were perhaps a million and a quarter of fresh Chinese troops. Until New Year's Day the build-up continued, with Russian-designed jet-propelled fighter planes appearing in considerable numbers for the first time. Then the offensive broke, all along the Korean front. At Lake Success, the advocates of a negotiated settlement had not lost heart. The next phase, however,

[28] Report of the cease-fire group, U.N. Document A/C.1/643, January 2, 1951.

was primarily up to the fighting men of 11 nations [29] who were resisting the aggressors on Korea's frozen and inhospitable ground.

4. Crisis in the North Atlantic Community

In one sense the European crisis opened by the Soviet note of November 3 was less intense than the simultaneous crisis in the Far East and the United Nations. In the Far East, a great Communist power was actually making war on the United Nations; in Europe, its superior partner was only hinting that it might make war if certain contemplated steps were taken by the North Atlantic Treaty powers. The difference, however, was at most a difference of degree. In both instances, the United States and a group of associated governments had taken up positions from which retreat would be difficult, but in which a refusal to retreat might prove extremely costly. Facilities for retreat were available in both cases: in the Arab-Asian proposals for a Far Eastern conference, and in the Soviet proposal for a conference on Germany. A good many governments clearly were for seizing the opportunity to fall back on positions that would be more easily defensible. In neither case, however, did the United States propose to yield to threats, sacrifice principles, or incur accusations of "appeasement."

Very many countries agreed with the United States that there were certain positions and certain principles that had to be maintained even in the face of great risks. The general support hitherto accorded to United States foreign policy, both in and outside of the United Nations, bore sufficient witness to this fact. The difficulty was that in the present crisis this country for the first time found itself attaching great importance to certain specialized views which the majority of its friends did not share. This was particularly true with respect to Formosa and Chinese representation in the United Nations; in a lesser degree it was true also of policy toward Western Germany.

[29] Australia, Belgium, France, Greece, Republic of Korea, Netherlands, Philippines, Thailand, Turkey, U.K., and U.S.

Beneath these specific divergences, moreover, was a difference of fundamental mood which was expressing itself in contrary approaches to the whole problem of relations with the Communist world. While other countries continued to place considerable hope in the possibilities of negotiation and compromise, the United States seemed to have lost faith in diplomacy and, while still officially committed to a policy of peace, to be willing to risk war rather than modify its position. When foreign governments revealed their lack of enthusiasm for such energetic leadership, some Americans were ready to conclude that both the United Nations and the North Atlantic Treaty had outlived their usefulness to this country.

That the incipient split among the North Atlantic allies did not grow wider was largely due to the clarifying effects of the Truman-Attlee conference on December 4-8. Although strictly bilateral in form, the conference actually dealt with much wider issues which vitally concerned the North Atlantic community and the free world at large. Before taking off across the Atlantic, Mr. Attlee received the French Prime Minister and Foreign Minister and assured himself that London and Paris were in essential agreement on the principal matters he was to take up with the President. In a very real sense he was acting as spokesman for the whole of Western Europe, which had shown the deepest concern over this country's apparent willingness to involve itself in war with China and relegate the interests of the Atlantic community to second place.

That the Attlee mission was aimed essentially at restraint of this country was understood equally well in Europe and in the United States, where denunciation of the British attitude went hand in hand with insistence on all-out action against Communist China. There was strong congressional agitation against the whole idea of accommodation with the British, which reached a climax in the midst of the conference when 24 Republican Senators endeavored unsuccessfully to secure passage of a resolution which would have required Senate ratification of any agreement or understanding that might be reached by the heads of the two governments.

On the critical issues of the Far East no real Anglo-American agreement was possible at that stage, although the frank exchange of views was helpful in reducing the problem to its true dimensions, while the development of the military situation in Korea made it possible to avoid any irrevocable decision for the time being. Mr. Attlee also was unable to obtain full satisfaction on the matter of the atomic bomb, whose use, the President had intimated in his press conference, lay entirely within American discretion notwithstanding the fact that this country was acting officially on behalf of the United Nations. From this position the President would not retreat, although he assured the Prime Minister that he hoped world conditions would never call for the use of the bomb and that he desired "to keep the Prime Minister at all times informed of developments which might bring about a change in the situation." [30]

The positive side of the conversations, apart from a reaffirmation of general principles, lay in the recognition of both governments that Far Eastern developments must not be allowed to throw their global policies out of balance. In considering the necessities of the Far Eastern situation, the two leaders declared, they had "kept in mind the urgency of building up the strength of the whole free world," and, in particular, were "in complete agreement on the need for all the North Atlantic Treaty countries to intensify their efforts to build up their defenses and to strengthen the Atlantic community." In other words, Europe retained all its importance in the world picture. Military capabilities must be built up as rapidly as possible, and on a basis of "mutual arrangements by which all will contribute appropriately to the common defense"; and a supreme commander for the North Atlantic defense forces should be named "soon."

Discussion of the always vexed question of military versus civilian requirements, on which the United States consistently took a more austere view than most of its allies, produced a statement that endeavored to do justice to the opinions of both sides. On the one hand, it was agreed that "the maintenance of

[30] White House communiqué, December 8, 1950.

healthy civilian economies is of vital importance to the success of our defense effort," and that "the essential civilian requirements of the free countries must be met so far as practicable"; on the other, it was stipulated that defense production would have to receive priority in the apportionment of scarce raw materials. Both governments promised to work together closely to increase supplies of scarce materials and promote their equitable allocation, and the British group agreed to a further sentence emphasizing the importance of preventing strategic items from flowing to "those who might use them against the free world."

No public statement was made about the critical question of German rearmament and the proposed four-power conference, to which the British and especially the French were known to look forward much more hopefully than did the United States. It was once again affirmed, however, that existing circumstances left the free nations no alternative to vigorously building up their defense forces; that their purpose was purely defensive; that the Communist leaders of the U.S.S.R. and China "could, if they chose, modify their conduct in such a way as to make these defense preparations unnecessary"; and that "we shall do everything that we can, through whatever channels are open to us, to impress this view upon them and to seek a peaceful solution of existing issues." [31]

Meanwhile, as representatives of the Big Three conferred in Paris about a reply to the Soviet note of November 3, the North Atlantic deputies in London were preparing the ground for another full-dress meeting of the 12 Atlantic Foreign Ministers. This fourth session of the North Atlantic Council in 1950 would, it was hoped, bring final agreement on the integrated defense force which had been in contemplation for so many weeks. The prospect was greatly improved because the pressure of world events had helped to break the interallied deadlock over German rearmament which had delayed this consummation through the autumn.

Since the New York meetings in September, the United

[31] *Ibid.*

States and most of its allies had continued to insist on the inclusion of German divisions in an integrated defense force; France had held out strongly for the Pleven plan of a European army. Eventually the difference was bridged by a compromise arrangement credited to Charles M. Spofford, the American chairman of the council of deputies. Under the "Spofford plan," Western Germany would be represented not by divisions but by "regimental combat teams"—self-contained units of less than divisional strength (not over 6,000 men), which would be small enough to overcome French misgivings but large enough, it was hoped, to constitute effective fighting contingents, and which might ultimately represent perhaps 20 percent of the Atlantic powers' total ground strength. In the first half of December this compromise was approved successively by the Military Committee and the Defense Committee, in preparation for its submission to the full North Atlantic Council in Brussels on December 18-19.

Under the circumstances prevailing in mid-December, the approval of this arrangement by the European members of the North Atlantic Treaty Organization required a certain courage. Important governments of the North Atlantic alliance were under fire from various quarters. The French cabinet was more than usually shaky. Britain faced a crisis in its relations with the Arab governments of the Middle East and a renewal of Spanish agitation on the Gibraltar issue. The Netherlands was seriously at odds with the new Republic of Indonesia over the future of Dutch New Guinea. In Europe, Soviet irreconcilability to the program for West German rearmament had been made known with increasing emphasis since the notes of November 3. On the very eve of the Brussels meeting, while Mr. Wu in New York was defying the United Nations, the Kremlin had dispatched new stiff notes to Britain and France, warning them of the dangers of a rebirth of German militarism and accusing them of violating the wartime Anglo-Soviet and Franco-Soviet alliance treaties.

The possibility that the Soviet Union really would make war over this issue could not be excluded; and, to fill the cup of

European consternation, there were increasingly plain intimations that the United States, after insisting that Germany be rearmed, might not shrink from leaving its European partners to face the consequences alone. The President and Secretary Acheson could be relied upon to uphold the American side of the partnership, but it was no longer possible to be sure they would be supported by public opinion. What, for instance, were Europeans to expect from those Republican congressmen of both houses who were questioning the whole European connection and who, on December 15, by overwhelming majorities, adopted resolutions declaring that Acheson and his department "have lost the confidence of the Congress and the American people and cannot regain it"?

Despite these disturbing portents, the ministers at Brussels smoothly carried out their prearranged tasks. They completed the arrangements for "the establishment in Europe of an integrated force under centralized control and command"; then they unanimously requested President Truman to designate General Eisenhower as "Supreme Allied Commander, Europe," and formally appointed him to the new post as soon as Acheson had conveyed the President's assent. General Eisenhower was to establish headquarters in Europe early in 1951; meanwhile he was assigned operational command of all United States Army, Air, and Naval forces in the European theater, and other powers prepared to follow the American lead by placing comparable forces under his command.

The North Atlantic Council further noted that a new and more powerful Defense Production Board was being set up to expand and accelerate production and promote efficient use of all available industrial capacity of the North Atlantic nations. Finally, it "reached unanimous agreement regarding the part which Germany might assume in the common defense," and invited the three occupying powers to "explore the matter" with the Bonn government.[32]

This language sounded rather less urgent than might have

[32] North Atlantic Council communiqué, December 19, and related documents in *Department of State Bulletin*, XXIV, January 1, 1951, 6-7.

been expected in view of the pressure the United States had been exerting to get Western Germany's rearmament under way. Accordingly, it was greeted in Europe with considerable relief. The United States, it appeared, had consented to some relaxation of the tempo as part of the price paid for agreement on the principle. French quarters even claimed that there was an escape clause providing that under certain circumstances the agreement might not have to be implemented at all. In any case, the "explorations" which the Allied High Commissioners were to undertake with Dr. Adenauer would require plenty of time. Meanwhile the Western countries would be forging ahead with their own rearmament programs. The United States, it was assumed, would be sending additional divisions to Europe, as well as equipment and a commander-in-chief; the President had repeated this promise in announcing the Eisenhower appointment. And there was always a possibility that the Russians might prove unexpectedly amenable if a four-power conference were to be held as the French and British seemed to expect.

In reality the most serious single obstacle to German rearmament had still to be faced in the attitude of the Germans themselves. Hitherto German acquiescence in the plan had been taken more or less for granted, if only because the objections from other quarters had been so much more pressing. Such optimism, however, was no longer possible in the light of recent developments within Germany. The Prague declaration and subsequent occurrences had crystallized German opposition to the whole idea of military partnership with the West and gone far to cut the ground from under the feet of Dr. Adenauer, its principal advocate. A series of state (*Land*) elections in the United States zone revealed the trend unmistakably. On November 19 the Social Democrats, by now clearly identified with opposition to the government's policy on rearmament, scored decisive victories in Hesse and Württemberg-Baden. A week later, to dispel any doubts, they repeated their success in Bavaria. Dr. Schumacher expressed confidence that a national election on the rearmament issue would sweep his party into office at Bonn, and redoubled determination to hold out for more favorable terms if the country was ever to be rearmed.

Thus there was a considerable aura of unreality about the meeting on December 21 at which Dr. Adenauer and the Allied High Commissioners decided to set up a committee which would examine the "scale and manner" of Western Germany's contribution to the collective defense of Western Europe. Although the High Commissioners tried to sweeten the pill by holding out the prospect of a further relaxation of allied controls over the Federal Republic, the plain fact was that the Germans, never enthusiastic about participating on Western terms, were more reluctant than ever now that the Russians had declared their opposition so strongly. The declaration of the Eastern European Foreign Ministers, with its insistence on German demilitarization and reunification, had produced a profound effect throughout Germany, and the East German Communists had kept the agitation alive with a propaganda campaign on the theme of "unity and neutrality." If, as the Communists implied, the alternative was war and invasion by Russia and the execution of all "warmongers," the average German could hardly doubt where his preferences lay.

The spear point of this Communist campaign within Germany was a highly conciliatory letter which East German Premier Otto Grotewohl had addressed to Dr. Adenauer, suggesting a meeting of East and West German delegates to discuss their country's reunification through a constituent council and "free" all-German elections.[33] Thus the Communists duplicated on a national level the parallel gestures already made by the Eastern European Foreign Ministers and by the Russians on the four-power level. Adenauer was too familiar with Communist methods to put much faith in their good intentions, no matter how loudly advertised. The same could not be said, however, for Dr. Martin Niemöller and other more or less prominent citizens of the Federal Republic to whom the notion of "unity for peace" was proving irresistibly attractive. Even the Bonn government, moreover, would have been somewhat

[33] Text (November 30, 1950) in *Europa-Archiv*, VI, February 5, 1951, 3716.

ill-advised to reject these overtures out of hand. With the
Western powers in a tight place and a four-power meeting on
the horizon, there was no guarantee that the U.S.S.R. might not
maneuver its opponents into some "deal" that would have serious implications for the future of the 15-month-old Federal
Republic.

Such uncertainties were not conducive to a strengthening of
the democratic and pro-Western trend which the Western
powers had hoped to bring about in Germany. One of the least
heartening features of the German situation was the continually increasing prominence of elements and attitudes which had
flourished under the Nazi regime. The evident disposition to
drive a hard bargain with the West on rearmament was only
one manifestation of a general nationalistic tendency which the
Russians were perhaps not wholly unjustified in calling to
Western attention. German democrats were discouraged by
such moves as Adenauer's designation of two former Hitler
generals to handle the rearmament negotiations. Genuine
democrats still had some voice in German affairs, but they
would be the first to suffer if Western Germany fell a victim to
totalitarian trends, whether foreign or domestic in origin. Other
elements whose attachment to democratic principles was less
secure—industrialists who were seeking markets in the East
and holding up completion of the Schuman Plan negotiations,
and military and other groups intent on securing special advantages from rearmament—seemed confident of their own ability
to stay afloat under any circumstances.

Conditions in Western Germany might leave much to be desired, but this did not mean that negotiations with the U.S.S.R.
were likely to lead to a satisfactory alternative. The Kremlin,
for all its recurrent expressions favoring German unity and demilitarization on the basis of the outmoded Potsdam agreement, had never displayed the least readiness to implement the
Potsdam principles in fact or to establish German unity on any
basis the Western powers could accept. The language of the
Prague declaration and the Soviet notes gave no reason to sup-
pose that Soviet aims had altered, while the contrasting char-

acter of the political regimes that had grown up in Eastern and
Western Germany meant that the country could not possibly be
knit together again unless very fundamental concessions were
made by one side or the other. Under normal circumstances no
one would have expected the Russian overture to lead to practical consequences. But the circumstances of late 1950 were far
from normal.

Acheson and Bevin, followed more hesitantly by their French
colleague, had made it clear that in their opinion negotiations
confined to the question of German demilitarization as suggested in the Soviet note of November 3 would be fruitless. A
discussion on so limited a basis, they intimated, would not even
come to grips with the realities of the German problem; and,
as Acheson pointed out, Germany itself was "not a problem
which can be isolated from the context of similar areas of tension elsewhere." [34] The State Department, which had consistently maintained that negotiations with the U.S.S.R. were
unlikely to succeed until the military strength of the free nations had been increased, seems to have been convinced from
the outset that nothing would result from a four-power meeting except another futile exchange of propaganda, in which
the Western powers might very well come off second best.

Yet obviously the invitation could not be turned down flatly.
Too many people in Europe believed something positive might
come of it. Left-wing and pacifist circles in the Labor party
were putting heavy pressure on Bevin to accept; in France the
government itself looked forward to a four-power meeting
with surprising optimism, fed no doubt by its own distaste for
German rearmament. In any case there were good arguments
for treating the Soviet proposal with deference. Russian intentions were always worth exploring, and at least it was hardly
likely that they would attack in Europe while a four-power conference was in the cards.

The minimum condition insisted upon by the United States,
and generally accepted by Britain and France, was that if any

[34] Statement of November 8, in *Department of State Bulletin*, XXIII, November 20, 1950, 818.

talks were held they must not be confined to Germany but must
cover a much broader range of East-West questions in Europe.
Some consideration was given to including the Far East as well,
but this idea was abandoned in the interest of avoiding another
argument over the participation of Communist China. But
there were other issues in Europe whose settlement was long
overdue and on which the Western legal and political position
was perhaps more difficult to misrepresent than it was in Germany. Two outstanding examples were the negotiations for an
Austrian treaty—still stalemated by Soviet insistence on bringing in the Trieste issue [35]—and the continuing rearmament of
Bulgaria, Hungary, and Rumania in excess of peace treaty
limitations.[36]

The identical notes in which the three Western powers eventually responded to the Soviet initiative were delivered at the
Kremlin on December 22, after an interval of just seven weeks.
They rejected the contentions embodied in the Prague declaration and the Soviet note, but offered to designate representatives to a preliminary four-power meeting—perhaps at United
Nations headquarters—which would seek a mutually acceptable basis for a meeting of the Foreign Ministers. "The Soviet
proposal to examine the question of the demilitarization of
Germany," they emphasized, "will not suffice to remove the
causes of the present tension. The only German military force
which exists at present is that which for many months in the
Soviet zone has been trained on military lines with artillery and
tanks. . . ."

As often happened, the Western powers found it necessary
to go to some pains to restate a problem which the Soviet communication had presented in distorted form. "The serious tension which exists at present," they continued, "springs neither

[35] On the failure of a new attack on the Austrian treaty problem by the Foreign
Ministers' deputies on December 15 cf. *ibid.*, December 25, 1950, 1008. On
November 10 and 22 the three powers had also filed protests at the Kremlin over
Soviet interference with Austrian police administration in Soviet-occupied sections
of the country (*ibid.*, November 20, 1950, 819 and December 4, 1950, 894-895).
[36] Details of the rearmament being carried out by the Balkan satellites were
offered by Marshal Tito—an interested but well-informed source—in an interview
published in *New York Times*, December 29, 1950.

from the question of demilitarization of Germany nor even
from the German problem as a whole. It arises in the first instance from the general attitude adopted by the Government of
the U.S.S.R. since the end of the war and from the consequent
international developments of recent months." Questions related to Germany, and to Austria, were obvious subjects for
four-power discussion, they said; but there was no point in discussing them in a vacuum. "Any discussions should include
equally the principal problems whose solution would permit a
real and lasting improvement in the relations between the Soviet Union and the United States, Great Britain, and France
and the elimination of the causes of present international tensions throughout the world. . . ." [37]

The Soviet reply, delivered on January 1, 1951,[38] neither accepted nor absolutely rejected such a broadening of the agenda;
thus the hint was conveyed that four-power talks on a wide
range of topics might eventually be arranged. For the United
States and the free world this prospect spelled both danger and
opportunity. The danger was that the Soviet Union, being presumably under no compulsion to beat a strategic retreat, would
so exploit its opportunity to play upon the hopes and fears of
the free world as to aggravate present disunities and perhaps
emerge with new tangible advantages. The opportunity which
was presented, conceivably for the last time, was boldly to seize
the moral and diplomatic initiative and outplay the Soviets at
their own game—not merely to put the U.S.S.R. in the wrong,
but to reaffirm, in a fashion unmistakable for men and women
on both sides of the Iron Curtain, the intrinsic strength of the
free world and the indefeasible superiority of its democratic
faith.

[37] U.S. note, *Department of State Bulletin*, XXIV, January 1, 1951, 11-12. The
United States released simultaneously a background statement stressing the
"futility" of past efforts to negotiate with the Soviet Union; cf. *ibid.*, January 15,
1951, 92-93.
[38] *Ibid.*, 90-92.

5. Crisis in American Foreign Policy

It must be acknowledged that conditions in the democratic world were scarcely propitious for a diplomatic counteroffensive which would require imagination, conviction, unity of purpose, and a reasonable assurance of public support. One of the Soviet objectives in dangling the bait of a four-power conference undoubtedly was to encourage the highly volatile tendencies that were manifesting themselves throughout the democratic community and especially within the United States itself. The Kremlin was watching developments in this country closely and with considerable satisfaction, as was apparent from various articles in the Soviet press which pointed to the fact that American opinion in late 1950 was in a condition of profound crisis. For once, moreover, the Soviet version did not greatly exaggerate the reality. Senator Kenneth D. McKellar of Tennessee told his colleagues on December 18 that he had not seen such disunity in 40 years of congressional service. Two days later Herbert Hoover made a speech whose effects were literally to rock the Atlantic community to its foundations.

Dissension within the United States did not apply equally to all aspects of foreign affairs. President Truman's declaration of a national emergency on December 16 had general support, as did the concurrent request for a meeting of American Foreign Ministers and the various measures of economic warfare undertaken against Communist China. There was little quarreling with the broad principles of the intensified national mobilization program outlined in a presidential broadcast on December 15, which called for a further expansion of the armed forces from 2.5 to nearly 3.5 million, a vast new increase in defense production, and stringent controls on the home front. At its short year-end session, Congress disregarded the President's plea for ratification of the Convention on Genocide, but enacted a $20,165 million supplemental defense appropriation bill (bringing total defense appropriations for the fiscal year to over $42 billion) as well as a national civil defense program and the authorization of emergency relief assistance to Yugo-slavia.[39]

That world conditions obliged the United States to strengthen itself was not seriously questioned; but few who had watched the development of American world policy over the last decade could have anticipated how little agreement there would be about the way in which our rapidly growing strength should be used. The military and foreign policy of this country rested on the supposedly well-established principle that American security was indivisible from the security of the free world as a whole, and that America's defensive frontiers lay beyond both oceans. This was the basis not only of the deployment of the national armed forces but also of solemn international cove-nants—the United Nations Charter, the Rio Pact, the North Atlantic Treaty. These engagements, however, had been en-tered into at a time when the eventuality of war had seemed comparatively remote, and when their implications had per-haps not been fully appreciated by the country at large. Now, when war suddenly seemed a definite possibility, there was a startling resurgence of the old feeling that by withdrawing into its own shell the United States could somehow avoid paying the price of its world position.

The exponents of this feeling did not, indeed, suggest a re-turn to complete isolation such as some people had favored in the 1930's. Some took the opposite road and called on the na-tion to blast its way out of the difficulty with atomic bombs. Others stopped short of this course, but showed an equal confi-dence in this country's ability to get along without allies and protect itself by air and sea power alone. Many who felt that the United States had assumed commitments in excess of its immediate military power demanded that the commitments be reduced forthwith. The areas selected for retreat were deter-

[39] Cf. above, p. 292. Another important mobilization step was the creation on December 21 of a Committee on International Security Affairs, embracing the State, Defense, and Treasury Departments, the Economic Cooperation Administra-tion, and the office of presidential assistant Harriman, to handle "international security matters and military and economic assistance for mutual defense." Thomas Dudley Cabot was named Director for International Security Affairs in the State Department and ex officio chairman of the committee.

mined by what was evidently considered a realistic appraisal of the military factors, uncontaminated by sentimental concern for foreign nations which had allegedly "let us down." Formosa, where the international position of the United States was weakest, was to be held under all circumstances. Korea, where it was strongest, might be abandoned. But the really decisive retraction was to occur in Western Europe, whose security had hitherto been deemed the central concern of American foreign policy and the key to the security of the United States itself.

The first serious intimation of the new trend was the favorable public response accorded to a speech by Joseph P. Kennedy on December 12, in which the former Ambassador to London described current American policy as "suicidal" and "politically and morally bankrupt," denounced the weakness of the United Nations and the ingratitude of our friends, and demanded withdrawal from "unwise commitments" beginning with Korea, Berlin, and the whole idea of defending Western Europe.[40] This, however, was as nothing compared to the sensation caused by ex-President Hoover in his radio address of December 20, the day after the appointment of General Eisenhower as Supreme Commander of the Allied Forces in Europe. Throughout the year the former President had proved himself the most effective spokesman of that group which sought salvation for the United States in such negative courses as nonrecognition of Communist China, expulsion of the U.S.S.R. from the United Nations, and lessened support for Western Europe. His speech of December 20 was a superb catalyst of all the negative emotions that had been gathering across the nation for many months, and the response showed that he had not misjudged the temper of the moment.

As a powerful statement of America's case against the world, the Hoover speech unquestionably merits study and preservation as an historic document. Here it must suffice to touch on its major foreign policy recommendations—preservation of the Western Hemisphere; holding of the Atlantic and Pacific oceans, in association with Japan, Formosa, the Philippines,

[40] Text in *Vital Speeches of the Day*, XVII, January 1, 1951, 170-173.

and (preferably) Great Britain and the Commonwealth; re-armament at sea and in the air; and not "another man or another dollar" to the nations of Western Europe until they themselves had produced "organized and equipped combat divisions of such huge numbers as would erect a sure dam against the red flood." With such policies, Mr. Hoover said, "even without Europe Americans have no reason for hysteria or loss of confidence in our security or our future. . . . It would be an uneasy peace but we could carry it on with these policies indefinitely even if the Communists should attack our lines on the seas. . . ."

Although the initial public reaction to this pronouncement was as favorable in the United States—and the U.S.S.R.—as it was unfavorable among non-Communist Europeans, some Americans immediately challenged Mr. Hoover's thinking; and his optimistic conclusions were to look less and less tenable as time went on. Administration dissent was to be expected. The President said Mr. Hoover's policy was nothing else but isolationism and the country was not going back to that. The Secretary of State returned from Brussels with a reasoned refutation which concluded in the assurance that "we are rejecting any policy of sitting quivering in a storm cellar waiting for whatever fate others may wish to prepare for us." [41] Although Senators Taft and Wherry appeared sympathetic to the Hoover thesis, a good many Republicans dissociated themselves from the former President's views or at least refrained from openly endorsing them. Intraparty differences among Republicans would clearly be a significant element in the "great debate" on American policy that was shaping up.

That there would be such a debate, that it would involve the very roots of American foreign policy, and that the free world would have to mark time while the issues were thrashed out, was now obvious. The principal question overtly in dispute would be the wisdom of persevering in the attempt to build an

[41] Remarks by Acheson, December 22, in *Department of State Bulletin*, XXIV, January 1, 1951, 3-6; by the President, December 28, in *New York Times*, December 29, 1950.

effective, integrated defense against aggression in Western Europe. More fundamentally, the question at issue was whether any nation, even the greatest, could still afford under twenti-eth-century conditions to think in terms of military, economic, and moral self-sufficiency. The nature of some of the argu-ments would be more or less novel, but the basic attitudes were familiar from comparable debates in earlier decades. On one side were those who were able to convince themselves that the United States could somehow keep its own health in the midst of a plague-stricken world; on the other, those who held that the free nations were united, for better or worse, in a common destiny from which no one of them could hope to separate itself.[42]

The ultimate outcome of the great debate was also scarcely more in doubt than that of the parallel debates in 1914–1917 and 1939–1941. The United States was not going to adopt the Hoover formula or any of its several variants, because too many Americans found validity in the opposite courses of ac-tion to which this country was already committed and which it was engaged in carrying out. The only question, therefore, was how seriously the attack on those policies, especially in regard to Western Europe, would weaken and delay their implementa-tion, and whether or not their opponents would succeed in hedging them about with so many limitations and restrictions as to render them ineffective. That the policy of collective defense in the free world was dangerous no one could deny, because the very situation that had called it into being was full of dangers. The only hope of success, therefore, lay in prosecut-ing it with vigor, discrimination, and fidelity to its underlying democratic principles.

The best judgment in Washington as the year closed was that the Soviet Union would not provoke full-scale war in 1951 —which seemed a reasonable hypothesis if one accepted the as-sumption that Moscow still preferred to avoid unnecessary risks and would rather let the free world succumb to the "in-

[42] The most effective statement of this latter view in the early days of the debate was a radio address by John Foster Dulles on December 30, 1950.

ternal contradictions" which had been so much in evidence of late. The prospect of a breathing space had important implications for the future course of American policy in relation to both the Soviet and non-Soviet worlds, since the manner in which the interval was used might spell success or ultimate failure of the great attempt to shield Western civilization against the hazards of an atomic world war.

The trend of Soviet diplomacy showed that the Kremlin already was seriously perturbed over the gathering material strength of the free world, and would overlook no possibility of halting the process by insinuations, threats, or conciliatory gestures aimed at slowing down the pace of rearmament. If these devices failed to shake the resolve of the free nations, another year might see them so strong that Moscow, always fearful of dissidence within its own camp, would no longer dare attack and would have to reconcile itself to a long-term stabilization in the relations of the "socialist" and "capitalist" worlds. But the very growth of American power might also, under certain circumstances, endanger the prospect of a peaceful outcome. By encouraging that current in American thinking which openly rejected the idea of peaceful "coexistence" between the two worlds, it might tend gradually to undermine the national dedication to a policy of peace. Already the advocacy of "preventive" war had ceased to horrify American opinion as it would once have done. And a conviction that warlike tendencies were gaining the upper hand in this country would be the surest inducement to the Politburo to anticipate the coming "capitalist crusade" by unleashing—or compelling the United States to unleash—the very catastrophe America was pledged to prevent by every honorable means within its power.

In relation to the non-Soviet world, the principal danger to the United States would lie in a failure to halt the disintegration and mutual distrust which had gained momentum among the free nations over the past six months. This was a task that would claim special attention from American officials responsible for the expanded foreign information program, but one which could not be carried through successfully by them alone since it involved the whole tendency and spirit of American policy. The United States, as the leading nation of the free world, had still to find the right formula for accommodating its individual national aims with those universal human aspirations whose satisfaction or violation would ultimately determine man's future course. Not without a very special utility to this country, in the years immediately ahead, would be a clearer exhibition of that "decent respect to the opinions of mankind" which had inspired our own Declaration of Independence.

The truth was that in this mid-twentieth century the United States needed to have the people of the world on its side, just as surely as the latter needed to rely on the continuing encouragement and support of the United States. A fundamental harmony of purpose was essential to all-round survival. Such a harmony—rudimentary enough, to be sure—had actually existed in 1947, 1948, and 1949. In 1950 it had suffered grave impairment. Not until it was restored could the freedom-loving peoples of the two hemispheres hope to move forward once again toward that wider and brighter future in which, at heart, Americans still believed.

SELECTED BIBLIOGRAPHY

No annual bibliography of world affairs can mention more than a small fraction of the literature that daily pours from the world's presses. The present selection, designed to provide a point of departure for both the student and the general reader, is necessarily limited to works that combine a high degree of relevance with reasonable accessibility. Additional materials of permanent interest will be found listed in earlier volumes of this series, and more extensive bibliographies are readily available in such specialized publications as the *American Political Science Review, Foreign Affairs,* and *International Organization.* A number of outstanding periodicals are listed by way of a reminder that much of the best current writing on international affairs appears in this medium. Except as otherwise indicated, all official United States documents are published by the U.S. Government Printing Office (Washington 25, D.C.), and all British documents by H. M. Stationery Office in London (obtainable in the United States through British Information Services, 30 Rockefeller Plaza, New York 20, N.Y.). United Nations publications may be ordered from the International Documents Service, Columbia University Press, 2960 Broadway, New York 27, N.Y.

GENERAL

Periodicals

American Journal of International Law. Washington, American Society of International Law, quarterly.

American Perspective. Washington, Foundation for Foreign Affairs, monthly.

Aussenpolitik: Zeitschrift für internationale Fragen. Stuttgart, Deutsche Verlags-Anstalt, bimonthly.

Chronique de Politique Étrangère. Brussels, Institut des Relations Internationales, monthly.

Current Developments in United States Foreign Policy. Washington, Brookings Institution, ten times a year. (Detailed chronicle of world events.)

Current History. Philadelphia, Events Publishing Company, monthly.

The Economist. London, The Economist, weekly. (Leading political and economic review.)

Europa-Archiv. Frankfurt am Main, Verlag Europa-Archiv, semimonthly.

Foreign Affairs. New York, Council on Foreign Relations, quarterly.

Foreign Policy Reports. New York, Foreign Policy Association, semimonthly except July and August.

International Affairs. London, Royal Institute of International Affairs, quarterly.

International Conciliation. New York, Carnegie Endowment for International Peace, monthly except July and August.

International Journal. Toronto, Canadian Institute of International Affairs, quarterly.

International Organization. Boston, World Peace Foundation, quarterly.
Politique Étrangère. Paris, Centre d'Études de Politique Étrangère, quarterly.
Relazioni Internazionali. Milan, Istituto di Studi Internazionali, weekly.
World Affairs. London, London Institute of World Affairs, quarterly.
World Politics. New Haven, Yale Institute of International Studies, quarterly.
The World Today. London, Royal Institute of International Affairs, monthly.

Reference Works and Documents

POLITICAL HANDBOOK OF THE WORLD: Parliaments, Parties and Press as of
January 1, 1951, edited by Walter H. Mallory. New York, Harper, for the
Council on Foreign Relations, 1951, 230 p.
THE DIPLOMATIC YEARBOOK, by the editors of the United Nations World
Magazine. New York, Funk & Wagnalls, 1951, 836 p. (A symposium.)
YEARBOOK OF INTERNATIONAL ORGANIZATIONS 1950. New York, Hafner,
1950, 902 p.
STATISTICAL YEARBOOK, 1949–50, prepared by the Statistical Office, United
Nations Department of Economic Affairs. U.N. Publication 1950. XVII. 3.
Lake Success, 1950, 555 p.
DEMOGRAPHIC YEARBOOK 1940–50. U.N. Publication 1951. XIII. 1. New York,
1950, 558 p. (World population statistics.)
PUBLICATIONS OF THE DEPARTMENT OF STATE, July 1, 1950: A Semiannual
List Cumulative from January 1, 1948. Department of State Publication 3881.
Washington, 1950, 61 p.
UNITED NATIONS DOCUMENTS INDEX: United Nations and Specialized Agen-
cies Documents and Publications. U.N. Document ST/LIB/SER E., Lake Suc-
cess, monthly.
BASIC DOCUMENTS OF INTERNATIONAL RELATIONS, edited by Frederick H.
Hartmann. New York, McGraw-Hill, 1951, 312 p.
DOCUMENTS ON AMERICAN FOREIGN RELATIONS, edited by Raymond Dennett
and Robert K. Turner. Princeton, Princeton University Press, for the World
Peace Foundation. Vol. XI (1950, 728 p.) covers the year 1949.
DOCUMENTS ON REGIONAL ORGANIZATIONS OUTSIDE WESTERN EUROPE, 1940–
1949. London, Royal Institute of International Affairs, 1950, 85 p.

World Politics, International Organization

INTERNATIONAL RELATIONS IN THE AGE OF THE CONFLICT between Democ-
racy and Dictatorship, by Robert Strausz-Hupé and Stefan T. Possony. New
York, McGraw-Hill, 1950, 947 p.
THE YEAR BOOK OF WORLD AFFAIRS, 1950, edited by George W. Keeton and
Georg Schwarzenberger. London, Stevens, for the London Institute of World
Affairs, 1950, 392 p. (A group of specialized studies.)
THE DEFENSE OF THE FREE WORLD, edited by John A. Krout. (*Proceedings
of the Academy of Political Science*, XXIV, No. 2, January 1951, 138 p.)
DEFENCE IN THE COLD WAR: The Task for the Free World, by a Study Group
under the chairmanship of Major General Sir Ian Jacob. London, Royal In-
stitute of International Affairs, 1950, 123 p.
REPRIEVE FROM WAR: A Manual for Realists, by Lionel Gelber. New York,
Macmillan, 1950, 196 p.
FUNDAMENTALS OF WORLD ORGANIZATION, by Werner Levi. Minneapolis,
University of Minnesota Press, 1950, 233 p.
PATTERNS OF COOPERATION. Department of State Publication 3735, Interna-
tional Organization and Conference Series I, 9. Washington, 1950, 130 p.

WHICH WAY TO WORLD GOVERNMENT?, by Alfred M. Lilienthal. Headline
Series, 83. New York, Foreign Policy Association, 1950, 62 p.
STRENGTHENING THE FRAMEWORK OF PEACE: A Study of Current Proposals,
by Alan De Rusett. London, Royal Institute of International Affairs, 1951,
225 p.
CHALLENGE AND DECISION: A Program for the Times of Crisis Ahead, by
Edgar Ansell Mowrer. New York, McGraw-Hill, 1950, 291 p. (Advocates
world federation under American leadership.)
A PLAN FOR PEACE, by Grenville Clark. New York, Harper, 1950, 83 p. (A
plan for world government.)
THE THEORY AND PRACTICE OF COMMUNISM, by R. N. Carew Hunt. New
York, Macmillan, 1950, 231 p. (An exposition of Marxist theory.)
THE FRONT IS EVERYWHERE: Militant Communism in Action, by William R.
Kintner. Norman, University of Oklahoma Press, 1950, 274 p.
VERDICT OF THREE DECADES, edited by Julian Steinberg. New York, Duell,
1950, 634 p. (Anthology of anti-Communist writings by former adherents.)
I BELIEVED, by Douglas Hyde. New York, Putnam, 1950, 312 p. (One of the
better ex-Communist autobiographies.)
THE VATICAN AND THE KREMLIN, by Camille M. Cianfarra. New York, Dut-
ton, 1950, 258 p.

Social and Economic Affairs

FREEDOM, POWER, AND DEMOCRATIC PLANNING, by Karl Mannheim. New
York, Oxford University Press, 1950, 384 p.
THE SOCIAL CRISIS OF OUR TIME, by Wilhelm Ropke. Chicago, University of
Chicago Press, 1950, 260 p.
THE OPEN SOCIETY AND ITS ENEMIES, by Karl R. Popper. Princeton, Princeton
University Press, 1950, 732 p.
"The World's Refugee Problem," by Fred W. Riggs. (*Foreign Policy Reports*,
XXVI, January 15, 1951, 190-199.)
CHILDREN OF EUROPE, by Dorothea Macardle. Boston, Beacon, 1951, 349 p.
WORLD ECONOMIC REPORT, 1949–1950, prepared by the [United Nations]
Secretariat. U.N. Document E/1910, January 29, 1951, 392 p.
WORLD OUTLOOK AND STATE OF FOOD AND AGRICULTURE, 1950. Washington,
Food and Agriculture Organization, October 1950, 81 p.
NATIONAL INCOME STATISTICS OF VARIOUS COUNTRIES, 1938–1948. U.N. Pub-
lication 1950. XVII. 2. Lake Success, 1950, 249 p.
NATIONAL AND PER CAPITA INCOMES, SEVENTY COUNTRIES, 1949 U.N. Docu-
ment ST/STAT/SER. E/1, September 20, 1950, 29 p.
THE INTERNATIONAL ECONOMY, by P. T. Ellsworth. New York, Macmillan,
1950, 922 p.
THE COMMERCE OF NATIONS, by J. B. Condliffe. New York, Norton, 1950,
884 p. (History and analysis of world trade problems.)
WORLD TRADE AND INVESTMENT: The Economics of Interdependence, by Donald
Bailey Marsh. New York, Harcourt, Brace, 1951, 594 p.
THE BALANCE OF PAYMENTS AND THE STANDARD OF LIVING, by R. G. Haw-
trey. London, Royal Institute of International Affairs, 1950, 158 p.
DOLLAR SHORTAGE AND OIL SURPLUS IN 1949–1950, by Horst Mendershausen.
Essays in International Finance, 11. Princeton, Princeton University Press,
1950, 34 p.
THE CUSTOMS UNION ISSUE, by Jacob Viner. New York, Carnegie Endowment
for International Peace, 1950, 221 p.
POINT IV AND THE WORLD ECONOMY, by J. B. Condliffe and Harold H.

Hutcheson. Headline Series, 79. New York, Foreign Policy Association, 1950, 62 p.

Atomic Energy

SOURCEBOOK ON ATOMIC ENERGY, by Samuel Glasstone. New York, Van Nostrand, 1951, 546 p. (A semipopular treatise sponsored by the U.S. Atomic Energy Commission.)

ATOMIC ENERGY AND THE HYDROGEN BOMB, by Gerald Wendt. New York, McBride, 1950, 192 p.

THE EFFECTS OF ATOMIC WEAPONS, released by the U.S. Atomic Energy Commission. Washington, 1950, 456 p.

THE HYDROGEN BOMB AND INTERNATIONAL CONTROL: Technical and Background Information, released by the Joint Committee on Atomic Energy, 81st Congress, 2nd Session. Washington, 1950, 41 p.

THE H BOMB, edited by Albert Einstein, with a commentary by George Fielding Eliot. New York, Didier, 1950, 175 p.

THE HELL BOMB, by William L. Lawrence. New York, Knopf, 1951, 198 p.

ECONOMIC ASPECTS OF ATOMIC POWER: An Exploratory Study, directed by Sam H. Schurr and Jacob Marschak. Princeton, Princeton University Press, 1950, 289 p.

Recent History

THE UNITED STATES AS A WORLD POWER: A Diplomatic History, 1900–1950, by Samuel Flagg Bemis. New York, Holt, 1950, 491 p.

THE UNITED STATES IN A CHAOTIC WORLD, and THE NEW DEAL IN WORLD AFFAIRS, by Allan Nevins. Chronicles of America Series. New Haven, Yale University Press, 1950. (U.S. foreign policy in the Roosevelt era.)

ROOSEVELT AND HOPKINS: An Intimate History, by Robert E. Sherwood. Revised edition, New York, Harper, 1950, 1021 p.

SEVEN DECISIONS THAT SHAPED HISTORY, by Sumner Welles. New York, Harper, 1951, 236 p. (By the wartime Under-Secretary of State.)

THE ROAD TO PEARL HARBOR, by Herbert Feis. Princeton, Princeton University Press, 1950, 356 p.

THE GRAND ALLIANCE and THE HINGE OF FATE, by Winston S. Churchill. Boston, Houghton Mifflin, 1950. (Third and fourth volumes of the author's personal World War II narrative.)

I WAS THERE: The Personal Story of the Chief of Staff to Presidents Roosevelt and Truman, by Fleet Admiral William D. Leahy. New York, McGraw-Hill, 1950, 527 p.

ROOSEVELT AND THE RUSSIANS: The Yalta Conference, by Edward R. Stettinius, Jr. New York, Doubleday, 1949, 367 p. (By the wartime Secretary of State.)

POSTWAR FOREIGN POLICY PREPARATION, 1939–1945. Department of State Publication 3580, General Foreign Policy Series 15. Washington, 1950, 726 p.

MAKING THE PEACE (1941–1945): The Diplomacy of Wartime Conferences, by William L. Neumann. Washington, Foundation for Foreign Affairs, 1950, 101 p.

THE MAN OF INDEPENDENCE, by Jonathan Daniels. Philadelphia, Lippincott, 1950, 384 p. (Close-up study of President Truman.)

TRUMAN, STALIN AND PEACE, by Albert Z. Carr. New York, Doubleday, 1950, 256 p. (By a former White House aide.)

BEHIND CLOSED DOORS, by Ellis M. Zacharias and Ladislas Farago. New York, Putnam, 1950, 367 p. (A self-styled "secret history of the cold war.")

U.S. POLICY

Periodicals

Department of State Bulletin. Washington, weekly. (The principal source of official documents and statements on U.S. foreign relations.)

Foreign Commerce Weekly. Washington, weekly. (Official organ of the Department of Commerce, valuable for statistics and special articles.)

General Aspects

THE AMERICAN PEOPLE AND FOREIGN POLICY, by Gabriel A. Almond. New York, Harcourt, Brace, for the Yale Institute of International Studies, 1950, 269 p.

MAJOR PROBLEMS OF UNITED STATES FOREIGN POLICY, 1950–1951. Washington, Brookings Institution, 1950, 416 p. (Latest volume in an annual series.)

OUR FOREIGN POLICY. Department of State Publication 3972, General Foreign Policy Series 26. Washington, 1950, 100 p.

STRENGTHENING THE FORCES OF FREEDOM: Selected Speeches and Statements of Secretary of State Acheson, February 1949–April 1950. Department of State Publication 3852, General Foreign Policy Series 28, 192 p. *Supplement, May–June 1950.* Publication 3852a, General Foreign Policy Series 28, 57 p. Washington, 1950.

WAR OR PEACE, by John Foster Dulles. New York, Macmillan, 1950, 274 p.

FAITH, PURPOSE AND POWER, by James P. Warburg. New York, Farrar, Straus, 1950, 180 p.

ADDRESSES UPON THE AMERICAN ROAD, 1948–1950, by Herbert Hoover. Stanford, Stanford University Press, 1951, 221 p.

PEACE CAN BE WON, by Paul G. Hoffman. New York, Doubleday, 1951, 188 p.

Organization and Operations

THE ADMINISTRATION OF AMERICAN FOREIGN AFFAIRS, by James L. McCamy. New York, Knopf, 1950, 364 p.

THE DEPARTMENT OF STATE. Department of State Publication 3745, Department and Foreign Service Series 14. Washington, 1950, 12 p.

SOME FACTS ABOUT THE FOREIGN SERVICE: A Short Account of Its Organization and Duties Together with Pertinent Laws and Regulations. April 1, 1950. Department of State Publication 3789, Department and Foreign Service Series 16. Washington, 1950, 70 p.

A GENERATION ON TRIAL: The Ordeal of Alger Hiss, by Alistair Cooke. New York, Knopf, 1950, 342 p.

STATE DEPARTMENT EMPLOYEE LOYALTY INVESTIGATION: *Hearings* before a subcommitte of the Senate Foreign Relations Committee pursuant to S. Res. 231, 81st Congress, 2nd Session, March 8–June 28, 1950. Washington, 1950, 3 pts., 2525 p. *Report* and Individual Views of Committee on Foreign Relations. S. Rept. 2108, July 20, 1950, 2 pts.

ORDEAL BY SLANDER, by Owen Lattimore. Boston, Atlantic (Little, Brown), 1950, 236 p.

DEPARTMENT OF STATE APPROPRIATIONS FOR 1951: *Hearings* before the Subcommittee of the House Appropriations Committee, 81st Congress, 2nd Session, Jan. 20–Feb. 2, 1950. Washington, 1950, 2 pts. *Hearings* [Departments of State, Justice, Commerce and the Judiciary Appropriations for 1951] before the Subcommittee of the Senate Appropriations Committee, Jan. 31–May 24, 1950. Washington, 1950, 2 pts.

LEGISLATIVE HISTORY OF THE [SENATE] COMMITTEE ON FOREIGN RELATIONS, 81ST CONGRESS. Senate Document 247, 81st Congress, 2nd Session. Washington, 1950, 66 p.

SURVEY OF ACTIVITIES OF THE COMMITTEE ON FOREIGN AFFAIRS, House of Representatives, Eighty-First Congress (January 3, 1949–January 2, 1951). Washington, 1951, 90 p.

GENERAL APPROPRIATION ACT, 1951 (Public Law 759, 81st Congress, approved Sept. 6, 1950—H.R. 7786). Hearings: Senate Appropriations Committe, March 10–June 20, 1950, 647 p. Reports: H. Rept. 1797, March 21, 1950; S. Rept. 1941, July 6, 1950. Conference Report: H. Rept. 2991, Aug. 24, 1950.

SUPPLEMENTAL APPROPRIATION ACT, 1951 (Public Law 843, 81st Congress, approved Sept. 27, 1950—H.R. 9526). Hearings: House Appropriations Committee (subcommittees), 3 pts.; Senate Appropriations Committee, 962 p. Reports: H. Rept. 2987, Aug. 24, 1950; S. Rept. 2567, Sept. 13, 1950. Conference Report: H. Rept. 3096, Sept. 18, 1950.

SECOND SUPPLEMENTAL APPROPRIATION ACT, 1951 (Public Law 911, 81st Congress, approved January 6, 1951—H.R. 9920). Hearings: Senate Appropriations Committee, Washington, 1950, 405 p. Conference Report: H. Rept. 3240, Jan. 1, 1951.

THE ADMINISTRATION OF UNITED STATES PARTICIPATION IN INTERNATIONAL ORGANIZATIONS, by John F. Meck and Louis W. Koenig. Chicago, American Society for Public Administration, 1950, 77 p.

PARTICIPATION OF THE UNITED STATES IN INTERNATIONAL CONFERENCES, July 1, 1948–June 30, 1949. Department of State Publication 3853, International Organization and Conference Series I, 12. Washington, 1950, 372 p.

UNITED STATES RELATIONS WITH INTERNATIONAL ORGANIZATIONS: IV. United States Participation in International Organizations During the Fiscal Year Ending June 30, 1949. Report of the Committee on Expenditures in the Executive Departments. S. Rept. 1274, 81st Congress, 2nd Session. Washington, 1950, 71 p.

—————. V. Internal Operations of the United Nations and Certain International Organizations in which the United States Participates. S. Rept. 90, 82nd Congress, 1st Session. Washington, 1951, 114 p.

ATLANTIC UNION: Hearings before the House Foreign Affairs Committee, 81st Congress, 2nd Session, on H. Con. Res. 107, January 23, 1950. Washington, 1950, 43 p.

REVISION OF THE UNITED NATIONS CHARTER: Hearings before a subcommittee of the Senate Foreign Relations Committee, 81st Congress, 2nd Session, Feb. 2-20, 1950. Washington, 1950, 808 p. Report of the Senate Foreign Relations Committee, S. Rept. 2501, Sept. 1, 1950. Washington, 1950, 63 p.

THE GENOCIDE CONVENTION: Hearings before a subcommittee of the Senate Foreign Relations Committee, 81st Congress, 2nd Session, on Executive O, Jan. 3–Feb. 9, 1950. Washington, 1950, 555 p.

Economic Policy

REPORT TO THE PRESIDENT ON FOREIGN ECONOMIC POLICIES [by Gordon Gray]. Washington, November 10, 1950, 131 p.

ECONOMIC REPORT OF THE PRESIDENT transmitted to Congress, January 12, 1951, together with the Report to the President, Annual Economic Review, by the Council of Economic Advisers. Washington, 1951, 241 p.

PARTNERS IN PROGRESS: A Report to the President by the International Development Advisory Board. Washington, 1951, 120 p.

BUILDING AMERICA'S MIGHT: Report to the President by the Director of Defense Mobilization. Washington, 1951, 45 p.

REPORTS TO CONGRESS OF THE ECONOMIC COOPERATION ADMINISTRATION: Eighth, January–March 1950, 137 p.; Ninth, April–June 1950, 156 p.; Tenth, July–September 1950, 147 p. Washington, 1950–1951.

ANNUAL REPORT OF THE SECRETARY OF COMMERCE: 38th, fiscal year 1950. Washington, 1950, 76 p.

EXPORT CONTROL AND ALLOCATION POWERS: Quarterly Reports . . . by the Secretary of Commerce. 10th (Feb. 1950)–13th (Nov. 1950). Washington, 1950.

REPORT OF THE NATIONAL ADVISORY COUNCIL on International Monetary and Financial Problems . . . October 1, 1949–March 31, 1950. Washington, 1950, 63 p.

SEMIANNUAL REPORTS OF THE EXPORT-IMPORT BANK OF WASHINGTON: 10th, Jan.–June 1950. Washington, 1950, 64 p.

FAR EASTERN ECONOMIC ASSISTANCE ACT OF 1950 (Public Law 447, 81st Congress, approved Feb. 14, 1950—H.R. 5330, S. 2319). *Reports:* H. Rept. 1571, Feb. 1, 1950; S. Rept. 748 (81st Congress, 1st Session), July 22, 1949; S. Rept. 1251, Feb. 3, 1950.

FOREIGN ECONOMIC ASSISTANCE ACT OF 1950 (Public Law 535, 81st Congress, approved June 5, 1950—H.R. 7797, S. 3101, S. 3304). *Hearings:* House Foreign Affairs Committee, on H.R. 7378 and H.R. 7797 (Economic Cooperation Act), Feb. 21–March 15, 1950, 2 pts.; on H.R. 5615 (Act for International Development), Sept. 27–Oct. 7, 1949 and Jan. 12-17, 1950, 2 pts.; on S.J. Res. 153 (Palestine Refugees), Feb. 16-17, 1950, 76 p.; Senate Foreign Relations Committee, on S. 3101 (Extension of European Recovery), Feb. 21–March 7, 1950, 413 p.; on S. 3304 (Act for International Development), March 30–April 3, 1950, 124 p. *Reports:* H. Rept. 1802 (on H.R. 7797), March 22-29, 1950, 5 pts.; S. Rept. 1371 (on S. 3304), March 24, 1950, 2 pts. *Conference Reports* (on H.R. 7797): H. Rept. 2117, May 19, 1950; S. Doc. 168, May 18, 1950.

YUGOSLAV EMERGENCY RELIEF ASSISTANCE ACT OF 1950 (Public Law 897, 81st Congress, approved Dec. 29, 1950—H.R. 9853, S. 4234). *Hearings:* House Foreign Affairs Committee, Nov. 29-30, 1950, 77 p. *Reports:* H. Rept. 3179, Dec. 7, 1950; S. Rept. 2588, Dec. 7, 1950. *Conference Report:* H. Rept. 3204, Dec. 15, 1950.

MEMBERSHIP AND PARTICIPATION BY THE UNITED STATES in the International Trade Organization: *Hearings* before the House Foreign Affairs Committee on H. J. Res. 236, April 19–May 12, 1950. Washington, 1950, 809 p.

EXPORT-IMPORT BANK GUARANTIES of U.S. Private Capital Investments Abroad (H.R. 8083): *Report* from the House Banking and Currency Committee. H. Rept. 1960, 81st Congress, 2nd Session, April 27, 1950.

THE UNITED STATES AND THE RESTORATION OF WORLD TRADE, by William Adams Brown, Jr. Washington, Brookings Institution, 1950, 572 p.

U.S. AGRICULTURE IN THE WORLD FOOD SITUATION, by Arthur P. Chew. Department of State Publication 3788, International Organization and Conference Series IV, UNESCO 11. Washington, 1950, 41 p.

SURVEY OF UNITED STATES INTERNATIONAL FINANCE, 1949, by Gardner Patterson. Princeton, Princeton University Press, 1950, 222 p.

PEACE BY INVESTMENT, by Benjamin A. Javits. New York, Funk and Wagnalls-United Nations World, 1950, 242 p.

FORMULATING A POINT FOUR PROGRAM, edited by Ernest Minor Patterson.

(*Annals of the American Academy of Political and Social Science*, CCLXX, July 1950, 1-149.)

BOLD NEW PROGRAM, by William R. Espy. New York, Harper, 1950, 273 p.

Military Policy

SEMIANNUAL REPORTS OF THE SECRETARY OF DEFENSE: July 1–Dec. 31, 1949, 283 p.; Jan. 1–June 30, 1950, 222 p.; July 1–Dec. 31, 1950, 31 p. Washington, 1950–1951.

DEPARTMENT OF DEFENSE APPROPRIATIONS FOR 1951: *Hearings,* House Appropriations Committee (subcommittee), Feb. 7–March 14, 1950, pts. 3-5; Senate Appropriations Committee (subcommittee) March 13–May 15, 1950. Washington, 1950, 915 p.

SEMIANNUAL REPORTS TO CONGRESS ON THE MUTUAL DEFENSE ASSISTANCE PROGRAM: First, Oct. 6, 1949–April 6, 1950. Department of State Publication 3878, General Foreign Policy Series 33. Washington, 1950, 74 p.

MUTUAL DEFENSE ASSISTANCE ACT EXTENSION (Public Law 621, 81st Congress, approved July 26, 1950—S. 3809). *Hearings:* House Foreign Affairs Committee, June 5-26, 1950, 164 p.; Senate Foreign Relations and Armed Services Committees, June 2-15, 1950, 113 p. *Reports:* H. Rept. 2538, July 12, 1950; S. Rept. 1853, June 21, 1950.

"United States Military Policy," by Blair Bolles. (*Foreign Policy Reports,* XXVI, December 15, 1950, 166-175.)

BACKGROUND INFORMATION on Use of United States Armed Forces in Foreign Countries: Report of House Foreign Affairs Committee pursuant to H. Res. 28. H. Rept. 127, 82nd Congress, 1st Session. Washington, 1951, 77 p.

HOW STRONG IS AMERICA? THE SCORE ON NATIONAL DEFENSE, by Robert S. Bird and Ogden R. Reid. New York, Duell, 1950, 79 p.

AIR POWER: Key to Survival, by Alexander P. de Seversky. New York, Simon and Schuster, 1950, 376 p.

SEMIANNUAL REPORTS OF THE ATOMIC ENERGY COMMISSION: Seventh, January 1950, 228 p.; Eighth, July 1950, 230 p.; Ninth, January 1951, 158 p. Washington, 1950–1951.

UNITED STATES CIVIL DEFENSE, released by the National Security Resources Board. Washington, 1950, 162 p.

Special Foreign Affairs Programs

SEMIANNUAL REPORTS OF THE UNITED STATES ADVISORY COMMISSION ON INFORMATION: Second, Jan. 1–June 30, 1949, 34 p.; Third, July 1–Dec. 31, 1949, H. Doc. 556, 81st Congress, 2nd Session, 15 p.; Fourth, Jan. 1–June 30, 1950, H. Doc. 648, 81st Congress, 2nd Session, 21 p. Washington, 1950.

SEMIANNUAL REPORTS OF THE UNITED STATES ADVISORY COMMISSION ON EDUCATIONAL EXCHANGE: Third, July 1–Dec. 31, 1949, H. Doc. 556, 81st Congress, 2nd Session, 16 p.; Fourth, Jan. 1–June 30, 1950, H. Doc. 648, 81st Congress, 2nd Session, 21 p. Washington, 1950.

TWO WAY STREET: International Educational and Technical Exchange in Fiscal Year 1950—Report of the United States Advisory Commission on Educational Exchange, [July 1, 1949–] June 30, 1950. Department of State Publication 3893, International Information and Cultural Series 12. Washington, 1951, 119 p.

BUILDING ROADS TO PEACE: Exchange of People Between the United States and Other Countries. Department of State Publication 3738, International Information and Cultural Series 11. Washington, 1950, 71 p.

EXPANDED INTERNATIONAL INFORMATION AND EDUCATION PROGRAM: *Hearings* before a subcommittee of the Senate Foreign Relations Committee, 81st Congress, 2nd Session, July 5-7, 1950. Washington, 1950, 165 p.

INTERNAL SECURITY ACT OF 1950 (Public Law 831, 81st Congress, became law Sept. 23, 1950—H.R. 9490, S. 4037). *Reports:* H. Rept. 2980, Aug. 22, 1950; S. Rept. 2369, 2 pts., Aug. 17 and 28, 1950. *Conference Report:* H. Rept. 3112, Sept. 19, 1950. *Veto Message:* H. Doc. 708, Sept. 22, 1950.

THE IMMIGRATION AND NATURALIZATION SYSTEMS OF THE UNITED STATES: Report of the Senate Judiciary Committee, 81st Congress, 2nd Session, pursuant to S. Res. 137, 80th Congress. S. Rept. 1515, Washington, 1950, 925 p.

AMERICAN IMMIGRATION POLICY: A Reappraisal, edited by William S. Bernard and others. New York, Harper, for the National Committee on Immigration Policy, 1950, 341 p.

DISPLACED PERSONS—ADMISSION TO U.S. (Public Law 555, 81st Congress, approved June 16, 1950—H.R. 4567). *Hearings:* Senate Judiciary Committee (subcommittee), March 25, 1949–March 16, 1950, 1237 p. *Reports:* H. Rept. 581, May 16, 1949; S. Rept. 1163, Oct. 12, 1949; S. Rept. 1237, Jan. 25, 1950; S. Rept. 1237, Part 2, Feb. 14, 1950. *Conference Report:* H. Rept. 2817, June 2, 1950.

UNITED NATIONS

Periodicals

United Nations Bulletin. Lake Success, Geneva, and Mexico City, U.N. Department of Public Information, semimonthly. (Indispensable summary of U.N. activities.)

Current Review of Economic and Social Problems in the United Nations. Washington, Department of State, monthly.

General

HOW TO FIND OUT ABOUT THE UNITED NATIONS: Materials Available and Where to Get Them. U.N. Publication 1950.I.4. Lake Success, 1950, 51 p.

EVERYMAN'S UNITED NATIONS: A Ready Reference to the Structure, Functions and Work of the United Nations and Its Related Agencies. Second edition. U.N. Publication 1950.I.9. New York, 1950, 313 p.

DOCUMENTARY TEXTBOOK ON THE UNITED NATIONS, edited by J. Eugene Harley. Second edition. Los Angeles, Center for International Understanding, 1950, 1470 p.

A COMMENTARY ON THE CHARTER OF THE UNITED NATIONS, by Norman Bentwich and Andrew Martin. New York, Macmillan, 1950, 239 p.

THE LAW OF THE UNITED NATIONS, by Hans Kelsen. New York, Praeger, for the London Institute of World Affairs, 1950, 903 p.

THE UNITED NATIONS IN ACTION, by Eugene P. Chase. New York, McGraw-Hill, 1950, 464 p.

THE UNITED NATIONS: Its Record and Its Prospects. New York, Carnegie Endowment for International Peace, 1950, 60 p.

YEARBOOK OF THE UNITED NATIONS, 1948–49, compiled by the United Nations Department of Public Information. U.N. Publication 1950.I.11. Lake Success, 1950, 1171 p. (Summarizes U.N. activities through 1949.)

ANNUAL REPORT OF THE [U.N.] SECRETARY-GENERAL on the Work of the Organization, 1 July 1949–30 June 1950. U.N. Document A/1287 (General Assembly *Official Records*, 5th Session, Supplement 1). Lake Success, July 1950, 143 p.

THE UNITED STATES IN WORLD AFFAIRS

THE UNITED NATIONS SECRETARIAT. United Nations Studies, 4. New York, Carnegie Endowment for International Peace, 1950, 96 p.

Political and Security Affairs

REPORT OF THE SECURITY COUNCIL TO THE GENERAL ASSEMBLY Covering the Period 16 July 1949 to 15 July 1950. U.N. Document A/1361 (General Assembly *Official Records,* 5th Session, Supplement 2). Lake Success, September 1950, 69 p.

DECISIONS TAKEN AND RESOLUTIONS ADOPTED by the Security Council during the Year 1950, prepared by the Department of Security Council Affairs. U.N. Document S/INF. 4, February 1, 1951, 24 p.

VOTING AND THE HANDLING OF DISPUTES IN THE SECURITY COUNCIL, by Eduardo Jiménez de Aréchaga. United Nations Studies, 5. New York, Carnegie Endowment for International Peace, 1951, 189 p.

REPORT OF THE INTERIM COMMITTEE OF THE GENERAL ASSEMBLY (3rd Session, 16 January–18 September 1950). U.N. Document A/1388 (General Assembly *Official Records,* 5th Session, Supplement 14). Lake Success, 1950, 38 p.

Economic and Social Activities

REPORT OF THE ECONOMIC AND SOCIAL COUNCIL Covering the Period from 16 August 1949 to 15 August 1950. U.N. Document A/1345 (General Assembly *Official Records,* 5th Session, Supplement 3). Lake Success, September 1950, 140 p.

ANNUAL REPORT OF THE ECONOMIC COMMISSION FOR EUROPE, 22 May 1949–15 June 1950. U.N. Document E/1674 (E/ECE/119). Geneva, June 15, 1950, 61 p.

ANNUAL REPORT OF THE ECONOMIC COMMISSION FOR ASIA AND THE FAR EAST, [April 6, 1949–May 20, 1950]. U.N. Document E/1710 (E/CN.11/241/Rev.1). Geneva, May 23, 1950, 158 p.

CATALOGUE OF ECONOMIC AND SOCIAL PROJECTS 1950. U.N. Publication 1950.-II.D.1. Lake Success, 1950, 515 p.

CURRENT TECHNICAL ASSISTANCE ACTIVITIES of United Nations and Specialized Agencies: Far East, Near East, Africa, Southern Asia, Latin America. Department of State Publication 3843, International Organization and Conference Series III, 49. Washington, 1950, 23 p.

UNITED NATIONS TECHNICAL ASSISTANCE CONFERENCE: Resolutions and Final Act. U.N. Document E/CONF.10/11, June 15, 1950 (as corrected).

THESE RIGHTS AND FREEDOMS. U.N. Publication 1950.I.6. Lake Success, 1950, 214 p. (Describes U.N. activities in the field of human rights.)

YEARBOOK ON HUMAN RIGHTS FOR 1948. U.N. Publication 1950.XIV.4. Lake Success, 1950, 535 p.

INTERNATIONAL LAW AND HUMAN RIGHTS, by H. Lauterpacht. New York, Praeger, 1950, 475 p.

UNITED NATIONS INTERNATIONAL CHILDREN'S EMERGENCY FUND. General Progress Report of Executive Director. U.N. Document E/ICEF/163, January 27, 1951, 22 p.

————. Final Report of the First Executive Board . . . 11 December 1946 to 31 December 1950. U.N. Document E/1908 (E/ICEF/L.8), January 13, 1951, 37 p.

PARTNERS: United Nations and Youth, by Eleanor Roosevelt and Helen Ferris. New York, Doubleday, 1950, 206 p.

Trusteeship and Non-Self-Governing Territories

REPORT OF THE TRUSTEESHIP COUNCIL Covering its First Special Session, and its Sixth and Seventh Sessions, 23 July 1949 to 21 July 1950. U.N. Document A/1306 (General Assembly *Official Records*, 5th Session, Supplement 4). Lake Success, August 1950, 215 p.

REPORT OF THE SPECIAL COMMITTEE ON INFORMATION Transmitted under Article 73e of the Charter. U.N. Document A/923 (General Assembly *Official Records*, 4th Session, Supplement 14). Lake Success, July 1950, 17 p.

Related Agencies

INTERNATIONAL COURT OF JUSTICE YEARBOOK, 1949–1950. Sales No. 44. The Hague, n.d., 193 p. (Proceedings of the Court are regularly listed in the *United Nations Documents Index*.)

FOOD AND AGRICULTURE ORGANIZATION OF THE UNITED NATIONS: Constitution and Rules and Regulations. Washington, F.A.O., 1950, 94 p.

—————. Work of FAO 1949/50. Washington, F.A.O., October 1950, 89 p.

—————. Report of the 5th Session of the Conference . . . 21 November–6 December, 1949. Washington, F.A.O., 1950, 92 p.

SECOND SPECIAL REPORT OF THE NATIONAL ADVISORY COUNCIL . . . on the Operations and Policies of the International Monetary Fund and the International Bank for Reconstruction and Development. Washington, 1950, 25 p. (Covers the two-year period ending March 31, 1950.)

REPORT OF THE INTERNATIONAL BANK FOR RECONSTRUCTION AND DEVELOPMENT. U.N. Document E/1873/Add. 1, Santiago, February 8, 1951, 23 p.

INTERNATIONAL MONETARY FUND: Annual Report of the Executive Directors for the Fiscal Year Ended 30 April 1950. Washington, I.M.F., n.d., 160 p.

INTERNATIONAL CIVIL AVIATION, 1949–1950: Third Report of the United States Representative to the International Civil Aviation Organization. Department of State Publication 3915, International Organization and Conference Series IV, ICAO 5. Washington, 1950, 47 p.

INTERNATIONAL LABOUR ORGANISATION: Fourth Report to the United Nations. Geneva, I.L.O., 1950, 345 p.

INTERNATIONAL REFUGEE ORGANIZATION: Annual Report of the Director-General for the Period 1 July 1949 to 30 June 1950. Geneva, I.R.O., August 23, 1950, 91 p.

—————. Statistical Report with 35 Months Summary. Geneva, I.R.O., May 1950, 40 p.

UNITED NATIONS EDUCATIONAL, SCIENTIFIC AND CULTURAL ORGANIZATION: Report to the United Nations, 1949 to 1950. UNESCO Publication 714, Paris, 1950, 198 p.

—————. Records of the General Conference, Fifth Session, Florence, 1950. UNESCO Publication 767, Florence, 1950, 729 p.

THE UNESCO STORY: A Resource and Action Booklet for Organizations and Communities. Department of State Publication 3931, International Organization and Conference Series IV, UNESCO 12. Washington, 1950, 112 p.

WAR AND THE MINDS OF MEN, by Frederick S. Dunn. New York, Harper, for the Council on Foreign Relations, 1950, 115 p. (A study of UNESCO.)

WORLD HEALTH ORGANIZATION: Annual Report of the Director-General to the World Health Assembly and to the United Nations, 1949. Geneva, W.H.O., March 1950, 113 p.

NORTH ATLANTIC AREA AND WESTERN EUROPE

General

THE NORTH ATLANTIC TREATY, THE BRUSSELS TREATY AND THE CHARTER OF THE UNITED NATIONS, by Sir W. Eric Beckett. London, Stevens, 1950, 75 p. (A legal study.)

EUROPE AND THE UNITED STATES, by Vera Micheles Dean. New York, Knopf, 1950, 349 p.

POLICY FOR THE WEST, by Barbara Ward. New York, Norton, 1951, 317 p. (Comprehensive analysis of the situation of the Western nations.)

"Military and Economic Strength of Western Europe," by Vera Micheles Dean and Howard D. Gary. (*Foreign Policy Reports,* XXVI, October 15, 1950, 118-128.)

THE SOCIALIST TRAGEDY, by Ivor Thomas. New York, Macmillan, 1951, 254 p. (By a disillusioned British Socialist.)

"Labor Unions and Politics in Britain and France," by Sidney Lens. (*Foreign Policy Reports,* XXVI, November 1, 1950, 130-139.)

Economic Cooperation

GENESIS OF THE EUROPEAN RECOVERY PROGRAM: A Study on the Trend of American Economic Policies, by Warren L. Hickman. Geneva, 1949, 297 p.

THE ECONOMICS OF FREEDOM: The Progress and Future of Aid to Europe, by Howard S. Ellis. New York, Harper, for the Council on Foreign Relations, 1950, 549 p.

EUROPEAN RECOVERY PROGRAM: Second Report of the Organization for European Economic Cooperation. Paris, O.E.E.C., February 1950, 277 p.

THE ORGANISATION FOR EUROPEAN ECONOMIC CO-OPERATION: Two Years of Economic Co-operation. Paris, O.E.E.C., July 1950, 46 p.

REPORT ON INTERNATIONAL INVESTMENT. Paris, O.E.E.C., 1950, 119 p.

INTERNAL FINANCIAL STABILITY IN MEMBER COUNTRIES. Paris, O.E.E.C., 1950, 122 p.

NINTH REPORT TO CONGRESS OF THE ECONOMIC COOPERATION ADMINISTRATION—Supplement: Economic Cooperation Agreements and Other Documents, July 1–December 31, 1950. Washington, 1951, 100 p.

THE PROPOSED EUROPEAN PAYMENTS UNION, submitted by the Joint Committee on Foreign Economic Cooperation. Senate Document 144, 81st Congress, 2nd Session. Washington, 1950, 11 p.

A EUROPEAN PAYMENTS UNION, and the Rules of Commercial Policy to be Followed by Member Countries. Paris, O.E.E.C., 1950, 24 p.

ANGLO-FRENCH DISCUSSIONS REGARDING FRENCH PROPOSALS for the Western European Coal, Iron and Steel Industries. Cmd. 7970, Miscellaneous No. 9 (1950). London, May–June 1950, 15 p.

EUROPEAN COAL AND STEEL COMMUNITY: Draft Treaty Constituting the European Coal and Steel Community; Draft Convention Containing the Transitional Provisions. Department of State Publication 4173, European and British Commonwealth Series 22. Washington, 1951, 126 p. (Texts of the Schuman Plan documents initialed in Paris on March 19, 1951.)

Political Cooperation

CAN EUROPE UNITE? by Vera M. Dean and J. K. Galbraith. Headline Series, 80. New York, Foreign Policy Association, 1950, 62 p.

THE UNION OF EUROPE: Declarations of European Statesmen. New York, American Committee on United Europe, 1950, 75 p.

EUROPE UNITE, by Winston S. Churchill. Boston, Houghton Mifflin, 1950, 506 p. (Speeches, 1947–1948.)

UNITE OR PERISH: A Dynamic Program for a United Europe, by Paul Reynaud. New York, Simon and Schuster, 1951, 214 p.

EUROPEAN UNITY: A Statement by the National Executive Committee of the British Labour Party. London, Labour Party, 1950, 15 p.

COUNCIL OF EUROPE: Compilation of Recommendations and Resolutions Adopted by the Consultative Assembly during its 2d Session (1st Part—August 1950). Strasbourg, n.d., 149 p.

————. Report on the Proceedings of the Committee of Ministers. *Fifth Session*, Strasbourg, Aug. 3-9, 1950. Cmd. 8082, Miscellaneous No. 15 (1950). *Sixth Session*, Rome, Nov. 3-4, 1950. Cmd. 8083, Miscellaneous No. 16 (1950). London, 1950.

HUMAN RIGHTS: Convention for the Protection of Human Rights and Fundamental Freedoms, Rome, November 4, 1950. Cmd. 8130, Miscellaneous No. 1 (1951). London, 1951.

Military Cooperation

COLLECTIVE DEFENCE UNDER THE BRUSSELS AND NORTH ATLANTIC TREATIES. Cmd. 7883. London, 1950, 27 p.

DEFENCE OF THE WEST, by B. H. Liddell Hart. New York, Morrow, 1950, 335 p.

DEFENSE OF WESTERN EUROPE, compiled by Walter M. Daniels. New York, H. W. Wilson Co., 1950, 242 p. (A collection of readings.)

United Kingdom

BRITISH POLITICS SINCE 1900, by D. C. Somervell. New York, Oxford University Press, 1950, 265 p.

CRISIS IN BRITAIN: Plans and Achievements of the Labour Government, by Robert A. Brady. Berkeley, University of California Press, 1950, 730 p.

THE CAUTIOUS REVOLUTION: Britain Today and Tomorrow, by Ernest Watkins. New York, Farrar, Straus, 1950, 456 p.

THE DECLINE AND FALL OF BRITISH CAPITALISM, by Keith Hutchison. New York, Scribner, 1950, 277 p.

NATIONAL INCOME AND EXPENDITURE OF THE UNITED KINGDOM, 1946 TO 1949. Cmd. 7933. London, 1950, 69 p.

UNITED KINGDOM BALANCE OF PAYMENTS, 1946 TO 1950. Cmd. 8065. London, 1950.

THE DOLLAR CRISIS: Causes and Cure, by T. Balogh. New York, Macmillan, 1950, 269 p.

ANGLO-AMERICAN ECONOMIC RELATIONS. Problem Papers, 2. Washington, Brookings Institution, 1950, 74 p.

THE BRITISH FOREIGN SERVICE, by F. T. Ashton-Gwatkin. Syracuse, University of Syracuse Press, 1950, 94 p.

UNITED KINGDOM ADMINISTRATION AND INTERNATIONAL ORGANIZATIONS: A Report by a Study Group of the Institute of Public Administration. London, Royal Institute of International Affairs, 1951, 55 p.

Other Western Countries

MODERN FRANCE: Problems of the Third and Fourth Republics, edited by Edward Mead Earle. Princeton, Princeton University Press, 1951, 522 p.

FRANCE: Setting or Rising Star? by Saul K. Padover. Headline Series, 81. New York, Foreign Policy Association, 1950, 64 p.

MONETARY AND FOREIGN EXCHANGE POLICY IN ITALY, by Friedrich A. and Vera C. Lutz. Princeton Studies in International Finance, 1. Princeton, Princeton University Press, 1950, 45 p.

SCANDINAVIA TODAY, by Franklin D. Scott. Headline Series, 85. New York, Foreign Policy Association, 1951, 62 p.

SCANDINAVIA: Between East and West, edited by Henning Friis. Ithaca, Cornell University Press, for the New School of Social Research, 1950, 388 p.

FINLAND: The Adventures of a Small Power, by Hugh Shearman. New York, Praeger, for the London Institute of World Affairs, 1951, 114 p.

SWITZERLAND: A Democratic Way of Life, by André Siegfried. New York, Duell, 1950, 223 p.

TREATY OF FRIENDSHIP, COMMERCE, AND NAVIGATION WITH IRELAND, with protocol relating thereto. Message from the President . . . transmitting a treaty . . . signed at Dublin on January 21, 1950. S. Ex. H, 81st Congress, 2nd Session, 18 p. *Report:* S. Ex. Rept. 8, June 26, 1950. (Ratified July 8, 1950.)

GREEK MONETARY DEVELOPMENTS, 1939–1948, by Dimitrios Delivanis and William C. Cleveland. Bloomington, Indiana University Press, 1949, 196 p.

REPORT OF THE UNITED NATIONS SPECIAL COMMITTEE ON THE BALKANS. U.N. Document A/1307 (General Assembly *Official Records,* 5th Session, Supplement 11). Lake Success, August 1950, 33 p.

GERMANY AND AUSTRIA

Germany

QUARTERLY REPORTS ON GERMANY, by the Office of the U.S. High Commissioner for Germany: First, Sept. 21–Dec. 31, 1949, 79 p.; Second, Jan. 1– March 31, 1950, 69 p.; Third, April 1–June 30, 1950, 99 p.; Fourth, July 1– Sept. 30, 1950, 112 p. Washington, 1950.

INFORMATION BULLETIN. Frankfort, Office of the U.S. High Commissioner in Germany, monthly (formerly biweekly).

REPORT OF THE CONTROL COMMISSION FOR GERMANY (BRITISH ELEMENT). London, monthly through Sept. 1950; quarterly beginning Oct.–Dec. 1950.

GERMANY: Promise and Perils, by Sigmund Neumann. Headline Series, 82. New York, Foreign Policy Association, 1950, 62 p.

WEST GERMANY: Protectorate or Ally? by Arnold Wolfers. Memorandum 35. New Haven, Yale Institute of International Studies, 1950, 49 p.

GERMANY AND THE FIGHT FOR FREEDOM, by General Lucius D. Clay, Ret. Cambridge, Harvard University Press, 1950, 83 p. (By the former U.S. Military Governor in Germany.)

"German Democracy 1950," by Franz L. Neumann. (*International Conciliation,* 461, May 1950, 249-296.)

THIS IS GERMANY, edited by Arthur Settel. New York, Sloane, 1950, 429 p. (Reports by foreign newspaper correspondents.)

ALL HONORABLE MEN, by James Stewart Martin. Boston, Little, Brown, 1950, 320 p. (Vicissitudes of the decartellization program.)

INDUSTRIAL RELATIONS IN GERMANY, 1945–1949. Cmd. 7923, Germany No. 1 (1950). London, 1950, 25 p.

"Social Democracy and Labor in Germany," by Sydney Lens. (*Foreign Policy Reports,* XXVI, November 13, 1950, 142-151.)

REPORT OF A SPECIAL SUBCOMMITTEE of the House Judiciary Committee, 81st Congress, 2nd Session, pursuant to H. Res. 238, A Resolution to Authorize

. . . a Study of Immigration and Nationality Problems. Washington, 1950, 87 p. (Analyzes Germany's refugee and population problem.)

EDUCATIONAL AND CULTURAL ACTIVITIES IN GERMANY TODAY. Frankfort, Office of the U.S. High Commissioner for Germany, 1950, 93 p.

FRANCE AND THE SAAR, 1680–1948, by Laing Gray Cowan. New York, Columbia University Press, 1950, 247 p.

AKTENSTÜCKE ZUR BEURTEILUNG DES GROTEWOHLBRIEFES, veröffentlicht im Auftrage der Bundesregierung. Bonn, Deutscher Bundes-Verlag, 1951, 71 p. (Documents on relations between East and West Germany.)

BERLIN COMMAND, by Brig. Gen. Frank Howley. New York, Putnam, 1950, 276 p. (Experiences of a U.S. Commandant in Berlin.)

NEWS FROM SOVIET GERMANY, by Fritz Löwenthal. London, Gollancz, 1950, 344 p.

DER VOLKSWIRTSCHAFTSPLAN 1950. Berlin, Deutsche Demokratische Republik, 1950, 127 p. (Schriftenreihe 1.) (Economic plan of the "German Democratic Republic.")

Austria

REPORT OF THE UNITED STATES HIGH COMMISSIONER, U.S. Element, Allied Commission for Austria. Vienna, quarterly. Processed.

THE AUSTRIAN ECONOMY SINCE 1945, by K. W. Rothschild. London, Royal Institute of International Affairs, 1951, 82 p.

SOVIET BLOC

Periodicals

Current Digest of the Soviet Press. Washington, Joint Committee on Slavic Studies, weekly.

Soviet Press Translations. Seattle, University of Washington, Far Eastern and Russian Institute, semimonthly.

New Times. Moscow, "Trud," weekly. (Presents the international "party line" on world affairs.)

USSR Information Bulletin. Washington, Embassy of the U.S.S.R., semimonthly. (Includes official texts of Soviet speeches and documents.)

Soviet Studies. Oxford, Basil Blackwood, quarterly. (Objective review of Soviet social and economic institutions.)

For a Lasting Peace, For a People's Democracy! Bucharest, Information Bureau of the Communist and Workers' Parties, weekly. (The official Cominform organ.)

U.S.S.R.—General

GEOGRAPHY OF THE U.S.S.R.: A Regional Survey, by Theodore Shabad. New York, Columbia University Press, 1951, 584 p.

GEOGRAPHY OF RUSSIA, by N. T. Mirov. New York, John Wiley, 1951, 362 p.

THE SOVIET UNION: The Land and Its People, by Georges Jorré. Second edition. New York, Longmans, Green, 1950, 353 p.

RUSSIA'S SOVIET ECONOMY, by Harry Schwartz. New York, Prentice-Hall, 1951, 592 p.

"The U.S.S.R.—Economic Strengths and Weaknesses," by Howard C. Gary. (Foreign Policy Reports, XXVII, April 1, 1951, 14-23.)

SOVIET POLITICS—THE DILEMMA OF POWER: The Role of Ideas in Social Change, by Barrington Moore, Jr. Cambridge, Harvard University Press, 1950, 503 p. (Scholarly analysis of the development of the Soviet system.)

460   THE UNITED STATES IN WORLD AFFAIRS

THE OPERATIONAL CODE OF THE POLITBURO, by Nathan Leites. New York, McGraw-Hill, 1951, 115 p.
PUBLIC OPINION IN SOVIET RUSSIA, by Alex Inkeles. Cambridge, Harvard University Press, 1950, 379 p.
TAMING OF THE ARTS, by Juri Jelagin. New York, Dutton, 1950, 333 p. (Report on Soviet artistic policies.)
JUSTICE IN RUSSIA: An Interpretation of Soviet Law, by Harold J. Berman. Cambridge, Harvard University Press, 1950, 323 p.
SOVIET TRADE UNIONS: Their Place in Soviet Labour Policy, by Isaac Deutscher. London, Royal Institute of International Affairs, 1950, 156 p.
THE CHOICE, by Boris Shub. New York, Duell, Sloan & Pearce, 1950, 205 p. (Reports mass disaffection in the U.S.S.R.)
ELEVEN YEARS IN SOVIET PRISON CAMPS, by Elinor Lipper. Chicago, Regnery, 1951, 310 p.
THE SOVIET AIR FORCE, by Asher Lee. New York, Harper, 1950, 207 p.

U.S.S.R.—Foreign Affairs

SOVIET DOCUMENTS ON FOREIGN POLICY, edited by Jane Degras. Vol. I: 1917–1924. New York, Oxford University Press, for the Royal Institute of International Affairs, 1951, 501 p.
THE SOVIETS IN WORLD AFFAIRS, 1917–1929, by Louis Fischer. Princeton, Princeton University Press, 1951, 2 vols. (Reprint of a standard work first published in 1930.)
BACKGROUND INFORMATION ON THE SOVIET UNION IN INTERNATIONAL RELATIONS, released by the House Foreign Affairs Committee. House Report 3135, 81st Congress, 2nd Session. Washington, 1950, 54 p. (A tabulation of unfavorable facts.)
THE NEW SOVIET EMPIRE, by David J. Dallin. New Haven, Yale University Press, 1951, 210 p.
AMERICA FACES RUSSIA: Russian-American Relations from Early Times to Our Day, by Thomas A. Bailey. Ithaca, Cornell University Press, 1950, 375 p.
THE SOVIET IMAGE OF THE UNITED STATES: A Study in Distortion, by Frederick C. Barghoorn. New York, Harcourt, Brace, 1950, 297 p.

The "People's Democracies"

TITO AND GOLIATH, by Hamilton Fish Armstrong. New York, Macmillan, 1951, 312 p. (The "Titoist" resistance in Yugoslavia and Eastern Europe.)
"Communist Regimes in Eastern Europe," by Samuel L. Sharp. (*Foreign Policy Reports*, XXVI, January 1, 1951, 178-186.)
CENTRAL AND SOUTH EAST EUROPE, 1945–1948, edited by R. R. Betts. London, Royal Institute of International Affairs, 1951, 227 p. (Contributions by several authors on the countries of the Soviet bloc.)
EAST OF THE IRON CURTAIN, by Vernon Bartlett. New York, McBride, 1950, 212 p. (An optimistic view.)
SOVIET TRADE WITH EASTERN EUROPE, by Margaret Dewar. London, Royal Institute of International Affairs, 1951, 123 p.
CZECHOSLOVAKIA ENSLAVED: The Story of the Communist Coup d'État, by Hubert Ripka. London, Gollancz, 1950, 339 p.
EAST WIND OVER PRAGUE, by Jan Stransky. New York, Random House, 1951, 245 p. (Personal observations of Communist methods in Czechoslovakia.)
R. VOGELER, E. SANDERS AND THEIR ACCOMPLICES BEFORE THE CRIMINAL COURT. Budapest, Hungarian State Publishing House, 1950, 309 p. (Official account of a celebrated espionage trial.)

Rumania: Political Problems of an Agrarian State, by Henry L. Roberts. New Haven, Yale University Press, 1951, 428 p.

NEAR EAST AND AFRICA
Periodicals

L'Afrique et l'Asie: Revue politique sociale et économique. Paris, L'Afrique et l'Asie, quarterly.
Middle Eastern Affairs. New York, Council for Middle Eastern Affairs, monthly.
Middle East Journal. Washington, Middle East Institute, quarterly.

General

THE MIDDLE EAST: 1950. London, Europa Publications, 1950, 375 p. (A reference volume.)
THE MIDDLE EAST, by W. B. Fisher. New York, Dutton, 1951, 514 p. (Physical and social geography.)
THE MIDDLE EAST: A Political and Economic Survey. London, Royal Institute of International Affairs, 1950, 496 p.
THE SECURITY OF THE MIDDLE EAST. Problem Papers, 1. Washington, Brookings Institution, 1950, 66 p.
THE UNITED STATES AND THE NEAR EAST, by Ephraim A. Speiser. Revised edition. Cambridge, Harvard University Press, 1950, 283 p.
AMERICANS AND THE MIDDLE EAST—PARTNERS IN THE NEXT DECADE: A Series of Addresses and Panel Discussions . . . at the Fourth Annual Conference on Middle East Affairs, March 17-18, 1950. Washington, Middle East Institute, 1950, 63 p.

Palestine

THE STRUGGLE FOR PALESTINE, by J. C. Hurewitz. New York, Norton, 1950, 404 p. (A history of the British mandate.)
THE REPUBLIC OF ISRAEL: Its History and Its Promise, by Joseph Dunner. New York, McGraw-Hill, 1950, 265 p.
NEW STAR IN THE NEAR EAST, by Kenneth W. Bilby. New York, Doubleday, 1950, 279 p. (A report on Israel.)
UNITED NATIONS CONCILIATION COMMISSION FOR PALESTINE: General Progress Report, Dated 2 September 1950, to the Secretary-General of the United Nations. U.N. Document A/1367, September 22, 1950, 70 p.
"Jerusalem and the United Nations," by Paul Mohn. (International Conciliation, 464, October 1950, 421-471.)
QUESTION OF AN INTERIM REGIME FOR JERUSALEM and Protection of the Holy Places: Special Report of the Trusteeship Council, July 1950. U.N. Document A/1286 (General Assembly Official Records, 5th Session, Supplement 9). Lake Success, 1950, 33 p.
THE PALESTINE REFUGEE PROBLEM. Department of State Publication 3757, Near Eastern Series 3. Washington, 1950, 39 p.
ASSISTANCE TO PALESTINE REFUGEES: Interim Report of the United Nations Relief and Works Agency for Palestine Refugees in the Near East. U.N. Document A/1451, October 1950, 55 p.

The Moslem World

HISTORY OF SYRIA, by Philip K. Hitti. New York, Macmillan, 1951, 749 p.
THE STORY OF THE ARAB WORLD, by John Glubb. London, Hodder and

Stoughton, 1950, 502 p. (By the British commander of Jordan's Arab Legion.)

MEMOIRS OF KING ABDULLAH OF TRANSJORDAN. New York, Philosophical Library, 1950, 278 p.

"Reform and Power Politics in Iran," by Georgiana C. Stevens. (*Foreign Policy Reports*, XXVI, February 15, 1951, 214-223.)

AFGHANISTAN: A Study of Political Developments in Central Asia, by W. K. Fraser-Tytler. New York, Oxford University Press, 1950, 330 p.

Africa

ANNUAL REPORT OF THE UNITED NATIONS COMMISSIONER IN LIBYA. U.N. Document A/1340 (General Assembly *Official Records*, 5th Session, Supplement 15). Lake Success, September 1950, 110 p.

REPORT OF THE UNITED NATIONS COMMISSION FOR ERITREA. U.N. Document A/1285 (General Assembly *Official Records*, 5th Session, Supplement 8). Lake Success, June 1950, 129 p.

DRAFT TRUSTEESHIP AGREEMENT FOR THE TERRITORY OF SOMALILAND UNDER ITALIAN ADMINISTRATION: Special Report of the Trusteeship Council. U.N. Document A/1294 (General Assembly *Official Records*, 5th Session, Supplement 10). Lake Success, August 1950, 11 p.

LAST CHANCE IN AFRICA, by Negley Farson. New York, Harcourt, Brace, 1950, 381 p. (Observations inspired by a visit to Kenya.)

BLACK AND WHITE, by Martin Flavin. New York, Harper, 1950, 332 p. (Illuminating travelogue.)

THE FAR EAST

Periodicals

Far Eastern Survey. New York, American Institute of Pacific Relations, biweekly.

Pacific Affairs. New York, Institute of Pacific Relations, quarterly.

General

GEOGRAPHY OF THE PACIFIC, edited by Otis W. Freeman. New York, John Wiley, 1951, 573 p.

A HISTORY OF THE FAR EAST IN MODERN TIMES, by Harold Vinacke. Fifth edition. New York, Appleton-Century-Crofts, 1950, 785 p.

MODERN FAR EASTERN INTERNATIONAL RELATIONS, by H. F. MacNair and D. F. Lach. New York, Van Nostrand, 1950, 681 p.

ECONOMIC SURVEY OF ASIA AND THE FAR EAST, 1949. U.N. Document E/Cn. 11/260, June 25, 1950, 485 p.

PUBLIC HEALTH AND DEMOGRAPHY IN THE FAR EAST: Report of a Survey Trip September 13–December 13, 1948, by Marshall C. Balfour and others. New York, Rockefeller Foundation, 1950, 132 p.

NEW FORCES IN ASIA, edited by Bruno Lasker. New York, H. W. Wilson Co., in association with the American Institute of Pacific Relations, 1950, 237 p. (A collection of reference material.)

EAST OF HOME, by Santha Rama Rau. New York, Harper, 1950, 303 p. (Feminine observations on the Far East.)

RED STORM OVER ASIA, by Robert Payne. New York, Macmillan, 1951, 309 p.

INSTITUTE OF PACIFIC RELATIONS, 11th Conference, Lucknow, 1950. Conference papers. (Full list in *Foreign Affairs*, XXIX, April 1951, 511.)

"Far Eastern Policy of the United States," by Harold M. Vinacke. (*Foreign Policy Reports*, XXVI, March 1, 1951, 226-235.)

TOWARD A NEW FAR EASTERN POLICY, by Edwin O. Reischauer. Headline Series, 84. New York, Foreign Policy Association, 1950, 61 p.

MACARTHUR: MAN OF ACTION, by Frank Kelley and Cornelius Ryan. New York, Doubleday, 1950, 191 p.

THE RIDDLE OF MACARTHUR: Japan, Korea and the Far East, by John Gunther. New York, Harper, 1951, 240 p.

BLUNDER IN ASIA, by Harrison Forman. New York, Didier, 1950, 190 p.

China

A HISTORY OF CHINA, by Wolfram Eberhard. Berkeley and Los Angeles, University of California Press, 1950, 375 p.

CHINA: A Short History, by Owen and Eleanor Lattimore. Revised edition. New York, Norton, 1950, 218 p.

CHINA AND THE SOVIET UNION, by Aitchen K. Wu. New York, John Day, 1950, 434 p. (A diplomatic history.)

THE GOVERNMENT AND POLITICS OF CHINA, by Tuan-Sheng Ch'ien. Cambridge, Harvard University Press, for the International Secretariat, Institute of Pacific Relations, 1950, 526 p.

TWO KINDS OF TIME: A Personal Story of China's Crash into Revolution, by Graham Peck. Boston, Houghton Mifflin, 1950, 725 p.

MAO TSE-TUNG: Ruler of Red China, by Robert Payne. New York, Henry Schuman, 1950, 303 p.

PEKING DIARY: A Year of Revolution, by Derk Bodde. New York, Henry Schuman, 1950, 292 p.

NEW CHINA: Three Views, edited by Otto B. van der Sprenkel. New York, John Day, 1951, 241 p. (All three views are optimistic.)

AMERICAN POLICY TOWARD CHINA: A Report on the Views of Leading Citizens in Twenty-Three Cities, edited by Joseph Barber. New York, Council on Foreign Relations, 1950, 49 p.

ROOF OF THE WORLD: Tibet, Key to Asia, by Amaury de Riencourt. New York, Rinehart, 1950, 322 p.

OUT OF THIS WORLD: Across the Himalayas to Forbidden Tibet, by Lowell Thomas, Jr. New York, Greystone, 1950, 320 p.

Japan

THE OCCUPATION OF JAPAN: Second Phase, 1948–50, by Robert A. Fearey. New York, Macmillan, for the International Secretariat, Institute of Pacific Relations, 1950, 239 p. (By a State Department official.)

SELECTED DATA ON THE OCCUPATION OF JAPAN. Tokyo, GHQ, SCAP, 1950, 214 p.

THE FAR EASTERN COMMISSION: Third Report by the Secretary-General, December 24, 1948–June 30, 1950. Department of State Publication 3945, Far Eastern Series 35. Washington, 1950, 48 p.

JAPANESE LAND REFORM PROGRAM, by Laurence I. Hewes, Jr. Natural Resources Section Report No. 127. Tokyo, GHQ, SCAP, 1950, 118 p.

"Politics and Public Opinion in Japan," by Robert A. Scalapino. (*Foreign Policy Reports*, XXVII, March 15, 1951, 2-11.)

ASPECTS OF JAPAN'S LABOR PROBLEMS, by Miriam S. Farley, with a supplement by William T. Moran. New York, John Day, for the International Secretariat, Institute of Pacific Relations, 1950, 283 p.

Korea

THE KOREANS AND THEIR CULTURE, by Cornelius Osgood. New York, Ronald Press, 1951, 387 p. (Anthropology and history to 1949.)

SOURCE MATERIALS ON KOREAN POLITICS AND IDEOLOGIES, compiled by Donald G. Tewksbury. New York, International Secretariat, Institute of Pacific Relations, 1950, 190 p. Processed. (Political documents, 1871–1950.)

THE EPIC OF KOREA, by A. Wigfall Green. Washington, Public Affairs Press, 1950, 136 p. (Korea's postwar history, especially 1945–1948.)

AMERICAN MILITARY GOVERNMENT IN KOREA, by E. Grant Meade. New York, King's Crown Press, 1951, 281 p.

BACKGROUND INFORMATION ON KOREA: Report of the House Foreign Affairs Committee pursuant to H. Res. 206. House Report 2495, 81st Congress, 2nd Session. Washington, 1950, 74 p.

WHY WAR CAME IN KOREA, by Robert T. Oliver. New York, Fordham University Press-Declan X. McMullen, 1950, 260 p. (By an American confidant of President Syngman Rhee.)

REPORT OF THE UNITED NATIONS COMMISSION ON KOREA Covering the Period 15 December 1949–4 September 1950. U.N. Document A/1350 (General Assembly *Official Records,* 5th Session, Supplement 16). Lake Success, October 1950, 43 p.

UNITED STATES POLICY IN THE KOREAN CRISIS. Department of State Publication 3922, Far Eastern Series 34. Washington, 1950, 68 p.

"The Fight against Aggression in Korea." (*Foreign Affairs Outlines: Building the Peace,* No. 24, Autumn 1950.) Department of State Publication 3971, Far Eastern Series 37. Washington, 1950, 8 p.

KOREA: Summary of Events Relating to Korea, 1950 (With Appendix and Annexes). Cmd. 8078, Korea No. 1 (1950). London, 1950, 32 p.

KOREA AND THE UNITED NATIONS: A *United Nations Bulletin* Reprint. U.N. Publication 1950.I.8. Lake Success, 1950, 86 p.

THE SOVIET UNION AND AMERICAN INTERVENTION IN KOREA: Documents. Supplements to *New Times,* Moscow, Nos. 28, 32, and 33, July 12, Aug. 9, and Aug. 16, 1950.

WAR IN KOREA: The Report of a Woman Combat Correspondent, by Marguerite Higgins. New York, Doubleday, 1951, 224 p.

RELIEF AND REHABILITATION OF KOREA: Report by the [United Nations] Secretary-General. U.N. Document E/1913, Santiago, February 12, 1951, 35 p.

Southeast Asia

THE LEFT WING IN SOUTHEAST ASIA, by Virginia Thompson and Richard Adloff. New York, Sloane, for the International Secretariat, Institute of Pacific Relations, 1950, 298 p.

THE CHINESE IN SOUTHEAST ASIA, by Victor Purcell. New York, Oxford University Press, 1951, 801 p.

HUMAN BONDAGE IN SOUTHEAST ASIA, by Bruno Lasker. Chapel Hill, University of North Carolina Press, for the Institute of Pacific Relations, 1950, 406 p.

BURMA, by D. G. E. Hall. New York, Longmans, Green, 1950, 184 p. (A short history.)

LAOS, 1950. [New York, French Press and Information Service] 1950, 154 p. (Official volume on the Kingdom of Laos.)

UNITED NATIONS COMMISSION FOR INDONESIA: Special Report to the Security

Council on the Round Table Conference. U.N. Document S/1417/Rev. 1, March 2, 1950 (Security Council *Official Records,* 4th Year, Special Supplement 6). Lake Success, 1950, 173 p.

REPORT BY THE CONSULAR COMMISSION AT BATAVIA TO THE SECURITY COUNCIL. U.N. Document S/586/Rev. 1, April 14, 1950 (Security Council *Official Records,* 4th Year, Special Supplement 4). Lake Success, 1950, 135 p.

MALAYA AND ITS HISTORY, by Sir Richard Winstedt. New York, Longmans, Green, 1950, 156 p.

REPORT TO THE PRESIDENT OF THE UNITED STATES BY THE ECONOMIC SURVEY MISSION TO THE PHILIPPINES. Department of State Publication 4010, Far Eastern Series 38. Washington, 1950, 107 p.

BRITISH COMMONWEALTH AND EMPIRE *

Periodicals

Journal of the Parliaments of the Commonwealth. London, Commonwealth Parliamentary Association, quarterly. (Abstracts of significant debates in the U.K. and Commonwealth representative bodies.)

The Round Table. London, The Round Table, quarterly. (A review of Commonwealth politics.)

The Colonial Empire

THE BRITISH COLONIES IN 1949. New York, British Information Services, 1950, 53 p.

COLONIAL DEVELOPMENT CORPORATION: Annual Report and Statement of Accounts, 1949. H.C. 105. London, 1950.

WEALTH OF COLONIES, by W. K. Hancock. New York, Cambridge University Press, 1950, 81 p. (A study of colonial development policies.)

SELF-GOVERNMENT FOR THE COLONIES, by W. R. Crocker. New York, Macmillan, 1950, 177 p.

THE GROUNDNUT AFFAIR, by Alan Wood. London, Lane, 1950, 264 p. (Difficulties of the famous East African peanut project.)

"Peoples, Politics and Peanuts in Eastern Africa," by Olive Holmes. (*Foreign Policy Reports,* XXVI, December 1, 1950, 154-163.)

The Commonwealth

"The British Commonwealth in the Asian Crisis," by Gwendolen M. Carter. (*Foreign Policy Reports,* XXVI, October 1, 1950, 106-115.)

COLOMBO PLAN FOR THE CO-OPERATIVE ECONOMIC DEVELOPMENT IN SOUTH AND SOUTH-EAST ASIA: Report by the Commonwealth Consultative Committee. Cmd. 8080. London, Sept.–Oct. 1950.

NEW HORIZONS IN THE EAST: The Colombo Plan for Co-operative Economic Development in South and South-East Asia. London, 1950. (A popular summary.)

OVERSEA SETTLEMENT: Migration from the United Kingdom to the Dominions, by G. F. Plant. New York, Oxford University Press, for the Royal Institute of International Affairs, 1951, 186 p.

* For the United Kingdom see "North Atlantic Area and Western Europe."

Canada, Australia, New Zealand

CANADA IN WORLD AFFAIRS, by F. H. Soward. New York, Oxford University Press, for the Canadian Institute of Intenational Affairs, 1950, 359 p. (A survey covering the years 1944–1946.)

CANADA, edited by George W. Brown. Berkeley and Los Angeles, University of California Press, 1950, 608 p.

TREATY WITH CANADA Concerning Uses of the Waters of the Niagara River: Message from the President . . . transmitting the treaty . . . signed at Washington, February 27, 1950. S. Ex. N, 81st Congress, 2nd Session. Washington, 1950, 8 p. *Report:* S. Ex. Rept. 11, Aug. 2, 1950. (Ratified Aug. 9, 1950.)

NEW ZEALAND, by Harold Miller. New York, Longmans, Green, 1950, 155 p. (A short history.)

India, Pakistan, Ceylon

SOUTH ASIA IN THE WORLD TODAY, edited by Phillips Talbot. Chicago, University of Chicago Press, 1950, 253 p. (A collection of lectures.)

INDIA, PAKISTAN, CEYLON, edited by W. Norman Brown. Ithaca, Cornell University Press, 1951, 234 p. (A series of political essays.)

THE POPULATION OF INDIA AND PAKISTAN, by Kingsley Davis. Princeton, Princeton University Press, 1951, 263 p.

INDIA, by Cyril H. Philips. New York, Longmans, Green, 1950, 176 p. (A short history.)

INDEPENDENCE AND AFTER, by Jawaharlal Nehru. New York, John Day, 1950, 403 p. (Speeches by India's Prime Minister.)

INDIA AND THE UNITED STATES: Political and Economic Relations, by Lawrence K. Rosinger. New York, Macmillan, for the American Institute of Pacific Relations, 1950, 149 p.

INTERVIEW WITH INDIA, by John Frederick Muehl. New York, John Day, 1950, 310 p. (Illuminating report on Indian village life.)

THE INTERNATIONAL POSITION OF INDIA'S RAW MATERIALS, by N. V. Sovani. New York, Oxford University Press, for the Indian Council of World Affairs, 1950, 332 p.

PAKISTAN: The Heart of Asia, by Liaquat Ali Khan. Cambridge, Harvard University Press, 1950, 151 p. (Speeches in the U.S. and Canada by Pakistan's Prime Minister.)

LETTER . . . FROM THE U.N. REPRESENTATIVE FOR INDIA AND PAKISTAN to the President of the Security Council Transmitting his Report. U.N. Document S/1791, September 15, 1950, 37 p.

Union of South Africa

SOUTH AFRICA: A Short History, by Arthur Keppel-Jones. New York, Longmans, Green, 1950, 212 p.

TWILIGHT IN SOUTH AFRICA, by Henry Gibbs. New York, Philosophical Library, 1950, 288 p.

"South Africa: Old Policies, New Leaders," by Whitman J. Severinghaus. (*Foreign Policy Reports*, XXVI, February 1, 1951, 202-211.)

LATIN AMERICA

Periodicals

Annals of the Organization of American States. Washington, Pan American Union, quarterly. (Official reports and documents.)

Inter-American Economic Affairs. Washington, Institute of Inter-American Studies, quarterly.

The Pan American. New York, Famous Features Syndicate, monthly. (Informative in popular style.)

General

LATIN AMERICA, by Preston E. James. Revised edition. New York, Odyssey Press, 1950, 848 p.

THE LATIN-AMERICAN REPUBLICS: A History, by Dana Gardner Munro. Second edition. New York, Appleton-Century-Crofts, 1950, 605 p.

ROOSEVELT'S GOOD NEIGHBOR POLICY, by Albert O. Guerrant. Albuquerque, University of New Mexico Press, 1950, 235 p.

PEACE IN THE AMERICAS: A Résumé of Measures Undertaken through the Organization of American States to Preserve the Peace, with Documents. Department of State Publication 3964, International Organization and Conference Series II, American Republics 6. Washington, 1950, 29 p.

ANNUAL REPORT OF THE SECRETARY GENERAL OF THE ORGANIZATION OF AMERICAN STATES, for the fiscal year ending June 30, 1950. Washington, Pan American Union, 1950, 199 p. Processed.

CHARTER OF THE ORGANIZATION OF AMERICAN STATES, Bogotá, April 30, 1948. S. Ex. A, 81st Congress, 1st Session. *Report:* S. Ex. Rept. 15, 81st Congress, 2nd Session, Aug. 24, 1950. (Ratified Aug. 28, 1950.)

THE ECONOMY OF LATIN AMERICA, by Wendell C. Gordon, New York, Columbia University Press, 1950, 434 p.

ECONOMIC DEVELOPMENT IN LATIN AMERICA, by Simon G. Hanson. Washington, Inter-American Affairs Press, 1951, 531 p.

THE ECONOMIC DEVELOPMENT OF LATIN AMERICA AND ITS PRINCIPAL PROBLEMS, by the U.N. Economic Commission for Latin America. U.N. Publication 1950. II.G.2. Lake Success, 1950, 59 p.

TRADE TRENDS AND POLICIES OF LATIN AMERICAN COUNTRIES, by the U.N. Economic Commission for Latin America. U.N. Document E/CN.12/165, Montevideo, May 1, 1950, 133 p.

AGRICULTURAL REQUISITES IN LATIN AMERICA: Report of the Joint ECLA/FAO Working Party. U.N. Publication 1950.II.G.1. Lake Success, 1950, 156 p.

Mexico, Central America, Caribbean

INDUSTRIAL REVOLUTION IN MEXICO, by Sanford A. Mosk. Berkeley, University of California Press, 1950, 331 p.

HONDURAS: An Area Study in Government, by William S. Stokes. Madison, University of Wisconsin Press, 1950, 351 p.

RURAL CUBA, by Lowry Nelson. Minneapolis, University of Minnesota Press, 1950, 285 p.

"United Nations Technical Assistance Programs in Haiti," by Marian Neal. (*International Conciliation*, 468, February 1951, 81-118.)

South America

THE SOUTH AMERICAN HANDBOOK 1950, edited by Howell Davies. New York, H. W. Wilson Co., 1950, 766 p.

RECENT DEVELOPMENTS IN THE FOREIGN TRADE OF ARGENTINA, by the U.S. Tariff Commission. Washington, 1950, 185 p.

THE BASIS OF A DEVELOPMENT PROGRAM FOR COLOMBIA: Report of a Mission Headed by Laughlin Currie and Sponsored by the International Bank for Reconstruction and Development in Collaboration with the Government of Colombia. Washington, International Bank for Reconstruction and Development, 1950, 642 p.

————. Summary, 76 p. (I.B.R.D. 1950. 1). Washington, I.B.R.D., 1950.

THE PERUVIAN ECONOMY. Washington, Pan American Union, 1950, 279 p.

TREATY OF FRIENDSHIP, COMMERCE, AND ECONOMIC DEVELOPMENT with the Oriental Republic of Uruguay: Message from the President . . . transmitting a treaty . . . together with a protocol, an additional protocol, and an exchange of notes, relating thereto, signed at Montevideo on November 23, 1949. S. Ex. D, 81st Congress, 2nd Session, 19 p. *Report:* S. Ex. Rept. 5, May 22, 1950. (Ratified Aug. 9, 1950.)

CHRONOLOGY OF WORLD EVENTS

JANUARY 1–DECEMBER 31, 1950

In a general chronology such as this the selection of items must be somewhat arbitrary. An attempt has been made to include international agreements and events, statements of policy, changes in government, and general elections of greatest significance. The division is along broad geographic lines, with the exception of an initial category entitled "United Nations and International." Items are located in the area of primary interest, e.g., the Prague Conference of Eastern European Foreign Ministers falls under "Germany and Austria." A more complete and detailed chronology may be found in the fortnightly *Chronology of International Events and Documents,* published by the Royal Institute of International Affairs.

UNITED NATIONS AND INTERNATIONAL

January

13. *Security Council*—Soviet delegate Yakov A. Malik walks out after failing to oust the delegate of Nationalist China, and declares that the Soviet Union will not participate in or recognize any Security Council action so long as Nationalist China remains.

19–April 4. *Trusteeship Council*—Sixth session is held in Geneva.

27. *Italian Colonies*—The Trusteeship Council approves an agreement placing former Italian Somaliland under Italian administration for ten years.

February

7–March 6. *Economic and Social Council*—Tenth session is held at Lake Success.

Kashmir—General A. G. L. McNaughton of Canada reports failure of his mediation efforts to the Security Council.

23–April 4. *General Agreement on Tariffs and Trade (G.A.T.T.)*—Fourth session of contracting parties is held at Geneva.

March

3. *U.N. Membership*—The International Court of Justice rules, 12-2, that the General Assembly cannot override the Security Council with regard to the admission of new U.N. members.

8. *China*—Secretary-General Trygve Lie expresses the view that representation in the U.N. is independent of recognition by member governments.

30. *Balkans*—The International Court of Justice rules, 11-3, that under the

peace treaties disputes exist with Bulgaria, Hungary, and Rumania regarding alleged violations of human rights.

April

4. *Jerusalem*—The Trusteeship Council adopts, 9-0, with the U.S. and the U.K. abstaining, a revised statute for internationalization of Jerusalem.

12. *Kashmir*—The Security Council appoints Sir Owen Dixon, Australian jurist, as mediator in the India-Pakistan dispute.

22–May 25. *Secretary-General* Lie visits major European capitals for peace discussions with chiefs of state.

May

8–27. *World Health Organization*—Third World Health Assembly is held in Geneva.

16–20. *Economic Commission for Asia and the Far East*—Sixth session is held in Bangkok, Thailand.

22–June 17. *UNESCO*—Fifth annual conference is held in Florence.

30–June 20. *I.C.A.O.*—Fourth session of the Assembly is held in Montreal.

31–June 15. *Economic Commission for Europe*—Fifth session is held in Geneva.

June

1–July 21. *Trusteeship Council*—Seventh session is held at Lake Success.

5–21. *Economic Commission for Latin America*—Third session is held in Montevideo, Uruguay.

6. *Secretary-General* Lie issues a ten-point peace program and reiterates his views on Chinese U.N. representation.

7–July 1. *International Labor Organization*—Thirty-third International Labor Conference is held in Geneva.

12–14. *Technical Assistance*—A U.N. Conference on Technical Assistance at Lake Success receives pledges totaling $20,012,500.

14. *Jerusalem*—The Trusteeship Council admits stalemate and decides to return the problem to the General Assembly.

25. *Korea*—The Security Council in emergency session orders an immediate cease-fire in Korea and the withdrawal of North Korean forces.

27. *Korea*—The Security Council calls on U.N. members to "furnish such assistance to the Republic of Korea as may be necessary to repel the armed attack and to restore international peace and security in the area."

July

3–August 16. *Economic and Social Council*—Eleventh session is held in Geneva.

7. *Korea*—The Security Council adopts a resolution recommending a unified U.N. command under a commander to be designated by the U.S. General of the Army Douglas MacArthur is so designated on July 8.

11. *South West Africa*—The International Court of Justice unanimously rules that South West Africa is still under mandate to the Union of South Africa, with the U.N. assuming the functions of the League of Nations.

14. *Korea*—Secretary-General Lie appeals for additional military support of the U.N. effort, especially ground forces.

18. *Balkans*—The International Court of Justice rules that an arbitration

commission cannot be set up if Bulgaria, Hungary, and Rumania, in contravention of their treaty obligations, refuse to participate in arbitral proceedings.

24. *Kashmir*—A five-day conference in New Delhi between Prime Ministers Jawaharlal Nehru and Liaquat Ali Khan and mediator Dixon ends in deadlock.

31. *Korea*—The Security Council requests the U.N. command to take necessary measures to coordinate civilian relief in Korea.

August

1. *Security Council*—Soviet delegate Malik returns as president and inaugurates a month of delay and procedural wrangling.

22. *Kashmir*—Mediator Dixon reports failure of his attempts to secure agreement on the demilitarization of Kashmir precedent to a plebiscite.

24. *China*—Communist Premier Chou En-lai demands U.N. condemnation of the U.S. for "its criminal act in the armed invasion of the territory of China" (Formosa).

25. *China*—The U.S. denies that it has encroached in China, asserts that the status of Formosa has still to be internationally fixed, and suggests a U.N. investigation into the Communist charges.

31. *China*—Answering Communist China's complaint to the Security Council that U.S. planes have bombed Manchuria, the U.S. urges an inquiry on the spot and proposes (September 1) an Indian-Swedish investigating commission.

September

6. *Korea*—The U.S.S.R. vetoes a Security Council resolution urging all members to refrain from action that might extend the conflict and use their influence to secure North Korean compliance with the cease-fire order.

7. *Korea*—A Soviet motion to condemn the U.S. for "barbarous and inhuman" conduct in Korea is rejected by the Security Council.

11. *China*—A Soviet proposal to the Security Council to invite an envoy from Peking to attend discussion of alleged U.S. violation of the Manchurian air space fails by one vote.

12. *China*—The Soviet Union vetoes the U.S. proposal to create an Indian-Swedish commission to investigate Communist China's complaint.

19. *General Assembly*—The Fifth Regular Session opens on Long Island, and Nasrollah Entezam of Iran is elected president.

China—Resolutions to seat Communist China (by India) and expel Nationalist China (by the Soviet Union) are rejected by the General Assembly.

28. *U.N. Membership*—Indonesia becomes the sixtieth member of the U.N. by unanimous vote of the General Assembly.

–April 1951. *G.A.T.T.*—The fifth series of G.A.T.T. negotiations, attended by 41 delegations, is held at Torquay, England.

29. *China*—The Security Council agrees, 7-4, to invite a Peking delegation to present its case on alleged American aggression against China.

October

7. *Korea*—The General Assembly adopts, 47-5, a resolution to restore stability in Korea by "all appropriate steps," thus by implication authorizing military operations above the 38th parallel.

12. *Secretary-General*—The Soviet delegate in the Security Council vetoes a proposal to recommend Trygve Lie for reelection as Secretary-General.

–December 13. *Economic and Social Council*—A special session is held at Lake Success to consider plans for Korean rehabilitation.

24. *U.N. Day*—On the fifth birthday of the U.N. President Truman tells the Assembly that the U.N. must use collective strength to curb aggression, and outlines the basic principles that must underlie an effective disarmament program.

November

1. *Secretary-General*—The General Assembly, 46-5, extends Lie's tenure as Secretary-General for three years.

3. *United Action for Peace*—The General Assembly adopts by heavy majorities a composite resolution including an American-sponsored collective security plan, a Soviet request for implementation of the Charter's military clauses, and a unanimous request by the Assembly for five-power talks.

Balkans—The General Assembly, 40-5, condemns Bulgaria, Hungary, and Rumania for failing to observe their obligations under the peace treaties.

4. *Spain*—The General Assembly, 38-10, revokes the ban on normal diplomatic relations with Spain and Spanish membership in the specialized agencies.

8. *Korea*—The Security Council votes to invite Communist China to participate in discussion of charges of Chinese intervention in Korea (see "Far East").

10. *Food and Agriculture Organization*—A special session of the F.A.O. Conference (November 3–11) admits the German Federal Republic, Spain, Vietnam, Cambodia, and Jordan to membership.

17. *Italian Colonies*—The General Assembly adopts, 50-0, a proposal for the creation of a unified and sovereign state of Libya.

Palestine—The Security Council adopts a comprehensive resolution on infringements of the armistice agreements and admonishes the parties to take all steps toward permanent peace.

20. *Peace plans*—The General Assembly endorses, 51-5, the Secretary-Geneearl's 20-year peace program and rejects Soviet counterproposals.

28. *Korea*—In the Security Council U.S. delegate Warren R. Austin calls Communist China an aggressor. The Peking representative, General Wu Hsiuchuan, accuses the U.S. of aggression and urges U.N. sanctions.

30. *Korea*—A Security Council resolution calling for the withdrawal of the Chinese Communists from Korea and promising to safeguard Chinese border interests is vetoed by the Soviet delegate.

December

1. *China*—The General Assembly approves, 35-17, a proposal referring Nationalist China's allegations of Soviet intervention and treaty violations to the Interim Committee.

Greece—The Assembly adopts a resolution urging all states harboring Greek children and military personnel to effect their voluntary repatriation, and continuing the U.N. Special Commission on the Balkans.

Korea—The Assembly approves the recommendations of the Economic and Social Council for the relief and rehabilitation of Korea.

2. *Italian Colonies*—The General Assembly adopts resolutions granting autonomy to Eritrea under the Ethiopian crown and approving the agreement for Italian trusteeship of Somaliland.

Palestine—The Assembly extends for 18 months the life of the U.N. Relief and Works Agency for Palestine Refugees.

4. *U.N. membership*—The Assembly adopts, 46-5, a resolution asking the Security Council to reconsider the applications of nine non-Communist states.

13. *Disarmament*—The Assembly votes to establish a committee to study the merger of the Atomic Energy Commission and the Commission on Conventional Armaments.

South West Africa—The Assembly reaffirms its desire that South West Africa be placed under the trusteeship system, and sets up a committee to work with the Union of South Africa to this end.

14. *Korea*—The Assembly decides, 52-5, to create a three-man cease-fire committee. Lester B. Pearson (Canada), Sir Benegal N. Rau (India), and Nasrollah Entezam (Iran) are appointed to membership.

15. The *General Assembly* recesses its plenary session pending the outcome of the cease-fire efforts.

22. *China*—The Communist government denounces the cease-fire committee, reiterates its charges of aggression by the U.S., and repeats its demands for admission to the U.N. and cessation of U.S. protection of Formosa.

UNITED STATES

January

3–January 2, 1951. The Eighty-First Congress holds its second session.

18. Myron C. Taylor resigns as the President's personal representative at the Vatican.

21. Alger Hiss is found guilty of perjury in connection with alleged transmission of confidential documents to a Communist espionage agent.

31. President Truman authorizes efforts to develop a hydrogen bomb.

February

8. Secretary Acheson declares that agreement with the Soviet Union will be useful only when it is backed by strength.

14. President Truman signs the Far Eastern Economic Assistance Act of 1950.

16. Secretary Acheson defines the current struggle in world affairs as one of "total diplomacy."

March

7. Judith Coplon and Valentin Gubichev are found guilty of conspiracy and attempted espionage, and Gubichev is ordered expelled from the U.S.

28. John Sherman Cooper is appointed consultant to the State Department.

31. Gordon Gray is appointed to make a special survey of U.S. foreign economic policy.

April

6. Sir Basil Brooke, Premier of North Ireland, arrives in the U.S. for a week's visit.

John Foster Dulles is appointed consultant to the Secretary of State.

12. President Gabriel Gonzalez Videla of Chile arrives in the U.S. on a 20-day state visit.

28. Herbert Hoover proposes that the U.N be reorganized without the Soviet Union and its satellites.

May

3–July 1. Liaquat Ali Khan, Prime Minister of Pakistan, visits the U.S.

June

5. President Truman signs the Foreign Economic Assistance Act, authorizing funds for the third year of the European Recovery Program and providing for a technical cooperation (Point Four) program.

16. W. Averell Harriman is named Special Assistant to the President for international affairs.

President Truman signs the new displaced persons bill, increasing to 341,000 the number of European refugees admissible to the U.S. outside the quota.

July

19. In a message to Congress on the Korean crisis President Truman calls for an increase in the size of the armed forces, greater military strength and preparedness, and a "substantial redirection of economic resources" to meet defense needs.

20. A report terming Senator Joseph R. McCarthy's charges of Communism in the State Department "a fraud and a hoax" is approved by the Senate.

26. President Truman signs the bill authorizing $1.2 billion for the Mutual Defense Assistance Program in 1950–1951.

August

25. Secretary of the Navy Francis P. Matthews endorses the thesis of a preventive war, and is rebuked (August 26) by the Department of State and the White House.

28. The Senate ratifies the Charter of the Organization of American States.

September

6. The President approves the General Appropriation Act, 1951, including $14.6 billion for defense, $1.2 billion for the Mutual Defense Assistance Program, $2.5 billion for E.C.A., $62.5 million for a loan to Spain, and $26.9 million for the Point Four program.

12. General George C. Marshall is appointed Secretary of Defense to replace the resigning Louis A. Johnson.

22. President Truman vetoes the McCarran Internal Security Act, but the act becomes law when Congress overwhelmingly overrides the veto on September 23.

Congress passes an emergency defense appropriation of $16.8 billion, including a further $4 billion for the Mutual Defense Assistance Program in 1950–1951. The President signs the bill on September 27.

25. Economic Cooperation Administrator Paul G. Hoffman resigns and is succeeded (September 29) by Deputy Administrator William C. Foster.

26. Lewis W. Douglas, Ambassador to the U.K., resigns, and Walter S. Gifford is appointed his successor (September 27).

November

1. Two Puerto Rican Nationalists make an abortive attempt to assassinate President Truman.

7. Congressional elections sharply reduce Democratic majorities in both houses.

12. The *Report to the President on Foreign Economic Policies,* prepared by a commission under Gordon Gray, recommends three to four more years' aid to Europe and an expanded economic development program.

24. Nelson A. Rockefeller is appointed chairman of the International Development Advisory Board.

30. At a press conference on the Korean crisis (see "Far East"), President Truman says that possible use of the atom bomb in the Korean conflict has always been under consideration.

December

4–8. President Truman and British Prime Minister Clement R. Attlee confer in Washington.

15. Senate and House Republicans pass resolutions demanding the replacement of Acheson as Secretary of State.

President Truman asks that the armed forces be increased to 3.5 million and outlines other mobilization steps.

16. President Truman declares a state of national emergency and names Charles E. Wilson head of the Office of Defense Mobilization.

19. Congress approves a $38 million grant for food relief for Yugoslavia.

20. Ex-President Herbert Hoover urges a reversal of U.S. world policy with primary emphasis placed on the Western Hemisphere.

21. The Senate passes a defense appropriation measure of $20.2 billion, which is then referred to a joint House-Senate conference committee. (The $20.2 billion measure is approved by Congress on January 2 and signed by President Truman on January 16, 1951.)

A Committee on International Security Affairs, headed by Thomas Dudley Cabot, is established to coordinate U.S. military and economic assistance for mutual defense.

NORTH ATLANTIC AREA AND WESTERN EUROPE

January

6. *North Atlantic Treaty Organization (N.A.T.O.)*—The third meeting of the North Atlantic Council in Washington approves recommendations for an integrated defense of the North Atlantic area.

11. *Italy*—The cabinet of Alcide de Gasperi resigns to permit the inclusion of right-wing Socialists in a reconstructed cabinet.

19. *Spain*—Secretary Acheson reveals that the U.S. is ready to support a U.N. resolution for the resumption of normal diplomatic relations with Spain.

21. *Ireland*—Ireland and the U.S. sign a treaty of friendship, commerce, and navigation.

27. *Italy*—President Luigi Einaudi approves a new de Gasperi cabinet composed of Christian Democrats, Republicans, and right-wing Socialists.

Mutual Defense Assistance Program—Bilateral agreements are signed in Washington with Great Britain, France, Italy, Denmark, Norway, Belgium, Netherlands, and Luxembourg. President Truman approves the recommendations of the North Atlantic Council for an integrated defense, thus clearing the way for implementation of the military aid program.

31. *Organization for European Economic Cooperation (O.E.E.C.)*—The O.E.E.C. Council adopts a proposal to appoint Dr. Dirk U. Stikker of the Netherlands as "Political Conciliator."

February

1. *O.E.E.C.*—The Council approves a resolution for the reduction of quantitative restrictions on imports.

3. *United Kingdom*—Atomic scientist Klaus Fuchs is arrested and sentenced (March 1) to 14 years' imprisonment for transmitting atomic information to the U.S.S.R.

4. *France*—The Socialists resign from the Bidault cabinet without, however, affecting its parliamentary majority.

23. *United Kingdom*—A general election reduces the Labor majority in the House of Commons to six seats.

March

3. *Saar*—France and the Saar sign five agreements, subject to a peace treaty with Germany, providing for economic union and granting limited autonomy to the Saar.

12. *Belgium*—In a national referendum 57.68 percent of the voters favor the return of King Leopold III from exile.

15–19. *Sweden*—The permanent committee of the Communist-controlled World Peace Congress meets at Stockholm and calls for signatures to a world-wide appeal against use of the atomic bomb.

18. *Belgium*—The government of Gaston Eyskens (Christian Social) resigns over the question of Leopold's return.

30. *Council of Europe*—Third session of the Committee of Ministers opens in Strasbourg and decides to invite Western Germany and the Saar to accept associate membership.

April

1. *N.A.T.O.*—The Defense Committee (Defense Ministers) at the Hague approves plans for "an integrated defense of the entire North Atlantic area."

16. *N.A.T.O.*—Premier Georges Bidault of France proposes the creation of an Atlantic High Council for Peace.

29. *Belgium*—The Regent dissolves parliament due to the failure of the parties to reach an agreement on the royal question.

May

9. *Schuman Plan*—Foreign Minister Robert Schuman of France proposes a plan for the pooling of Europe's coal and steel production under a single supranational authority.

11–14. *Western Foreign Ministers*—The Foreign Ministers of the U.S., U.K., and France at London discuss European defense and the coordination of policies throughout the world and declare that Germany should "reenter progressively the community of free peoples of Europe."

15–18. *N.A.T.O.*—The fourth session of the North Atlantic Council at London agrees on the creation of "balanced collective forces" and decides to establish a standing committee of deputies.

June

3. *Schuman Plan*—A joint French-German-Italian-Benelux communiqué announces the decision to proceed with negotiations.

Council of Europe—The fourth session of the Committee of Ministers is held in Paris.

4. *Belgium*—Elections give the pro-Leopold Christian Social party a majority in the Chamber of Deputies. A Christian Social government under Jean Duvieusart is formed June 8.

Schuman Plan—The U.K. declares its unwillingness to join negotiations or commit itself in principle until the full economic and political consequences of the plan have been explored.

20. *Schuman Plan*—A six-power conference opens in Paris. A French working draft is published (June 27), five study groups are set up (July 4), and

on July 25 Schuman announces that common agreement has been reached by the six delegations on the main points of the French proposals.

24. *France*—The Bidault government falls when the Assembly fails to give it a vote of confidence.

July

7. *European economic cooperation*—The Council of the O.E.E.C. approves the principles of a European Payments Union, which is established as of July 1 after final agreement is reached September 19.

11. *France*—René Pleven (Independent) is confirmed as Premier after five candidates fail to form a government, and his cabinet is approved (July 13) by the National Assembly.

19. *Council of Europe*—Western Germany and the Saar are formally admitted as associate members.

20. *Belgium*—Parliament votes to end the Regency and bring back King Leopold. Leopold returns on July 22 to the accompaniment of Socialist and Liberal opposition and a fortnight of strikes and rioting.

25–August 1. *N.A.T.O.*—The first meeting of the Council of Deputies in London under the chairmanship of Charles M. Spofford (U.S.) calls for accelerated efforts to achieve an effective integrated defense.

August

1. *Belgium*—Leopold, to avert a possible civil war, agrees to delegate royal power to his son.

3. *Defense*—In response to an inquiry by the U.S., the U.K. announces plans to spend £3,400 million for defense during the next three years.

Council of Europe—Fifth session of the Committee of Ministers is held at Strasbourg.

6. *Defense*—France announces an increase in national rearmament targets, including the creation of 15 new and fully equipped divisions during the next three years.

7–28. *Council of Europe*—The second session of the Consultative Assembly convenes at Strasbourg and reelects Paul-Henri Spaak of Belgium as president. Iceland, Western Germany, and the Saar are represented for the first time.

10. *Belgium*—Parliament passes a bill transferring royal prerogatives to Prince Baudouin, who takes the oath of allegiance on August 11. The Duvieusart government resigns, and a new Christian Social government takes office (August 15) under Joseph Pholien.

11. *Council of Europe*—The Consultative Assembly calls for the immediate creation of a unified European army under a European Minister of Defense.

September

9. *Defense*—President Truman approves a "substantial increase" in the strength of U.S. forces to be stationed in Europe.

15–26. *N.A.T.O.*—The North Atlantic Council meets in New York, agrees on the creation of an integrated European defense force under a supreme commander, and declares that Germany should be "enabled to contribute" to the defense effort.

October

12–15. *Defense*—The French Defense and Finance ministers, Jules Moch and Maurice Petsche, discuss defense needs with U.S. authorities in Washington. Moch announces (October 18) that the U.S. will provide aid to the value of $2-2.6 billion, including help for Indochina.

24. *N.A.T.O.*—The Military Committee meets in Washington and announces (October 26) agreement on defense measures to be taken in the event of an emergency, and recommendations to be submitted to the Defense Ministers.

Defense—Premier Pleven of France proposes the creation of a European army under a European Ministry of Defense as an alternative to German re-armament. The National Assembly approves the project October 25–26.

27. *O.E.E.C.*—The O.E.E.C. Council in Paris agrees on further measures to reduce import quotas.

28–31. *N.A.T.O.*—The Defense Committee meets in Washington, approves recommendations of the Military Committee on an integrated defense force, and refers the German question to the Council of Deputies and the Military Committee for further study.

November

3–5. *Council of Europe*—The Committee of Ministers in Rome decides to avoid discussion of the Consultative Assembly's recommendation for the creation of a European army, and approves (November 4) a Convention on Human Rights.

14. *O.E.E.C.*—The Council takes measures to rectify the situation caused by Western Germany's heavy deficit in the European Payments Union.

18–25. *Council of Europe*—The Consultative Assembly meets in Strasbourg and approves (November 24) a recommendation for West German participation in a European army on the basis of equality.

December

8. *Defense*—President Truman and Prime Minister Attlee in Washington announce agreement on the need for immediate action by the North Atlantic countries to intensify defense efforts and appoint a supreme commander as soon as an integrated defense plan is approved.

13. *United Kingdom*—Announcement is made that Marshall Plan aid to the U.K. will be suspended on January 1, 1951 because of its improved balance-of-payments position.

N.A.T.O.—The Deputies and the Military Committee announce agreement on political and military recommendations for German participation in an integrated European defense force.

18–19. *N.A.T.O.*—Meetings of the Defense Committee and the North Atlantic Council in Brussels result in completion of arrangements for the establishment of an integrated defense force under the supreme command of General Dwight D. Eisenhower, and unanimous agreement that Western Germany should contribute to the defense force. President Truman appoints General Eisenhower (December 19) as Supreme Allied Commander, Europe, with operational command of U.S. Army, Navy, and Air Force units in Europe.

Western Foreign Ministers—A separate conference of the U.S., U.K., and French Foreign Ministers in Brussels announces that the Allied High Commissioners have been authorized to explore German association with European defense plans with the Bonn government (see also "Germany and Austria").

27. *Spain*—The U.S. resumes normal diplomatic relations with Spain with the naming of Stanton Griffis as Ambassador.

GERMANY AND AUSTRIA
January

9. *Austria*—The Deputies of the Council of Foreign Ministers resume negotiations for an Austrian treaty in London. On January 24 they adjourn without progress.
18. *Austria*—The U.S., U.K., and French Ambassadors in Moscow visit the Soviet Foreign Ministry to discuss the Austrian treaty.

February

15. *Austria*—The Deputies meet in London, make no progress, and adjourn until March 1.
27. *Austria*—A Soviet note to the Austrian Government places responsibility for delay in the treaty negotiations on the Western powers.

March

1. *Austria*—The Deputies make no progress in the treaty negotiations and adjourn until April 26.
4. *Saar*—Chancellor Adenauer strongly criticizes the agreements of March 3 between France and the Saar. (See "North Atlantic Area and Western Europe.")
21. *France-Germany*—Chancellor Adenauer proposes a Franco-German economic union as the first step toward a political union and as a nucleus for a wider European union.
22. *German unification*—The Bonn government proposes an all-German constituent assembly, elected under U.N. or four-power supervision, to draft a constitution for submission to a national referendum.

April

26. *Austria*—The four Deputies make no headway and adjourn until May 22.

May

4. *Prisoners of War*— TASS states that the Soviet Union has completed the repatriation of German prisoners of war.
Austria—The Deputies meet at the request of the Soviet delegate, but make no progress after he charges that Austria has failed to carry out denazification measures and that the U.S. and U.K. have turned Trieste into a naval base.
9. *Council of Europe*—The Bonn cabinet accepts the invitation to join the Council of Europe as an associate member. (The Bundestag approves on June 25.)
15. *East Germany*—The U.S.S.R. announces a 50 percent reduction in East German reparations obligations.
19. *Austria*—The U.S., U.K., and France announce that civilian high commissioners will be appointed to replace the military high commissioners.
22. *Austria*—The Soviet Deputy declares that the Soviet Union will not sign an Austrian treaty until a reply is received to the Soviet note of April 20 on Trieste. (See "Greece, Turkey, Yugoslavia, and Trieste.")
23. *East Germany*—The U.S., U.K., and France protest to the U.S.S.R. against the remilitarization of Eastern Germany.
25. *German unification*—The three Western High Commissioners send a letter to the head of the Soviet Control Commission with proposals for achieving German unification on the basis of a freely elected all-German government.

28. *German youth rally*—A demonstration of 500,000 "Free German Youth" is held in the Soviet sector of Berlin.

June

7. *German-Polish boundary*—The "German Democratic Republic" and Poland conclude an agreement permanently fixing their common boundary on the Oder-Neisse line. The Bonn government (June 9) denounces the agreement as "null and void."

12. *Austria*—The U.S., U.K., and France send identic notes to the Soviet Union reaffirming their desire for the early conclusion of a treaty.

23. *East Germany*—The "German Democratic Republic" and Czechoslovakia sign cultural, technical and scientific, and financial agreements at Prague. All German claims to the Sudetenland are renounced.

July

10. *Austria*—The Deputies, deadlocked as a result of continued Soviet insistence on prior settlement of the Trieste issue, adjourn until September 7.

14. *Prisoners of war*—Similar U.S., U.K., and French notes ask Moscow to permit investigation into the actual fate of German war prisoners reportedly still in Soviet hands.

20–24. *East Germany*—The third conference of the Socialist Unity (Communist) party in East Berlin approves a five-year economic plan.

September

7. *Austria*—At the Deputies' 257th meeting the Soviet delegate refuses to proceed with negotiations until the Soviet note on Trieste is answered.

12–19. The *Western Foreign Ministers* meet in New York and announce the following decisions on Germany: to end the state of war by legislation, to reinforce the occupation troops, to consider any attack on West Germany or Berlin as an attack on the Western powers, to permit the creation of a foreign ministry and a mobile police force, and to relax occupation restrictions.

29. *East Germany*—Admission of the "German Democratic Republic" to the Council of Mutual Economic Assistance is announced.

October

2. *Prisoners of war*—The Soviet Union rejects the three-power demand for more information concerning German war prisoners.

15. *East Germany*—In general elections 99.71 percent of the valid votes endorse the single (Communist) National Front ticket.

20. *German remilitarization*—A Soviet note to the U.S., U.K., and France rejects charges that the East German police force is being organized as a military force and declares that the Soviet Government "will not tolerate" the remilitarization of West Germany.

–21. *Prague proposals*—A conference of East European foreign ministers at Prague denounces as illegal the New York decisions of the Western powers on Germany and proposes the following program: opposition to remilitarization, immediate conclusion of a peace treaty, restoration of German unity, withdrawal of occupation troops within one year after the signing of a peace treaty, and the formation of an all-German Constituent Council on the basis of parity between East and West Germany.

November

3. *Four-power conference*—A Soviet note to the three Western powers proposes a Big Four meeting to discuss German demilitarization on the basis of the Prague program.

19. *West Germany—Land* elections in Hesse and Württemberg-Baden register gains for the Social Democrats at the expense of the Christian Democrats.

26. *West Germany*—Elections in Bavaria bring the Social Democrats substantial gains and commensurate losses to the Christian Social Union.

December

15. *West German rearmament*—Soviet notes to the U.K. and France allege that West German rearmament is a violation of the Potsdam agreement and the U.K.-Soviet and French-Soviet treaties.

Austria—The Deputies hold another inconclusive meeting and adjourn for three months.

21. *European defense*—The Western High Commissioners and Chancellor Adenauer discuss German contributions to European defense and announce that Bonn will be consulted on future moves that concern Germany.

22. *Four-power conference*—In identic notes to the U.S.S.R. the Western powers reject Germany alone as the basis for a four-power conference but offer to discuss a suitable agenda.

31. *Four-power conference*—The U.S.S.R. partly accepts the Western powers' proposal for a preliminary conference of deputies to fix an agenda.

GREECE, TURKEY, YUGOSLAVIA, AND TRIESTE

January

5. *Greece*—Premier Alexander Diomedes and Commander-in-Chief Alexander Papagos resign. A new government is formed by John Theotokis on January 6, and Papagos withdraws his resignation.

March

1. *Yugoslavia*—The U.S. Export-Import Bank grants a $20 million credit to Yugoslavia.

5. *Greece*—A general election is held, with none of the major parties receiving a clear majority.

23. *Greece*—A new government is formed under Liberal party leader Sophocles Venizelos.

24. *Turkey and Italy* sign a treaty of friendship.

26. *Yugoslavia*—Parliamentary elections give 93 percent of the total vote to candidates of the People's Front.

April

6. *Trieste*—Premier Marshal Tito of Yugoslavia says the question of Trieste must be solved in such a way as to make cooperation with Italy possible.

8. *Trieste*—Italian Foreign Minister Carlo Sforza appeals for direct negotiations with Yugoslavia on Trieste and affirms that Italy bases its position on the three-power declaration of March 20, 1948, supporting the return of the territory to Italy.

14. *Greece*—The Venizelos government resigns. General Nicholas Plastiras forms a new coalition government which is sworn in on April 15.

16. *Trieste*—Elections in the Yugoslav zone give the Yugoslav People's Front 88 percent of the vote.

20. *Trieste*—A Soviet note accuses the U.S., U.K., and France of violating the Italian peace treaty by establishing a naval base in Trieste and demands implementation of the treaty provisions and withdrawal of foreign troops.

28. *Trieste*—Tito says the Trieste issue is not of vital importance but declares Italy's recent proposals unacceptable as a basis for negotiations.

May

14. *Turkey*—A general election ousts President Ismet Inönü's Republican People's party, continuously in power since 1923, and gives the five-year old Democratic party an overwhelming majority. Democratic leader Celal Bayar is chosen President on May 22.

June

16. *Trieste*—The U.S., U.K., and France reject the Soviet note of April 20 and place responsibility for failure to implement the Italian peace treaty on the Soviet Union.

August

17. *Greece*—The Liberal party withdraws from the Plastiras government, causing its resignation on August 18; on August 21 Venizelos forms a new all-Liberal government.

September

7. *Greece*—Venizelos fails to get a vote of confidence and resigns. A new coalition government under Venizelos is formed on September 11.

November

2. *Greece*—The Venizelos coalition government resigns due to local scandals, and a new Venizelos cabinet of Liberals and Democratic Socialists is sworn in November 3.

24. *Yugoslavia*—President Truman authorizes the diversion of $16 million from Mutual Defense Assistance Program funds to provide food for Yugoslav armed forces. The Export-Import Bank extends a $6 million credit to Yugoslavia for food.

December

19. *Yugoslavia*—The U.S. Congress approves a $38 million grant for food relief for Yugoslavia.

23. *Yugoslavia and Italy* sign economic agreements settling reparations and war claims questions under the peace treaty.

28. *Yugoslavia and Greece* agree to restore full diplomatic relations.

SOVIET BLOC

January

3. *Hungary*—The U.S. requests the closing of Hungarian consulates in New York and Cleveland.

6. *Balkans*—The U.S., U.K., and Canada ask Bulgaria, Hungary, and Rumania to designate commissioners to discuss violations of the human rights provisions of the peace treaties.

19. *Bulgaria* declares U.S. Minister Donald R. Heath *persona non grata* and requests his recall.

23. *Bulgaria*—Prime Minister Vasil Kolarov dies. Vulko Chervenkov forms a new government on February 1.

February

15. *Finland*—Dr. Juho K. Paasikivi is reelected president.

20. *Bulgaria*—The U.S. suspends diplomatic relations with Bulgaria.

21. *Hungary*—A Hungarian court sentences an American and a British businessman to prison terms of 15 and 13 years respectively on espionage charges.

23. *Hungary* requests a reduction in the U.S. and U.K. legation staffs.

24. *Balkans*—The U.S. "freezes" the assets of Bulgaria, Hungary, and Rumania due to delays in the payment of American claims.

28. The *Soviet Union* revalues the ruble and places it on a gold rather than a dollar basis.

March

4. *Hungary*—A U.S. note terms the Vogeler trial (February 21) a travesty of justice and dismisses the request for a reduction in the legation staff as improper and irrelevant.

12. *Soviet Union*—A general election is held with 99.98 percent of the electorate voting.

14. *Czechoslovakia*—Vladimir Clementis resigns as Foreign Minister and is succeeded by Deputy Foreign Minister Viliam Siroky.

April

8. *Baltic plane incident*—A U.S. patrol plane disappears over the Baltic. On April 11 a Soviet note protests an alleged violation of Soviet territory by an American bomber which was fired upon by Soviet planes when it refused to land as directed.

18. *Baltic plane incident*—A U.S. note declares that the missing plane, an unarmed patrol plane on a routine training flight, had not transgressed Soviet territory, and asks for an apology, punishment of the offenders, and an appropriate indemnity. On April 21 a Soviet note denies the U.S. charges and reasserts that responsibility for the incident was the plane's.

21. *Czechoslovakia*—The U.S. closes the Czech consulate in Chicago in retaliation against the closing of the U.S.I.E. libraries in Prague and Bratislava. On April 28 Czechoslovakia demands a two-thirds reduction in the staff of the U.S. Embassy and the U.S. closes the Czechoslovak consulates in Pittsburgh and Cleveland.

May

5. *Baltic plane incident*—A U.S. note condemns the Soviet action as a violation of international law and practice.

10. *Czechoslovakia* gives the U.S. Embassy one week's notice to effect the requested reduction in personnel.

13. *Rumania* accuses the U.S. diplomatic staff of espionage and requests that the staff be reduced to ten. On May 22 the U.S. denies the accusations, agrees

to reduce the staff as requested, and curtails the movement of Rumanian diplomats in the U.S.

23. *Czechoslovakia* requests a further reduction in the U.S. diplomatic staff. The U.S. complies on May 27 and closes the Czechoslovak Consulate General in New York.

June

12–19. *Soviet Union*—The Supreme Soviet of the U.S.S.R. meets in Moscow and reelects N. M. Shvernik as Chairman of the Presidium.

October

16–18. *Soviet Union*—The second all-U.S.S.R. Conference for Peace is held in Moscow.

November

6. *Soviet Union*—Deputy Prime Minister N. A. Bulganin on the thirty-third anniversary of the Russian Revolution contrasts the "peace" policy of the Soviet Union with Anglo-American "imperialism."

16–22. *Peace congress*—The second World Peace Congress of the Communist-controlled Partisans of Peace is held in Warsaw.

NEAR EAST AND AFRICA

January

3. *Egypt*—A general election returns the Wafdists to power in a decisive victory; Mustafa al-Nahhas Pasha forms a new government on January 12.

11. *Iran*—The cabinet resigns, and the outgoing Prime Minister, Muhammad Sa'id, forms a new government on January 14.

14. *Israel*—The Knesset proclaims Jerusalem the capital of Israel.

February

1. *Iraq*—Prime Minister Ali Jawdat al-Ayyubi resigns, and Tawfiq al-Suwaidi forms a coalition government on February 5.

March

19. *Iran*—The government of Muhammad Sa'id resigns, and Ali Mansur forms a new government on March 22.

April

1. *Arab League*—The Council agrees unanimously to expel any member that negotiates a separate peace with Israel.

6. *Arab League*—With Jordan absent, the Political Committee approves with some reservations the U.N. plan for the internationalization of Jerusalem.

13. *Arab League*—The Arab states, including Jordan, provisionally approve a collective security pact.

24. *Palestine*—King Abdullah of Jordan announces the annexation of Arab Palestine.

27. *Palestine*—The U.K. gives *de jure* recognition to Israel and, at the same time, recognizes Jordan's annexation of Arab Palestine.

May

15. *Arab League*—The Political Committee deadlocks on the question of expelling Jordan for its unilateral action in Palestine.

25. *Near Eastern arms*—The U.S., U.K., and France announce a policy of supplying arms to Israel and the Arab states in the interest of Near Eastern security.

June

12. *Arab League*—The Council meets in Alexandria, and Egypt, Syria, Lebanon, and Saudi Arabia call for the expulsion of Jordan.

17. *Arab League*—Egypt, Saudi Arabia, Syria, Lebanon, and Yemen sign a collective security pact, with Iraq abstaining and Jordan not in attendance.

26. *Iran*—The cabinet of Ali Mansur resigns, and General Ali Razmara forms a new government.

September

4. *Iraq*—Prime Minister Tawfiq al-Suwaidi resigns, and General Nuri al-Sa'id forms a new government on September 16.

5. *Syria*—The Chamber of Deputies adopts a new constitution and elects Hashim al-Atasi President of the Third Republic. A new government under Nazim al-Qudsi is formed on September 8.

October

12. *Jordan*—The government resigns, and the outgoing Prime Minister, Sa'id Pasha al-Mufti, forms a new government on October 14.

15. *Israel*—Prime Minister David Ben-Gurion resigns due to the withdrawal of the religious bloc from his cabinet, but forms a new coalition cabinet on October 30.

19. *Iran* and the U.S. sign a technical cooperation agreement, the first major project under the Point Four program.

November

16. *Egypt*—King Farouk demands immediate and complete British evacuation from Egypt, unification of the Nile valley under the Egyptian crown, and termination of the 1936 treaty with the U.K. On November 20 British Foreign Secretary Ernest Bevin declares that the 1936 treaty with Egypt will abide until changed by mutual consent.

25. *Libya*—A Libyan National Constituent Assembly convenes in Tripoli.

December

3. *Libya*—The Emir Sayid Idris al-Sanusi is proclaimed King by the National Constituent Assembly.

FAR EAST

January

1. *Japan*—General MacArthur declares that Japan's renunciation of armed forces should not be interpreted as "complete negation of the inalienable right of self-defense against unprovoked attack."

2. *Formosa*—Ex-President Herbert Hoover and Senator Robert A. Taft in separate statements call for use of the U.S. Navy, if necessary, to help defend Formosa.

4. *Japan*—Soviet delegate K. N. Derevyanko walks out of the Allied Council in Tokyo when asked to account for Japanese prisoners of war still in Soviet hands.

5. *Formosa*—President Truman declares there will be no U.S. armed interference in or military aid to Formosa. Secretary Acheson says Formosa is a part of China and advises against premature recognition of Communist China.

6. *China*—After breaking off relations with Nationalist China (January 5), the U.K. accords Communist China *de jure* recognition and offers to establish diplomatic relations with Peking.

12. *U.S. policy*—Before the National Press Club Secretary Acheson defines U.S. policy in the Far East, accuses the Soviet Union of imperialism in China, and warns against any "ill-conceived adventures" by the U.S.

14. *China*—The Peking government seizes U.S. consular property in China. U.S. consular officials are recalled from China.

19. *Far Eastern Commission*—Soviet delegate A. S. Panyushkin walks out after failing to depose the delegate of Nationalist China.

29. *Indochina*—The French National Assembly ratifies, 401-193, accords recognizing Vietnam, Cambodia, and Laos as independent states within the French Union.

31. *Indochina*—The Soviet Union recognizes the insurgent Vietminh regime.

February

1. *Japan*—A Soviet note urges that the Emperor Hirohito be tried as a war criminal. The U.S. rejects the proposal on February 3.

7. *Indochina*—The U.S. and U.K. extend full recognition to Vietnam, Cambodia, and Laos.

10. *Indonesia*—The Export-Import Bank extends a $100 million economic reconstruction credit to Indonesia.

13–15. *Southeast Asia*—A conference of U.S. heads of mission at Bangkok, Thailand, recommends military and economic aid to Southeast Asian countries resisting Communist aggression.

14. *Soviet-Chinese treaty*—The Soviet Union and Communist China sign a 30-year treaty of friendship, alliance, and mutual assistance, and the Soviet Union agrees to extend a $300 million loan to China over a five-year period.

March

1. *China*—Generalissimo Chiang Kai-shek resumes the presidency of the Nationalist government.

April

7. *Korea*—The U.S. informs the Republic of Korea that economic aid will be terminated unless steps are taken to halt inflation.

21. *Japan*—TASS reports that repatriation of Japanese war prisoners has been substantially completed.

May

8. *Indochina*—After conferring with Foreign Minister Schuman in Paris, Secretary Acheson announces that the U.S. will send economic and military aid to Indochina.

26. *Conferences of Asian states*—A conference of representatives of seven Southeast Asian states (Pakistan, India, Indonesia, Philippines, Thailand, Ceylon, and Australia) at Baguio in the Philippines adopts a broad resolution urging economic, social, and cultural cooperation.

30. *Korea*—A general election in the Republic of Korea registers a setback for the Syngman Rhee government when Independents gain 128 of 210 seats.

June

4. *Japan*—Elections to the upper house of the Diet brings losses to the government Liberal party and the Communists and gains for the Socialists.

5. *Japan*—Following Communist-inspired disorders General MacArthur orders 24 members of the Communist central committee disqualified from public office.

7. *Korea*—The North Korean regime calls for nationwide elections to choose a unified legislature for all Korea.

25. *Korea*—North Korean forces invade South Korea, overrunning light resistance and capturing (June 28) the capital city of Seoul.

27. *U.S. policy*—President Truman orders U.S. air and sea forces to support South Korean troops, orders the U.S. Seventh Fleet to prevent any attack on Formosa or action from Formosa against the mainland, and announces intensified military aid to the Philippines and Indochina.

Korea—A U.S. note to the Soviet Union asks the Soviet Government to use its influence to effect the withdrawal of North Korean forces.

29. *Korea*—A Soviet note to the U.S. attributes the conflict to South Korean provocation and disclaims intervention in Korean internal affairs.

China—Foreign Minister Chou En-lai asserts that Formosa will always be a part of China and that China will fight "to liberate Taiwan (Formosa) from the grasp of the American aggressors."

30. *Korea*—President Truman authorizes the U.S. Air Force to conduct missions above the 38th parallel, orders a naval blockade of the Korean coast, and authorizes the use of U.S. ground units in the conflict.

July

4. *Korea*—Soviet Deputy Foreign Minister A. A. Gromyko accuses the Republic of Korea of initiating the conflict, condemns the U.S. as an aggressor in Korea and Formosa, and declares the Security Council resolutions illegal.

13. *Korea*—In messages to the U.S. and the Soviet Union, Prime Minister Jawaharlal Nehru of India proposes a localization and speedy pacific settlement of the Korean conflict by seating Communist China in the U.N. Stalin's reply (July 15) welcomes the Indian initiative and agrees that Communist China should be admitted to the U.N. Secretary Acheson's reply (July 18) declares that a Korea settlement is not contingent on the determination of other questions before the U.N. which must be settled on their own merits.

31. *China*—General MacArthur and Chiang Kai-shek hold military discussions on Formosa.

August

28. *Formosa*—General MacArthur's message on Formosa to the Veterans of Foreign Wars is withdrawn by order of the President.

September

4. *Aircraft incident*—A Soviet bomber is shot down by U.S. fighter planes under U.N. command over the Yellow Sea.

14. *Japan*—President Truman says the U.S. will initiate informal discussions with interested governments on the subject of a Japanese peace treaty.

15. *Korea*—U.N. forces make an amphibious landing behind North Korean lines at Inchon.

26. *Korea*—Seoul is liberated by U.N. forces.

30. *China*—Foreign Minister Chou En-lai, on the first anniversary of the Chinese People's Republic, says that China is determined to liberate Tibet, wrest Formosa from the "American aggressors," and not stand aside if "imperialists" invade the territory of its neighbors.

October

1. *Korea*—General MacArthur broadcasts a surrender demand to the North Korean forces as South Korean troops cross the 38th parallel.

9. *Korea*—General MacArthur "for the last time" calls upon the North Koreans to surrender.

Aircraft incident—The U.S.S.R. protests an attack on a Soviet airfield by U.S. planes under U.N. command.

11. *Korea*—Peking denounces the crossing of the 38th parallel and declares that China "cannot stand idly by."

15. *U.S. policy*—President Truman and General MacArthur meet on Wake Island to discuss U.S. Far Eastern policy.

24. *Tibet*—The Peking radio says that Chinese troops have been ordered to "liberate" Tibet.

26. *Japan*—John Foster Dulles confers with Soviet U.N. delegate Yakov A. Malik on the Japanese peace treaty question.

Tibet—The Indian Government in a note to Peking expresses "surprise and regret" at the decision to invade Tibet.

28. *Philippines*—The report of the U.S. Economic Survey Mission to the Philippines emphasizes the need for agricultural and administrative reforms and urges the provision of $250 million in loans and grants.

30. *Tibet*—A Communist Chinese note to India asserts that Tibet is a domestic problem and that India's policy is being influenced by foreign governments. India (October 31) denies any foreign influence on its policy and says China should not impose a decision in Tibet by force.

November

5. *Korea*—General MacArthur announces the intervention of Communist Chinese troops in Korea.

6. *Nepal*—The King of Nepal is deposed and given asylum in the Indian Embassy at Katmandu. An emergency session of parliament (November 7) unanimously proclaims the three-year-old son of the Crown Prince as Nepal's new king. Insurrectionists enter Nepal from India (November 10) and set up a "provisional government" (November 12). The Indian Ministry of External Affairs declares (November 12) that the raid was a complete surprise and that measures are being taken to prevent the use of Indian territory for armed operations against Nepal. India on November 15 bans the movement of arms and troops across the Nepalese frontier.

13. *Tibet*—Tibet appeals to the U.N. for aid against Chinese aggression.

20. *Japan*—A Soviet aide-mémoire to the U.S. raises various questions with regard to the proposed peace treaty with Japan.

24. *Korea*—General MacArthur launches an offensive designed to "end the war" in Korea.

Japan—The U.S. releases the text of a memorandum outlining its views on a Japanese peace treaty.

Tibet—The U.N. General Assembly suspends consideration of the Tibetan appeal due to the Indian contention that an honorable and peaceful settlement could be reached on the spot. Meanwhile Communist China establishes a "Tibetan Autonomous Region" under its control in Western Sikang.

26. *Korea*—Communist Chinese forces open a massive counteroffensive against U.N. troops.

December

1. *Korea*—In a special message to Congress President Truman denounces Chinese intervention in Korea as deliberate and unprovoked aggression.

4–8. *Truman-Attlee conference*—A conference between Prime Minister Attlee and President Truman reveals differences in the Far Eastern policies of the U.K. and U.S. but common agreement that aggression will not be appeased.

5. *Japan*—Chou En-lai demands Peking representation in Japanese peace treaty negotiations, attacks the U.S. peace treaty proposals, and charges that the U.S. is turning Japan into a colony.

21. *Nepal*—Nehru reveals that India in a memorandum to Nepal has advised the election of a constituent assembly and other reforms.

29. *Japan*—A U.S. aide-mémoire to the Soviet Union declares that a peace treaty with Japan cannot be dictated or frustrated by any one power.

BRITISH COMMONWEALTH

January

2. *Australia*—Minister for External Affairs P. C. Spender emphasizes the need for Commonwealth cooperation with the U.S.

6. *India-Pakistan*—Prime Minister Nehru reveals that India has proposed to Pakistan a joint declaration barring any war between the two states.

9–14. *Colombo conference*—A conference of Commonwealth foreign ministers at Colombo recommends measures and sets up permanent machinery for economic development in Southeast Asia.

26. *India*—The Republic of India is formally proclaimed and Dr. Rajendra Prasad is sworn in as president.

February

16. *Oil purchases*—The U.K., despite U.S. objections, restricts oil imports to the sterling area from dollar sources.

23. *India-Pakistan*—Nehru calls the communal riots in Bengal, raging since early February, a "major tragedy" and alleges that the riots in (Pakistani) East Bengal were far more serious than in (Indian) West Bengal.

27. *India-Pakistan*—Liaquat Ali Khan places responsibility for incitement of the Bengal riots on India and says that their remedy lies in "an honest acceptance of the fact of partition."

March

28. *India-Pakistan*—Liaquat Ali Khan accepts Nehru's invitation to seek a solution to the problem of communal rioting.

April

3. *Oil purchases*—A Commonwealth conference in London approves proposals to limit dollar oil purchases.
8. *India-Pakistan*—Nehru and Liaquat Ali Khan at New Delhi sign an agreement for the protection of minorities in India and Pakistan.

May

15–19. *Commonwealth conference*—A Commonwealth Consultative Committee, established at the Colombo conference, holds its first meeting in Sydney to discuss economic aid to Southeast Asia.

July

7. *India*—Nehru announces Indian acceptance of the Security Council resolution of June 27 on Korea (see "United Nations"), but declares that this does not alter India's independent foreign policy.

September

25–October 4. *Commonwealth conference*—The Commonwealth Consultative Committee on economic development of South and Southeast Asia meets in London and approves a three-year technical aid program costing up to £3 million.

November

28. *Colombo Plan*—The report of the Commonwealth Consultative Conference recommends six-year development programs for British and Commonwealth territories in South and Southeast Asia at an over-all cost of £1,868 million.

December

15. *India*—Deputy Prime Minister Sardar Vallabhbhai Patel dies.
27. *India* and the U.S. sign a technical cooperation agreement under the Point Four program.

LATIN AMERICA
January

6. *Organization of American States*—The Council of the Organization appoints a fact-finding committee to study disturbances in the Caribbean area.
20. *Bolivia*—The coalition government resigns, and a new government is formed (January 28) with all but one ministry assigned to members of the Republican Socialist Unity party.

February

3. *Chile*—The 12-month-old "national concentration" cabinet resigns following a wave of strikes in protest against a bill to freeze wages. President Gabriel Gonzalez Videla swears in (February 7) a new cabinet composed entirely of his own Radical party.
19–24. *Argentina*—Assistant Secretary of State Edward G. Miller, Jr. visits Argentina and sees President Juan D. Perón.

March

19. *Organization of American States*—The Council publishes the report of the fact-finding committee, which accuses Cuba, Guatemala, and the Dominican Republic of plots and conspiracies that have kept the Caribbean in turmoil for three years, and recommends sanctions if they fail to keep the peace.

20–April 10. *Inter-American Economic and Social Council*—A special session in Washington draws up a program for hemispheric technical cooperation.

26–29. *El Salvador*—In a general election Major Oscar Osorio, head of the revolutionary government council since 1948, is elected President by a large majority.

April

8. *Organization of American States*—The Council unanimously agrees to order Cuba, Guatemala, and the Dominican Republic to take steps to prevent further unrest in the Caribbean.

May

7. *Haiti*—The cabinet presents its resignation to President Dumarsais Estimé. On May 10 President Estimé resigns in favor of a military junta.

Nicaragua—General Anastasio Somoza is unanimously chosen President by a special session of congress following the death of President Roman y Reyes. In an election on May 21 Somoza is elected to the presidency.

17. *Argentina*—The U.S. Export-Import Bank extends a $125 million credit to a consortium of Argentine banks.

June

24. *Bolivia*—The government resigns and President Mamerto Urriolagoitia appoints (June 29) a new cabinet composed of nine Republican Socialist Union members and one Independent.

28. *Organization of American States*—The Council declares its "firmest support" of the U.N. decisions regarding Korea.

Argentina—The Chamber of Deputies approves the Inter-American Treaty of Reciprocal Assistance (Rio Treaty). The ratification is deposited August 21.

July

2. *Peru*—General Manuel Odría, head of the ruling military junta until he resigned to run for the presidency, is elected President in an unopposed election.

15. *Ecuador*—Former Minister of the Interior C. G. Morena leads an unsuccessful revolt against the government.

16. *Paraguay*—National elections are held and Dr. Federico Chaves, the sole candidate, is elected President.

21. *Argentina* suspends meat shipments to the U.K. because of failure to reach an agreement on prices.

August

28. *Organization of American States*—The U.S. Senate ratifies the Charter of the Organization, signed in Bogotá in 1948.

September

2. *Mexico*—The Export-Import Bank extends a $150 million credit to Mexico for economic projects.

26. *Bolivia* deposits its official ratification of the Rio Treaty.

October

3. *Brazil*—Getulio Vargas, dictator from 1930 to 1945, decisively wins the presidential election on the Labor party ticket.

8. *Haiti*—The first Haitian presidential election is won by Colonel Paul E. Magliore, who had resigned from the ruling junta to run for the presidency.

18. *Bolivia* ratifies the Charter of the Organization of American States.

November

13. *Guatemala*—Lieutenant Colonel Jacobo Arbenz Guzman is elected President by a large plurality.

Venezuela—Lieutenant Colonel Carlos Delgado Chalbaud, head of the military junta, is assassinated.

26. *Uruguay*—In a national election Andres Martínez Trueba of the Colorado party is elected President.

December

2. *Paraguay* and the U.S. announce the establishment of a Joint Commission for Economic Development.

20. *Organization of American States*—The Council unanimously adopts a U.S.-sponsored resolution calling for a conference of American Foreign Ministers to discuss urgent economic, political, and defense matters.

21. *Brazil* and the U.S. sign an agreement for technical cooperation under the Point Four program.

INDEX

Acheson, Dean, 194, 197; and atomic energy, 69-70; and Austria, 162; and China, 192, 195, 356; and Europe, 430; and Far East, 53; and Formosa, 52, 209; at General Assembly, 356, 369; and Germany, 105, 171, 269, 273, 408; and Hiss, 54-5; and Indochina, 129, 179; on isolationism, 440; and Japan, 181; and Korea, 92, 185, 200, 226-9, 418; and Latin America, 335, 339; and Lie, 195-6; and Mediterranean, 285-6; and North Atlantic defense, 128, 131, 286, 430; political attacks on, 47, 54-8, 210, 251, 397, 413, 430; on Prague declaration and four power conference, 410, 434; on Schuman Plan, 143; and Southeast Asia, 180, 332; and Spain, 288; Acheson plan, 369-72

Adenauer, Konrad, 114; and Franco-German problems, 114, 116, 118, 143, 146; and defense problems, 168, 267, 270, 273, 275, 431-3

Afghanistan, 19, 57, 162, 320-21, 356

Africa, 160, 294, 307

Albania, 378-9, 409

Algeria, 283

Ali Razmara, 314

American Bar Association, 82

American Federation of Labor, 82

American Foreign Ministers, 335-6, 340, 437

American Legion, 82

Anglo-Egyptian Sudan, 311

Anglo-Iranian Oil Co., 313-14

Antarctic, 163

Anze Matienzo, Eduardo, 388

Arab League, 309, 311-12, 421

Arab states, Arab world, 28, 212-13, 307-14, 357, 361, 393, 429

Arab-Asian bloc, 212, 315, 352, 421-2, 425

Argentina, 60, 289, 338, 340, 342-3, 357, 370

Armstrong, Hamilton Fish, 76

Asia, 2, 3, 8, 39-40, 294, 306; and East-West conflict, 30-31, 40-41, 174, 178-9, 315-16, 347, 401, 403, 416, 422, 424; and U.S., 24-5, 27, 53, 315, 412

Asia, Southeast, 36-9, 326-7; and East-West conflict, 177-80, 321-2, 330; and U.S., 27, 53, 178-9, 253, 322, 330

Atatürk, Kemal, 285

Atomic bomb, atomic energy, 11, 24, 61-84, 191; and Communist propaganda, 64, 157-60; international control, 41, 64, 72; see also United Nations and country names

Atomic Energy Commission, (U.S.), 382

Attlee, Clement R., 104, 145, 300, 418-20, 426-8

Austin, Warren R., 202-3; in Security Council, 210-11, 234, 239-41; in General Assembly, 373, 416, 422

Australia, 182, 297, 299, 384; and Korea, 198, 214, 243, 295, 360, 363, 425

Austria, 16, 30, 71, 161-2, 196, 264, 379-80, 384, 435; treaty negotiations, 32, 165-6, 435-6

Baltic plane incident, 162-3, 242

Bangkok conference, 38

Bao Dai, 38-9, 323, 325

Bayar, Celal, 285

Belgium, 75, 134, 140, 147, 243, 263, 425

Bell, Daniel W., 329

Benelux countries, 141, 144, 146, 289

Bennett, Henry G., 302

Berlin, 112, 162, 168-9, 173, 196, 270, 439

Bevin, Ernest, 107, 111, 128, 166, 196, 269, 312, 434

Bidault, Georges, 110-11, 128, 147, 268

Bogotá conference, 337

Bolivia, 338, 341, 374, 388

Bonin Islands, 332

Borneo, North, 304

Bradley, Omar N., 63, 126, 131-2, 184

Brazil, 301-2, 340-41, 345, 360, 380

Bridges, Styles, 57

British Commonwealth, 38, 100, 160, 180, 184, 214, 296-7, 299, 301, 304, 440

Brunei, 304